S0-CFU-147

937
TIB

A8227

A8227

937

937
TIB

AUTHOR
Marsh, F. B.
TITLE
Reign of Tiberius

DATE DUE	BORROWER'S NAME
MAY 1 1970	R. Porter
OCT 1 1970	Larry Brown
MAR 22 1972	Nick Stunt
out + 46	Corday Mahry
	Overdue
MAR 2 4 2004	
1 - 11 - 10	

Seattle Preparatory School Library
Seattle, Washington

HEFFER REISSUES OF STANDARD BOOKS

THE REIGN OF TIBERIUS

BY

FRANK BURR MARSH

CAMBRIDGE

W. HEFFER AND SONS, LTD.

1959

ORIGINAL EDITION: 1931 (Oxford University Press)

Photographically reprinted by permission,
without alteration, for W. Heffer & Sons, Ltd.: 1959

Printed in Great Britain by Lowe & Brydone (Printers) Ltd.
London, N.W.10

PREFACE

IT was my original intention that this work should be simply a continuation of my book *The Founding of the Roman Empire*, but the nature of the subject and the problems raised by the sources combined to give it a distinctive character. In view of this fact it seemed desirable to supply such a background in the first chapters as would make this study an independent work, complete in itself. Nevertheless the two books remain closely linked together, in my mind at least. In the first I have endeavoured to show how and why the republican principate came to be established by Augustus, while in this I have sought to trace the causes which were responsible for its collapse under Tiberius. My success in either undertaking is of course a matter for the reader to judge.

A word of explanation may be called for in regard to the footnotes. In general I have not considered it worth while to give references to Tacitus when the passage in question could be readily found by the reader. In citing modern works I have given only the author's name where but one of his works has been referred to in the course of this study, but I have provided the necessary bibliographical information in the 'List of Works Referred to in the Notes' at the end of the volume. This course seemed to me to have the double advantage of avoiding encumbering the notes with titles and of making it easier for the reader to verify any statement. All references to Tacitus and Suetonius are to the *Annals* and to the life of Tiberius respectively unless otherwise specified.

In my quotations from Tacitus I have in most cases borrowed from Ramsay's admirable translation. I do not always agree with him, but I recognize clearly that I cannot hope to improve upon his version, which has in a remarkable degree preserved the peculiar quality of the original. Nevertheless, in a few instances I have, for special reasons, given a rendering of my own, which the reader will all too easily detect apart from the lack of any acknowledgement to Ramsay.

It only remains to acknowledge my obligations to numerous

friends, and especially to Professor Paul M. Batchelder of the
University of Texas, who kindly read the manuscript and
offered many valuable suggestions. I wish also to express my
gratitude to the adviser of the Clarendon Press, to whose helpful
criticism I am deeply indebted.

F. B. M.

AUSTIN, TEXAS,
  December 1930.

CONTENTS

APPENDIXES

CONTENTS

I

TIBERIUS AND HIS HISTORIANS

PERHAPS no Roman emperor has been the subject of more bitter controversy than Tiberius. The ancient historians pictured him as a monster, and until recent times this portrait has been accepted as authentic. In the last century, however, a decided reaction made itself felt, and a number of scholars undertook to clear his character. These efforts have met with a considerable measure of success, and few historians now hold entirely to the older view.

Before attempting any consideration of the actual events of his reign it seems necessary to consider briefly the testimony of antiquity against him. If Tiberius were not really as black as he has been painted, how did it come about that he was so misrepresented? In this connexion our primary concern is with Tacitus, from whose pages we derive by far the greater part of our information concerning Tiberius. If we can adequately explain the view of Tacitus, we shall find ourselves in a better position to estimate the extent of his prejudices and to allow for them in dealing with his testimony. What we learn of his life, of the sources which he used, and of the manner in which he handled his material are thus of obvious importance.

It is now admitted that the great Roman historian had a strong bias against Tiberius, but the explanations of it hitherto offered do not seem wholly satisfactory. It is very probable that the root of Tacitus' hostile attitude lay in the very fact which gives to the reign of Tiberius its historical significance, namely, that it was a period of transition, in which the constitutional principate of Augustus was transformed into the tyranny of Caligula, Claudius, Nero, and Domitian. To appreciate this point it is essential to consider one or two circumstances in the life of Tacitus which must have contributed powerfully to influence his outlook. This is the more necessary because the historian was in these respects a typical Roman of his time and probably accepted in the main the estimate of Tiberius then common, so that his view is substantially the same as that of our other principal sources, Dio Cassius and Suetonius.

Our knowledge of the life of Tacitus is very meagre. He was born at about the time of Nero's accession (A.D. 54), and so witnessed the events of the year of the four emperors as a boy of about fourteen. Under the Flavians he found his way into the aristocratic society of Rome, if he did not belong there by birth,[1] for in A.D. 78 he married the daughter of Julius Agricola, who had been consul the year before. Perhaps it was this alliance which won Tacitus the favour of Vespasian, who in the last year of his reign named the young man as one of the imperial candidates for the quaestorship. This office Tacitus probably held under Titus; under Domitian he was advanced to the praetorship, and after performing the duties of this office he spent several years in the provinces. When he returned to Rome it was to become a helpless participant in the reign of terror which marked the last years of Domitian's life, voting submissively in the senate for the condemnation of innocent men who had aroused the suspicion of the tyrant. This experience left an impression which nothing could efface. Having seen with his own eyes the abuse of the law of treason, he came to hate it with passionate intensity. But better days soon dawned; Domitian was murdered and Nerva succeeded him on the throne. The new reign was brief, but the aged emperor raised Tacitus to the consulship and thus to the highest rank of the Roman nobility. On the death of Nerva the crown passed to his adopted son Trajan, one of the ablest and best of the emperors. Throughout his reign Tacitus seems to have occupied himself largely with his historical works; he first produced the *Histories*, dealing with the period from the death of Nero to that of Domitian, and then, turning back, wrote the *Annals*, covering the period from the death of Augustus to that of Nero. The latter work was probably composed about A.D. 116, and the historian must have died at very nearly the same time as Trajan. The *Histories* and *Annals* taken together formed a complete history from A.D. 14 to 96, but large portions of both works have been lost. We have, however, that part of the *Annals* dealing with the reign of Tiberius almost entire—that is, we have approximately five out of the original six books. There is one

---

[1] His father seems to have been a knight originally, but he may have made his way into the lower nobility before his death.

large gap in the only surviving manuscript; most of Book V and the beginning of Book VI, treating the events from early in A.D. 29 till towards the end of 31, have perished, so that we lack his guidance for about three years out of the twenty-seven of the reign.

It is evident that Tacitus can have known little of the reign of Tiberius except from written sources, although the interval between the death of the emperor and the birth of the historian was not so great as to make it impossible for Tacitus in his youth to meet contemporaries of Tiberius and to draw upon the recollections of men who were living at the time of the events narrated in the *Annals*.[1] In one case we have the historian's own word that he used information from such a source, but his language implies that this was exceptional. Nevertheless there are a number of places in which he seems to have been more or less influenced by the family traditions preserved among the great Roman houses. He himself says that when he wrote many were still living whose ancestors had suffered under Tiberius,[2] and to their version of the transactions in which those ancestors were involved he sometimes attached considerable importance.[3] Yet when due allowance is made for the use of such material it is still clear that the *Annals* are almost entirely based either directly upon documentary sources or upon the works of previous historians. Both of these deserve a word or two of explanation and comment.

Of the documentary sources at the disposal of Tacitus the most important was the archives of the senate (the *acta senatus*), which consisted of the official record of the proceedings of that body and could be consulted by all senators. How full or complete this record was we cannot determine with certainty, but it undoubtedly included the motions offered, the names of the speakers, the letters and speeches of the emperor (at least when written out beforehand and read to the senate). When trials were conducted before the senate it is probable that a summary of the evidence, if not the whole of it, was included in the record. In many cases the speeches of the advocates on each side were probably filed in the archives, as these would

[1] *Ann.* 3, 16.   [2] *Ann.* 4, 33.
[3] See my article on 'Tacitus and Aristocratic Tradition' in *Classical Philology*.

often be carefully prepared in advance. Of extemporaneous speeches delivered in the course of a debate it is probable that only the general sense was taken down by the officials who reported the proceedings. It is obvious that the senate's archives contained an immense mass of historical material, but this material was defective in two ways. In the first place some of the most important departments of the government lay outside the jurisdiction of the senate altogether. Concerning foreign affairs or military events on the frontiers the senate received only such information as the emperor, for one reason or another, chose to impart. All communications between the emperor and his legates in the imperial provinces were kept apart in the imperial archives, which were not open to the scrutiny even of the senators. Roman historians have often been blamed for their preoccupation with events in Rome and their neglect of what was passing in the empire as a whole, but this was more or less inevitable in view of the sources available. It is true that most of them were closely connected with the senatorial nobility and that this nobility constituted the public for which they wrote, but even if Tacitus had risen to the conception of a general history of the empire he could not have written one when all documents relating to those provinces where the most important events occurred were inaccessible. He might perhaps have done more than he has, but it is not impossible that he wrote as full an account as he was able with the sources at his command. A second defect of the documents in the senate's archives was their official character; this made them unquestionably trustworthy in some matters, but it robbed them of much of their value in others. It was easy to determine the exact wording of a senatorial decree, but there were many documents which could not be implicitly relied upon. If a general gained a victory or suffered a defeat, it might suit the emperor's policy to exaggerate or mininize it,[1] or to distort the circumstances under which it had occurred. Often no doubt the imperial announcements in the senate represented more accurately what the government wished the public to believe than the real facts, and there were at

---

[1] For example, Tacitus (4, 74) says that Tiberius entirely ignored a defeat suffered by the Romans at the hands of the Frisians in A.D. 28.

hand only very imperfect means of verifying or correcting them.

In addition to the *acta senatus* there were the *acta diurna*, a sort of daily bulletin posted by the government and containing all sorts of announcements, for the most part of ephemeral interest and of strictly official character. There were also the published speeches of various orators, some of them doubtless included in the archives of the senate. Last of all there were the memoirs and letters of various persons. We know that the younger Agrippina left memoirs which Tacitus had read,[1] and it is hardly likely that she was the only one who did so. Even if the practice of publishing letters had not then become common, such documents must have been preserved to some extent by the surviving noble families, and no doubt an historian would at times be able to consult them. To what extent such sources existed and how much they were used by Tacitus or his predecessors must remain uncertain, but the probability seems to be that they were not of great importance.

Besides these primary sources, Tacitus could draw upon the works of preceding historians. We know of three writers whose works, unfortunately lost, dealt with the reign of Tiberius, namely, Servilius Nonianus, Aufidius Bassus, and the elder Seneca, and no doubt there were others whose very names have failed to reach us. We still possess the brief history of Velleius Paterculus, which covers the first part of the reign, but it is doubtful if Tacitus made any use of him.[2] The works of these earlier authors must have been not only secondary sources, but to some extent primary sources as well. They were all contemporaries of Tiberius, and they were thus able to supplement the material in the archives by their own recollections and by information gathered privately from eye-witnesses and participants in the various events, as well as by the gossip and rumour of the time. Thus, for example, all three could have known officers who had seen the mutinies on the Rhine and in Pannonia

---

[1] We know of but one fact taken from the memoirs of Agrippina. Tacitus here cites her as his authority (4, 53) because the incident was not mentioned by other historians. He may, however, have been influenced in his judgement of events by these memoirs.

[2] He is valuable chiefly as showing the official view of various events, which Tacitus often rejects.

and who had fought under Germanicus in Germany or accompanied him to the East. Moreover, Servilius Nonianus was a senator during most of the reign and could, therefore, draw on his own memory for details not mentioned in the official records.

The question of how Tacitus used the material at hand has been much discussed by modern scholars. Probably he compared the various secondary sources carefully and supplemented them by a more or less frequent consultation of the archives. It seems clear that the *acta senatus* is the ultimate source for a very large part of those books of the *Annals* which deal with Tiberius, though much has been added from other sources.

But in what spirit did Tacitus treat his material and how did he handle his authorities? It has been held that he deliberately blackened the character of Tiberius, and that to accomplish this he not only misrepresented the emperor at every turn but filled his pages with rumour, gossip, and malicious insinuations.[1] Such a view is upon the whole untenable. Tacitus had a very bad opinion of Tiberius, and in consequence he often imputes unduly sinister motives to the emperor; nevertheless, he sought to tell the truth, and it is this combination of honest intentions hampered by strong prejudices which exposes him to attacks on his veracity. His style is also partly responsible; he was a brilliant rhetorician and a lover of sententious brevity who could paint a vivid picture with a concise and telling phrase. Unfortunately his terse phrases are sometimes obscure and leave an impression on the reader different from that at which the author aimed. It is thus an easy matter to misunderstand Tacitus, and since his prejudices often blinded his judgement his brilliant rhetoric not infrequently seems designed to conceal the truth. Yet he did not hesitate to record details which were inconsistent with his own ideas, and it is by his candid admissions that it is mainly possible to correct his picture, a fact which in itself seems to exclude any theory of deliberate dishonesty.

Our confidence in Tacitus is increased if we compare his account with those of Suetonius and Dio. Suetonius seems to have gathered a large amount of material from sources of very

[1] Ritter and Jerome are perhaps the best exponents of this view, but all defenders of Tiberius seem to hold it in some degree.

different degrees of reliability. Apparently he made no effort to apply any kind of historical criticism to the stories he collected, but merely selected those that suited his purpose, arranged them in a more or less logical order, connected them with loose general statements, and so constructed a biography. In his *Lives* we find anecdotes which must have been drawn from the gossip of aristocratic society side by side with others which were probably much better attested. In his generalizations he was often careless, paying more attention to effect than to accuracy, a fault which he shared with Dio, and one from which Tacitus is by no means wholly free. It is clear, therefore, that the modern historian must use Suetonius with caution, but he ought not for that reason to be ignored. If some of his sources were worthless, others were trustworthy, and we can at times supplement or correct Tacitus by details which the biographer has preserved.

The history of Dio was written much later than either the *Annals* or the *Lives of the Caesars*, but Dio seems to have made little, if any, use of either. It is this circumstance which gives to his work much of its importance. He compiled it from the works of earlier historians, which were doubtless among those consulted by Tacitus, but which were not his chief sources. Here again the advantage plainly lies with Tacitus, who made a much more extensive comparison of different writers and was a far more serious critic of his authorities. In general his account is more sober and apparently more accurate than that of Dio, but the latter, if less trustworthy, at least shows us that a different version of certain events existed and sometimes supplies us with what seem to be authentic details. In particular, Dio and Suetonius enable us to fill up after a fashion the gaps in our information due to the loss of a portion of the *Annals*.

Since Tacitus is not only our fullest but also our most trustworthy authority, it becomes all the more necessary to determine as far as possible how he handled his material, what critical standards he applied to it, and how far he was influenced by his prejudices in weighing evidence. He himself has furnished us with some hints as to his methods, and further light may be obtained by a careful examination of his practice. He began by a comparison of the most important of the preceding historians, and where their accounts agreed he regarded the matter as settled.[1] Where they differed he investigated the point in dispute further and decided between the conflicting opinions if he could. If he found himself unable to arrive at a definite judgement, he gave the version which he thought most probable and added the other as something which some writers reported or which was believed by many. In his search for the truth he sometimes went to the archives and sometimes, no doubt, to special works which he regarded as peculiarly trustworthy on some particular subject, and from these various sources he added occasionally to what he found in his main authorities. Such a method certainly falls short of modern standards, and in particular it seems a little naïve to assume that the agreement of writers whom he himself regarded as prejudiced[2] settled all questions. If, as he declares, preceding historians were unreliable, it would seem that a fresh and thorough examination of the whole subject was called for, but an agreement in untruth due to a common bias does not seem to have occurred to Tacitus as possible. We may regret that it did not, but, at least, he seems to have applied his own standard conscientiously, as is shown by the frequency with which he found himself embarrassed by facts which did not fit his own conceptions. Although he tried to apply his critical tests honestly, Tacitus was unable to do so impartially, since the indelible impression left by his own painful experiences under Domitian constantly distorted his judgement. His hatred of informers was so bitter that he attached little or no weight to their testimony. In his eyes the law of treason was an engine of tyranny and every man prosecuted under it a victim. With such prepossessions it was easy for him to distort the record. If the accused committed suicide the case was usually dropped at that point, so that much of the evidence was never presented to the senate. When the defendant was conscious of guilt or knew that the informers had a strong case against him, he not infrequently ended the matter before the trial was even begun, and there might thus be on file in the archives only the charge or charges on which he had been arraigned. In such a case Tacitus had no faith in the

---

[1] *Ann.* 13, 20. For a fuller discussion see the appendix on 'The Sources of Tacitus'.
[2] *Ann.* 1, 1.

truth of the charges, and if he does not always venture to declare the suicide's innocence in explicit terms, he often implies
it. That informers sometimes brought false charges is true
enough, but there can be little doubt that Tacitus allowed his
prejudice to carry him too far. Every suicide is presented
more or less as a martyr, and it is generally implied that the
prosecution had some sinister motive behind it. Tacitus entirely
overlooks the possibility that Tiberius might have permitted a
man to be brought to trial because there was really strong, if
not conclusive, evidence of a crime, and might thus have acted
with honest intentions, even if the accused preferred death to
the production of that evidence in the senate.

Perhaps it was in part this profound distrust of informers, this
deeply rooted conviction that their evidence had often been
trumped up for the occasion, and the consequent suspicion that
the reasons for a prosecution were frequently quite different
from those publicly alleged, that led Tacitus to attach so much
importance to the version of events handed down in the surviving noble families,[1] hoping to find there a clue to the hidden
motives of which the official records gave no hint. Such traditions
ought not to have been entirely ignored, but he was perhaps
over-ready to accept them and failed to make sufficient allowance
for the fact that the motives attributed to the emperor by the great
families, who were naturally anxious to excuse their ancestors,
might be fully as untrustworthy as the charges of the informers.

Yet if Tacitus sometimes followed aristocratic family
traditions, he paid little attention to mere gossip and rumour,
and his use of these has been both misunderstood and exaggerated by modern scholars. In the first place, however great
his contempt for them, as an historian he could not altogether
neglect them. Popular opinion, even when most erroneous and
absurd, influenced the course of events, and if the events were
to be understood it was necessary to mention the beliefs which
determined them. Thus, for example, Tiberius ordered Piso
to be tried before the senate because of the reports in circulation
regarding the death of Germanicus,[2] and it was therefore clearly

---

[1] For a fuller discussion of the use of this source by Tacitus see my article
on 'Tacitus and Aristocratic Tradition'.
[2] *Ann.* 4, 11. Similarly the gossip about Livia mentioned in the first book

impossible to explain the public trial without mentioning these reports. But although Tacitus was forced to take account of gossip and rumour, he despised them, and he has seldom, if ever, made a positive assertion without some better authority.

If in gathering his facts Tacitus employed methods which leave much to be desired from the standpoint of modern historical research, he was at least more critical and more conscientious in the pursuit of truth than any other Roman historian whose works have been preserved. The attacks upon his honesty are based mainly on the manner in which he treated his material after it had been collected. His veracity is open to question for three chief reasons, namely, his candour, his preconceived opinions, and his literary genius. His candour often led him to add details and to make admissions which are inconsistent with his own views, and since he would not alter his opinions to fit the facts he was driven to colour the facts so as to conceal the discrepancy from himself as well as others. This he did by the free use of rhetorical touches, which his genius rendered singularly effective. When once the falsity of the colour which he thus imparted to the facts was suspected, the natural reaction led many critics to go too far and to see in such touches the subtle art of a malicious and mendacious rhetorician purposely seeking to conceal the truth. Such critics seem oblivious to an insurmountable difficulty in their theory: if Tacitus had not been scrupulously honest according to his lights they would have had no means of detecting his perversions, since he would have omitted those details on which they fasten to refute and to expose him. That his portrait of Tiberius can be shown to be false by the evidence he has himself supplied would seem a guarantee that he was not intentionally or deliberately untruthful.

Admitting then that, in his account of Tiberius, Tacitus laboured under the handicap of a preconceived bias which constantly led him to give a false colouring to the facts, we need to seek some explanation of this bias. It is probable that he derived it in the first place from the tradition of the aristocratic society

(10), whatever the intention in recording it, does actually serve to explain how she could later be suspected of playing a part in the murder of Germanicus, and this suspicion could not be omitted if the attitude of Agrippina towards Tiberius and his mother was to be intelligible.

in which he lived. The impression which he received in these
circles was strengthened and confirmed by his general conception
of the history of the empire and by his personal experiences. It
was inevitable that as he looked back upon the past the recent
tyranny of Domitian should darken all his views. One victim
of tyranny impresses one's imagination more than several years
during which the emperor abstained from evil. Thus in the
reign of Tiberius the death of Libo Drusus in A.D. 16, as described
by Tacitus, is far more striking than the fact that in A.D. 18
there was not, so far as we can learn, a single prosecution, and
the reader of the *Annals* cannot fail to be more deeply influenced in his judgement of the emperor by the story of Titius
Sabinus in A.D. 28 than by the fact that the only man accused
in the preceding year was not even brought to trial. The cruelty
that was committed inevitably makes a far deeper impression
than the negative fact that in many years no atrocities were
recorded. When Tacitus looked back over the history of the
empire after the reign of Augustus, he saw some periods of good
government, notably in the first years of Tiberius and of Nero,
but, apart from such occasional lucid intervals, the record was
one of capricious and suspicious tyranny. Under Trajan, it is
true, the empire had found glory and happiness, but Tacitus
must have realized how insecure and unstable this felicity was.
The machinery of oppression in the shape of the law of treason
was there, and though it stood idle for the moment it required
but the whim of an irresponsible despot to set it in motion once
more. One may even go further and surmise that the tranquillity of Trajan's government did not wholly conciliate the
historian, since it might be attributed as much to contempt as
to humanity. A soldier who spent much of his time at the head
of his army could safely ignore the senate and the aristocracy
not from respect but because he was convinced of their entire
impotence. The tolerance of Trajan may have stung the nobles
as really if not as much as the suspicions of Domitian. The
tyrant had at least so far respected the conscript fathers as to
fear them, but now even this compliment might seem to be
denied. As an aristocrat Tacitus lamented the decline of the
nobility, even though, as a practical man, he recognized the
necessity of the empire. The reign of Augustus seemed to offer

a profound contrast; then the nobles had been respected without being oppressed, and the historian might readily conclude that somewhere in its course the development of the empire had taken a wrong turn. If he felt thus he could not doubt where this had occurred; the reign of Tiberius marked the transition between the principate of Augustus and the tyranny of the later Caesars. It was then that the apparatus of oppression was elaborated and set in motion, and that the law of treason developed into a potential engine of cruelty and injustice. It was this law, used as it had been, which had broken the nobility and forced the once proud aristocrats to cringe before their master. It was wholly natural, therefore, that Tacitus should loathe it and should transfer some of his loathing to the emperor under whom its sinister possibilities first became apparent. With his personal experience of its abuse under Domitian, Tacitus would have been more than humanly impartial if he had been able to treat the reign of Tiberius with perfect fairness, or to tr .ce the development of the law with a calm detachment which made full allowance for all the circumstances of the case.

The prevalent modes of thought also militated against impartiality on the part of Tacitus. The Romans had but a weak perception of economic or political causation in human affairs and turned naturally to the personality of the actors to explain the course of events. If the republic fell, it was in their eyes simply because Caesar was ambitious, and apparently it did not occur to them that the republic must have been profoundly undermined if it was really so weak that the ambition of one man, however great, could destroy it. One searches in vain for any clear insight into the social and economic causes which had slowly and silently destroyed the foundations of the republic before Caesar was born. In this respect Tacitus was in no wise in advance of his fellow countrymen, and like them, when he was confronted by an obvious transformation in the working of the imperial government, he sought its explanation in the personal character of the emperor under whom the change first became visible. Seeing that it was in the reign of Tiberius that the constitutional principate of Augustus broke down and was replaced by an autocracy equipped with all the apparatus of the later tyranny, he drew the conclusion that this must have been due to the depravity and wickedness of Tiberius himself. It was probably with such preconceptions that Tacitus approached the study of his sources, and if he found in them anything that did not harmonize with such a view he had an explanation ready to hand in the prevalent tradition which ascribed hypocrisy to the emperor along with other vices. Thus it was always possible to construe the facts in such a way that they supported, instead of overthrowing, the historian's initial prejudices.

Moreover, Tacitus had weaknesses which helped to blind him to the real meaning of the facts which he discovered. He was lacking beyond some of his contemporaries in both political insight and historical imagination. He had little or no perception of the general bearings of a situation and could see nothing but its personal aspects. Neither did he grasp the changes which the course of events had brought about in familiar institutions. Informers must always have been precisely what he had known them to be under Domitian, and if Domitian had often inspired their prosecutions, it was taken for granted that Tiberius had done the same. It never occurred to Tacitus that the first accession of a new emperor was an unprecedented event and that it happened while the constitutional theory of Augustus still retained its force, and as a consequence he judged the language of Tiberius on this occasion exactly as he would similar expressions in the mouth of Trajan. It never dawned upon his mind that the Flavian senate of which he had been a member was a very different body from the senate of Tiberius, and he interpreted its conduct accordingly. If a verdict of guilty had meant nothing under Domitian, it meant nothing under Tiberius, nor could he see that the fact that the senate of Tiberius often acquitted the accused was of the slightest significance. Tacitus seems never to have realized that the changing circumstances of Tiberius' position might have influenced his policy, and this was due to his complete inability to see that the circumstances had changed. As the situation in which the emperor found himself could therefore never furnish an explanation of his conduct, Tacitus was forced to seek for purely personal motives, for old grudges, or long-cherished suspicions. In military matters the same defect is visible as in political. If the campaigns of Germanicus had any definite plan or purpose

Tacitus has failed to give us any hint of it; as he describes them, the expeditions of his hero are aimless adventures filled with unintelligible blunders.

Since Tacitus was forced to find the causes of events so largely in the characters of the main actors, it was an added handicap that his psychology was superficial. He conceived of character as a wholly static and immutable thing. If Tiberius acted differently at the beginning and at the end of his reign, Tacitus refuses even to consider the possibility that an old man betrayed by his best friend might have grown morose and bitter, for this would have meant that his character had altered. If in his last days he showed himself harsh and suspicious, then he must always have been so, and to much the same degree. That the qualities in question were not manifested earlier Tacitus explains by assuming that the emperor was a hypocrite who at first dissembled his evil qualities, and dropped the mask when he had ceased to be afraid. That a man could successfully conceal his real character till he was nearing seventy and then throw off the disguise does not seem to Tacitus in any way improbable. In this the historian showed less insight than some Romans, who offered suggestions which he refused to heed. In his own pages he has recorded a speech of L. Arruntius in which Tiberius is described as a man whose nature had been distorted and changed by the weight of sovereignty,[1] a view which shows Arruntius to have been a better psychologist than Tacitus.

However, when all is said in criticism of Tacitus, his merits still remain. He made a sincere effort to weigh the evidence and to get at the truth. If his preconceived opinions and his limitations combined to prevent his attaining it and dominated his presentation of the results, he has at least this to his credit, that he would not set down in malice what was not proved according to his standards of proof, and that he would not conceal what was so established even when it did not fit his theories. In his statements as to facts he is far more reliable than either Suetonius or Dio, and his candour is so great that we may confidently hope to correct many of his errors by his own testimony.

In attempting to reconstruct the history of the reign of Tiberius the method to be followed is fairly obvious from what

[1] *Ann.* 6, 48.

precedes. For the facts, in so far as we can now recover them, we must depend mainly upon Tacitus. In view, however, of his limitations we should not neglect other sources by which we may at times be able to correct or supplement his account. Yet if the *Annals* furnish us with the bulk of our material, the facts must be separated entirely from the rhetoric in which Tacitus has enveloped them and must be allowed to speak for themselves. We must judge Tiberius by what he did, considered carefully in the light of what we know of the circumstances under which he acted, and not by the motives which Tacitus has ascribed to him. Like any other man accused of villainy, Tiberius is entitled to a fair hearing. We are bound to acquit him of all evil qualities of which we can find no evidence in his deeds. In estimating his conduct we should place upon it neither the most favourable construction nor the most unfavourable, but the most reasonable. In this we must have as little hesitation in agreeing with Tacitus as in disagreeing with him. An older generation of scholars assumed that Tacitus was invariably right, while some more recent ones seem to take it for granted that he was invariably wrong. In reality he was not infallible. He had at times clear flashes of insight, and he knew many facts which he has not recorded. Moreover, the legendary picture of Tiberius which lived in men's memories must have had some foundation. If the emperor was not a hypocrite, there was at any rate something in his character or conduct which made such a charge seem plausible. We ought not, therefore, to ignore the opinions of Tacitus unless we can explain them, or to set them aside when there is evidence, even though it be not quite conclusive, to support them. In weighing the conflicting statements of our authorities, the accuracy of Tacitus is in general so much greater than that of Dio or Suetonius that his account should be followed unless there appears reason to suspect his testimony. The present work is an attempt to write the history of the reign of Tiberius in this spirit and by this method. That the attempt will be entirely successful is too much to hope, and certainly the conclusions reached will not be so solidly established as to convince all readers. It will be enough if some light is thrown on an important period and the way rendered in some respects easier for others.

II

THE LEGACY OF AUGUSTUS

TO understand the reign of Tiberius we must bear constantly in mind that he succeeded Augustus and felt himself bound to carry on his predecessor's system of government, the nature of which must, therefore, be clearly grasped at the outset.[1] It was in fact a complex and delicately adjusted system, where the realities were carefully disguised by elaborate legal fictions. This was not due primarily to the devious policy of Augustus, but rather to the peculiar nature of the problem which faced him after the battle of Actium. That victory in leaving him the military dictator of the Roman world imposed upon him the unavoidable duty of establishing some stable form of government. The whole course of recent events had demonstrated that while at any given moment public opinion was helpless against the swords of the legions, yet in the long run the soldiers could not escape from the influence of the general sentiment of Italy. It followed from this that, if the rule of Augustus was to be stable, he must find some means of reconciling it with the wishes and feelings of the Roman people. The demands of public opinion at the moment were two: first, that Augustus should remain at the head of the army with such powers as would suffice to guarantee peace and order, and, second, that the old republican constitution should be restored. These demands might seem to be in violent contradiction, but they were so only in appearance. What the Romans really required of Augustus was that he should bring his supremacy within the accustomed forms of Roman law. Modern writers too often forget that the Roman world cared little for liberty in our sense of the word. Most men were quite willing that Augustus should be an autocrat in fact if he would exercise his powers in accordance with the legal forms; they were willing to submit to his authority, but they resented being subject to his caprice. They hated the name of king largely because in their minds it signified a ruler who stood outside of and above the law. Augustus met

[1] The government of Augustus is more fully discussed in my book *The Founding of the Roman Empire.*

the demands of his contemporaries by the organization of the principate. He solemnly proclaimed the restoration of the republic and set its antiquated and moribund machinery once more in motion, but at the same time he took advantage of the precedents of the last century to have himself invested with such powers as he thought essential to his own supremacy. In its decline the republic had frequently entrusted to one man the government of several provinces for a number of years. To guarantee the peace of the world Augustus, making use of this device, had the sole command of the most important provinces and the troops stationed in them formally conferred upon him. In this way he became practically the commander-in-chief of the army and was able to control both the frontier and the foreign policy of Rome. Italy and the remaining provinces were to be ruled by the traditional methods, and within this portion of the world the restored republic was permitted to try its hand at governing.

Thus Augustus created what modern scholars have called a diarchy, as the government of the world was divided between him and the republic.[1] Under this arrangement Augustus, as princeps, ruled the frontier provinces and commanded the army, most of which was stationed in these provinces, by virtue of the proconsular *imperium* conferred upon him by the formal vote of the Roman people for a definite term of years, the grant being renewed whenever the term for which it was given was about to expire. The republic administered under the old forms all parts of the empire which had not been expressly entrusted to the princeps. In constitutional theory there was no division of authority, since Augustus was simply a proconsul of the republic invested with an exceptional authority by the people, an authority of which the people could deprive him at any time by repealing the law which conferred it. His position was, therefore, constitutionally the same as that held by Pompey under the Gabinian and Manilian laws, or that of Caesar during his proconsulship in Gaul. In spite of this theory, however, the constant renewal of his *imperium* made Augustus in fact

---

[1] The diarchy is usually explained as a division of the world between the emperor and the senate. I think it more accurate to describe it under Augustus as a division between the emperor and the republic.

independent of the republic, and it is evident at once that two such powers could not remain wholly separate from each other without grave risk of a collision. To remove this danger some connexion between the princeps and the republic was imperative, and this connexion took the form of conceding to the princeps the means of controlling the working of the republican machine. Such an arrangement was inevitable under the circumstances. The world, taught by experience, was insistent that Augustus should control the army, and if he did so he was always the master whenever he chose to resort to force. It was, therefore, a matter of common sense to eliminate the need for an appeal to arms by conferring on Augustus such powers as would remove all possibility that such an appeal would become necessary.

The control of the princeps over the republican machine was secured by the tribunician power and by certain special privileges. In the last days of the republic a close connexion had grown up between the great proconsuls and the tribunes; both Pompey and Caesar had found it necessary to safeguard their positions by securing the election of one or more tribunes devoted to their interests. In conferring on Augustus the tribunician power the Roman people in substance merely gave him the right to do in person what his predecessors had done by deputy. He thus secured the right to veto (or forbid) any act of any magistrate and any law or resolution of senate or people. These powers protected him against any interference on the part of the republic, and incidentally rendered it impossible for the republican machine to work in a way seriously contrary to his wishes. Had the Roman republic been in fact what it was in theory, the proconsular *imperium* and the tribunician power would have sufficed the emperor, and they always remained the legal bases of his position. Theory and fact were, however, widely divergent, and as a consequence the princeps was compelled to assume still greater powers and to encroach steadily upon the sphere assigned to the republic.

The Roman republic throughout its history was always aristocratic in its actual government. Democracy might be established in law, as it was after the plebeians secured equal rights with the patricians, but the Roman mind remained stubbornly hostile to democracy in practice. The holding of office conferred distinction on the descendants of the holder, and was the basis of the Roman nobility, the nobles being simply the descendants of the men who had been raised to the highest offices of the republic by the votes of their fellow citizens. They had no legal privileges, and their honorary distinctions would have mattered little if it had not been for the fact that the Romans were a conservative and deferential people. To them it seemed only natural that the son of a consul should seek the consulship in his turn, and they even recognized that he possessed a sort of right to hold it if he were not manifestly unworthy. The result was to create a ring of office-holding families among whom the magistracies were passed around from generation to generation. Only occasionally did an outsider succeed in forcing his way to the front, and when he did so he merely created a new noble family. Thus while the offices were in theory open to all, they were nearly always filled from the members of a small governing class, one of whose deepest instincts was to keep itself as narrow and exclusive as possible; hence it opposed bitterly the advancement of a new man (one whose ancestors had not held office) to the higher magistracies. For a long time the nobility was able to maintain a firm grip on the government of the Roman world. In one way or another the aristocracy could normally control the assembly and fill the offices with its members, and it also dominated the senate which was made up of the ex-magistrates. During their year of office the magistrates governed Rome and Italy under the direction of the senate; after their year of office the consuls and praetors took charge of the provinces and commanded the armies of the republic as proconsuls and propraetors, again under the direction of the senate, so that the supremacy of the nobles was practically complete.

Naturally enough differences of rank gradually developed and became important. In the senate a sharp distinction was made between the members on the basis of the dignity of the office which each had held, the offices being arranged in a fixed order of precedence; and it became a rule that a man must mount in regular sequence from one to another. Thus a Roman began his career with the quaestorship, which gave him a seat in the senate, where he was known as a quaestorian. From this rank at the bottom of the scale he might in due time rise to the praetorship, and after serving for a year as one of the judges in Rome he would then be made governor of a province for a year or more, as the senate might determine. When his provincial governorship terminated he returned to Rome as a praetorian senator; and he might now become a candidate for the consulship. If successful, he was one of the chief magistrates of Rome for a year and then governed another province for a year or more, returning to Rome as a consular. Both the consulship and the praetorship conferred nobility upon the descendants of their holders,[1] but with a distinction of rank. There were thus two kinds of rank within the Roman aristocracy—the rank of the family and the actual rank of any particular noble. A member of a consular family must pass through the same round of offices as any other man, though his chances of election were greatly increased by the distinction of his birth. Among the quaestorians in the senate there would always be many young men belonging to consular families along with others whose ancestors had never risen so high.

The consular families were the cream of the nobility; with the praetorian families they constituted the governing class, and the senate, dominated by them, was merely their instrument of government. To the aristocracy the republic was identified with the supremacy of the senate, and liberty meant primarily the right of the nobility to rule; a government in which they did not hold the offices and direct the policy through the senate was not a free republic, but either anarchy or despotism. This point of view possessed considerable plausibility, since the influence of the nobles was so great that with really free elections they had little difficulty in maintaining themselves in power under normal conditions. In fact their control was seldom

---

[1] Gelzer (*Die Nobilität*) contends that the Romans, at least under the republic, used the term noble only of the consular families. Even if this conclusion be accepted, modern usage has extended the term to include the prætorian families as well, and it seems on the whole better to adhere to the modern usage. The prætorian families were certainly considered superior to the knights, though inferior to the consular families. If we accept Gelzer's limitation we shall have to invent a new term. It will be simpler to call both the consular and the prætorian families nobles and distinguish where necessary by using the words higher and lower nobility. Thus employed, 'the nobility' will mean the entire group of families forming the governing class.

seriously shaken except by disorder within the city or by armed force from without. It was, therefore, natural that the great body of Roman citizens should accept with little question the aristocratic conceptions of liberty and the republic, more or less identifying both with the supremacy of the senate and the rule of the nobility.

In the last century of the republic, however, the influence of the nobility was undermined by a variety of causes. The wars with Carthage and the conquest of the Mediterranean world had resulted in a serious transformation in Italian agriculture. In many parts of the peninsula the small farmer had been driven from his land and replaced by great landholders, who turned their estates into cattle and sheep ranches or worked them by slave labour. The peasants flocked to the cities, especially Rome, where they formed a turbulent rabble over whom the nobles had less and less control. At the same time the conquests of Rome abroad had built up a powerful capitalist class, known as the knights, whose interests were often at variance with those of the senatorial aristocracy. Armed with wealth, the knights could exert a formidable influence, and when they chose to ally themselves with the rabble the combination had little difficulty in dominating the popular assembly. While such an alliance never lasted for any length of time, its occasional occurrence and its constant possibility made the hold of the nobility upon the government precarious. The result was disorder, confusion, and incoherence, since a steady and consistent policy was no longer possible.

The agricultural crisis had other results which were more obviously fatal to the republic. The decline in the number of the small farmers in Italy at length forced a change in the character of the military system. Rome won her empire with an army of peasant soldiers, drawn from their farms for a campaign and returning to them when the fighting was over. This was possible as long as the peasants were numerous and the wars both short and carried on in or near Italy. But the empire of the Mediterranean brought with it not only a rapidly diminishing peasantry but long wars fought at a distance. Thus at the same time the class from which the legions were recruited shrank in numbers and such as remained grew steadily more reluctant to enter the service. At length a fundamental change in the composition of the army became necessary. Marius was the first to take the momentous step of calling for volunteers instead of resorting to the traditional method of conscription, and by so doing he created a proletarian army. The men who responded to his call had nothing to lose, and were induced to join his standard by their confidence in him and by the hope of reaping profit from his victories. They were no longer an army of the Roman state, fighting for the state under such leaders as it might appoint, but an army of Marius, fighting for the rewards he promised them and unwilling to follow any leader but the one under whom they had enlisted. From this time on an army belonged to its commander, not to the state, and was prepared to support him against the state if necessary. This last was true because, if their general was superseded or lost his influence, he would be unable to fulfil his engagements. To secure recruits each general in turn was obliged to promise not only pay and plunder but in addition a bonus from the state in the form of an allotment of land after the victory was won.

Thus while the nobility lost their former control over the assembly, the senate lost all serious influence over the legions. The danger to the republic was too clear to be overlooked or misunderstood, but the senate was powerless to avert it. The conscript fathers strove vainly for peace against the inexorable pressure of circumstances which drove them into war. Once the sword was drawn, it became necessary to place in command some general whose name would attract recruits, and when the victory was won the senate had to get rid of its general and his army in whatever way was possible. The republic had no longer any solid support on which it could rely, and it could meet the physical force of a successful general only by the prestige of its glorious past and by an appeal to his own patriotism. Under such circumstances the tottering aristocracy was compelled to play off one military chief against another until at last Caesar overthrew their supremacy when he defeated their champion, Pompey, at Pharsalia. From that time until the restoration of the republic by Augustus the Roman nobility was in eclipse and the world was governed by the sword. But, broken by defeat and decimated by proscription, the fallen nobility still retained a strong hold on the imagination of mankind, which their misfortunes only intensified. Moreover, the governments which were set up by the army after Caesar's death did little to win men's affection or respect; on the contrary they brought nothing but civil war, confiscation, and proscription. Under such circumstances it was natural that the world should demand the restoration of the republic and should identify the republic with the senate and nobility. Yet a real revival of the republic was rendered impossible by the very causes which had brought about its ruin. The army was still bound to its leader rather than to the senate, and there was no way of changing this condition. The situation was so plain that men were seized with panic at the very thought of the retirement of Augustus, for all could see that if he laid down the supreme command of the army a renewal of civil war was almost certain. At bottom what the world desired was a return to the rule of law and a guarantee of order; but law was bound up with the republic, and order seemed incarnate in Augustus. Whatever powers Augustus needed to maintain peace the Romans were willing and even eager to confer upon him, if he would bring these powers within the scope of the old constitution. The restoration of the republic was necessarily in some degree a sham if Augustus was left in control of the physical force of the state, but it could be accepted if the old forms were observed and the nobility brought back to a position of honour and distinction. To make his government stable by basing it upon public acceptance as well as on the swords of his legions, Augustus was compelled to arrive at some sort of reconciliation with the fallen aristocracy. Broken by a long series of disasters, the old noble families that still survived were ready to accept his supremacy if he would concede their claims as a governing class. In essence, therefore, the diarchy was a government resting on the support of the army but carried on by officials chosen from the noble families. In other words it was a government of the emperor, through the nobles, for the people.

It was not enough for Augustus to restore the republic and surrender to its control the tranquil provinces of the empire while he remained at the head of the turbulent frontiers and the army stationed there. The reaction was so strong, or he so shared the prevalent feeling, that he went further and chose the chief officers of his army from the senatorial nobility. When he employed new men of proved capacity in his portion of the world, he felt it necessary, or at least desirable, to confer noble rank in the senate upon them before appointing them to important posts in his service. His chief officers were always consulars, and the rest were taken mainly from among the praetorian senators, and it was only in minor positions that he ventured to choose his agents outside the senatorial aristocracy altogether.

If such a system was to work, it is obvious that the emperor must be given some control over the membership of the senate, so that he could secure the necessary rank for the men whom he wished to employ. This was accomplished by conferring on him the special power of presiding over the elections and of commending to the people candidates whom they chose without question. Thus some of the quaestors and praetors were each year practically appointed by the emperor, and as the presiding magistrate at the election he could reject the name of any candidate to whom he seriously objected. Although he does not seem to have applied his right of commendation to the consulship, Augustus was able by his power of rejection to narrow the people's range of choice so as to make certain the return of any new man to whom he wished to give consular rank. If he chose to exercise his powers to their fullest possible extent, he could reduce the elections to a farce and leave the people nothing to do but ratify his will.

In the earlier years of his reign Augustus took care to preserve a show of freedom by leaving the choice of the magistrates very largely to the voters. But as time passed he found this increasingly difficult and narrowed more and more the people's part in the elections until they retained only the rather barren right of rejecting one or two of the least popular candidates whose names were presented to them by the emperor.[1] Many causes doubtless contributed to this result, but among them was certainly the steadily increasing need of the princeps for men of noble rank, even if not of noble birth, to carry on the administration of his provinces. At first he was able to govern them and

[1] For further discussion of the elections under Augustus see the appendix on 'The Elections under Tiberius'.

command his armies largely from the circle of his own family. But the number of his relatives grew less rather than greater and the number of the places to be filled increased steadily as the frontiers were extended and the new territory thus acquired was organized. The nobles might have preserved the vitality of the republic for a somewhat longer time if they had been prepared to sacrifice their monopoly of office, but to this their instincts as a class opposed an insurmountable obstacle. In the last analysis they cared little how the elections were conducted so long as they could maintain their position as a governing class, and the people—a pauper mob dependent on the bounty of the state for their daily bread—were unable, even if they wished, to make any serious objection to the steady abridgement of their power. Thus the tendency of the principate to develop into what was practically a despotism went on without serious opposition from any quarter.

By the time of his death Augustus had become in fact an autocratic monarch, though the reality was still elaborately veiled and the constitutional theory of a republic carefully preserved. The result may be described as a constitutional despotism, a government in which the absolute authority of the emperor was exercised under the names and forms of a republican constitution. The emperor was still legally but one magistrate among a number of others, more powerful than his colleagues but in no sense their superior, and like them ultimately responsible to the senate and the people. While he retained the *imperium* he could not be brought to trial for his acts, and though this *imperium* was conferred on him for a limited period only, yet its constant renewal made Augustus in fact an irresponsible ruler. Nevertheless he carefully observed the letter of the law, exercising no authority not expressly granted him, and constantly consulting the senate and accepting its advice. This could give rise to little inconvenience, since he possessed such efficient means of influencing the conscript fathers that they were unlikely to offer serious opposition to his wishes. Yet though the senate was unable to resist the emperor openly, it was far from being a negligible factor in the government, since from its ranks were chosen all the emperor's important officers, and this fact compelled the autocrat to pay some attention to its wishes and opinions. A breach between him and the nobility would make difficult the smooth working of the imperial administration; hence Augustus, and after him the better emperors, carefully sought to maintain a good understanding with the senate, partly because a quarrel with that body might entail disloyalty among the commanders of the army and the governors of the imperial provinces.

The subservience of the senate was at first due less to fear than to the control of the elections by the emperor and to the attraction of the imperial patronage. Every man who aspired to rise in rank must take care not to displease the princeps upon whom his advancement depended. To gain a seat in the senate he must be chosen quaestor; to become more than an insignificant member of that body and to become eligible for any office of real importance he must gain the praetorship; and to reach the highest positions in the state, the consulship was a prerequisite. His social standing and that of his family were involved in the success of his official career, and no man who had either political or social ambition could afford to offend the princeps. The man who lacked all ambition to rise was seldom disposed to give trouble, and in the vast majority of cases was content to live at ease. Hence as a body the conscript fathers bowed humbly to the imperial will, and their discontent took the shape of intrigues and plots. The republican theory of the constitution made these forms of opposition peculiarly dangerous, for there could be no fixed succession to the throne, and any noble might hope to seize the principate by a successful rebellion or conspiracy. This danger naturally created fear, and the fear exaggerated the danger, with the inevitable result of tyranny. The cruelty of Domitian had its root in such a situation; the monarch who oppressed and insulted the senate went in perpetual dread of the aristocracy on which he trampled, and died at last by the hand of an assassin.

But such suspicions and such fears were absent in the reign of Augustus. In his early years his immense services gave him an indisputable pre-eminence, and the nobles were grateful to the man who had restored the aristocracy to much of its old dignity and splendour after a long period of disaster and political eclipse. In later years the length of his reign, his venerable age, and the prosperity of the world under his rule combined to invest him, even before his death, with something of the halo of divinity. His genial and gracious bearing made it easy to accept his authority, so that even the proudest noble was hardly conscious of servility in deferring to the judgement of the aged monarch. Some bitterness there was and some malicious gossip, but they were harmless, and Augustus, secure in his position, did not deign to treat them seriously, knowing that his throne was firmly based on universal consent and his person protected by universal reverence. Even those who slandered him had probably little real hostility and meant merely to display their wit. In later years men looked back upon his reign as a kind of golden age. Dio records that at his death the Romans mourned him deeply, among other reasons, because 'joining monarchy with democracy he guarded their liberty while preserving order and security, so that, being free from the licence of democracy and the arrogance of despotism, they lived in a sober liberty under a monarchy without terror; they were subjects of a king but not slaves, and citizens of a democracy without dissensions'.[1]

But if Augustus seemed to have combined monarchy and liberty, the combination was unstable and depended too much on his personal character and personal pre-eminence to endure permanently. The liberty was largely an illusion which depended on the tact of the sovereign, and if the illusion were dispelled the reality was certain to be resented as a tyranny by the proud and exclusive aristocracy whom Augustus had contrived to dominate without offence. Tiberius was destined to be hated by the nobles, not so much because he really oppressed them as because under him they felt for the first time their own impotence.

It may be well in conclusion, even at the risk of somewhat tedious repetition, to sketch briefly the working of the imperial government at the death of Augustus. At the head of affairs was of course the emperor, but with him were closely associated the magistrates of the republic and the senate, while

---

[1] Dio, 56, 43. Dio must have drawn his picture from Roman writers. Perhaps it represents the feelings of the nobility afterwards, contrasting his reign with those of later emperors.

the popular assembly still retained a nominal place in the constitution. Each year the people formally elected the magistrates, and though the most important of them were actually named by the emperor, Augustus took care always to leave a few positions to be filled by the popular vote.[1] The lowest of the offices was the quaestorship, which conferred upon its holder a seat in the senate. There were twenty quaestors chosen each year, and this number sufficed to keep the senate a body of approximately six hundred members. Above the quaestors in rank were the six aediles and ten tribunes, and one or both of these offices was a normal part of an official career.[2] Next in order came the twelve praetors, and this office, the first of real importance, could not be held until at least five years after the quaestorship. Highest of all in dignity was the consulship. At first there were normally two consuls for each year as under the republic, but in the latter part of the reign it became usual for one or both to resign in the middle of the year, in which case additional consuls known as *consules suffecti* were chosen to fill out the terms of those who had retired. The emperor had the power to name outright a number of the lesser magistrates and to compile the lists of candidates from among whom the people must elect the rest. He could exclude any man from office by refusing to receive his name as a candidate, and he could push forward any man by commending him to the people. But although he possessed the power of exclusion, he was probably reluctant to exercise it with any frequency; the nobles claimed the offices as a quasi-hereditary right, and the monarch did not care to dispute their pretensions. In general it may be assumed that he contented himself with holding back a few conspicuously worthless or unfriendly nobles and pushing forward a few conspicuously useful new men.[3] When the magistrates laid down their offices they at once assumed their appropriate places in the senate. In the case of the praetors and consuls, however, there was a further career in the provinces.

The functions of the actual magistrates were confined to

[1] *Ann.* 1, 15.

[2] At any rate for a plebeian; a patrician might omit both.

[3] The right of *adlectio*, that is, the right of conferring rank without the actual holding of the office, seems to have been very little used by either Augustus or Tiberius.

Rome and Italy, but the vast bulk of the Roman world consisted of the provinces; these were divided into two groups, the senatorial and the imperial. The governors of the senatorial provinces were chosen from the ex-praetors and ex-consuls by lot with the requirement that at least five years must elapse between the magistracy and the provincial governorship. Of the senatorial provinces there were two classes, the consular and the praetorian. The consular provinces were Asia and Africa, the governors of which usually served for two years. The praetorian provinces were Bithynia, Cyprus, Crete and Cyrene, Achaia, Macedonia, Sicily, Sardinia and Corsica, Narbonensis, and Baetica—nine in all. Thus a senator whose career lay strictly within the republic after holding the minor offices and attaining the praetorship would remain in Rome as a praetorian senator for three years, when he would be eligible as a candidate for the consulship. If successful, he would then become a consular, and after a year or two he would draw by lot one of the senate's praetorian provinces, where he would serve for a year as governor. Returning to Rome he would, after a longer interval, draw one of the senate's two consular provinces and rule either Asia or Africa for two years. The remainder of his life he would spend in Rome as a consular, and as such a member of the highest rank of the Roman aristocracy

But besides the senate's provinces there were fourteen imperial provinces which were governed by legates appointed by the emperor and holding office at his will, often for a number of years. Although apparently bound by no definite law in the choice of his legates, the emperor always selected them from among the consular and praetorian senators. The provinces where more than one legion was stationed, namely Syria, Moesia, Pannonia, Dalmatia (or Illyricum), Upper and Lower Germany, and Tarraconensis, were almost invariably entrusted to consulars, while the legates of Pamphylia, Galatia, Aquitania, Lugdunensis, Belgica, and Lusitania were senators of praetorian rank. Three minor provinces (Noricum, Raetia, and the districts known as *Alpes Maritimae*), as well as the very important kingdom of Egypt, were governed by knights. In addition to his legates the emperor had still other uses for senators of high rank. In his army the highest commands were held by the legates of the provinces, but they were usually assisted by a staff of other senators. If a member of the imperial family was placed at the head of an army his staff often included one or more consulars, and the commanders of the separate legions were often senators of praetorian rank.

Thus a career in the senate's provinces was only a small part of the career of a really successful Roman. In addition to what was offered in the senatorial provinces there were the various positions open in those of the emperor, and these were the most important and attractive to a man of energy and ambition. Military honours and distinctions were to be won there, and efficient service was frequently rewarded by a command prolonged for years. Thus the great prizes of an official career were absolutely at the disposal of the emperor, a fact which was responsible for much of the servility of the senate. Moreover this condition was one which no emperor could change in any essential respect. As long as all important positions in the imperial administration were filled from the ranks of the senatorial nobility it was impossible for the senate to act with independence. The personality and immense prestige of Augustus enabled him to conceal with some degree of success the loss of real freedom under polite forms and legal fictions, but it was beyond the power of any successor to prevent the ultimate realization of the truth.

That there must be a successor to Augustus was not, perhaps, realized at first, since when the principate was established its founder was careful to conform to established precedent by having his proconsular *imperium* conferred upon him for a definite term of years, thus giving to his position the appearance of a temporary office, created to meet the special circumstances of the moment. He, however, must soon have seen that the conditions which rendered an emperor necessary were permanent, and that the Roman world could not dispense with a commander-in-chief of the legions without the gravest risk of civil war. To avert this risk might seem to Augustus his manifest duty to the state, and this duty could only be fulfilled by the practical designation of a successor to the throne. In constitutional theory this was a matter to be determined wholly by the senate and the people, who, at the death of Augustus, would decide whether another emperor was necessary, and if so would raise to the throne whatever person they might choose. In fact, however, it was easy for Augustus to make it inevitable that their choice should fall upon the man whom he had selected in advance.

This result could be achieved in two ways. Augustus might content himself with pointing out in an unmistakable fashion the man whom he considered most worthy to succeed him, in which case it was in the highest degree probable that his wishes would be accepted without serious question. But it was also possible for Augustus during his own life to confer the essential imperial powers upon his candidate, since the proconsular *imperium* and the tribunician power could both be held at the same time by two persons, one of whom was subordinate to the other. In this way Augustus could give himself a colleague in the principate who upon his death would be already emperor in fact, and all that would remain possible for the senate and people would be to confer on the new princeps the various dignities and special powers which his predecessor had enjoyed. Since it was thus possible for Augustus to designate his successor, he might reasonably feel that it was his duty to do so rather than to leave a matter so vitally important to the peace of the world to the chances of political intrigue or the arbitrament of civil war.

If Augustus undertook to provide for the succession it was very natural that he should prefer some member of his own family. It must have seemed probable that the army would be reluctant to accept a commander-in-chief who had never seen service in the field except as a subordinate officer, and that the senate and people would hesitate to place the government of more than half the world in the hands of a man who had never demonstrated his capacity for administration. Even if Augustus did not make his chosen successor his colleague in the principate, it would be necessary to give him an opportunity to win distinction in the imperial provinces, and this was only possible if he were appointed to some position of the first importance there. While his power was still newly established, Augustus apparently shrank from trusting members of the old nobility unrelated to himself with commands wherein disloyalty would be dangerous, for during the first part of his reign he seems to have kept the principal armies in the hands of men closely connected with himself. Caution and family affection thus combined to narrow the emperor's field of choice and led him to seek for a successor among the members of the Julian house. In his later years, when such caution had become less necessary, he might still feel that the aristocracy, accustomed for years to accept the ascendancy of the Caesars, would be far less willing to see one of their own number on the throne than a member of the family that had so long enjoyed an undisputed pre-eminence. This was a point of real importance; the Aemilii Lepidi, for example, would submit far more readily to a new Caesar than to the elevation of a Calpurnius Piso. Augustus might reasonably believe, therefore, that the peace of the world required that his successor should be closely related to himself and should, if possible, inherit his blood and bear his name.

The domestic and frontier policy of Augustus was thus intimately connected with his dynastic plans. If he feared the possible disloyalty of the old nobility he was forced to make use of his own relatives in carrying on his administration and in the command of his armies, a necessity which conditioned his choice of a successor, since under these circumstances only his relatives could gain the necessary prominence to be considered; moreover, he could not venture on an aggressive policy unless there were members of his family fit to be entrusted with the leadership of his armies. Although his policy on the frontiers and his family affairs were thus bound together, it will be advisable to consider them separately.

Whatever motives inspired his policy, Augustus spent the first years of his reign in organizing and consolidating the government of the imperial provinces. Here there was much work to be done which it was imperative to accomplish before any extension of the frontiers could be undertaken with safety. In Spain the mountain tribes were still unsubdued, and in Gaul the Civil War had forced Caesar to leave the work of organizing the newly-conquered parts incomplete. In the East the Parthians were always a potential menace, and the settlement of that region which Augustus had carried out after Actium was still recent and probably somewhat unstable; it was necessary to keep a watchful eye on the whole region lest serious disturbances should arise. With such tasks before him the emperor divided responsibility with his ablest general, Agrippa.

As soon as he had officially restored the republic Augustus turned to Gaul and Spain, where he spent some three years. On his return to Rome he dispatched Agrippa to Syria in 23 B.C., leaving him in charge there till 21. In that year Augustus determined to visit the East himself and recalled Agrippa. Since his general was to take charge in Rome and the West, the emperor, to remove all temptation to disloyalty, arranged that Agrippa should marry his only child, Julia, and thus not only bound the general to himself by the bond of marriage but very clearly indicated his intention that Agrippa should succeed him. From 21 to 18 B.C. Augustus was busy in the East, while Agrippa represented him in Rome and suppressed revolts in Gaul and Spain. On returning to Italy, Augustus had the tribunician power conferred upon his son-in-law, and in 16 B.C. he dispatched him again to Syria to oversee the East while he himself went to Gaul resolved to adopt a new policy on the frontiers. This policy deserves a word of explanation.

Augustus was a statesman rather than a soldier, and he seems never to have meditated a policy of conquest. He had no wish to rival Alexander the Great; to conquer Parthia, or to plunge at the head of his legions into the unknown wilderness inhabited by barbarians. He was content to organize and govern the territory which Rome already had, but he meant to hold that firmly and to rule it with a maximum of safety and a minimum of trouble and expense. This desire, modest in itself, necessitated at the least a rectification of the frontiers at certain points. A large part of the northern boundary rested on no natural barrier and was, therefore, extremely difficult to hold. On the eastern coast of the Adriatic the Romans had effectively occupied little more than a narrow strip along the coast, and their possessions there, known as the province of Illyricum, were exposed to constant raids by the mountain tribes of the interior. In Macedonia likewise the northern frontier was bordered by turbulent barbarians who gave continual trouble and threatened not only Macedonia but Greece itself in case of any disaster to the Roman arms. In neither Illyricum nor Macedonia was any permanent peace or real security possible until the Roman power had been pushed forward to some natural frontier, and the nearest such frontier was the Danube. To extend the empire to that river was, therefore, not so much an expansion of territory as an attempt to gain a frontier which could be more easily held and which would afford a better protection to the actual possessions of the empire.

In Gaul, Rome already possessed the Rhine as a frontier, but the restless German tribes across the river were a standing menace, and the best means of protecting the provinces annexed by Caesar might seem an open question. It was not unreasonable to think that the most effective method might be the conquest of Germany, at least so far as some convenient and easily-held barrier, which would in fact mean to the Elbe. The annexation of this territory, if the sacrifices required were not too great, would put an end to border warfare along the Rhine, and as the line of the Elbe was shorter it might be held more easily than that of the Rhine.[1]

In the early part of the reign both Augustus and Agrippa were too much occupied with other matters to undertake the military operations which the consolidation of the frontiers would require, and the emperor seems to have been reluctant to entrust the command of his armies to any of the nobles, lest success should make them dangerous, if not to himself at any rate to his plans for the succession. Now, however, that his stepsons were reaching an age when they might be put in charge, and that Spain and Gaul seemed well in hand, the situation was changed. With possible generals of his own family, in whose loyalty he felt confidence, he was better prepared to undertake a more aggressive frontier policy, and after 16 B.C. circumstances thrust the question of the frontier to the fore.

When Augustus married Livia she was already the mother of one son, Tiberius, and was about to become the mother of a second, Drusus. The two boys were educated under the eye of Augustus and displayed unusual promise. Tiberius was now twenty-six years of age and Drusus twenty-two. Both had already been introduced into public life by their stepfather,

---

[1] I can see no evidence in support of Baker's theory (51–4) that Augustus and Tiberius were opposed to the conquest of Germany, but that Augustus was persuaded by Drusus to sanction the attempt.

who had conferred upon them the privilege of holding the regular
offices five years before the legal age; by virtue of this dis-
pensation both had held the quaestorship, and for 16 B.C.
Tiberius had been chosen praetor. He had previously accompanied Augustus to Spain and Syria, where he had gained some
military experience under the supervision of the emperor.
When in 16 B.C. Augustus departed for Gaul he took Tiberius
with him, the senate having authorized Drusus to exercise the
functions of the praetorship in his brother's place.

The departure of the emperor for Gaul was perhaps hastened
by the defeat there of the imperial legate, M. Lollius, at the
hands of German invaders. The legate set promptly to work to
retrieve his reverse, and his preparations, combined with the
appearance of Augustus himself on the scene, led to the retirement of the invaders, who submitted to the emperor and gave
hostages for their future good behaviour. The need for immediate action against the Germans thus disappeared, but the
incident must have led Augustus to consider carefully the
question of the best method of dealing with them. Other disturbances took place about this time along the whole northern
frontier, and probably had a part in deciding the emperor to
adopt a forward policy. Before embarking upon it, however,
he tested the capacity of his stepsons, Drusus having now
joined him in Gaul, by giving them the command of some
minor operations against the troublesome tribes inhabiting the
Raetian Alps; their success in this task seems to have convinced Augustus that they were fully capable of undertaking
more serious responsibilities. When the emperor returned to
Rome he left Drusus in charge of Gaul, while Tiberius accompanied him to the capital, where he was given the office of
consul in 13 B.C. Augustus seems now to have resolved upon a
serious advance along the frontier, for he recalled Agrippa from
Syria and placed him in charge of Pannonia, where a formidable
outbreak seemed imminent. In the next year, 12 B.C., Agrippa
died and Tiberius replaced him in command. In the same year
Drusus invaded Germany, and the policy of an aggressive
defensive on the northern borders was really launched; Tiberius
was occupied with the task of subduing Pannonia and extending
the Roman frontier to the Danube, while his brother undertook

the conquest of Germany as far as the Elbe. For some time it seemed as if the emperor's plans would be carried out with comparative ease, for though both his stepsons had hard fighting to do, both proved able generals and won substantial successes. In 9 B.C., however, a blow befell Augustus in the death of Drusus in the midst of his German conquests. Tiberius was hastily summoned from Pannonia and took over the command of Germany. After two years more of fighting the conquest of Germany seemed so far complete that Tiberius returned to Rome, where he celebrated a triumph and enjoyed the honour of a second consulship in 7 B.C.

Although in 7 B.C. the position of Augustus seemed more brilliant than ever with the conquest of new provinces in Germany and along the Danube, it was really weakened seriously by the deaths of Agrippa and Drusus. He had hitherto governed the imperial provinces largely through the members of his family, and had made comparatively little use of the old nobility.[1] Now that his family circle had shrunk till only Tiberius was left he found himself in a new position and was forced to decide upon some other method of administration. In view of the general sentiment of the Roman world it was scarcely possible for him to rule his provinces except by the help of men of noble rank, if not of old noble families, and he was forced to draw upon the senatorial aristocracy for his officials to a much greater extent than he had hitherto done. Up to this time he had taken his officers and governors, if we may judge by such of their names as have been preserved, chiefly from the new men whom he had promoted and ennobled by conferring on them the praetorship or the consulship. Such men could hardly become serious rivals, especially as they usually acted under the general control of some relative of the emperor. In the early years of the reign such promotions could be made without serious friction, for the civil wars and the proscriptions had left many gaps in the ranks of the old republican aristocracy. But this condition was a thing of the past; by 6 B.C. the gaps in the aristocracy had been largely filled by the creation of new

---

[1] The only member of an old consular family who held a position of great importance in the first part of the reign was L. Domitius Ahenobarbus, and he was related to Augustus.

noble families, and the promotion of new men was becoming difficult without excluding some of the young aristocrats who felt themselves to have an hereditary right to such honours and offices as their fathers had enjoyed. Thus, while the need for men of high rank increased through the deaths of his relatives and the creation of new provinces, it was becoming less and less easy to promote new men, and the emperor was being forced into a position where he must either trust the existing nobility or take the risk of offending it.

The question of the succession complicated matters still further. As we have seen, Augustus had chosen his son-in-law Agrippa as his heir, but the sudden death of the general had destroyed this arrangement. The emperor's grandsons, Gaius and Lucius Caesar, were still too young to be considered, and Augustus, anxious to make some definite provision for the future, selected the elder of his stepsons to succeed him. Tiberius was obliged to divorce his wife Vipsania, to whom he seems to have been genuinely attached, and in 11 B.C. he married the emperor's daughter Julia, for whom he felt no affection. This alliance plainly indicated to the Romans the new position of Tiberius as the probable heir to the throne. In 6 B.C. the emperor went a step further and caused Tiberius to be invested with the tribunician power, thus making him his colleague. This had hardly been done, however, when Tiberius abruptly abandoned public life, and withdrew into seclusion in Rhodes.

The reasons for this step must always remain conjectural. It is certain that the marriage of Tiberius and Julia was unhappy and that her dissolute conduct had become a public scandal, of which no one was ignorant but her father. Tiberius thus found himself in an intolerable position; he could not pretend ignorance himself, and he shrank from attempting to open the eyes of Augustus to his daughter's true character; under such circumstances retirement from public life may have seemed to him the only way of escape. Another reason suggested by ancient writers may have had its share in determining his course. This was the marked favour with which Augustus regarded his grandsons; they had been too young to be considered in 11 B.C., but as they grew older it became evident that the emperor was more and more desirous of leaving his throne to one of them. Tiberius had no wish to enter upon a rivalry, which would probably have been unsuccessful, and preferred to stand aside before such a rivalry developed.

Whatever the motives of Tiberius may have been, his action seems to have taken Augustus and the Roman world by surprise. The emperor bitterly resented it, and Tiberius finally discovered that at Rhodes he was not so much a private citizen as an exile. The anger of Augustus was perhaps due to the fact that the withdrawal of Tiberius came at an inopportune moment. The emperor would probably have preferred to have his stepson continue as heir to the throne for a few years longer, until in short Gaius Caesar was old enough to step into his place. Perhaps Tiberius might have consented to this if it had not been for Julia, but, as matters were, he was inflexible and insisted upon taking his own course. The consequence was that for the next few years Augustus was compelled to manage the imperial provinces without the help of any member of his family. He was thus forced to depend more than ever on the senatorial nobility, and he appears to have tightened his control over the elections, perhaps as a direct consequence. It seems significant that the last law against electoral corruption was enacted in 8 B.C., two years before the retirement of Tiberius. After this time we may surmise that the imperial control became so complete that bribery of the voters was no longer a serious matter.

Augustus also began regularly to curtail the length of the consul's term of office; before this he had sometimes induced one or both of the consuls to resign before the year was over and so create a vacancy which was filled by the election of one or two *consules suffecti*, but this practice had been exceptional. Now, however, it offered a solution of the problem which the growing need of the emperor for men of consular rank in his provinces, combined with the increasing pressure of the claims of the aristocracy, had made acute.[1] If the emperor had not

[1] From A.D. 2 to 13 inclusive there would under the republican system have been but twenty-four consuls. During these years twenty-five members of consular families held the office; there were also seventeen consuls from families which had never before attained that dignity, and one whose name has perished except for the last three letters. Of these seventeen, seven are known to have held commands in the imperial provinces.

increased the number of the consuls by thus shortening their
term he would have been obliged to draw his most important
officers wholly from the families already noble, or to refuse the
honours which they claimed to a number of the young aristocrats. With the beginning of the Christian era the device of
having one or both of the consuls retire in July or August
became a regular part of the governmental system. This
shortening of the consul's term, together with the increasing
control of the emperor over the elections, necessarily resulted in
making the republic more and more of a sham, because all
possibility of independence on the part of either the senate or
the magistrates was now inevitably destroyed. In the early
days of the principate, while the people still possessed a real
voice in the elections and while the nobles could hope for little
in the imperial provinces, men might safely venture to act with
some degree of freedom, but this condition rapidly changed
when the attainment of office came to depend almost wholly on
the favour of the emperor. Even unambitious men were driven
to court his good will, since a Roman noble felt that his social
standing and that of his family depended on his success in
gaining his appropriate rank in the senate, so that a member of
an old consular family regarded the holding of the consulship
as necessary to maintain the honour of his name. The ambitious
had not only these motives but others as well, for an immense
mass of patronage, including all the most attractive and important provincial governorships, was at the emperor's sole
disposal, and these positions were now open to senators of high
rank if they could gain the imperial confidence. Thus all alike
were driven by an almost irresistible pressure to pay diligent
court to the monarch. This necessity caused little humiliation
to the nobles as long as Augustus lived, because the veneration
which he inspired, combined with his genial tact and gracious
manners, made it easy to yield to his wishes, and even flattery
had so much sincerity behind it that it seemed little more than
courtesy; but no successor could really inherit his position, and
his death was certain to be followed by a bitter realization of
the true situation by an aristocracy which had retained its old
pride in the midst of its new servility.

After the retirement of Tiberius Augustus pushed his grand-

sons rapidly to the front, and made it clear that he intended the
elder, Gaius Caesar, to be his successor. In 5 B.C. Gaius assumed
the *toga virilis* with unusual state, and was soon given a seat in
the senate. He was designated as consul for A.D. 1, and in 1 B.C.
was dispatched to the East on a special mission. In view of his
youth and inexperience the emperor sent several advisers with
him, who no doubt were expected to exercise the real power.
The young man remained in the East for several years, but his
mission ended disastrously, for he was wounded in an engagement with the Armenians and died in A.D. 4. Two years previously his younger brother, L. Caesar, had died in the West,
and thus a new plan for the succession was necessary.

During the life of C. Caesar a partial reconciliation had
taken place between Augustus and Tiberius. One barrier which
separated them was removed when in 2 B.C. the former at length
discovered the vicious life of Julia. In his shame and anger
the old emperor dealt sternly with his daughter, divorcing her
from Tiberius and banishing her from Rome. At first it seemed
that her fall was destined to be of little advantage to her former
husband, for a considerable time elapsed before Tiberius was
permitted to return to Rome. Even after his return, whether
by choice or from necessity, he took no part in politics but
resided in the city as a private citizen.

When Augustus undertook his final settlement of the succession his only remaining descendants, except his exiled daughter,
were his granddaughter Agrippina and his grandson Agrippa
Postumus, both children of Julia and Agrippa. Agrippa
Postumus, however, was manifestly unfit for the throne, being
coarse and brutal in his disposition,[1] and the emperor not only
set him aside but finally relegated him to an island as a state
prisoner. There were but two other relatives who could be
considered, namely, his stepson Tiberius and his grandnephew
Germanicus, son of his younger stepson Drusus and his niece
Antonia, daughter of his sister Octavia and Antony. In A.D. 4,
however, Germanicus was only nineteen years of age, and so too
young for the immediate succession. In his case, as in that of
C. Caesar, Augustus might have been content to wait if cir-

---

[1] He has been considered insane by some historians, but the evidence seems
hardly sufficient to warrant more than is said above.

cumstances had permitted, but his own health may have given him cause for anxiety, and in any case the situation on the frontiers was so menacing that it was necessary immediately to place some general at the head of a large army and to give him very extensive powers. The situation was too critical for the emperor to trust such an army in the hands of an inexperienced youth, and the only general of his own family, and the best perhaps that Rome possessed, was Tiberius. Augustus therefore determined to place him in charge of the principal armies, and to remove all temptation to disloyalty and all resentment for the past by formally designating him as his immediate heir. He accordingly adopted Tiberius as his son and made him his colleague by conferring on him the proconsular *imperium* and the tribunician power.

But though he seems to have felt himself obliged to accept Tiberius as his immediate successor, Augustus still desired to bring his own descendants ultimately to the throne. To accomplish this he induced Tiberius to adopt Germanicus, and arranged a marriage between that prince and his granddaughter Agrippina. The purpose and meaning of this arrangement were obvious. Tiberius was undoubtedly pledged to leave the crown to Germanicus rather than to his own son Drusus, and the children of Germanicus, who were the direct descendants of Augustus, would succeed their father. Tiberius would thus occupy the place of a regent, and he was so much older than Germanicus that it was probable that the latter would become emperor while still in the prime of life. The reign of Tiberius would, therefore, serve to give Germanicus a chance to gain experience and to fit himself for the responsibilities of empire before he was called upon to ascend the throne.

As soon as these arrangements were complete Tiberius hastened to Germany, where he gained some successes; but before he had achieved anything of decisive importance a great revolt broke out in Dalmatia and Pannonia, and he was called upon to undertake its suppression. Four years were needed for this task, and the young Germanicus was sent to learn the art of war under the eye of the leading general of Rome.

Hardly had this uprising been crushed when news arrived of the greatest disaster that had befallen the Roman arms during the reign of Augustus. In Germany Tiberius had been succeeded as governor by Quinctilius Varus. The province then extended from the Rhine to the Elbe, but it was neither well organized nor thoroughly subdued,[1] the Romans having been content with forcing the restless tribes to acknowledge their supremacy without interfering more than was necessary in their local affairs. Apparently it was believed that if peace and order were steadily maintained the Germans would gradually settle down and acquire the habits of civilized life. For the task of administering such a dependency Varus was quite unsuited, and in three years he succeeded in provoking a widespread revolt. Bad generalship was added to bad government, with the result that Varus at the head of three legions was entrapped by the Germans. The disaster was complete, for the general committed suicide and his army was destroyed. It was many years since the Romans had suffered such a defeat, and for a time the danger seemed acute. The Germans, however, failed to take advantage of their victory, and Tiberius hastened to the scene, where he promptly took measures to assure the safety of Gaul.

In consequence of this reverse Augustus decided to abandon the attempt to extend the frontiers of the empire beyond the Rhine. One important reason for this decision may have been the difficulty of finding soldiers for the legions. This difficulty had already made itself felt, for when Germanicus was sent to assist Tiberius in Pannonia it had been impossible to find enough recruits, and Augustus was forced to fill the ranks with freedmen, even buying slaves and freeing them for the purpose.[2] To replace the legions which had perished with Varus, it was found necessary to take recruits of such poor quality that they were later a cause of serious trouble.[3] Now that disaster had revealed the magnitude of the task of conquering and holding Germany, Augustus made up his mind that the enterprise was an unprofitable one and determined to content himself with inflicting such punishment on the Germans as would suffice to restore Roman prestige. For two years Tiberius was occupied

[1] Oldfather and Canter in their monograph on the defeat of Varus seem to have shown this clearly, but their conclusion that Augustus never intended the annexation of Germany seems to me an error.

[2] Dio, 55, 31.

[3] *Ann.* 1, 31; Suet., *Augustus*, 25; Dio, 56, 23.

with the defence of the Rhine and with punitive expeditions
into Germany, but in A.D. 11 he finally returned to Rome,
where he celebrated a triumph early in the next year. Henceforth he remained in Italy, and seems to have directed the
government for the old and infirm emperor.

From A.D. 4 to 11 there was thus continuous fighting on the
frontiers. During this time, although Tiberius was in charge at
the point of greatest danger, numerous generals of high rank
had been needed to carry on the operations. Either Augustus
still distrusted the old nobility, or else he found military talent
somewhat rare among them, for he advanced new men to the
consulship more frequently than in any other period of his
reign. In the eight years from A.D. 3 to 10 inclusive he conferred
the honour on no less than sixteen men not belonging to
consular families, while in the eight years from 6 B.C. to
A.D. 2 he had promoted only five such persons, and in the
preceding eight years (from 14 to 7 B.C.) but six. During the
frontier troubles, therefore, new consular families were created
on a more extensive scale than ever before, and this must have
been highly displeasing to the old aristocracy, for the rapid
promotion of new men threatened to modify the character of
the nobility and to undermine the position of the old families.
From the past policy of Augustus it might be expected that he
would draw his officials mainly from the new consular families,
with the result that the great republican houses would be more
than ever restricted to a purely senatorial career. Even here
any considerable intrusion of new men worked to their disadvantage in every direction; the shortening of the consul's
term made the office less important when they reached it, and
the increased number of consulars lengthened the interval
which must elapse before they could obtain one of the senate's
consular provinces. Moreover, since every consul must have
held the praetorship, the influx of new men in the highest
office must have made it more difficult for them to secure the
lower one. It is suggestive in this connexion that in A.D. 11
Augustus allowed the election of sixteen praetors instead of the
usual twelve, Dio says because there were that number of
candidates, and he did not wish to offend any of them.[1] We

[1] Dio, 56, 25.

may surmise that the special cause in this case was the number of members of old families who had been obliged to wait for the office in order that the unprecedented number of new men might be pushed forward.

With the return of Tiberius to the capital a marked change set in; from A.D. 11 to the death of Augustus he appears to have directed the government and to have been distinctly favourable to the old nobility, for the rapid advancement of new men ceased, and some members of the republican houses received appointments in the imperial provinces. At the death of Augustus such men were in charge of Spain, Syria, and Dalmatia. This change of policy must have been welcome to the old nobility, but it can hardly have been agreeable to the new consular families or to the lesser nobles who were still striving for promotion to the highest grade of the aristocracy. Perhaps in the last years of the reign of Augustus may be found the origins of the party strife destined to break out under his successor.

In A.D. 12 Germanicus held the consulship for the whole year, after which he was dispatched to Gaul. While in command of this region Tiberius had so far repaired the defeat of Varus as to check invasion of the Germans, but it was felt that more was necessary to prevent raids across the Rhine at the first convenient moment. It seems to have been intended that Germanicus should invade Germany in order to strike terror into the barbarians, although all idea of a permanent occupation of the country had been abandoned. In A.D. 14 Tiberius set out for the frontier again, but he was recalled by the last illness of Augustus. The aged emperor, whose health had always been delicate, expired somewhat suddenly at Nola, and a new epoch in the history of the Roman empire was opened.

III

THE ACCESSION OF TIBERIUS

AS the principate of Augustus was a new form of government, the death of its founder created a situation without precedent. Although there was no doubt as to who his successor would be, it was far from clear by what precise steps he should be placed upon the throne. It might even be argued that, since Tiberius already held the proconsular *imperium* and the tribunician power independently of, though in subordination to, Augustus, the death of the latter left Tiberius the reigning emperor, and that he had merely to go on governing the Roman world, only now in his own name instead of in that of Augustus. If this view were adopted all that Tiberius need do was to summon the senate and ask it to grant him such honorary distinctions as he desired and such of the special prerogatives of his predecessor as he thought it convenient to possess. But while this course would have been legal it would have violated the whole theory of the principate, by which the office of emperor was regarded as a temporary one, created especially for Augustus, after whose death the senate and people might confer it upon any person whom they pleased or abolish it altogether.[1] If Tiberius wished to respect this theory, he could not openly assume that he would succeed Augustus, or that, if he did, he would be given the same powers; he must leave to the senate the appearance of perfect freedom, and this necessity forced him to play a part in a comedy. The senators can have felt no doubt that Tiberius intended to mount the throne, and to give their recognition of him the semblance of an election it was necessary for him to feign reluctance and to yield only to their earnest solicitation. In this there was no real hypocrisy but only an observance of constitutional fictions. Tiberius wished to reign as the choice of the senate rather than as the nominee of Augustus, and probably the senate preferred that, if he became emperor, it should be in this fashion. Whether

---

[1] They might be held to have settled the matter when they conferred the proconsular *imperium* and the tribunician power on Tiberius. Nevertheless, since his powers had been subordinate to those of Augustus, it was theoretically possible for them to prefer some one else as the actual head of the government.

if the conscript fathers could have acted with real freedom they would have selected him must remain uncertain, but it is not improbable that under any circumstances the result would have been the same,[1] since he was the outstanding candidate, and, although he must certainly have had enemies, we know of no one whom the majority of the senate would have been likely to prefer. The populace might, perhaps, have chosen Germanicus, but it seems very doubtful whether the old republican nobility would have favoured him; at any rate they seem never to have displayed any enthusiasm either for him or his family.

Whatever the secret wishes of the senate may have been, in some respects Tiberius was by far the best qualified candidate for the throne. He was a man of great ability and long experience in public affairs, and no other living Roman could show a record of achievement as a soldier or administrator that was comparable to his. His character, moreover, commanded respect and inspired confidence. Even Tacitus admits this, for he says that up to the death of Augustus the conduct of Tiberius was admirable and that he was held in high esteem.[2] The historian sets this down as evidence of hypocrisy, but he is forced to concede that until this time Tiberius had maintained a successful pretence of virtue. In A.D. 14, then, Tiberius stood out as a man of high character and as the ablest general and statesman of Rome; yet he had some defects which may have caused misgivings among those who urged him to accept the crown. In his temperament and manners he presented a marked contrast to his predecessor; he was cold and reserved, lacking in tact, and inclined to be both haughty and aloof. He had spent many years in the camp and in the provinces where he had acquired the habit of command. Neither his natural disposition nor his training fitted him to play the part of Augustus, to lead while seeming to follow, to manage the senate while outwardly deferring to its advice, to respect the sensitive pride of the

---

[1] I think that Baker (135–43) is wrong in construing the scenes in the senate as revealing an undercurrent of hostility to Tiberius; neither can I see any evidence that there was ever a serious legitimist or republican party in that body (Lang, 36). The view that Tiberius seriously contemplated a republican restoration and was thwarted by an imperialist opposition in the senate seems to me still farther from the truth (Kuntz, 42–4).

[2] *Ann.* 6, 51.

nobility while yet maintaining a firm control over the government. Some modern writers have held that in spite of his ability he was distrustful of himself[1] and disposed to rely on others, at first on his mother Livia and later on his favourite Sejanus. Of this there seems little evidence, and it is hardly likely that a man of this type could have distinguished himself as a general. The facts seem to show that throughout his reign Tiberius acted largely for himself. His dependence on his mother appears to have been only a reluctance to quarrel openly with her, but from the first he resolutely refused to allow her any serious influence in the government. He may at times have yielded to her intercession in the matter of individuals, but this is all that is attested by any recorded facts. As to Sejanus, the evidence goes to show that he could deceive Tiberius, but could not control him. In other respects the character of Tiberius in the first part of his reign seems obvious enough. Though somewhat stern in manner, he meant to act justly, but he was wholly lacking in the qualities which win popularity. In spirit he was a man of an earlier generation, dignified in bearing, hating flattery, frugal in his personal habits, and cordially detesting the frivolous luxury then common in high society; in short, he possessed in large measure the *gravitas* of the old Roman. An aristocrat by birth, he felt a profound contempt for the mob and took little or no interest in the shows in which they delighted. He had a high sense of duty and held himself bound to the continuance of his predecessor's policy and to the rigid observance of the agreement by which he had secured the throne.

On the death of Augustus the course which Tiberius followed was in strict accordance with the constitutional theory of the principate. He accompanied the body of the late emperor, which was borne at night from town to town by the leading

---

[1] Baring-Gould (256) says: 'A feeling of uncertainty, of self-mistrust, was an integral feature of the character of Tiberius . . .' He further holds that this is shown at his accession. Tiberius was accustomed to a camp, but he had had no dealings with the senate; he intended to succeed Augustus, but at the last moment his heart failed him and he hesitated to accept the principate. This interpretation seems to me very strained. Tiberius had certainly had extensive dealings with the senate, for he had long been a member of that body and had twice held the consulship. I can see no evidence throughout his reign of any self-distrust.

citizens of each until at Bovillae it was received by Roman knights and carried into the city, where it was placed in the vestibule of the palace. From Nola, by virtue of the proconsular *imperium*, Tiberius issued such orders to the army as seemed immediately necessary, and he made use of the tribunician power to convene the senate, but he refrained from assuming the imperial title and, in appearance at least, allowed the whole question of the succession to remain open. At the first meeting of the conscript fathers the will of Augustus was read and the arrangements made for his funeral, but all other business was postponed. Tiberius professed a strong desire to withdraw from public life altogether on account of age and near-sightedness, replying to the expostulations of his friends that they were ignorant of what a monster the empire was.[1] When the last rites for the dead monarch had been celebrated with due pomp and his ashes deposited in the Mausoleum, the senate met again on September 17.[2] After the solemn deification of Augustus had been voted, the consuls proposed a decree declaring Tiberius emperor.[3] This motion he opposed, and urged the division of the imperial authority among several persons, saying that only the mind of the divine Augustus was equal to so vast a burden. This suggestion met with no favour, and the senators implored Tiberius to accept the principate. In reply he ordered a document in the handwriting of Augustus to be produced and read. This so-called Breviary of the Empire[4] contained a statement of its military and financial resources and obligations, closing with an injunction to restrict it within the existing frontiers. This document made no impression on the senate, and the entreaties to Tiberius were renewed with undiminished fervour. For a

[1] I am inclined to think that this wish was expressed in conversations with his friends in the interval between the two meetings of the senate, though he may have said something of the sort at either or both its sessions. His reply to Asinius Gallus (*Ann.* 1, 12) might be taken to imply that his wish was known to the senators.

[2] For the date see the entry in the *Fasti Amiternini* (*C.I.L.*, vol. i, 2nd edition).

[3] This is made clear by the speech of Scaurus.

[4] The term is from Suetonius (*Aug.* 101). Dio (56, 33) makes two documents of the Breviary and seems to me clearly wrong both as to the time when it was read in the senate and as to its contents. He appears to have confused the injunctions of the Breviary with the proposal of Tiberius for a divided emperorship. I cannot believe that any such scheme was advised by Augustus.

time he continued to urge a division of power, and would only agree to undertake a part of the government; but at length, wearied by the clamorous insistence of the conscript fathers, he consented to act as princeps until the senate should think it reasonable to grant some repose to his old age. After this outwardly reluctant and temporary acceptance had been secured, the motion of the consuls was at once passed and Tiberius was formally proclaimed emperor.[1]

The provisional character of Tiberius' acceptance not only kept up the appearance of reluctance on his part, but it led to his receiving the imperial powers for an indefinite period, and hence practically for life, even the proconsular *imperium* which had hitherto been held only for a fixed term of years being so conferred. If legal subtleties had still retained any serious meaning this change would have been a matter of importance, but in reality it merely did away with the empty form of renewing from time to time the most essential of the emperor's prerogatives. Yet the conferring of the *imperium* by the senate instead of by the people, taken in connexion with the implied promise of Tiberius to retire at the pleasure of the conscript fathers, might seem to transform his position from that of an independent magistrate to that of a prime minister responsible to the senate. Some of the speeches of Tiberius as reported by Suetonius[2] would show that he realized clearly this new conception of his office and accepted it, at least in words.

[1] The chief sources for the accession of Tiberius are Tacitus (1, 5–13), Suetonius (23–5 and *Aug.* 100–1), and Dio (57, 2–7). I have followed Tacitus in the main but have added some details which seem authentic from Dio and Suetonius. The subject has been discussed by Fabia (*L'Avènement*), whose conclusions are attacked by Lang (5–26) and Rietra (1–4). I agree in general with Fabia, but I am unable to accept some of his views. I do not see that Tacitus and Suetonius differ materially. Suetonius, indeed, says that Tiberius refused the principate, while Tacitus mentions no direct refusal; but the proposal to divide the authority might well be described as a refusal of an office which such a measure would practically abolish. There may, however, have been a more explicit refusal which Tacitus has omitted because the discussion turned principally on the suggested division of power. The final acceptance of Tiberius, as reported by Suetonius, seems to agree with the language of Tacitus, since Tiberius only consented to undertake the government provisionally, and nothing less could have put an end to the debate. I think further that there were only the two meetings of the senate described by Tacitus, and that Dio is wrong in postponing the acceptance till the suppression of the Rhine mutiny was known at Rome, which must have been sometime in October.

[2] Especially that in Suet. 29.

D

Although we may find it impossible to believe that Tiberius was sincere in his professed reluctance, nevertheless his conduct on this occasion involved no real hypocrisy but only a strict adherence to the theory of the constitution. He seems, however, to have blundered in holding back too long and so overdoing the part which he felt obliged to play. A few of the senators, becoming wearied of the farce, used somewhat plain language in their endeavour to force him to a decision, and one cried out in the midst of the clamour 'Let him take it or leave it'—a sentiment with which many doubtless sympathized.

Before he had formally assumed the title of emperor,[1] Tiberius had been confronted with the problem of dealing with certain prisoners of state. One of these was Agrippa Postumus, whom Augustus had banished to an island, where he was closely guarded.[2] Some of the counsellors of Tiberius and Livia regarded him as dangerous, and as soon as Augustus breathed his last an order was dispatched for his immediate execution. Of this order Tiberius was ignorant—perhaps he was absent from Nola when it was sent—and on learning the fate of the unhappy prince he threatened to have a thorough investigation made by the senate, but, yielding to his advisers, he finally allowed the matter to drop. Events soon made it clear that a grandson of Augustus, even in prison, was a real menace to the throne. The death of Agrippa having been hushed up, a pretender assumed his name, and might have given serious trouble to the government but for the prompt action of the authorities. One murder is laid to the emperor's account by Tacitus, namely, that of Sempronius Gracchus, a former lover of Julia, who had given Tiberius especial cause for resentment. Julia herself did not long survive. Tiberius seems to have made no change in the conditions of her captivity, but, with his accession and the death of her youngest

[1] The statement of Suetonius (26) that Tiberius refused the title of Augustus and never assumed it except in correspondence with monarchs is incorrect, for he certainly used it in the provinces. An instance in point is found in his letter to the town of Gythium (Seyrig, 86-7). Other instances are cited by Rietra (19). In a law passed by the town of Gythium itself he is styled 'father of his country', a title which we know that he consistently rejected. Probably the law was passed at the beginning of his reign before his rejection of it had become generally known.

[2] The story told by Tacitus (1, 5) of a last visit of Augustus to Agrippa is universally discredited.

son, she abandoned all hope of leniency or pardon and ended her life by suicide.[1]

Although the senate had accepted Tiberius with the outward show of enthusiasm, his position was far from secure. He was necessarily weaker than his predecessor, since he could not inherit the veneration which had been felt for Augustus. Great as his services to the empire had been, they were not of such a character as to silence all rivalry. He was the foremost general of Rome, but there were other commanders who might feel that they could have done as much with the same opportunities. His distinction was largely due to his relationship to Augustus, which had given him an ample field for the display of his ability. Moreover, his exploits had not been so striking as to give him any strong hold on the imagination of the common soldiers, and on the frontier the death of Augustus was immediately followed by formidable mutinies, the news of which may have reached Rome before September 17 and have had some influence in causing Tiberius to accept the principate in a provisional fashion so as to leave the way open for a compromise if it should be found necessary.

The difficulty which Augustus had encountered in the last years of his reign in finding recruits for the army had led to two important consequences. In the first place, he had been forced to lengthen the term of service, and, in the second, he had been driven to make use of poor material in time of emergency. In 13 B.C. he had enacted that the praetorian guards should be discharged after twelve years and the ordinary legionaries after sixteen, and that when they left the service they should receive a bonus in money.[2] In the course of time these conditions were found to be too liberal, so in A.D. 5 a new law was passed by which the legionaries were to serve for twenty years and the praetorians for sixteen; at the same time a special fund (the *aerarium militare*) was set aside for the payment of their bonuses.[3] These changes can hardly have made the service more attractive, and Augustus was forced to enlist freedmen and the city rabble

---

[1] Suetonius (50) says that Tiberius made her imprisonment harsher, but Tacitus (1, 53) does not mention this. I do not think Tacitus means to imply that Tiberius caused her to be put to death, but only that his failure to alleviate her captivity led her to starve herself, a common mode of suicide among the Romans.   [2] Dio, 54, 25.   [3] Dio, 55, 23 and 25.

for the legions in Pannonia and on the Rhine.[1] When the difficulty of finding recruits was so great, the government yielded
to the temptation of evading or ignoring the law as to the
discharge of the soldiers, keeping them in the legions long after
their term of service had expired. Discontent under such circumstances was inevitable and had long been accumulating,
but hitherto the awe felt for Augustus had been sufficient to
hold it in check. With his death this check was removed, and
outbreaks in Pannonia and on the Rhine were the immediate
consequence.

In Pannonia the mutineers forced their commander, Junius
Blaesus, to send his son to Rome as an envoy to demand their
discharge at the end of sixteen years' service, other demands
being postponed for the moment. After his departure the
attempts of Blaesus to restore some sort of discipline only
caused worse disorder, and the situation became highly critical.
On learning of the mutiny, Tiberius dispatched his son Drusus
with a distinguished staff and two praetorian cohorts to deal
with it. On his arrival Drusus was readily admitted within the
camp, but here he found himself face to face with a threatening
mob. Obtaining silence with difficulty, he read a letter from his
father, the language of which was somewhat vague, as was
natural enough since the emperor was not yet informed as to
the demands of the mutineers. He wrote that he had sent his
son to grant immediately such concessions as were possible, and
promised to bring other grievances before the senate. The men
replied through one of their number, demanding an increase in
pay and a full discharge with the promised bonuses after sixteen
years' service. Drusus declared that such concessions could be
made only by the senate[2] and the emperor. This reply was
regarded as an evasion and merely increased the anger and
resentment. While Drusus himself was not attacked, one
eminent senator on his staff, Cn. Lentulus, was nearly killed.
The outbreak seemed about to take an even more violent turn
when an eclipse of the moon took place, which was regarded by

---

[1] Suet. *Aug.* 25; Dio, 55, 31; *Ann.* 1, 31.

[2] Baker (152–3) regards the reference to the senate as absurd, but according
to Dio (55, 23 and 25) the conditions of military service seem to have been
regulated by a decree of the senate, and its consent was technically necessary
to change them.

the superstitious soldiers as a plain indication of the wrath of heaven. Taking prompt advantage of this change in their mood Drusus succeeded in restoring discipline and punishing the ringleaders of the revolt. His mission thus accomplished, he returned to Rome, whither he had been preceded by envoys from the army commissioned to lay the grievances of the men before the emperor.

While these events were taking place in Pannonia an even more formidable mutiny had broken out among the soldiers stationed on the Rhine.[1] The legions guarding that river were divided into two armies, the Upper under C. Silius and the Lower under A. Caecina. Both legates were under the supreme command of Germanicus, who at the moment was occupied in taking a census of Gaul. In his absence the soldiers of the Lower army mutinied, but the Upper was kept quiet by its general. The causes of the outbreak were much the same as in Pannonia, namely, real grievances on the part of the men and the presence among them of a considerable number of recruits of poor quality. According to Tacitus the men were also influenced by the hope, soon proved to be vain, that Germanicus would claim the throne and grant their demands in order to secure their support.

In any case, when the news of the death of Augustus reached the army, the recruits recently enlisted from the lower classes in the city of Rome began stirring up their comrades, and the result was a violent outbreak in which the soldiers set upon their officers, beating and killing many of them. As soon as Germanicus learned what had happened he hastened to the spot, where he was admitted to the camp and allowed to address the mutineers. After expressing his reverence for Augustus, he praised Tiberius and the unanimity with which he had been accepted as emperor. This was greeted with silence or slight murmurs from the audience. Coming to the matter of the mutiny, he asked what had become of their discipline and their officers. The answer was an uproar, in which the men tumultuously voiced their grievances, and in the midst of which some of the soldiers offered him their support if he would claim the principate.[2]

[1] Throughout my account of the Rhine mutiny I have followed Tacitus and ignored Dio (see the appendix on 'Kessler's Theory').

[2] If the soldiers really counted on Germanicus to lead them to Rome why

On hearing this he sprang down from the tribunal, but the men barred his way and threatened him if he did not remount it. Drawing his sword, he declared that he would rather die than play the traitor, and attempted to stab himself. The attempt was promptly stopped by the bystanders, who seized his arm, and was greeted with open jeers by some of the crowd; one man even offered Germanicus a sword which he declared was sharper than his own. This was going a little too far for the majority, and a pause ensued, during which Germanicus was hurried away by his friends.

After consulting his officers Germanicus decided to try the effect of concessions. A letter was written in the name of Tiberius, granting a full discharge after twenty years' service, with a partial release from duty at the end of sixteen, and promising the men a double donative. This device did not meet with entire success, for the soldiers suspected the forgery and demanded the immediate fulfilment of the promises. Germanicus was forced to yield; the discharges were made out at once and all the money at hand, whether in the military chest or in the private possession of the prince and his friends, was handed over to the mutineers. After this two legions marched off to their winter quarters under Caecina, while Germanicus hastened to the Upper army, where no disorders had as yet broken out. The oath to Tiberius was obtained without difficulty from three of the four legions composing it, but the fourth hesitated, so Germanicus at once granted them the same concessions that had been given to the Lower army.

As soon as the allegiance of the Upper army had been secured Germanicus returned to the winter quarters of the mutinous legions. Here envoys from the senate met him, and their arrival precipitated new disorders. The soldiers, afraid that the envoys would cancel the concessions, began rioting again and broke into the house of Germanicus, demanding their standard and threatening the envoys with death. The prince found the situation so serious that he was obliged to hurry the senators

did not all of them offer him the principate at once ? Perhaps they had heard of his having taken the oath to Tiberius, and, somewhat uncertain of his attitude, waited for him to speak before they acted. If so, his words must have convinced most of them of the vanity of their hopes. Perhaps also only a part of the army had ever thought of placing him on the throne.

away under an escort of cavalry. Something like quiet followed, but since no one could tell how long it would last Germanicus resolved to send his wife and son to a place of greater safety. Their departure was open and public, probably intentionally so, and it produced a strong revulsion of feeling among the men.[1] Taking advantage of this, the prince succeeded in working upon the emotions of the soldiers till they begged for pardon. This Germanicus granted, but only on condition that they should first punish those responsible for the outbreak. A wholesale lynching was the immediate result, after which the subordinate officers were brought before the men, and Germanicus dismissed those to whom the soldiers objected. Two of the four legions of the Lower army were thus reduced to obedience, but the other two continued defiant, and Germanicus determined to crush them by force if necessary. Already his staff had blamed him for not appealing to the Upper army for support instead of making concessions to the mutineers, and he now resolved to follow their advice. Nevertheless, he still shrank from the responsibility of dealing with the leaders of the sedition. To avoid the unpopularity which might result from severity, he sent a warning to the legions, declaring that, if they did not themselves punish the guilty, he would put them all to the sword. The threat was effective, and an indiscriminate massacre ensued. When Germanicus arrived at the camp he saw with tears the result of his policy, which seems to have been success-ful beyond his wishes. Discipline seemed to have been re-estab-lished, but Germanicus deemed it wise to distract the attention of the men by action, so he decided to make a raid into Germany before the army settled down for the winter.

Though he succeeded in putting down the mutiny it is difficult to feel much admiration for Germanicus.[2] In similar circumstances Drusus bore himself with much more dignity and courage. Probably the Pannonian mutiny was less formidable

[1] Baker (161–2) attributes the revulsion to the fear of the Upper army. The soldiers were probably uneasy on this score and somewhat dismayed by their own violence, so that it needed little to change their mood, but emotion seems to have been the decisive factor.

[2] Baring-Gould (263) goes too far in saying that 'Germanicus deserved to be court-martialled and put to death. A more despicable and discreditable pro-ceeding is not to be found in all military records'. Still there is some ground for such a judgement.

than that on the Rhine, yet nevertheless a commander who
stoops to forgery and delegates the task of punishment to a
mob [1] inspires little respect. His course was censured by his
own officers, who ought to have been competent to judge the
situation, and we can hardly escape the conviction that he
should have followed their advice, standing firm and calling on
the Upper army for support, and that his avoidance of responsibility for the punishment of the ringleaders was an act of
cowardice, moral if not physical. His conduct in refusing the
principate has been extravagantly praised, but the narrative of
Tacitus strongly suggests that in this case prudence and virtue
were upon the same side. The offer was made by some soldiers
among a mutinous rabble which had just refused to obey his
orders and which greeted his theatrical attempt at suicide with
derision. To place himself at the head of such a force against
Tiberius might well seem the height of folly. Many of the
soldiers had given no sign of support, and even if all finally
joined the movement, to march on Rome was by no means a
simple matter, since between the mutineers and Italy lay the
Upper army, fully as strong and as yet loyal to Tiberius.[2] Had
Germanicus accepted the offer he might have won, but to say
that he could easily have seized the throne is to go far beyond
the facts. Certainly he had no desire to begin a civil war under
the circumstances, and we have no reason to doubt that he was
loyal to his uncle and prepared to wait until the course of nature
should call him to the throne. In this he was honest and well
intentioned, but he can hardly be credited with superhuman
virtue.

The news of the mutinies caused a panic in Rome, and
Tiberius was bitterly blamed for not going at once to the scene
of the outbreaks but he remained unmoved, believing that his
proper place was in Rome until it should become clear that
Drusus and Germanicus could not deal with the situation. If
either of them failed he planned to set out immediately for the

[1] Baker (162) thinks that the resort to mob law was intended to prevent a
real investigation, but I can see no ground for such a suspicion. The mutiny
seems to me spontaneous and due to real grievances of the men.

[2] Later Silius was a partisan of Agrippina, but that fact throws little light
on his attitude at this time. Unless Germanicus was sure of his support an
attempt to seize the throne would have been a rash adventure.

point of danger, and with this purpose he selected his staff, collected his baggage, and had ships held in readiness for instant departure. As we have seen, the two princes were successful, and there was no occasion for him to leave the city, but his preparations have been construed by some modern writers as proof of indecision.[1] Such a view seems little short of absurd, since his course was obviously dictated by mere common sense. To rush to Pannonia without knowing whether his presence were not more urgently required on the Rhine would on the face of it have been stupid, and to be unprepared to act quickly if necessary would have been equally so. The facts speak for themselves and reveal Tiberius meeting a sudden emergency with coolness and good judgement, but without the least indecision.[2]

Though the mutinies were suppressed, Tiberius had still to deal with the military grievances which had produced them. Drusus had restored order in Pannonia without committing himself to any definite promises, but Germanicus had granted important concessions to the army on the Rhine. It was obvious that any discrimination would be dangerous, and Tiberius decided to extend these concessions to the Pannonian legions,[3] but at the same time to restrict them to those who would immediately profit by them; for the future he declared that the men must serve for twenty years before receiving their discharge, and this on the express ground that the government could not afford to pay them their bonuses at the end of a shorter period.[4] He must have realized that such a measure would perpetuate discontent in the legions, and it is probable that he adopted it only under pressure of necessity; the difficulty of finding recruits, perhaps, influenced his decision, as well as the condition of the treasury. In any case the mutinies had revealed a seditious spirit in the army, and Tiberius cannot have imagined that the final settlement was satisfactory to the

[1] Baring-Gould (264) says: 'One of his fits of indecision was on him. He was unable to make up his mind what to do.' This is a good instance of the evidence on which indecision due to a lack of self-confidence is attributed to Tiberius.

[2] Tacitus (1, 47) says that Tiberius was resolved not to leave the city, but the next words suggest indecision. I believe, however, that Tacitus regards the preparations as due to dissimilation rather than to any uncertainty as to what course to adopt.

[3] Dio, 57, 6.

[4] Dio, 57, 6; *Ann.* 1, 78.

soldiers; it may have been the consciousness of this that prompted his remark, often repeated, that he held a wolf by the ears.[1] Neither can he have been wholly pleased with the way in which Germanicus had handled the outbreak on the Rhine; to meet mutiny by sentimental appeals and to punish the guilty by mob violence was not a course likely to win the approval of a strict disciplinarian like Tiberius, or to inspire him with confidence in the firmness or capacity of his acknowledged heir.

Military sedition was not, however, the only danger which the new emperor had to face, for events soon showed that conspiracy among the nobles was by no means impossible. Although Tiberius was by birth a member of one of the great houses of the old republican aristocracy, there were others whose descent was equally distinguished, and not all of them were prepared to acquiesce in his supremacy. Early in his reign he received information of a plot against his life. The chief, and perhaps the only important, conspirator was a noble named Libo Drusus, by birth a member of the Scribonian *gens* but adopted into the Livian. He seems to have been a stupid young man, ambitious beyond his ability, and heavily in debt. Among his ancestors was the great Pompey, and he was related to that Scribonia who had been the first wife of Augustus and the mother of Julia, and these family connexions seem to have filled his mind with wild hopes of seizing the throne. While Germanicus was at the head of the army on the Rhine his plans could be only idle dreams, and though they were early reported to Tiberius he outwardly ignored them, merely keeping a close watch on Libo and his proceedings. This may have been partly to see if the malcontent could enlist any really serious support, but it is equally probable that the emperor did not regard him as dangerous, at least for the time being. Libo, however, appears to have had little backing, and he relied upon assassination for success. If Tiberius had been the only obstacle in his way he might have found a chance, but to murder the emperor was·useless while Germanicus and Drusus were alive; it was obviously necessary to remove all three at once, and, even then, there were several prominent men more likely than himself to gain the prize. He planned, therefore, to seize the first oppor-

[1] Suet. 25.

tunity to strike down Tiberius, Germanicus, and Drusus, and his most formidable rivals in the senate at the same time. A favourable occasion for such a crime was difficult to find and did not promise to present itself before the end of A.D. 16 or the beginning of 17. Germanicus had been recalled from the Rhine and Drusus had been appointed to the chief command of the legions in Dalmatia and Pannonia; between the arrival of the former and the departure of the latter there was likely to be an interval during which they would both be present in Rome, and Libo must perforce make use of this opportunity. Before the time for action had come, however, an informer named Fulcinius Trio learned that the conspirator had been engaged in magic practices and had sought to raise the dead. Feeling that he had sufficient grounds for an accusation, he at once reported the matter to the consuls, and the senate was convened for an investigation. The suddenness of this blow found Libo unprepared, and he could attempt little in the way of defence. As the news of his designs leaked out his friends and relatives deserted him, and he found no one willing to plead his cause. Really ill from anxiety, or feigning sickness to excite pity, he was carried to the senate in a litter and vainly appealed for mercy to Tiberius, who maintained an attitude of cold impartiality. The charges were read in order and Libo answered each in turn. The first ones seemed rather trivial, but a document was finally produced, said to be in Libo's writing, which consisted of a list of names, including the members of the imperial family and a number of prominent senators, with mysterious marks after each. Libo denied the authorship of the list, and it was necessary to examine his slaves, who were transferred to the treasury so that they might testify against their master. Seeing no hope of escape, Libo begged for an adjournment; this was granted, and he returned under guard to his own house, where he killed himself. In the senate the investigation was continued, and severe decrees were passed against his memory and rewards were voted to those who had exposed the plot. Tiberius declared that, whatever Libo's guilt, he would have asked the senate to spare his life if this had not been prevented by his suicide.[1]

[1] Tacitus stands alone in his treatment of this episode. He (2, 27–32)

This was the first tragedy due to the delators, and if any injustice was committed Tiberius was obviously not responsible. He himself had taken no action against Libo, but he could not decently forbid an investigation by the senate of a conspiracy which was alleged to threaten the lives of some of its leaders; neither was he to blame because Libo preferred to die rather than await the issue of the investigation. The whole affair, however, must have gone far to convince him that delation could not be suppressed with safety. The plot was stupid, but its essential stupidity lay, not in the difficulty of assassinating the emperor, but in the necessity of a rather extensive massacre if the murder was to be of any advantage to Libo. It was clear that Tiberius must take some precautions to guard his person, and the delators were the only means then actually at hand.

At the beginning of his reign Tiberius was forced to declare his policy in regard to certain questions, of which the most important was the law of treason. Under the republic the technical term for treason was 'diminishing the majesty of the Roman people'. Many attempts had been made to define the meaning of this somewhat vague phrase, with the general result that to incite mutiny in the army or to bring the constituted authorities into contempt was treason equally with the overt bearing of arms against the state. Thus slander of the magistrates might come within the law if the purpose was seditious. With the establishment of the empire no outward change was made, but, since the emperor was now the highest magistrate, the law could easily be invoked to protect him from vilification and abuse. Augustus, feeling secure in his position, refrained from so employing it, and treated those who ridiculed or defamed him with contemptuous indulgence. Towards the end of his reign, however, he sought to put a stop to scurrilous writings and banished at least one man, Cassius Severus,[1] for

represents Libo as a harmless fool, and implies that he was frightened into suicide by the baseless suspicions of Tiberius. From his account we would suppose that the case turned almost wholly on magic. Quite another impression is given by Velleius (2, 130), Seneca (*Epist.* 70, 10), Dio (57, 15), and Suetonius (25). Probably Tacitus derived his view from the descendants of Libo's sister, some of whom were still prominent in public life under Trajan (see my article on 'Tacitus and Aristocratic Tradition'). The nature of Libo's plot is revealed by an entry in the *Fasti Amiternini* for Sept. 13 (*C.I.L.* i, 2nd edition).

[1] *Ann.* 1, 72; Dio, 56, 27. Dio uses the plural without names; Tacitus,

attacks, not upon himself, but on some of the most distinguished
men and women in Rome. Whether this involved any extension
of the law is doubtful, but certainly from this time on defamatory libel came within its scope, though it had not yet been
applied to slander of the emperor. Soon after the accession of
Tiberius one of the praetors inquired whether charges of treason
should be allowed to come to trial, and the emperor replied
simply that the law must be enforced. The praetor can hardly
have been in doubt as to the course to be followed if any one
were charged with inciting mutiny in the army, so the question
must have referred to the recent action of Augustus in regard
to libel. Tacitus attributes the very natural answer of Tiberius
to the irritation which he felt at certain anonymous verses in
which he was accused of harshness and arrogance, and in which
his differences with his mother were commented upon. Yet the
facts seem to refute this explanation. Augustus had sought to
uphold the dignity and moral weight of the senate by shielding
its leading members from slander, and Tiberius, here as elsewhere, simply followed his predecessor's policy. For a number
of years he regularly dismissed all charges of slander directed
against himself and refused to use the law in any way as a
personal protection; indeed, it is not clear that in his entire
reign any one was punished for mere libel of the emperor.
Tacitus gives but a single instance of such punishment, and
the circumstances strongly suggest that in this case the charge
was seditious libel rather than simple slander.[1]

Adherence to the policy of his predecessor, however, required
one change in the constitution which Augustus had planned but
had not lived to carry out, namely, the introduction of a new
system of electing the republican magistrates. Hitherto the
forms of popular election had been carefully preserved, though
the reality had been reduced to a shadow. Thus in the case of
the praetors, whose number was normally twelve, Augustus had
'commended' some candidates, who were automatically elected
by the assembly, and had submitted a list of other candidates

however, gives only one instance with no hint that there were others. There
may have been other cases which Tacitus has omitted, but the vague plurals
of Dio are untrustworthy (see the appendix on 'Tacitus, Suetonius, and Dio').

[1] *Ann.* 4, 42. The man was Votienus Montanus. The case will be considered
later. Another man, C. Cominius, was convicted but pardoned (*Ann.* 4, 31).

from among whom the people selected the rest.[1] It was now determined that such right of selection as had been exercised by the assembly should be transferred to the senate. No law was necessary to introduce the new system, since the emperor in drawing up the list of candidates was not bound to submit more names than there were places to be filled. All that Tiberius did, and all that Augustus had intended, was to let the senate exercise the power of reducing the list to the required number instead of doing it himself or allowing the assembly to do it.[2] The chief change made by the new system was to relieve the candidates from the necessity of bribing and courting the mob; it took no real power from the people and gave none to the senate, for the emperor could control the elections to whatever extent he chose under both systems. In theory any person eligible for an office might give his name to the consuls, if the emperor refused to receive it, and might be elected by the senate; in practice, however, such a thing could hardly occur without the emperor's permission, so that a Roman's public career still depended on the good will of the monarch, a fact which no one was likely to forget.

That Tiberius desired to work in harmony with the senate is clear from every act recorded in the early years of his reign; but this was less easy for him than it had been for his predecessor, partly because he lacked the genial manners and immense prestige of Augustus, and partly because of the bitter party strife which developed among the nobles. Unfortunately we have no explicit information from any ancient source as to the character of the parties; nevertheless, a brief consideration of the composition of the senate at the accession of Tiberius will enable us to reach some probable, or at least plausible, conclusions.

When Augustus established the principate he carefully purified the senate of many unworthy members who had gained

[1] *Ann.* I, 15. Augustus had sometimes named all the magistrates (Dio, 55, 34), but this was unusual. Tiberius reduced the number of candidates for the praetorship to whom he gave his commendation to four. Probably Augustus had normally commended a larger number (see the appendix on 'The Elections under Tiberius').

[2] Dessau, ii, pt. i, 37–8, seems to hold the view of the change set forth above, but gives less freedom to the senate, and thinks that Augustus had named the consuls while Tiberius gave the senate a voice.

admittance in the confusion of the civil wars. Just what that body was like in 22 B.C. it is impossible to say, but since the principate was based on a reconciliation between Augustus and the republican aristocracy it is likely that they were strongly represented, and it seems certain that they soon came to predominate. The consular *fasti* [1] for the reign of Augustus are nearly complete, and from them we can form a clear idea of his policy, at least in regard to the consulship, where he showed marked favour to the republican nobility. New men were from time to time advanced, but the majority of the consuls were taken from families already consular. From 18 B.C. to A.D. 3 there were thirty-eight consuls from the higher aristocracy [2] and only fourteen lesser nobles or new men. When it is remembered that men promoted to the highest rank, if the promotions were gradual, would in the course of time naturally assimilate the sentiments and opinions of the class among whom they took their place, it is easy to see that the bench of consulars was almost certain to be controlled by the great republican houses whose representatives were so decidedly in the majority. It is, moreover, unlikely that, if Augustus favoured them so pronouncedly in the consulship, he was unfriendly to them in the lower offices, although their predominance there was probably less marked. It was only when the frontier became the seat of serious fighting that new men were pushed forward in large numbers.

At the accession of Tiberius we may safely assume that the old aristocracy dominated the higher ranks of the senate, where they must have formed a fairly compact group which would naturally seek to promote its own special interests as against those of the lesser nobles and new men both within and outside the senate. There is no evidence that they cherished any illusions as to the possibility of reviving the republic, but they were nevertheless the heirs of the old optimate party. This party derived its vitality chiefly from its spirit of aristocratic exclusiveness, and this spirit was in no wise inconsistent with

[1] The *fasti* here referred to were simply lists of the magistrates for each year. The consular *fasti* are much the best preserved.

[2] Not counting members of the imperial family, namely Tiberius, Drusus, and Gaius Caesar. Two of the thirty-eight died in office.

an acceptance of the empire. All it required was that the emperor should accept the higher nobility as the governing class and should allow them a more or less complete monopoly of the most important offices, not only in the republican magistracies but in his own service as well.

Opposed to this group stood the families of the lesser nobility and the new men seeking advancement. To some extent they were heirs of the old popular or democratic party, in that their main object was to break down the barriers set up by the higher nobility and force themselves to the front. This had been the essential principle of the democrats under the republic, but since the aristocracy had acted in politics mainly through the senate their opponents had attacked the senate and appealed to the assembly against it. The democratic leaders had sought to gain votes by putting forward a programme of more or less popular measures and thus constituting themselves the champions of the lower classes and the mob. Under the new conditions of public life, the assembly being politically moribund, their chief hope of breaking down the aristocratic barriers lay in the imperial prerogative. To pose as a friend of the people and to advocate popular measures was no longer a road to office, and so the democratic party abandoned its former appeals to the mob, retaining only its antagonism to the ring of noble families with their pretensions to a monopoly of office. The presence of such a party within and without the senate was fatal to any sort of independence on the part of the conscript fathers, for the lower nobility paid servile court to the monarch in the hope of gaining his favour, and the higher were forced to follow their example through fear of their success.

We can hardly doubt that the rivalry of the two parties ran the whole gamut of the offices for the possession of which they silently, but none the less earnestly, contended. Some modern scholars have held that the republican magistracies lost their importance under the early empire. In fact their importance was not diminished but only changed; if they were no longer sought through agitation in the forum, this was simply because the path to them no longer lay in that direction. It is quite true that a praetor or a consul was not now as important a person in Rome as he had been in the past, but even under the later republic men had striven for these offices chiefly because they were followed by the governorship of a province. This importance they retained, since the higher magistracies were still the indispensable preliminaries to a career, and the careers to which they opened the way were more splendid and alluring than ever. If the establishment of the principate had reduced the chances of gaining wealth by checking the plunder of the provincials, nevertheless in the imperial service a governor might hold office for many years, and not merely for one or two as had been usual under the republic.

The praetorship thus possessed a very real importance; to reach it meant not only the acquisition of noble rank and an assured position in the exclusive society of Rome, but it led to the command of a legion in the army, to a place on the staff of some distinguished general, or to the governorship of one of the minor imperial provinces.

The consulship was much the same. If the importance of the office in Rome had greatly declined, it still conferred upon the holder and his family the highest social rank, and was the prerequisite to the most important positions in the empire. We should expect that the existing consular families would seek by every means possible to keep this office in their own hands, because if they succeeded in this they would automatically secure for their class the cream of the imperial patronage, the command of the armies and of the principal provinces. As none but a praetorian senator was eligible for the consulship they would naturally desire to monopolize the praetorship as well, and to fill the quaestorship and the lesser magistracies which led to the praetorship from among the younger members of their class. Since their success in such an attempt depended upon the attitude of the emperor, the consular families could not venture to oppose his wishes.

Looked at in this light the struggle between the parties seems mean and sordid, yet it is not probable that it was wholly so, for the jealous exclusiveness of the great houses and the aggressive office-seeking of the new men could both disguise themselves under more respectable names and take the colour of genuine principles. Two rival theories were in conflict, neither of which was in itself base or selfish. If the aristocrats strove to keep power in their own hands they might, and no doubt often did, persuade themselves that they were the proper governing class, having behind them a long tradition of government and having been trained from early youth for the service of the state. They had as part of their inheritance the administrative experience of Rome, and the glory of his ancestors often served as a spur to bring out the better qualities of a young noble. The career of Otho is a good example of this. An idle and profligate courtier in his youth, he was no sooner sent to Spain as governor than he revealed himself in a new character and administered his province efficiently and well. If, therefore, the higher aristocracy clung tenaciously to power, it was not wholly sordid self-interest that inspired them but a sincere conviction of their superior fitness to rule.

On the other side, the new democracy could hold up the ideal of Napoleon, namely, a career open to talent. There were enough unworthy members of the old families to give force to a demand that the world should be governed by its best men regardless of the accident of birth; an illustrious name was not enough to make a man competent to lead the armies and guard the frontiers of the empire. An able officer who had won his position by hard fighting would very naturally desire the honours which he felt that he had earned and would resent his exclusion from all chance of high promotion.

In assuming such aims for the two parties we have assumed more than our sources tell us, yet hardly more than seems a legitimate inference from the general conditions. We have explicit testimony that two parties existed, and all the available facts concerning them point to the conclusion that they coincided approximately with the two classes of the higher and lower nobility.[1] If this was really their character it furnishes an explanation of a somewhat singular incident which occurred soon after the accession of Tiberius. At the first elections under the new system the emperor fixed the number of praetors at twelve, which had been the usual number under Augustus. When the senate besought him to increase this number he not only refused but swore never to sanction any increase. The motive of those who clamoured for a larger number is clear

[1] See my article on 'Roman Parties under Tiberius'.

enough, since it would facilitate the rise of new men to the lower rank of the nobility. Although the consular families seem to have offered no opposition in the senate, it is most unlikely that they desired any increase. Probably they were silent because they knew that the decision rested with the emperor and that opposition to his will was useless. As to the attitude of Tiberius it is incredible that at the beginning of his reign, while he was studiously seeking to make the senate appear as a great governing body, he deliberately insulted the conscript fathers by taking a solemn oath that he would never yield to their wishes. We can only explain his conduct if we suppose that he was well aware that an important section of the senate would welcome his emphatic refusal. His oath thus seems to have amounted to an assurance to the higher nobility that he intended to respect their claims and to lean on their support. Such an attitude was bound to alienate the lesser nobles, who would be likely to court the favour of his destined successor in consequence.

Such an interpretation of this incident derives some support from other circumstances. Tiberius was by birth and temperament an aristocrat, and his choice of consuls shows clearly that he was inclined to favour the old nobility as against the new men. As has been already pointed out, during the frontier wars Augustus had dealt liberally with the lesser nobles, and from A.D. 4 to 11 inclusive the consulship had been held by fifteen members of consular families, by three members of families of praetorian rank under the republic, and by eleven new men. The return of Tiberius to Rome was followed by a sharp change, and from A.D. 12 to 15 inclusive the office was held by two members of the imperial house,[1] by seven members of consular families, and by one new man.

While the manifest leaning of Tiberius towards their opponents would seem likely to drive the lesser nobles to rally around Germanicus, there was another cause working towards the same result. The prince soon came to be the champion of an aggressive frontier policy, aiming at the reconquest of Germany, while Tiberius, adhering to the final decision of Augustus,

[1] Germanicus in A.D. 12 and Drusus in 15. In 13 there was a consul whose name has perished except for the last three letters.

opposed expansion and sought to maintain the existing boundaries with as little fighting as possible. Recent experience had shown that war opened the way for promotion to the new men, so that they were naturally drawn to Germanicus. On the other hand, the same considerations must have tended to cause the higher nobility to support Tiberius, however little they may have liked him personally. Moreover, the fact that the lesser nobles were seeking the favour of Germanicus, apparently with success, must have made the consular families look forward with serious misgivings to the day when he would mount the throne.

The position of Tiberius was a difficult one at best, and such factional strife would only make it worse. Under the arrangement of Augustus he was a sort of emperor-regent for Germanicus, and this in itself was bound to create a delicate situation, especially since he was required to disinherit his own son in favour of his nephew. However loyally he may have meant to carry out his compact with his predecessor, it was nearly impossible for him to avoid suspicion; men could not help believing that in his heart he felt a preference for his own blood, and such a belief bred fear and distrust among the supporters of Germanicus and hope among his enemies.[1] Thus it is not surprising that the court soon came to be sharply divided between the adherents of Germanicus and those of Drusus, as Tacitus expressly informs us was the case,[2] and that the question of the succession became involved in the strife of parties, with results disastrous in the end to all concerned.

[1] It seems to me incredible that there should have been a party openly attached to Drusus unless his partisans believed that it would be possible to secure for him the succession to the throne. The only foundation for such a hope seems to have been the conviction that the arrangement of Augustus was so much in conflict with the natural feelings of Tiberius that he could ultimately be persuaded to set it aside.

[2] *Ann.* 2, 43.

IV

GERMANICUS

WITH the suppression of the mutinies in the army Tiberius might feel himself securely seated on the throne. Such discontent among the nobles as was represented by the conspiracy of Libo Drusus was hardly to be reckoned as a real danger, since it was apparently confined to one stupid and ambitious young man. Yet the position of the new emperor was not free from embarrassment, for his relations with his destined successor constituted a somewhat difficult problem. Germanicus had been placed in command of Gaul and of the armies on the Rhine by Augustus in A.D. 13 with the definite mission of avenging the defeat of Varus so as to restore Roman prestige in the eyes of the restless German tribes. When Augustus died he had not yet begun his military operations, but was still busy with a census of Gaul. The mutiny of the Lower army resulted in an immediate invasion of Germany, for as soon as some degree of order had been restored Germanicus crossed the Rhine in the hope that active service in the field would distract the minds of the soldiers from their grievances and facilitate the complete re-establishment of discipline. The summer was too far advanced for him to accomplish much, but in his raid he succeeded in surprising and massacring some of the Marsi; he then divided his army into four columns and laid waste a considerable extent of country with fire and sword, sparing neither age nor sex. The only result was to infuriate the neighbouring tribes, who attacked him on his retreat; however, he beat off his assailants and led his army back to its winter quarters in safety.

It is hardly likely that Tiberius regarded the achievements of Germanicus during this summer with much satisfaction, but whatever his private feelings it was obviously unwise to censure the acknowledged heir to the throne, so the emperor praised Germanicus in public and granted him the honour of a triumph. We are not informed as to the reasons officially assigned for the triumph, and it is impossible to discover from the pages

of Tacitus anything which Germanicus had done to merit it.[1]
Probably the motive was political, and the undeserved honour
was intended to allay any suspicion of ill-will or jealousy on the
part of the emperor.

During the winter Germanicus made preparations for a
campaign on a large scale in the summer of A.D. 15. For his
military operations in this and the following year we are forced
to rely on Tacitus, whose account is singularly unsatisfactory.
Germanicus occupies the centre of the stage, and many important facts have obviously been omitted. Thus at the close of 15
the triumphal ornaments were bestowed on L. Apronius and C.
Silius for their services under Germanicus; but what those services
were Tacitus has neglected to tell us.[2] In his account of the
campaign Silius is not even mentioned, and of Apronius we
learn only that at the very beginning of the expedition he was
left behind to guard the roads and bridges. It is certainly strange
that a general who merely watched roads and bridges in the
midst of complete tranquillity and another general who did
nothing worth recording should have received such honours.
The strategy of Germanicus, as it appears in the pages of Tacitus,
is also remarkable; it seems to have been his usual practice to
retreat after a victory, and the more brilliant the victory the
more difficult he found it to make his escape. In the course of
two years these repeated escapes had so discouraged the Germans that they were ready to surrender when the hero was
recalled. Because he avoided the fate of Varus, his admirers
compared him to Alexander the Great,[3] much to the disadvantage of the latter, and Tacitus quotes the comparison
with obvious approval; yet if Alexander had retreated every
time he defeated the Persians, it seems unlikely that he would
have conquered the East. If Germanicus was really an able
general, he has been most unfortunate in his historian. Tacitus

----

[1] A triumph could not be given for the suppression of the mutiny, for this
would have been a triumph over Romans. The slaughter of the Marsi and the
successful retreat were certainly not exploits which merited such an honour.

[2] Germanicus took both the Upper and the Lower army on this expedition;
the Lower was commanded by its general Caecina, and the prince himself had
charge of the Upper. Silius probably accompanied him and may have been
responsible for such success as was achieved, or perhaps there was a political
motive in the honour to Silius, as he had kept his legions loyal during the
mutiny.   [3] *Ann.* 2, 73.

has carried his idolatry of the prince to such lengths, and has so greatly exaggerated and so little understood his achievements, if he achieved anything of importance, that we can make out nothing more than the broad outlines of his campaigns.

Germanicus began his operations in A.D. 15 by establishing a fort on Mount Taunus.[1] His plan being to strike first at the Chatti, he dispatched Caecina with four legions to create a diversion and prevent the Cherusci from coming to the help of their neighbours while he himself launched his attack. An unusual drought enabled him to march with such rapidity that he took the enemy unprepared and so was able to ravage the country of the Chatti without serious resistance and to retreat unmolested towards the Rhine. Caecina, his mission accomplished, also withdrew after an engagement with the Marsi. While the armies were falling back a message was received from Segestes, one of the chiefs of the Cherusci. This tribe under Arminius had been foremost in the revolt against Varus, but Segestes, though forced to join the rebels, had always been friendly to the Romans and was besides a bitter personal enemy of Arminius. He was now besieged by his foes and begged for help. Germanicus returned, drove off the besiegers, and retired across the Rhine, bringing with him Segestes, to whom he promised a home in Roman territory.

Among the Germans who accompanied Segestes was his daughter Thusnelda, the wife of Arminius. The capture of his wife infuriated the rebel leader, who at once set himself to rouse his people against the Romans; the Cherusci responded and were joined by the neighbouring tribes. Alarmed at this movement Germanicus undertook another expedition. Dividing his army into three divisions, he sent Caecina with four legions through the country of the Bructeri, the cavalry through that of the Frisii, while he himself with four legions proceeded by boat to a point on the river Ems, where he met the other divisions. The united army now proceeded to lay waste the entire country of the Bructeri between the Ems and the Lippe. As they were then near the Teutoberg Forest, where Varus had met his great

---

[1] For the campaigns of Germanicus I have followed Tacitus closely. Modern attempts to determine what really happened, while often plausible, seem to me unconvincing. Perhaps the best discussion is to be found in the work of Knoke.

disaster, Germanicus visited the spot and performed the customary funeral rites in honour of the Roman dead. As yet, however, nothing had been done against Arminius, who retired before the Romans into a trackless country, where he hoped to entrap them as he had Varus. He came near to success, but Germanicus extricated his army and retreated to the Ems; even Tacitus does not claim that his hero was victorious in the battle, a fact which is most significant. On arriving at the Ems, Germanicus again divided his army; Caecina with his four legions was directed to retreat by an old route known to the Romans but long disused,[1] while P. Vitellius led two legions along the coast, and Germanicus with the remaining two legions returned by boat. The routes selected for Vitellius and Caecina seem to have been badly chosen. Vitellius was caught on low ground by heavy tides, and his men with difficulty and not without losses struggled through the waters to higher ground, where they were picked up by the ships of Germanicus. Caecina was attacked by Arminius, who must have been following the Romans, under heavy disadvantages owing to the nature of the ground, which was much better known to the Germans than to himself. For a time he seemed likely to meet the fate of Varus, but he was an experienced soldier, and the blunders of the Germans finally enabled him to cut his way through and reach the Rhine in safety.

Germanicus had accomplished little by the campaigns of the year; he had invaded Germany at the head of eight legions, had ravaged some territory, and had retreated. His only real battle was not a victory, and a large part of his army had been nearly destroyed, apparently as a result of his bad judgement in the choice of the routes for the retreat. There may have been reasons for the choice, but if Tacitus knew of any he did not see fit to mention them. All things considered, one can hardly help feeling that Germanicus was fortunate to get back to Gaul without serious disaster.

During the winter Germanicus constructed a large fleet, and

---

[1] It was a narrow causeway which had been constructed by L. Domitius across a swamp. It cannot have been recently in use, since Tacitus says (I, 63) that the bridges were broken through age. Why Germanicus did not send Caecina back the way he had come is a mystery.

at the beginning of the summer of A.D. 16 he concentrated his whole army at the Batavian delta, transporting it in his ships to the mouth of the Ems. Here he landed on the wrong side of the river,[1] which he was forced to cross under difficulties after marching inland for some distance. He had hardly gained the other side when he learned that one of the tribes in his rear, the Ampsivarii, had revolted; a force of cavalry was dispatched to ravage their country while he pushed on to the Weser to fight Arminius and the Cherusci. Arminius hoped to surprise the Romans, but Germanicus discovered his plans in time, and a battle was fought in which the prince won a great victory with little loss. Tacitus says that the Cherusci in despair were preparing to withdraw beyond the Elbe when they were aroused to fury by seeing the Romans erect a trophy on the field of the recent battle,[2] whereupon they suddenly changed their minds and attacked the Roman army on the march. Again the Romans were victorious, with the result that the Ampsivarii submitted, and the conquering hero was able to retreat to the Ems without further fighting. As it was now the middle of summer, Germanicus sent a part of his army back by land, but embarked most of it on his ships. The fleet, when it reached the ocean, encountered a storm in which many of the ships were wrecked with considerable loss of life. Germanicus himself was able to land in the country of the Chauci, where for some time he wandered on the shore, reproaching himself for the disaster and meditating suicide,[3] from which he was with difficulty dissuaded by his friends. After a time, however, the scattered and disabled ships reassembled, many of the men who had been cast ashore were rescued, and the more or less damaged army succeeded finally in reaching Gaul.

The report of the disaster to the fleet aroused the Germans again, and Germanicus felt it necessary to raid their territory once more in spite of the lateness of the season. He sent Silius

---

[1] Tacitus evidently knew of no excuse for what appears to have been an act of exceptional stupidity, for he admits frankly that Germanicus blundered.

[2] Their change of mind is too sudden and the motive for it too trivial to be very convincing. Probably they never intended to abandon their country.

[3] It is impossible to determine from Tacitus how great the losses really were. As the fleet had been badly scattered Germanicus must at first have believed the disaster much more serious than it turned out to be.

with 30,000 men to attack the Chatti while he himself with a
still larger army marched against the Marsi who, having lately
submitted, were now again in revolt. Meeting with little resistance, Germanicus pushed farther into the interior than he had
intended, devastating the country as he went, and finally
brought his army back to its winter quarters without serious
fighting. From prisoners taken in the raid he learned that the
Germans were terrified and convinced that the Romans were
invincible. Whether solely from these reports or on other
grounds as well, the prince was confident that the subjugation
of Germany was nearly achieved and that one more campaign
would re-establish Roman authority from the Rhine to the
Elbe.

It is difficult to see any basis for this confidence on the part of
Germanicus. His captives were naturally discouraged, but aside
from this there is nothing to suggest that the spirit of the Germans was broken or that they had any intention of submitting.
If the Cherusci had not yielded after two defeats, there was no
reason why successful raids on the Marsi and Chatti should
cause them to despair or bring them any nearer to surrender.
Apparently Germanicus had made no progress in the conquest
of Germany, and if this was to be accomplished a complete
change of policy was necessary;[1] the warlike tribes could never
be subdued by victories followed by immediate retreats, but
only by the permanent occupation of their country. Nevertheless Germanicus could claim that his campaigns had restored
Roman prestige among the barbarians, and, since this was the
purpose for which he had been given the command, Tiberius
determined to treat his mission as successfully accomplished
and to put an end to the war by recalling him to Rome.

Even if Germanicus was right in believing that in another
summer he could recover all that Varus had lost,[2] the question
still remained of whether the reconquest of this territory was
desirable. Augustus had deliberately abandoned it and had left
behind him a solemn warning against any attempt to extend

[1] Most modern writers have reached this conclusion. See, for example,
Knoke, 505–12 and Dessau, ii, pt. i, 11.

[2] Tacitus may have derived his information as to the confidence of Germanicus indirectly from some of the prince's staff (see the appendix on 'Kessler's
Theory').

the boundaries of the empire. This warning Tiberius was firmly
resolved to heed, and it is not impossible that he himself had inspired it.[1] The reasons for such a decision may be easily inferred.
The complete success of Germanicus against the rebellious
Germans would be of little or no advantage unless the work were
carried further and Rome's hold on the Elbe–Danube frontier
thoroughly secured. For the achievement of this object the
recovery of the old province of Germany must be followed by
the overthrow of a powerful state in Bohemia, where a German
king named Maroboduus, who had acquired some knowledge of
Roman civilization, had established the supremacy of his own
people, the Marcomanni, and had organized a strong army
drilled in Roman fashion. To link the Elbe with the Danube it
was necessary to incorporate a considerable portion of this
monarch's dominions in the empire, and in A.D. 6 Tiberius had
undertaken this task. The magnitude of the enterprise in
Roman eyes is shown by the extent of the preparations; two
armies with a combined strength of twelve legions[2] were to
invade Bohemia simultaneously, one from the Rhine under
Sentius Saturninus and the other from Pannonia under Tiberius
in person. The great revolt in Pannonia, however, broke out in
the midst of the campaign, and Tiberius was obliged to conclude
an indecisive peace with Maroboduus[3] so that he might devote
all his energy to the suppression of the uprising. This had hardly
been accomplished after three years of fighting when the news
arrived of the defeat of Varus. Although Maroboduus had remained quiet during the Pannonian war, he could not be
expected to look on passively while Rome reconquered Germany,
since he had received ample warning of what her occupation of
that country would mean for him. Under these circumstances
Augustus made up his mind to renounce once for all the Elbe-
Danube frontier and fall back upon the Rhine. The recent
victories of Germanicus had in no way altered the strategic
situation, for however indifferent Maroboduus might be to
punitive invasions of Germany, if the Roman operations
assumed a more serious character he was almost certain to be
drawn into the conflict. Tiberius was determined not to risk
so formidable a struggle nor to permit Germanicus to reverse

[1] Baker, 145. [2] *Ann.* 2, 46. [3] *Ann.* 2, 46; Dio, 55, 28.

the policy of Augustus by reopening the closed question of the northern frontier.

Nor were these the only aspects of the matter which Tiberius was bound to consider. There is sufficient evidence to justify the conclusion that the wars in the last years of Augustus had drained the resources of the empire both in men and money. We have seen what desperate measures were found necessary to fill the ranks of the legions, and the grievances of which the soldiers complained during the mutinies of A.D. 14 suggest a scarcity of money as well as of recruits, a suggestion confirmed by the reason given by Tiberius when he cancelled the concessions which had been granted to the mutineers, namely, that the treasury was unequal to the burden they imposed.[1] No doubt the empire possessed men enough and wealth enough for the conquest of the Germans and Maroboduus combined, but neither the men nor the money could be made available without a more or less profound modification of the military and fiscal system of Augustus. That no temporary expedients would suffice was clear from the fact that success would make necessary a permanent increase in the army and the revenues, since the eight legions on the Rhine were plainly inadequate for the double task of guarding effectively the Elbe-Danube frontier and at the same time maintaining order in Gaul,[2] and it was impossible to expect that the new provinces which might be acquired could be made to defray the cost of the additional legions necessary for their defence. To changes so important and so far-reaching in their effects Tiberius was strongly opposed,[3] and it is, therefore, not surprising that he should have refused to continue a war which had now become at once useless and dangerous.

Moreover, even had Tiberius been willing to sanction an attempt to conquer Germany, he must have felt grave doubts as to whether Germanicus was the right man for the work. The prince's campaigns had so far shown heavy losses without appreciable results, for in A.D. 16 he was still fighting the Marsi,

[1] *Ann.* 1, 78.

[2] The necessity of a considerable force for this purpose was shown by the revolt of Sacrovir in A.D. 21 (*Ann.* 3, 40–7).

[3] His probable reasons will be discussed in chapter vi, where his policy as a whole is considered.

one of the tribes nearest to the Rhine and the first he had attacked, and it must have been far from reassuring to observe
how narrowly he had escaped an appalling disaster on several
occasions. Tiberius evidently experienced such misgivings, for
we are told[1] that he spoke of Germanicus' deeds as wholly unimportant and his victories as ruinous to the state. This
language may be exaggerated, but Tiberius had good grounds
for distrusting the prince's generalship and for refusing to allow
him to run further risks which could serve no useful purpose.
Whatever the emperor's private feelings towards Germanicus
may have been, he was justified in declining to permit the prince
to win glory for himself at the expense of the best interests of
the empire, especially as the glory was uncertain, while Rome
was bound to lose whatever happened.

Tiberius may also have had private reasons for the recall of
Germanicus, for, though the latter had refused the offer of the
mutinous soldiers to proclaim him emperor, it might seem un-
safe to trust entirely to his loyalty for an indefinite period. His
wife Agrippina was ambitious; she was openly at odds with the
empress mother Livia, and very probably she was unfriendly to
Tiberius himself. She was, apparently, zealously courting
popularity with the army, mingling freely with the soldiers,
in defiance of what old Roman custom regarded as proper. It
must have seemed possible that her influence and that of his
soldiers might in time prevail with the weak and amiable
prince, and that he might ultimately accept what in a sudden
crisis he had rejected. At any rate Tiberius can hardly be blamed
for hesitating to stake the security of his life and throne upon
the firmness of one man. The longer Germanicus remained on
the Rhine the greater the danger became, because, whatever his
capacity as a general may have been, he possessed those gifts
which make for popularity and was rapidly becoming the idol
of the most powerful of the Roman armies.[2] A sense of public
duty blended with more personal reasons, perhaps, to lead
Tiberius to decide that the German campaign in the summer
of A.D. 16 should be the last, and that Germanicus should be

---

[1] Suet. 52.
[2] Tacitus, Dio, and Suetonius have probably exaggerated the popularity of
Germanicus, but it was doubtless real nevertheless.

removed from the command. This was clearly necessary if the attempt to conquer Germany was to be stopped, and on this the emperor was firmly resolved.

Although determined to recall Germanicus, Tiberius was anxious to prevent the recall from appearing to the public in the light of a disgrace. Such a course was obviously dictated by prudence, for so able a man as Tiberius must have seen than an open breach with his heir would greatly enhance the difficulties of his own position. Unless and until he was prepared to set aside the arrangement of Augustus as to the succession it was highly desirable to keep on outwardly good terms with the emperor-designate. On the point that Germanicus should return Tiberius was inflexible, but he was ready to shower honours upon the prince. In vain Germanicus begged for one more year to complete the conquest of Germany; the emperor, while lavish of compliments and excuses,[1] was insistent on his return. In the end the prince obeyed, and with a heavy heart laid down his command.

The reason publicly assigned for the recall of Germanicus was the imperative need of his presence in the East, where a critical situation had recently developed. The defence of the empire in this region had long been recognized as one of the most serious problems confronting the government, since this was the only quarter in which Rome found herself in contact with a powerful and civilized people whom she had been unable to subdue. Her attempts to conquer the Parthians had taught her that a war with them could hardly fail to prove disastrous, for victory was impossible except at a ruinous cost, and defeat might mean the loss or devastation of some of her fairest provinces. It was natural, therefore, that such far-sighted statesmen as Augustus and Tiberius should direct their Eastern policy to the maintenance of peace. Before discussing this major problem, however, it will be well to glance briefly at some of the minor ones with which it was involved.

When Augustus settled Eastern affairs after the death of Antony he deemed it wise to allow a number of vassal king-

---

[1] Tacitus represents the excuses as insincere, and there can be no doubt that he was right, but under the circumstances Tiberius could hardly assign his real reasons more clearly than Tacitus represents him as doing.

doms to remain, and contented himself with a change of monarchs in some of them. After his reorganization there were two senatorial provinces, Asia and Bithynia-Pontus, and one imperial province, Syria, while a group of dependent states extended from the Black Sea to the Mediterranean. The most important of these states were Galatia and Cappadocia in the centre, with Pontus to the north, and Commagene and Cilicia to the south. To the east of Pontus and Cappadocia lay the kingdom of Armenia, and beyond the frontiers of Commagene and Syria stretched the dominions of Parthia. Such an arrangement obviously lacked the elements of permanence, however useful it might be as a temporary expedient. It was inevitable that Rome should sooner or later seek to unite her separated provinces and that she should be reluctant to rely indefinitely on the fidelity of client kings who were exposed to the seductions and intrigues of potentially hostile powers and who occupied positions of strategic importance. Augustus might be willing to trust the kings on whom he had himself bestowed the crown, but the ultimate annexation of these kingdoms could be only a question of time. It is not unlikely that Augustus regarded the matter in this light, for the process of annexation was promptly begun. In 25 B.C., on the death of Amyntas, king of Galatia, his kingdom was made a Roman province. Here, however, Augustus paused, and when in 8 B.C. Polemo, king of Pontus, was killed in war, his widow Pythodoris, a granddaughter of Mark Antony, was allowed to govern Pontus as queen.[1] The motive in this case is not difficult to guess, for there would have been little gain in annexing Pontus as long as Cappadocia remained a vassal state, and a royal house there might prove a useful weapon in dealing with Armenia and the kingdom of the Cimmerian Bosporus.

It seems altogether reasonable to conclude that Augustus intended to annex the other petty kingdom as occasion arose in the same fashion as Galatia, and that no further steps were taken in this direction simply because the occasion did not arise, for all the kings except Polemo and Amyntas survived him, and their conduct was doubtless such as to furnish no motive or justification for their deposition. No sooner was Augustus

[1] On Pythodoris see the *Prosopographia*.

dead, however, than events began to move rapidly. Tiberius apparently had made up his mind to the prompt annexation of Cappadocia, whose king, Archelaus, was summoned to Rome in A.D. 17 and there tried before the senate on a charge of treason. He was acquitted but died soon afterwards, and his kingdom was declared a Roman province. It is impossible to determine with certainty what the motives of Tiberius were in this case. Both Tacitus and Dio attribute his action to a grudge against Archelaus dating back to the time of the exile at Rhodes, but the circumstances suggest that there were probably other and more weighty reasons. The king was old, crippled with gout, and his mental faculties were believed to be impaired.[1] The charge of treason seems plausible in connexion with the disturbed condition of Armenia at the time, for it is not unlikely that intrigues were being hatched in Cappadocia and that Tiberius became convinced that, whether Archelaus was involved in them or not, he was no longer fit to be trusted with the government. If this be true, it is probable that Tiberius had no desire to have the king condemned to death, but simply wished the senate to depose him. Of course the emperor could have accomplished his purpose without consulting the senate, but such a consultation was in line with his whole policy in the early part of his reign. It seems unnecessary to seek for old animosities to explain why a man concerning whose loyalty or capacity there was any doubt should not be allowed to remain in a position where his weakness or treachery might have the gravest consequences.

At about the same time that Archelaus was removed the kings of Commagene and Cilicia died, and their kingdoms were also promptly annexed. By these steps Rome's possessions in Asia Minor were consolidated and linked with Syria. Only one client kingdom of any importance remained, that of Pontus, and this was not only so situated that it could do little harm, but its royal family seemed likely to be of great service to Tiberius in dealing with the Armenian question. Probably these considerations protected it, and Pythodoris continued to rule it as queen, although she had been married to Archelaus, and it might have

---

[1] *Ann.* 2, 42 ; Dio, 57, 17. Tacitus says nothing of insanity, but Dio admits that the king's mind had given way once before, although at the trial his dementia was feigned.

been expected that she would share his downfall. The extinction of the kingdoms of Commagene and Cilicia is attributed by Tacitus to the fact that the deaths of their kings left them in disorder and that the majority of their people wished to be brought under the direct government of Rome.[1] Such an attitude is easily understood when we consider that both of them were small in size and that the maintenance of a royal court was likely to be decidedly more expensive than the cost of the imperial administration. The wishes of the people would probably not have deterred Tiberius had they run counter to his policy, but if the people were ready to submit quietly to the Roman authority the last motive for continuing the existence of these petty states was swept away.

The settlement of these newly annexed districts was part of the mission of Germanicus; another and much more delicate task was to deal with Parthia and Armenia, where disturbances had recently occurred which required serious attention. The Parthian monarchy had been founded in the middle of the third century B.C. in what was then an outlying province of the Seleucid empire by a king named Arsaces, and it had grown with the increasing weakness of the Seleucids until by 127 B.C.[2] its kings had secured possession of Mesopotamia. Its westward expansion was checked at the Euphrates, partly by internal dissensions and partly by the development of Roman power in Syria; but it remained a constant menace to the Asiatic provinces of Rome. Caesar had planned the conquest of Parthia, and after his murder Antony had tried to carry out his plans, but the attempt ended in failure, and Augustus definitely abandoned the project. With the renunciation of all aggressive designs the policy of Rome was directed solely to the maintenance of peace, but nevertheless it was at times attended with serious difficulties. The Arsacids had founded their kingdom by the help of Scythian nomads, and these nomads remained the dominant element and the basis of their power. The army was composed chiefly of mounted archers while the infantry was little developed, and in this fact lay at once the strength and the

---

[1] *Ann.* 2, 42.

[2] For dates and details, where no other reference is given I have followed Eduard Meyer's articles in the *Britannica*.

E

weakness of the Parthians. Against their mobile cavalry the Romans had found their legions practically helpless, so that an invasion of Parthia was a dangerous undertaking, and the nature of the Parthian army made it a formidable weapon for attack. It was not, indeed, probable that such an army could permanently hold any of the eastern territories of Rome, but it might easily devastate them if an opportunity for invasion presented itself. It was thus a matter of great importance to hold the Parthians in check, and this was rendered difficult by the fact that direct retaliation involved greater risks for the Romans than for the Parthians. It was therefore necessary to resort to indirect means, and for this reason Armenia became an essential factor in Rome's Eastern policy.[1]

The geographical position of Armenia was such that its control was of the utmost significance both to Rome and to the Arsacid kings. As long as it remained in close alliance with Rome there was little danger that the Parthians would venture on an invasion of her provinces. The territories directly governed by the Arsacids 'consisted of a rather narrow strip of land, stretching from the Euphrates and north Babylonia through southern Media and Parthia as far as Arachosia (north-west Afghanistan)',[2] with vassal states upon all sides. If the Parthian army advanced into Syria, the Armenians by descending from their mountains into Mesopotamia might effectually cut off its retreat, and if this occurred it was not unlikely that the vassal states would seize the opportunity to revolt and attack the more or less defenceless kingdom. A king devoted to Rome on the throne of Armenia thus constituted the best available insurance against a war with Parthia, and both Augustus and Tiberius were fully alive to this fact. On the

[1] Commercial reasons have been suggested for Rome's desire to control Armenia. It is certain that a considerable trade in spices, silks, and precious stones was carried on with India and China. In part this trade passed through Mesopotamia, but there was another route to the north of Armenia through Turkestan and the Caspian region. If Armenia was friendly this route could not be interfered with by the Parthians. In view of the character of Tiberius it seems unlikely that he was much concerned about the traffic in these eastern luxuries, the use of which was condemned by conservative Roman opinion. Whatever may have been the case with later emperors, it is probable that his policy was dictated almost wholly by political considerations (Charlesworth, 104-11; and Warmington, 33).

[2] Quoted from Meyer in the *Britannica*, xvii, 576 (14th edition).

other hand, if the Arsacids could contrive to place the Armenian crown on the head of a prince allied to them they could venture an attack with comparative impunity. Whether they would desire a war with Rome might depend almost entirely on the internal situation at any given time, for the Parthian kings were never able to organize a really stable government, and their power was liable to collapse suddenly, for, while the Parthian magnates clung to the royal house, they had little loyalty to the reigning sovereign. Kings were banished and restored with bewildering frequency, and were forced to guard themselves constantly against rivals and conspiracies. Under such conditions a war with Rome might seem to involve too great a risk, or it might appear the best means of rendering the position of the king secure, according to the circumstances of the moment. But in any case an aggressive policy was hardly possible unless the king was well assured as to the attitude of Armenia in the struggle; her neutrality was essential to safety, and her active support would be of the utmost importance, since her forces could distract the attention of Rome by invading Cappadocia as easily as they could threaten the Parthians by invading Mesopotamia. It was, therefore, inevitable that both Rome and Parthia should seek to control a kingdom which occupied a strategic position of such importance. Their rivalry kept Armenia in an almost continuous turmoil, and neither was able to gain a permanent success. At the beginning of his reign Augustus found Armenia in close alliance with Parthia as a result of Antony's policy, but he secured possession of two princes of the royal house whom Antony had brought as prisoners to Alexandria. In 20 B.C. circumstances enabled the emperor to place the elder of these princes on the Armenian throne. The new king, Tigranes II, had a brief reign and was succeeded by his son and daughter, Tigranes III and Erato, as joint sovereigns.[1] Since they showed Parthian leanings,[2] Augustus set up the younger of the two princes who had fallen into his hands, but the Armenians soon expelled. him.[3] The mission of C. Caesar to the East was partly intended to recover Armenia, and with the help of the able advisers who accom-

[1] *Ann.* 2, 3. [2] Dio, 55, 9.
[3] *Ann.* 2, 4 and the *Prosopographia* under Artavasdes (no. 956).

panied him he made Ariobarzanes, king of the Medes, ruler of
Armenia as well. This occurred in A.D. 1 or 2,[1] but the Mede soon
died and his son, who succeeded him, was killed in the last years
of the reign.[2] After this Armenia fell into a condition of anarchy
which lasted until a new and somewhat remarkable claimant
appeared upon the scene.

In his relations with Parthia Augustus had been so successful
that Phraates IV had been induced to send four of his sons to
Rome as hostages in 9 B.C. Probably the motive of the Parthian
was as much to rid himself of possible rivals as to give security
to Augustus, but whatever the motive the Romans thus acquired a weapon of which they afterwards made use. In A.D. 8
a faction in Parthia induced Augustus to send them one of these
princes, Vonones by name, and he was placed upon the throne.
His reign was short, however, for his foreign manners gave
offence to his subjects, and there were many who resented the
fact that Rome seemed to have given them a king.[3] Under these
circumstances a pretender was soon found in the person of
Artabanus, who was related to the royal house through his
mother.[4] By A.D. 11 Artabanus was successful, and the defeated
Vonones sought refuge in Armenia, where he took advantage
of the existing anarchy to seize the crown. Artabanus was not
disposed to allow his rival to reign quietly in the new kingdom
which he had won, but prepared to drive him out by arms. It
was while matters were in this state that Tiberius became
emperor and assumed the responsibility for dealing with the
Eastern situation. Vonones at once requested recognition as
king of Armenia, but this Tiberius refused to grant.[5] His
motives are probably stated correctly by Tacitus, though they
are ascribed to the legate of Syria rather than his master.[6] To
support Vonones might result in a war with Artabanus, and
Tiberius had no desire to incur such a risk; moreover, he must
have felt grave doubts as to the ability of Vonones to maintain
himself in Armenia, whose people had as little love of foreign
manners as the Parthians.[7] Considered from this point of view

---

[1] Dio, 55, 10 *a*.

[2] *Ann.* 2, 4 and the *Prosopographia* under Artavasdes (no. 957).

[3] *Ann.* 2, 2–4.   [4] *Ann.* 6, 42.   [5] Josephus, *Antiquities*, 18, 2, 4

[6] *Ann.* 2, 4.   [7] This is suggested by *Ann.* 2, 56.

Vonones was likely to be a liability rather than an asset, and it seemed the part of prudence to leave him to his fate without wasting Roman blood or Roman gold in his cause. The wisdom of Tiberius was speedily shown, for Vonones, seeing no hope of resisting the Parthians, fled to Syria, where the Romans kept him as a state prisoner. The refusal to aid Vonones did not mean that Tiberius had given up the idea of controlling Armenia, whose people were asking for Zeno, a prince of the royal house of Pontus, as their king. This solution was highly satisfactory to Tiberius, and the really vital part of the mission of Germanicus was to place this prince on the throne of Armenia if it could be done without endangering the peace. The task was obviously one of considerable delicacy, since it can hardly be doubted that Tiberius was prepared to drop his candidate rather than involve the empire in a war with Artabanus, whose attitude must have been somewhat uncertain. How far it was safe to go and when it was necessary to make concessions would have to be decided by the man on the spot, and could not be too rigidly determined in Rome. Apart from political considerations Tiberius might not have selected Germanicus for such a mission, although the reputation which the prince had gained by his campaigns in Germany, whether it was wholly deserved or not, and his prestige as the emperor's heir might be thought likely to give him a real advantage in dealing with the Parthians and Armenians.

Germanicus was received at Rome with the highest honours. In A.D. 17 he celebrated a splendid triumph and was named as consul with Tiberius for the next year. At the emperor's request the senate voted him a special command and exceptional powers over the eastern provinces. Not only was Tiberius thus careful to make his recall appear as a distinction rather than a disgrace, but care was also taken to conciliate his partisans. Whatever may have been the state of Roman parties at the emperor's accession, by the time of the prince's recall they had rallied round Germanicus and Drusus respectively. Whether Germanicus desired it or not, the lesser nobility had come to centre their hopes upon him, and in consequence the great consular families turned to the emperor's own son as a potential rival who might be set up against him. The court was thus torn by fierce dissension, but as yet it did not touch the two princes themselves, who remained on cordial and affectionate terms. If the higher nobility dreamed of setting Germanicus aside and placing Drusus on the throne, Drusus himself refused to play the part of a pretender. Neither did Tiberius give any sign that he regarded the succession as an open question, but none of these circumstances deterred the hostile parties; even if the men of the imperial family were friendly and united, there were feuds among the women, and time might bring many changes. It is possible that some of the criticisms of the conduct of Germanicus by Tiberius had become more or less public,[1] but in any case men could always fall back on the conviction that in the end natural affection would assert itself. In his heart Tiberius *must* prefer his own son to his nephew, and this feeling could be worked upon; Drusus, likewise, *must* have some latent ambition which might ultimately be aroused. The enmity of Livia and Agrippina may also have been counted on to create dissensions between Tiberius and Germanicus, while Livilla, the wife of Drusus, even though she was the sister of Germanicus, could hardly be expected to wish that her brother's children should inherit the empire to the exclusion of her own.

With the nobility thus divided, Tiberius seems to have felt the need of caution. The lesser nobles had favoured the conquest of Germany because it seemed likely to afford them an opportunity for advancement, and the recall of Germanicus was a distinct blow to them.[2] The emperor had no wish to see the prince surrounded by embittered partisans after his return to Rome, and considered it expedient to make large concessions in order to placate them; at least this supposition seems to furnish the best explanation of the fact that after Tiberius had resolved on the recall of Germanicus he reversed his policy in regard to the consulship. In the three years from A.D. 13 to 15 inclusive no member of the lower nobility had received this coveted

---

[1] Dessau (ii, pt. i, 12) treats their publicity as certain, but I think it somewhat improbable. Tacitus gives some criticisms, but he may have got them from the memoirs of Agrippina; it is not clear that they were known at the time.

[2] Asbach (14) recognizes this, but fails to distinguish between the two sections of the nobility. If the abandonment of the conquest of Germany was a blow to the lesser nobles, it was probably pleasing to the higher nobles.

honour,[1] but in the three years from A.D. 16 to 18 out of fourteen consuls, not counting Tiberius and Germanicus, only three came from the higher aristocracy, while eleven were either lesser nobles or new men. At no other time in the reign of Tiberius did the popular party enjoy such favour.[2] In the nine years that followed, from A.D. 19 to 27 inclusive, only five members of the lesser nobility gained the consulship as against eighteen from the higher, not counting Tiberius and Drusus. No doubt the promotion of his officers and friends was intended as a compliment to Germanicus, but it was well calculated to conciliate his partisans and to soften their exasperation at his recall and at the resumption of a purely defensive frontier policy. Perhaps Tiberius somewhat overdid the matter, and by making their advancement seem so plainly due to the influence of Germanicus he may not only have bound them more strongly to the prince but have widened the gulf between the parties, and thus, by increasing the fears with which the higher aristocracy regarded Germanicus, have driven them to a firmer determination to replace him in the succession by Drusus. It is possible, therefore, that the sudden favour shown the lesser nobles from A.D. 16 to 18 helped to augment the party strife to which Tacitus bears witness in the next year.

Although Tiberius sent Germanicus to the East it was with obvious misgivings as to the possible results, for, whatever the prince's abilities as a general, he seems to have had no diplomatic experience, and the emperor was determined to settle the Parthian and Armenian problems rather by negotiations than by arms. Moreover, the readiness with which Germanicus had transformed a punitive campaign against the Germans into a war of conquest was far from reassuring in this connexion. There was, perhaps, little danger that he would disobey specific instructions, but the nature of the case required that he should be left with a very considerable discretion. Tiberius, therefore, can hardly be blamed for feeling that it was necessary to find some means of preventing him from involving the empire in a

---

[1] Unless the consul in 13, whose name has perished except for the last three letters, was one.

[2] Only in the last years of the reign did they receive half the consulships (see my article on 'Roman Parties under Tiberius').

Parthian war.[1] But while we may admit that such precautions
were neither unwise nor unnatural, yet the measures adopted
for this purpose turned out to be very unfortunate if not very
ill-judged, though the consequences might not have proved
serious had it not been for events which could not be foreseen.
In view of the circumstances it was clearly undesirable to give
Germanicus complete control of the army in the East, since, if
he could dispose of a large force only in case of actual necessity,
he would be obliged to rely on diplomatic methods, and would
be unable to support his negotiations by military movements
which, although intended merely to impress Artabanus, might
easily frighten him into some hostile act. The legions in the
East were under the direct command of the legate of Syria, and
Tiberius felt it essential that this post should be held by a man
sufficiently independent and courageous to check Germanicus
if necessary. The legate then in charge, Q. Caecilius Metellus
Creticus Silanus, seemed ill-suited for this task, perhaps on
account of his personal character, perhaps because his daughter
was betrothed to the eldest son of Germanicus;[2] Metellus was
accordingly recalled, and in his place the emperor appointed
Cn. Calpurnius Piso. The new governor was the son of a bitter
and obstinate republican who had fought to the last against
Caesar and had followed Brutus and Cassius after Caesar's
murder. Pardoned and permitted to return to Rome, he had
long stood aloof from public life, and it was only at the solicitation of Augustus that he condescended to accept the consulship
in 23 B.C. The son inherited the proud and violent temper of his
father, but he had so far accepted the empire as to enjoy an
official career; he had held the consulship as the colleague of
Tiberius in 7 B.C., and had afterwards served as imperial legate
in Spain. What other positions, if any, he may have held we do
not know, but he was a friend of Tiberius and seems always to
have stood by him faithfully.[3] We may confidently assume that

[1] Schiller (i, 292) among others ascribes this motive to Tiberius.

[2] The two were little more than children. Nero, the eldest son of Germanicus,
was then about eleven years old; his betrothed was probably younger. She died
before the marriage took place.

[3] See his last letter to Tiberius (*Ann.* 3, 16), where any misrepresentation on
his part, at least regarding his relations with Tiberius, would have been the
height of folly.

he was an adherent of Drusus rather than of Germanicus, and this, combined with his haughty temper, may have appeared to the emperor a guarantee of his independence and fidelity. A man who, as Tacitus tells us, would hardly admit the superiority of the monarch himself, and who regarded the emperor's sons as his inferiors, was not likely to be too subservient or deferential. The choice of Piso seems readily comprehensible without the aid of any far-fetched conjectures,[1] but Tiberius overlooked the fact that his pride and his violent temper, combined with his unfriendly attitude towards Germanicus, might lead him to go much further than was intended.

Before Piso set out Tiberius gave him private instructions as to his mission as adviser (*adiutor*) to Germanicus and legate of Syria, the nature of which, though not positively known, may be readily inferred.[2] He was to restrain the prince's impetuosity and to prevent him from involving the empire in a Parthian war. In order to check Germanicus if necessary it was essential that Piso should keep a firm hold on the Syrian legions, and this may have seemed desirable from another point of view; Germanicus was already the favourite of the army on the Rhine, and if he gained a similar influence over the army in the East Tiberius might appear to retain the crown only by the permission of his heir. The emperor was naturally unwilling to place himself in such a position, and, whatever his confidence in Germanicus, it is not unlikely that he regarded those who surrounded him with some suspicion.

---

[1] Such as that of Furneaux (i. 140) that Tiberius distrusted both Piso and Germanicus, and balanced one against the other.

[2] These secret orders have given rise to many different theories. Liebenam (*Bemerkungen*, 870–1) disbelieves in them altogether while Stahr (107), Duruy (iv, 310), Domaszewski (*Geschichte*, i. 279 and 281), and others think that Piso misunderstood his instructions. A complete misunderstanding seems to me inadmissible, but some misconception is quite possible. Tacitus (2, 43) asserts that Piso never doubted that he was sent to the East to hold in check the hopes of Germanicus (*ad spes Germanici coercendas*). This in connexion with the fact that Piso later declared that he had been driven out of Syria to facilitate a rebellion would suggest that the governor thought his mission to be that of safeguarding the emperor against treason on the part of the prince. It seems rather unlikely that Tiberius had such suspicions, but Piso may have assumed that this was one of the objects of his mission. At any rate the evidence shows clearly that Tiberius did not disapprove of the governor's earlier acts. I can see no reason to attribute the orders to Livia (Tarver, 349–52) or to Sejanus (Willenbücher, 12 and 13, note 1).

The conduct of Piso makes it clear that he construed his orders in somewhat the sense indicated above. Arriving in Syria before Germanicus, he took immediate steps to secure the allegiance of the Syrian legions to himself and so to Tiberius. He sought the favour of the common soldiers by a lenient discipline,[1] and removed those officers who were friends of Germanicus, replacing them by men of his own. His wife Plancina seconded his efforts by imitating the example of Agrippina, mixing freely with the men and watching their drill and military exercises. In no long time Piso acquired the name of 'the father of the legions' and felt himself strong enough to disregard the orders of Germanicus whenever he thought proper,

An occasion for disobedience soon presented itself. Germanicus promptly undertook an expedition to Armenia in order to place Zeno, the Roman candidate, on the throne of that country. As the Armenians had asked Rome's consent to his becoming their king, there seemed no reason to anticipate any difficulty. Whatever trouble might arise with Artabanus in the future, geography made it impossible for him to strike without warning, and the only opposition to be feared was, therefore, that of those Armenians who were hostile to Zeno and inclined to an alliance with Parthia. Although the existence of such a faction can hardly be doubted, the course of events shows clearly that it was a powerless minority, but Germanicus may have formed an exaggerated idea of its strength, or he may have wished to impress Artabanus by a display of force. At any rate he decided to take with him a strong body of troops, and he accordingly ordered Piso or his son to accompany him with part of the Syrian legions. This order Piso ignored, probably believing that such a military display would endanger peaceful relations with Parthia, since, if Germanicus went about a task which required a mere escort of soldiers at the head of an army, Artabanus might infer that the expedition had other objects than those publicly avowed, and that the prince secretly intended to attack him, hoping to bring about his overthrow with the help of the former adherents of Vonones. If this was Piso's view of the situation he was probably well within the instruc-

---

[1] Tacitus (2, 55 and 3, 13) seems obviously to have followed the exaggerated version of Piso's conduct given at his trial by the friends of Germanicus.

tions of Tiberius in refusing to place at the disposal of Germanicus a force for which the prince had no legitimate use.[1]

Although he failed to get the soldiers from Piso, Germanicus pushed on into Armenia, where he installed Zeno as king, and then returned to Syria to demand an explanation from the governor. Tacitus affirms that Germanicus was inclined to moderation, but that his friends eagerly fanned his resentment against Piso with exaggerations and falsehoods. The two held a conference in the presence of a few friends in which the prince restrained his anger while Piso displayed an insubordinate spirit,[2] and they parted open enemies. It is hard to understand the attitude of Germanicus unless we suppose him to have been in some degree aware of Piso's secret orders. His authority had been flouted, yet instead of dismissing his subordinate he merely asked for an explanation, and when defied he contented himself with making no attempt to hide his resentment. Such conduct can only mean that Germanicus either had not the power to remove Piso,[3] or did not dare to exercise it. Neither is an impossible supposition. His *imperium* was superior to that of the provincial governors in the East, but while this entitled him to their obedience it is not certain that it gave him the right to dismiss them. Even if he had the right, he might hesitate to exercise it in the case of Piso, whom the emperor had expressly appointed as his adviser, and it might seem sufficient to report the matter to Tiberius,[4] since, if Germanicus had no suspicion of any secret orders, he would naturally expect that his report would lead to Piso's prompt recall, or to such a rebuke as would prevent further insubordination.

[1] The lack of any real need for the troops was pointed out long ago by Ihne (42).

[2] As witnesses were present at the interview, what passed could have been brought out at the trial, or have become known otherwise.

[3] Mommsen (*Staatsrecht*, i. 262, note 4) holds that the *maius imperium* gave Germanicus the right to dismiss Piso, and Schiller (i. 275) agrees. I do not see how we can reach such a conclusion without knowing the exact terms of the senate's decree which conferred the *maius imperium*. As the decree has not been preserved the question seems to me insoluble. It is impossible to argue from the practice of later times as Mommsen appears to do. In spite of the report recorded by Tacitus (2, 70) I do not believe that Piso was ever dismissed.

[4] It seems incredible that Piso and Germanicus did not both report the matter to Tiberius, since each would naturally suppose that the other would do so, and each would wish to place his side of the case before the emperor.

For whatever reason, the prince turned his attention to the other business of his mission, leaving his dispute with Piso unsettled. We have already seen that Tiberius had determined on the annexation of Cappadocia and Commagene, and Germanicus now incorporated them in the empire. Cappadocia was organized as a province, and, to reconcile the people to the change, the taxes hitherto levied by the king were reduced; Commagene was at the same time made a part of Syria.[1] There was also trouble in Cilicia, and both Syria and Judaea were complaining of the tribute.[2] It is probable that here too Germanicus made an adjustment of some kind, and one which did not meet with the approval of Piso.

Differences with the legate, however, continued to arise. Artabanus took the crowning of Zeno quietly enough, either because he had gained his immediate object in driving out Vonones, or because his position in Parthia and the reputation of Germanicus made him reluctant to risk a war. At any rate he sent envoys to negotiate a friendly treaty with Rome, and Germanicus readily agreed to his conditions, one of which was that Vonones should be removed from the frontier so that he could no longer keep in touch with the Parthian magnates. To this concession Piso was strongly opposed,[3] perhaps believing that Artabanus would observe his promises only so long as Vonones remained dangerous. In this matter Germanicus was probably right, for the wisdom of continuing to frighten and provoke Artabanus after making peace with him must seem very doubtful. Whatever the precise instructions of Germanicus, the later course of events makes it clear that in this instance he intelligently carried out the real intentions of Tiberius, for after the death of Vonones, which occurred soon afterwards, the peace of the East remained undisturbed for more than twenty years.

With his mission in the East successfully concluded Germanicus, partly perhaps to escape from the constant quarrels

---

[1] *Ann.* 2, 42 and 56. [2] *Ann.* 2, 42.
[3] *Ann.* 2, 58. Tacitus, looking always for personal motives, finds them for both Piso and Germanicus. Piso had been corrupted by gifts of Vonones to Plancina and Germanicus removed Vonones from the frontier partly in order to insult Piso. It is curious that Tacitus does not see that such a suggestion is a serious reflection on his hero. As to Piso the motive may have been taken from the testimony of the friends of Germanicus at his trial.

with Piso, paid a visit to Egypt, where he entertained himself with the sight of its wonders and antiquities. In doing this he exceeded his authority, for his *imperium* did not extend over Egypt, and he also broke a rule of Augustus which forbade Roman senators entering the valley of the Nile without the special permission of the emperor. Germanicus might naturally feel that such a rule was not intended to apply to a man in his exceptional position,[1] and during his visit to Alexandria he went so far as to order a distribution of grain to the citizens for the purpose of relieving a famine, no doubt justifying what was strictly a usurpation of power on the ground of emergency.[2] Tiberius, however, strongly disapproved of the conduct of the prince in violating established regulations, and he spoke bitterly in the senate concerning the trip to Egypt, of which he had not heard in time to forbid it.

If Germanicus hoped that during his absence Tiberius would send such a reprimand to Piso as would compel him to adopt a different attitude he was doomed to disappointment. Apparently the emperor expressed no dissatisfaction with his legate's conduct,[3] for Piso remained defiant, and reversed as far as

[1] Liebenam (*Bemerkungen*, 870-1) thinks that the whole quarrel between Germanicus and Piso arose in the East and was due to the tendency of the prince to set himself above the law. Against this theory, however, is the fact that Piso's course is consistent throughout and that he began his attempts to win the army before Germanicus arrived in Syria. Such measures seem to me to point clearly to secret instructions of some sort from the emperor rather than simply to personal differences between the two men.

[2] Suetonius (52) calls the famine *immensa* and *repentina*, and says that Germanicus went to Egypt on account of it. Tacitus, however, does not suggest it as a reason for the journey. Cichorius (*Röm. Stud.* 382) and Dessau (ii, pt. i, 20, note 2) think that the action of Germanicus may account for the rise in the price of grain in Rome during this year, but it seems to me that Wilcken has conclusively refuted this view and has shown that the grain distributed to the Alexandrians could not have been intended for the Roman people.

[3] There was ample time for Tiberius to interfere if he so desired. Riepl (225-6) estimates that it took a message seventeen or eighteen days to reach Rome from Judaea, but this can have been true only under favourable conditions. The data given by Friedländer (i. 340) would show that it required about forty days when navigation was closed (Nov. 11 to March 5). The expedition of Germanicus to Armenia must have occurred in the summer of A.D. 18, and his quarrel with Piso can hardly be put later than September. If an account of the quarrel was sent on the first of October, a dispatch from Tiberius could certainly have reached Syria before the end of January, 19. The only difficulty is that according to Tacitus (2, 64) the news of the enthronement of Zeno was not announced in Rome till A.D. 19, and apparently not till summer. However,

possible all the arrangements which Germanicus had made in
Syria. As a consequence, when the prince returned from Egypt,
the quarrel between the two became more violent than ever,
until finally the governor found his position intolerable. Probably, in the presence of Germanicus, Piso could not carry his
insubordination beyond a certain point without actual civil war,
and his pride would not permit him to give way. At any rate,
he at length resolved to return to Rome, but he had hardly
reached this decision when he abandoned it because of a serious
illness of Germanicus. The prince's health speedily improved,
and at the news the people of Antioch who had offered vows in
the temples for his recovery hastened to fulfil them. These
demonstrations of rejoicing were promptly stopped by Piso,
probably on the ground that such vows were disloyal to the
emperor.[1] While this may have relieved the feelings of the
governor it did not render his position in Syria more comfortable.
Leaving Antioch, he went as far as the port of Seleucia, where
he lingered on hearing that the prince had suffered a relapse,
and it was here that he received a letter from Germanicus
formally severing all friendly relations with him in accordance
with an old Roman custom. After this Piso at length set sail
and actually left the province, but he proceeded slowly, and at
Cos learned of the prince's death. Both Piso and his wife,
Plancina, were delighted at the news, and made no effort to
conceal their joy. Their conduct was as unwise as it was inde-
cent, and later furnished their enemies with material for charges
against them. The only explanations of their folly seem to be

Steup has advanced strong reasons for believing that the order of the chapters
has suffered a disturbance at this point. His view was accepted by Nipperdey,
and the force of his arguments is acknowledged by Furneaux. If Steup's
rearrangement of the chapters is rejected, the only explanation of the apparent
fact that Tiberius learns of the trip to Egypt before the news arrives of the
enthronement of Zeno seems to be that Tiberius held back the announcement
of the achievement of Germanicus till he could announce a success of Drusus,
so that the senate might vote honours to both princes at the same time.

[1] Mommsen, *Staatsrecht*, ii. 825. The actual illegality seems to me somewhat
doubtful. Tiberius later forbade vows for the safety of the sons of Germanicus,
but it was on grounds of expediency (*Ann.* 4, 17). It seems highly probable
that Piso based his action on the pretext that such vows were in some way
disloyal to Tiberius, since Tacitus tells us (2, 78) that Piso on his return to
Syria definitely accused Germanicus of treason, and to offer vows for the
recovery of a traitor was obviously a manifestation of disloyalty to the
emperor.

that they were either so carried away by their hatred as to forget everything else, or that they regarded Germanicus as a traitor to Tiberius. In favour of the latter is the fact that Piso wrote to the emperor alleging that he had been driven from Syria to facilitate a rebellion.[1] In support of such a charge he could point out that after enthroning Zeno Germanicus had struck coins with his own head upon them, and that he had assumed the *imperium* in Egypt.[2] In view of the general attitude of Germanicus up to his death, however, neither of these things could be taken seriously by any one not blinded by animosity. If the prince had intended a revolt he would naturally have begun it in Syria rather than in Armenia or Egypt, but probably the feelings of Piso and his wife had become so bitter that common sense and prudence were unheeded for the moment.

The malady which proved fatal to Germanicus seems to have been some kind of intermittent fever. In his last days, however, the idea that he had been poisoned took possession of his mind and was accepted by his wife and friends. That his death was due to natural causes is now generally believed,[3] but the Romans of that day were very credulous of poisoning and magic, two things which were closely associated in their minds. As soon as the illness of Germanicus was attributed to human wickedness, a search was made for signs of witchcraft, which were duly found in the shape of fragments of human bodies and lead tablets inscribed with imprecations against him concealed behind the walls and under the floors of his house. The significance of this is difficult to estimate. If the discoveries were genuine, some one must have desired the prince's death, and desired it strongly, but it seems not unlikely that the search was made by slaves who found what they knew they were expected to find. From what we know of Agrippina we can easily imagine that her slaves might think it unwise to disappoint her in any matter on which her heart was set.[4] The

[1] *Ann.* 2, 78.

[2] Liebenam, *Bemerkungen*, 870.

[3] I believe no scholar now takes the charge of poisoning seriously. Tacitus never asserts it except as something which some people believed. I do not think he believed it himself.

[4] This theory is implied by Baring-Gould (277), and it seems to me very plausible.

discovery of the objects in question, if it was genuine, would be no evidence of poisoning, nor would it point particularly at either Piso or Plancina.[1]

Germanicus was now entirely convinced that he was a victim of foul play, and on his deathbed he implored his friends to tell Tiberius of his wrongs and to demand the punishment of Piso and his wife, on whom he fixed as responsible for his fate.[2] His friends swore to avenge him, and he then addressed some words of caution to Agrippina, beseeching her for the sake of their children to remember the difference in her position which would result from his death and to curb her violent temper, so as to avoid irritating those in power. This was said publicly, and afterwards, when the dying man talked to his wife in private, it was conjectured that he warned her against Tiberius. Although this last was a mere guess it is not unlikely that it was near the truth; if the prince gave her such a warning, it was probably because he could foresee that her pride and recklessness might easily provoke the emperor if there was no one to act as a mediator between them. Shortly after this scene Germanicus died. His body was burned after being exposed naked in the forum of Antioch, presumably to exhibit to the public what were then supposed to be the outward signs of poisoning, and Agrippina, bearing his ashes, and accompanied by some of his friends, set out for Rome.

The officers of the dead prince at once set about the choice of a temporary governor to take charge of affairs in Syria until Tiberius should have time to make a regular appointment. After a long dispute between Vibius Marsus and Cn. Sentius Saturninus, Marsus finally gave way to his rival, and Saturninus was selected. The friends of Germanicus also promptly arrested a woman named Martina, who was said to have been intimate

[1] They might have been placed in the house he was expected to occupy before his return from Egypt by any one who hated him. It could hardly have been done after he took up his residence in the house. He may have had many enemies besides Piso, Vonones for example.

[2] I am strongly inclined to believe that the substance of this part of the speech of Germanicus was to be found in the archives of the senate. The friends of the prince who prosecuted Piso would probably refer to his last injunctions and their own oath. If Tacitus got his information from this source the failure of Germanicus to accuse Tiberius cannot be regarded as so significant as Baring-Gould (278) considers it.

with Plancina and who had the reputation of being a poisoner.[1] She was sent as a prisoner to Italy, where she died soon after her arrival without any apparent cause, a circumstance which seemed suspicious to many.

Piso, as has been already stated, heard the news of the death of his enemy at the island of Cos, and he immediately began to consider his next step. His son Marcus urged him to proceed to Rome and meet boldly any accusations which might be brought against him, but some of his friends advised him to return to Syria. He was, they argued, still the legal governor and had only left the province under compulsion; Rome was at the moment plunged in grief at the death of the popular idol, and it would be wise to delay his return so as to give the public feeling time to subside. Moreover, he could meet the charges far better as governor at the head of a great army than as a private citizen. He might indeed count on the secret favour of Livia and Tiberius, but at that moment they could not openly protect him. Yielding to such counsel and to his own violent temper, Piso decided to return, in spite of the warnings of his son that in doing so he was certain to precipitate a civil war. The event soon justified the fears of Marcus, and Piso, who had counted on his popularity with the soldiers, found that he had deceived himself, for the bulk of the army obeyed Saturninus, and Piso was forced to surrender and return to Rome to face his accusers.

The news of the death of Germanicus had been received at Rome with profound sorrow. The grief of the people produced wild suspicions and absurd rumours; it was whispered that he had been murdered because he cherished the design of restoring the liberty of the people, and Tiberius and Livia were regarded by many as in some way responsible. The funeral increased rather than diminished these suspicions, for although the last rites in honour of Germanicus were celebrated with splendour, it was noted that neither Tiberius nor Livia appeared in public on this occasion. Many believed that the emperor was secretly

[1] Tacitus asserts (2, 74) that Martina was a favourite of Plancina and a notorious poisoner as though both statements were certain. Probably, however, both were merely the assertions of the prosecution. If Martina was a notorious poisoner, an open intimacy between her and Plancina is improbable, and if Plancina wished to kill Germanicus, incredible.

pleased at the death of his nephew and that he stayed away for
fear that he might not be able to conceal his joy.[1] It is probable
that his real reason was the exact opposite. Tiberius was a
Roman of the old type who regarded any public display of
emotion as a lowering of his dignity. Antonia, the mother of
Germanicus, also remained away, and it was suspected that she
was detained at home by Tiberius to make his own absence and
that of his mother less conspicuous.[2] Some other honours were
omitted, the absence of which excited remark, and the mourning
of the people continued for so long a time that the emperor was
forced to issue an edict bidding them return to their usual
occupations and pleasures. The edict was obeyed, but grief and
suspicion still smouldered in the hearts of the populace.

It was in this mood that Piso found the city when he finally
reached it. Popular feeling was immediately turned against him
as the agent through whom Tiberius and Livia had poisoned
Germanicus. Conscious of his innocence, Piso demanded an
investigation, and both he and his accusers, the friends of
Germanicus, readily agreed that the whole question should be
referred to Tiberius. The emperor naturally shrank from
assuming such a responsibility, for he was well aware that many
suspected him, however unreasonably; he probably did not
believe that any crime had been committed, yet if he acquitted
Piso, he knew that the belief would instantly arise that he was
protecting his accomplice, so he determined that the case should
be publicly tried. In accordance with this resolve, after a formal
examination of the evidence, he referred the whole matter to
the judgement of the senate.

Tiberius presided at the trial and attempted to act in a wholly
impartial manner. At the opening of the proceedings he urged
the conscript fathers to be guided by the evidence rather than
their own feelings, and to distinguish sharply between actual
crime and conduct which was merely unbecoming. If Piso had
murdered Germanicus, he must pay the penalty, but, if he had

[1] Tacitus says (3, 2–3) that every one knew that Tiberius was pleased and
suggests that he feared to betray the fact. I take it, however, that this was the
explanation given by those who thought they knew his secret feelings,
since Tacitus himself seems inclined to think that Tiberius remained away
because he was reluctant to parade his feelings in public.

[2] Tacitus at any rate inclines to this belief (3, 3).

only rejoiced at the prince's death, this was a different matter. Although he himself would never forgive Piso for such rejoicing, he would revenge private wrongs not as emperor but as a private citizen; he would withdraw his friendship from Piso and banish him from court. The senators must consider only offences against the commonwealth, and he exhorted them to weigh the evidence laid before them carefully and without prejudice.

The prosecution brought forward a number of charges against the unhappy governor, ranging from murder to military insubordination and including treason on account of his return to Syria and his attempt to regain control there by civil war. Against most of these the defence could make little headway. One charge alone Piso was able to answer, namely that of poisoning. The friends of Germanicus were unable to suggest any plausible way in which Piso could have poisoned the prince, and on this count the prosecution broke down, though a suspicion still remained in the minds of many that a murder had been committed. Such a suspicion, even if groundless, was not wholly absurd. That the guilt could not be fixed on Piso did not prove him innocent, and if he had not poisoned the prince himself, his wife Plancina might conceivably have done so. On the other charges the prosecution was more successful; Piso could not deny that he had tried to make himself popular with the soldiers, that he had disobeyed the orders of his superior officer, that he had returned to Syria and attempted to recover possession of it by force. He battled manfully against his accusers, but he made little impression on the senate. He had confidently expected the protection of Tiberius, but the emperor showed himself implacable because of the return to Syria, and Piso finally realized that he had no chance of escape. Some of the charges he might have answered by the production of his orders, but on this count of the indictment he could make no defence. In leaving his province he had forfeited his *imperium*, and in attempting to resume his command he was technically guilty of treason. He may have imagined that under the circumstances Tiberius would approve his course, but he could produce no instructions which would justify his act.[1] If the emperor

[1] There had been no time for Tiberius to learn that Piso had left Syria before his return.

pressed this point against him, the display of his orders would
avail him nothing, but might ruin his family. Hence when the
senate called for the production of certain papers, probably the
correspondence between Piso and Tiberius,[1] both the emperor
and the accused joined in refusing. Seeing himself doomed, Piso
put an end to his difficulties by suicide, first addressing a
letter to Tiberius imploring mercy for his innocent sons; the
only crime of which he confessed himself guilty was that of
returning to Syria, and for this he expressed his sorrow and
regret.[2]

It seems clear from the letter of Piso and from the whole
course of events that he had expected the emperor's protection
and that he was conscious of possible offence only in this one
particular. But if he had corrupted the army and disobeyed
his superior officer, it seems impossible that he could hope that
Tiberius would publicly condone or overlook such conduct. The
only reasonable explanation seems to be that in these matters
he had acted in accordance with his instructions, and that he
believed he would be able to vindicate himself by producing
them. Why then did the emperor fail him? Perhaps because
he was genuinely angry at the return to Syria and felt that the
interest of the state forbade him to pardon it, but it is also
possible that he shrank from the storm which an attempt to
shield Piso would have provoked in Rome. The imaginary
crime of poisoning, added to the real offences of the governor
against the popular hero, had roused the people to a veritable
frenzy. During the trial the mob was clamouring for Piso's
death and a guard of soldiers was necessary to protect him from
its fury. Even among the senators who had heard the evidence
many believed that Germanicus had been murdered, and the
mob out of doors was doubtless entirely convinced; to shield
Piso would be construed as a confession on the part of the
emperor that he had instigated the assassination. Neither could
Tiberius venture to permit the production of his orders, for they
would exhibit him in the light of one who, while heaping public

[1] There is a gap in the text of Tacitus at this point (3, 14), so that we cannot be certain as to the nature of the documents.

[2] As Tiberius read the letter to the senate, it must have been filed in the
archives of that body, and there seems no reason to doubt that Tacitus has
accurately reported its substance, if not its words.

honours on the dead prince, had secretly sought to check and thwart him, and this, in the existing state of public feeling, would have confirmed the wild suspicions then afloat. Men would have reasoned that, if Tiberius was thus jealous and fearful of his adopted son, he must have wished that son out of the way, and hence had probably procured his death. That his orders said nothing of the kind was not likely to allay such suspicions, since he would hardly commit such a command to writing. It seems clear that at the time of the trial Tiberius had reason to fear the effect of the production of his correspondence with his legate or of any attempt to protect him. If Piso was to be abandoned, the best course was to insist on the one act of treason which his instructions would not cover, namely the return to Syria. The only risk was that, if driven to despair, Piso might lay his orders before the senate regardless of consequences. But Piso saw clearly that this would be a blunder, for, if the public wrath were turned against the emperor, he might not dare to shield Piso's innocent sons and he certainly could not save Piso himself; hence Piso kept his orders to himself, and begged in return for the imperial protection for his children.

In the senate Tiberius shielded the two sons of Piso from the vengeance of their father's enemies. In his letter the unhappy governor had said no word as to his wife, and her fate was determined by the empress-mother. Plancina had at first identified her cause with that of her husband, but, having assured herself of the protection of Livia, she hastened to separate her fate from his. The complete failure of the prosecution to make out the charge of poisoning against Piso led many who were convinced that the death of Germanicus was not natural, to turn their suspicions upon her. Tiberius was almost certainly convinced that no murder had been committed and that, therefore, Plancina was innocent, so he was probably quite ready to save her from punishment, but her open rejoicing at the death of Germanicus was something that it was difficult to ignore entirely. He had declared in the case of Piso that, if such a charge were found to be true, the offender, though not punished by law, should forfeit his friendship and be banished from his court. Livia did not share his feeling in the matter and

refused to part with her friend. Her attitude put Tiberius in
an embarrassing position; in the senate he requested that no
action should be taken against Plancina, giving as his reason
the entreaties of his mother. Since Tiberius was in general
strongly disinclined to allow Livia any open share in politics,
the pains he took on this occasion to parade her interference
seems strange.[1] Perhaps the most probable conjecture as to his
motives is that he hoped in this way to dispel the suspicions of
whose existence he was only too well aware. Men might believe
that he had contrived the death of his nephew in order to make
his son the heir to the throne, but it would be less easy to
imagine that Livia had murdered one grandson to clear the
way for another. By making it clear that the immunity of
Plancina was due wholly to her Tiberius may have hoped that
the myth of poisoning would be set at rest, but, if this was really
his motive, he miscalculated the effect, for he merely brought
suspicion and hatred on his mother without in any appreciable
degree removing them from himself.

The death of Germanicus and the trial of Piso mark a turning-
point in the reign. The suspicion of Tiberius which then arose
was never afterward dissipated; as the years passed a thick
cloud of popular hatred gathered around him and men were
more and more disposed to put the worst possible construction
upon his every word and act. That the suspicion was unjust
cannot be seriously doubted, for even if we suppose that Germanicus was murdered, which is wholly unlikely, it is impossible
to believe that Tiberius was in any way responsible. A very
simple dilemma is here presented to us: if Piso was sent to the

---

[1] Tacitus says that Tiberius made his plea with obvious shame. I doubt if
he would have made a positive assertion of this sort without some authority,
perhaps the writers who were senators at this time whom he has previously
cited (2, 88). Embarrassment might be interpreted as shame by contemporaries
who were suspicious, then or later. In the early years of his reign Tiberius
treated his mother with great deference and allowed her to act with a certain
amount of independence, at least in appearance. Thus, in his letter to the
people of Gythium (Seyrig, 102–3) he states that she will herself reply to them
after hearing their embassy as to the honours offered her, and at the trial of
Appuleia Varilla he consulted her before declaring that no words reflecting on
her should be considered as criminal (*Ann.* 2, 50). His action in regard to
Plancina might, therefore, seem in line with his general attitude, but it certainly went much further, for the charges against Plancina was not matters
which especially concerned Livia, still less which concerned her alone.

East to poison Germanicus, why did he wait so long before carrying out the deed, and above all, why did he quarrel with his victim and thus diminish his chances of success? The openness and violence of the quarrel is clear evidence that murder had no place in Piso's mission. What then was his mission? Tacitus affirms that Piso never doubted that he was sent to hold Germanicus in check. His conduct was in perfect harmony with this conception, and the failure of Tiberius to recall him promptly shows that the governor had not misunderstood the intentions of his master. But it seems obvious that, if Tiberius sent Piso to check Germanicus, he could have had no anticipation of the prince's death. If he were marked out to die, there was no need of checking him, since it would have been actually easier to murder him at once than to wait for a considerable time and put him on his guard by the disputes engendered by the checking process. It is impossible to believe that Tiberius bungled the matter so completely. Everything seems to indicate that the death of Germanicus came as a complete surprise to the emperor and that it placed him in an unexpected and difficult position. Had the prince lived and returned to Rome there might have been a quarrel, but it need not have been an open one; Germanicus might have been conciliated by a reprimand to Piso, and outwardly friendly relations preserved. As it was, the death of Germanicus made it impossible to avoid a public trial, which left Tiberius and his mother exposed to much unjustified suspicion, a result which seriously weakened the emperor's position.

Though the suspicions which many Romans cherished against Tiberius were unjust, they were not wholly unnatural. He had opened the trial with a show of impartiality and instructed the senate to make a thorough investigation, yet when the senate asked for certain documents he refused to permit their production. The obvious inference was that something was being covered up, and this left a bad impression. Then the charge which the emperor had pressed against Piso was his return to Syria rather than the one which roused the greatest indignation, namely his conduct toward Germanicus, and this attitude must have seemed to the latter's friends like an evasion of the real issue. These facts, together with such other incidents as the mysterious death of Martina, who had been sent to Rome as a witness for the prosecution, the conspicuous absence of both Tiberius and Livia from the funeral, and the protection of Plancina, combined to make possible a sinister interpretation of the emperor's conduct. He had never been popular, but hitherto he had been respected; respect now gave way to suspicion, and unpopularity began to ripen into hatred.

V

THE EARLY GOVERNMENT OF TIBERIUS IN ROME

ALTHOUGH there is no reason to believe that Tiberius rejoiced at the death of Germanicus, he may nevertheless have felt that the political situation was simplified by that event. Before the prince left for the East, the imperial court and the senate had been torn by factions which it had doubtless often been difficult to restrain. All this was suddenly changed, since the eldest of his sons was too young to be considered as the immediate successor to the emperor, now over sixty years of age, and Drusus became the inevitable heir to the throne. The party strife was at once suspended, for opposition to Drusus under the circumstances was both futile and dangerous. Moreover, it is possible that towards the end of his life Germanicus was becoming a problem to the emperor. Tiberius had no intention of being a mere puppet, and it was difficult to assert himself without clashing with his heir, especially as Germanicus had come to stand for a policy directly opposed to that which the emperor was determined to pursue. Tiberius succeeded in checking the prince's warlike ambitions in Germany and found a pretext for sending him to the East, but, if he had lived to return to Rome, the situation would have been extremely delicate and it would not have been easy to find another mission for him. This difficulty was now removed, and Tiberius could follow his own course without compromise, and could transmit the empire to his own son.

At this point it is desirable to consider the general character of the government of Tiberius in the first nine years of his reign, that is up to A.D. 23, in which year occurred the death of Drusus. In this connexion we have the emphatic testimony of a hostile witness, namely Tacitus, who says:

It may be convenient that I should here review the other parts of the administration, and explain on what methods it was conducted up to that time; since it was in this year that the change for the worse in the government of Tiberius set in. First, then, all public business, and the most important private business also, was transacted in the Senate. Its leaders had liberty of debate, and the

Emperor himself checked any lapses into sycophancy. In bestowing public offices, he paid regard to a man's birth, his distinction in war, or his eminence in civil pursuits, making it plain that no better person could have been appointed. The Consuls, the Praetors, enjoyed the dignity of their offices; the authority of the lesser magistrates was sustained; and the laws, except in cases of High Treason, were well administered. The public taxes, both in corn and money, as well as the rest of the public revenue, were managed by companies of Roman knights; his own affairs Tiberius entrusted to persons of the most approved character, some of them known to him only by reputation; once appointed, they would be kept on in office indefinitely, most of them continuing in the same employments till old age. The populace, no doubt, suffered from the high price of food, but for this the Emperor was not to blame; he did everything that money and forethought could do to provide against bad seasons and stormy seas. He took care that the provincials should not be disturbed by new imposts, and that the avarice and cruelty of magistrates should not add to the burden of the old ones. Corporal punishment and confiscations were unknown. The Emperor's own estates in Italy were few, his slaves modest in demeanour, his retinue of freed-men small; if he had disputes with private citizens, they were decided in the Courts of Law. Such was the government of Tiberius, not tempered indeed with any graciousness—for his manner was always rough, and often terrifying—but such it continued to be till all was changed by the death of Drusus.[1]

Aside from the emperor's ungracious manners, the one blot on his record which Tacitus can discover is the law of treason. Elsewhere he admits that even this law was not abused in the first part of the reign,[2] but he blames Tiberius bitterly for having revived it,[3] a quite unmerited censure, since the law had never been suspended either in theory or in practice. In the last years of his life Augustus had apparently extended it to include defamatory libel of the aristocracy; Tiberius merely continued to enforce it as it had come to him from his predecessor, steadily checked all attempts to extend it further,[4] and consistently

---

[1] *Ann.* 4, 6–7. I quote from Ramsay's translation. A casual remark of Seneca (*de Clem.* 6) shows that this judgement of Tacitus was generally accepted.

[2] *Ann.* 1, 73. When Tacitus says that at first Tiberius restrained the evil it seems to me a practical admission that he could find no serious abuse of the law.　　　　　　　　　　　　　　[3] *Ann.* 1, 72.

[4] *Ann.* 1, 73 and 3, 70. See also the appendix on 'The Law of Treason under Tiberius'.

refused to use it for his own protection.[1] Whether the nobles
ever invoked it in the praetorian courts to shield themselves
from slander we do not know, but we hear of no such prosecutions being brought before the senate.

The Roman law of treason was obviously open to grave
abuses. In the first place, it was vague and could be stretched
to almost any extent. There was, perhaps, little danger of this
being done for the benefit of senators or nobles, but it might
happen easily if the emperor chose to employ if for his own defence. In that case, any word or act which could be construed
as implying disrespect for the sovereign would furnish the basis
for an accusation.[2] It may have been because he realized this
possibility that Tiberius refused to allow prosecutions for
slanders against himself, or he may have despised such things
and seen that by treating them as crimes he would only give
them notoriety and importance, but more probably he simply
followed the example set him by Augustus. Whatever the
motive, he consistently maintained this attitude to the end of
his life.[3]

But though Tiberius prevented this abuse of the law, there
was another danger against which it was less easy to guard.
This lay in the Roman method of criminal procedure; there was
no public prosecutor, but it was left to any citizen who happened
to know of a crime to institute a prosecution. It was clear that
a mere sense of public duty was insufficient where the offence
was against the state rather than an individual, and that some
added inducement was necessary. It was, therefore, provided
that the accuser should receive a pecuniary reward if he secured
a conviction. Most offences were punished by a fine, and when
more severe penalties were imposed they were usually accompanied by the confiscation of the offender's property either in
whole or in part, and a portion of the fine or of the confiscated
property was assigned to the informer. Moreover, the Romans
attached great importance to oratory, and the courts offered an
excellent opportunity to acquire such a reputation for eloquence

---

[1] *Ann.* 1, 74 and 2, 50. [2] Somewhat as in Germany before 1914.

[3] Suetonius (58 and 61) asserts the contrary, but gives no names. Tacitus
fails to mention most of the cruelties referred to by Suetonius, or to confirm
his sweeping assertions. In such a connexion the silence of Tacitus seems to
me decisive.

as might pave the way to a career in public life ; thus the prosecution of delinquents became a recognized means by which an ambitious man could rise in the world. The financial rewards which successful prosecution offered to the accuser were a very obvious danger, for the bringing of serious charges against the rich might be made a lucrative business, with the result that the delator, or professional prosecutor, soon made his appearance. The empire did not create him, but it gave him a wider field. To prosecute successfully it was necessary to gather information, and for this purpose the delator organized a sort of private detective bureau. At a time when every man of means was attended by a considerable number of slaves, it was often easy to obtain the services of highly efficient spies in the households of the great, and the fact that there was known to be a market for information of a certain kind brought constant grist to the mill of the informer. Doubtless many of the delators were ready to supplement their real evidence with fabrications when necessary, since, if they failed to secure a conviction, they not only lost all reward but ran the risk of punishment as well. Unless restrained and made to feel the danger of false charges, they were likely to develop into a genuine evil. The least encouragement from the emperor was certain to lead to an abundant crop of prosecutions for treason, since the vagueness of the law and the richness of the spoil combined to make this charge a favourite one with the delators.

Before the accession of Tiberius the dangers inherent in such a system had caused little trouble, and throughout his reign he tried consistently to hold the informers in check ; nevertheless he could not prevent the growth of delation, and he was forced to turn it against the aristocracy. Under Augustus the nobles seem to have been little troubled by charges of treason, so that when such charges began to be brought against them, delation appeared in their eyes as an altogether new institution, and they hated Tiberius as the inventor of the system. Yet the emperor was almost helpless in the matter, and the growth of delation was really due to the growing insecurity of his position and the increasing danger of conspiracies against him among the nobles. Although the system might be a bad one, Tiberius could not abolish it unless he was prepared to set up some new method of

enforcing the laws.[1] If he is to be blamed for not finding a
substitute, a much more severe censure must be passed on
Nerva, Trajan, Hadrian, Antoninus Pius, and Marcus Aurelius,
for these emperors lived after the worst evils of delation had
been clearly revealed, yet, like Tiberius, they retained it and
sought merely to repress its abuses. Even in the light of modern
experience it is not easy to suggest a satisfactory substitute.
Since the emperor had to guard against conspiracies, a spy
system of some sort was inevitable. As it was he trusted to the
delators for protection; without them he would have had to
organize a secret police of his own. In the hands of a Domitian
such a police would probably have been no improvement, and
his spies would have been neither less greedy nor more scrupulous than the delators.

One of the chief charges against Tiberius is that he extended
the law of treason and encouraged delation till the two became
a veritable scourge, and a brief consideration of the facts seems
desirable at this point. Tacitus certainly regarded Tiberius as
guilty, and announces with a rhetorical flourish that he intends
to trace the beginning and progress of the evil, showing how
Tiberius, though at first restraining it, stealthily fostered it,
finally suffering it to break forth like a devouring conflagration.[2]
For any such view, however, his pages furnish very inadequate
evidence.

At the accession of Tiberius the delators were already in
existence, and they were not slow to test the attitude of the new
monarch. In A.D. 15 they brought charges of treason against
two knights, Falanius and Rubrius by name. The acts alleged
were trivial, but they were offences against the divinity of
Augustus, and Tiberius had shown such profound reverence for
his predecessor that it might reasonably be supposed that he
would be more willing to entertain such a charge than one which
concerned only himself. The manœuvre was unsuccessful,
however, for the emperor promptly dismissed both cases,
writing to the consuls that his father had not been raised to a
place in heaven that he might become a danger to Roman

---

[1] On one occasion Tiberius declared that rewards for the delators were
necessary to secure the enforcement of the laws (*Ann.* 4, 30). Under the existing
system this statement was perfectly true.   [2] *Ann.* 1, 73.

citizens on earth. He showed the charges against Falanius to be
frivolous, and that against Rubrius, of having broken an oath
taken in the name of Augustus, he dismissed with the remark
that the offence did not differ from the violation of an oath
where Jove had been invoked, and that it was the business of
the gods to avenge their own majesty.

Having failed on this line the delators soon tried another.
They accused Granius Marcellus, a former governor of Bithynia,
of a mild form of extortion [1] and added a charge of treason on
the grounds that he had slandered Tiberius, that he had a
statue of himself taller than one of the emperor, and that he had
substituted the head of Tiberius for that of Augustus on another
statue. When these charges concerning the statues were read
in the senate Tiberius lost his temper [2] and declared that he would
give his vote in the case openly and on oath. It was pointed out,
however, that this would abridge the freedom of the senate,
since if he voted first the senators would feel bound to follow
his example, while if he voted last they could hardly venture to
acquit the defendant for fear of seeming to condone the slanders.
Tiberius recovered his habitual self-control, Marcellus was
acquitted of treason, and the charge of extortion was referred to
a commission of senators.

These three cases occurred in A.D. 15, and in the next year we
have that of Libo Drusus. [3] He was certainly accused, rightly
or wrongly, of what would be considered treason by any
government. It is probable that he was guilty, since he committed suicide and the senate declared him a public enemy after
his death. [4]

In A.D 17 Appuleia Varilla, a grand-niece of Augustus, was
accused of adultery and treason. On this occasion Tiberius
categorically declared that no words against himself or his
mother should be taken into account; as a result Appuleia was

---

[1] I think Anderson (48) is clearly right in holding that the charge of extortion
was brought under the provisions of the edict of Augustus found in Cyrene.
If so, the charge was rather a suit for damages than a criminal prosecution.

[2] The language of Tacitus implies that it was these frivolous charges which
provoked the anger of Tiberius rather than the slanders of himself. The
slanders were probably of the same sort as the anonymous verses which
Tacitus has just mentioned.

[3] See chapter iii.

[4] The decrees against his memory imply such a declaration.

acquitted of treason, but was left to be banished by her family for adultery.

During the next three years the delators seem to have kept quiet, for the prosecution of Piso cannot be regarded as their work, but in A.D. 21 the trials for treason began again. A praetor accused of this crime was acquitted and the delators punished for bringing the charge, and in the praetorian courts a leading man of Macedonia was acquitted of adultery and then (Tacitus says at the instance of Tiberius) tried for treason and banished to an island. In both these cases our information is too meagre to permit of any definite judgement. It is during this year, however, that we find what appears to be the first instance of the straining of the law. While Tiberius was absent from the city a knight named Clutorius Priscus was tried by the senate. He had written a poem on the death of Germanicus for which he had been rewarded; later when Drusus fell ill and was expected to die, he composed a poem in anticipation of this event. On the recovery of the prince Clutorius foolishly read his elegy to a number of his women friends. The matter reached the ears of the delators, who promptly brought a charge of treason against the poet. The senate, indignant at such an attempt to profit by the death of the emperor's son and probable successor,[1] condemned Clutorius to death, only one senator protesting against such severity, and the sentence was immediately carried out before the emperor had an opportunity to interfere. Tiberius evidently disapproved of the execution, but he was anxious to avoid an open collision with the senate. Without severely censuring the majority he commended the senator who had spoken in favour of a milder penalty, and to prevent such hasty action in the future he caused the senate to pass a decree requiring an interval of ten days between a death-sentence and its execution.

[1] Ciaceri (160–1) believes that the fact that Clutorius composed his poem on the death of Drusus during the illness of the prince led the senate to regard him as guilty of magic. Such a view would make the whole matter more intelligible, but there is no definite evidence to support it. The speech which Tacitus attributes to Manius Lepidus, the dissenting senator, implies that the offence of Clutorius did not come clearly within the law of treason, perhaps because Drusus had not yet received the tribunician power, or perhaps because such a poem was not in itself treasonable even if the emperor had been its subject.

In A.D. 22 a former proconsul of Asia, C. Silanus, was indicted both for treason and for cruelty and extortion in his province.[1] He was undoubtedly guilty of gross maladministration and was condemned, though Tiberius mitigated the sentence of the conscript fathers in some particulars. In this same year another governor accused of both treason and extortion was condemned for the latter crime.[2] The delators also attempted to bring a charge of treason against a knight on the ground that he had melted down a silver statue of the emperor and converted it into plate for ordinary use, but Tiberius at once dismissed the case. Against this intervention one eminent jurist protested, declaring that, while the emperor had a right to be lenient in matters which concerned himself, the senate ought to be left free to act in cases where the state was injured. This protest had no effect and may have been intended simply to flatter Tiberius,[3] but it is possible that some senators thought that the majesty of the imperial office should be more sternly upheld,[4] since the awe felt for the emperor had no inconsiderable part in maintaining the peace of the world.

In A.D. 23 two men were accused of supplying grain to Tacfarinas, an African chieftain then in rebellion against Rome. It is probable that they were indicted on a charge of treason, as the offence alleged would certainly come within that law. Both were acquitted by the senate, but Tacitus takes occasion to remark that one of them would have been convicted if two prominent consulars had not come to his defence. If this statement is more than a mere opinion of the historian, it can only mean either that the evidence was strong, or that Tiberius preferred to allow a guilty man to escape rather than to offend influential senators.

From this brief review of the facts it is clear that in the first nine years of his reign Tiberius prevented any extension of the

[1] Tacitus says that the charge of treason was added to prevent the friends and relatives of Silanus from defending him, but the force of this suggestion is diminished by his statement (3, 38) that a charge of treason was regularly added to every indictment. Possibly Tacitus was influenced by a family tradition of the Junii Silani. For a fuller discussion see my article on 'Tacitus and Aristocratic Tradition'.

[2] *Ann.* 3, 38 and 70.   [3] Tacitus so regards it.

[4] If the case of Clutorius Priscus did not turn on magic it might be taken as showing the existence of such a feeling.

law of treason and restrained delation, refusing to allow trivial acts or slanders against himself to be treated as criminal. His attitude toward the laws in general was openly stated at the time of the trial of Silanus. A senator then denounced the personal character of the guilty proconsul and made a motion that no man of dissolute morals should be eligible to draw lots for one of the senatorial provinces, and that the emperor should be the judge in the matter. In defence of his motion he argued that the law only dealt with the offence after it was committed, and that it would be better to prevent the crime than to punish it. To this Tiberius replied that:

He had been aware of the reports current about Silanus; but decisions should not be based on rumour. There were many men who in the command of the provinces had disappointed the hopes, or the fears, which had been formed in regard to them. Some were stimulated to higher things by having great things to do; others were paralyzed by it. The Princeps could not embrace everything within his own knowledge; and it was not expedient that he should be led by the interested views of others. The law was appointed to deal with accomplished facts, because the future was uncertain; hence our forefathers had laid it down that when misdeeds had gone before, punishment should follow after. Let them not upset arrangements wisely devised and approved by experience. Princes had burdens enough as it was; enough of power also. Every increase of prerogative was a weakening of the law; the Imperial authority should not be invoked so long as recourse to the laws was open.[1]

Up to A.D. 23 Tiberius maintained this wise and enlightened policy in regard to the law of treason as well as other laws, permitting no one to be brought to trial except for overt acts or actual conspiracy. Did he in his later years change his policy? Tacitus affirms that he did, and most modern historians have accepted this view. Yet it is impossible to find really solid evidence in support of it. It is true that Suetonius asserts that one man was tried and condemned in the senate for changing the head on a statue of Augustus, and that after this men were punished for the most trivial acts which could be construed as showing disrespect for Augustus,[2] but it is a singular

---

[1] *Ann.* 3, 69. I quote from Ramsay's translation.

[2] Suet. 58. Is Suetonius thinking of the case of Granius Marcellus, which is the only one in which changing the head of a statue is mentioned by Tacitus? If so, then Suetonius is wrong in his specific as well as in his general statement,

circumstance that Tacitus says nothing whatever of these cases, or of any straining of the law to protect the divinity of Augustus. Since Tacitus consistently pictures Tiberius as a cruel tyrant, his silence seems to me conclusive against the accuracy of Suetonius, for it is surely incredible that *all* these cases occurred in the few years of the reign for which the text of Tacitus is lost, or that he deliberately refrained from using material so well adapted to enhance the effect of his picture. It seems evident that the biographer has here reported random gossip and vague abuse for which the historian found no basis in his sources.

After A.D. 23 there were more cases of treason tried before the senate than in the earlier years of the reign, but this may readily be explained by the simple fact that there were more conspiracies then than previously, and it does not necessarily mean that the law was stretched or modified in any way. There are, it is true, a number of instances where, if we take the narrative of Tacitus at its face value, we might conclude that men were punished for comparatively harmless and trivial acts, or even for mere words. Yet an examination of these cases will raise grave doubts. Often, if we read the account of Tacitus carefully, we find that it fails to support our first impression, and where we can obtain any additional information from other sources this first impression is entirely dispelled. Thus if we read what Tacitus says of the suicide of Mamercus Scaurus without close attention to unobtrusive details, we gather that the ruin of Scaurus was due to a tragedy he had written containing some lines which Tiberius construed as a reflection on himself. If we read carefully, however, we note that it was not Tiberius but Macro who was responsible, and that the tragedy did not figure in the charges. Apparently, therefore, the anger of Tiberius had only this result, that he did not interfere with the ordinary course of justice to protect Scaurus from being tried for other offences.

When all the facts are duly weighed there is no evidence that Tiberius at any time strained the law of treason or allowed careless words or acts to be treated as crimes.[1] From first to last he

---

for Marcellus was acquitted of treason. Probably he was convicted of extortion and Suetonius confused the two counts of the indictment.

[1] See the appendix on 'The Law of Treason under Tiberius'.

seems to have adhered to the same policy, and the account of Tacitus himself, if we can only disregard his rhetoric, reveals the emperor consistently striving to secure justice, inclining to mercy rather than severity, and tolerating with remarkable patience offences which affected merely his own honour or good name.[1]

In the administration of all other laws Tacitus emphatically commends the emperor (at least in the first nine years of his reign) even while constantly asserting his harshness and cruelty.[2] Some modern scholars have sought to escape from the obvious contradiction by assuming that Tiberius was a legal pedant who enforced the law with undue severity. This assumption makes nonsense of Tacitus' commendation, and in addition it is in conflict with such facts as he records. In his pages we see the emperor constantly interfering to mitigate the penalties imposed by the senate. In but two instances does Tacitus represent him as urging severity; in one case the historian admits that he was right,[3] and in the other after the sentence was pronounced he modified it in the direction of leniency.[4]

Aside from the law of treason Tacitus praises the early government of Tiberius highly, especially his choice of magistrates and his attitude towards the senate. As to the magistrates, we have seen that Tiberius steadily favoured the great consular families, advancing new men to the consulship rather infrequently. Whatever contemporaries of the emperor may have thought of such a policy, it evidently met with the approval of Tacitus, and probably of the Roman aristocracy in Trajan's day. By that time the old republican nobility was nearly extinct, but its memory was still fondly cherished and the preference shown for it by Tiberius during the greater part of his reign was likely to be applauded by the Flavian senate.

[1] As far as we know only two men were actually punished for slandering the emperor during the entire reign. One was Votienus Montanus (*Ann.* 4, 42), who was probably accused of seditious libel rather than simple slander (see chapter vii); the other was Sextius Paconianus (*Ann.* 6, 3 and 39), who was already in prison for another offence. A third man was convicted but pardoned (*Ann.* 4, 31).

[2] *Ann.* 1, 72 and 74; 3, 37, for example.   [3] *Ann.* 4, 31.

[4] *Ann.* 3, 68. In one case he insisted that a provincial who had been acquitted of adultery should be tried afterwards for treason. (*Ann.* 3, 38). Tacitus constantly asserts or implies that Tiberius was harsh and cruel, but he fails to produce any facts to support the charge.

The relations between Tiberius and the senate have been a theme for many rash conjectures. One modern writer has suggested that Tiberius wished the senate to co-operate with him in the government in an advisory and subordinate capacity, but that the senate, filled with memories of its former greatness, could not reconcile itself to such a role, and that, as the emperor came to realize this, he grew suspicious and stood on the defensive until the death of Germanicus and the trial of Piso put an end to any co-operation.[1] Of all this there is no evidence whatever. Unless Tacitus has completely misrepresented the attitude of the senate, that venerable body was willing to play a secondary role and to accept the imperial leadership and authority not only before the death of Germanicus but afterwards, nor is there any reason to think that the attitude of Tiberius toward the conscript fathers was changed by that event. If republican memories were still alive, we should expect to find them strongest among the great republican houses and the later consular families which had been long and intimately associated with them, and if Tiberius distrusted the senate, it would seem likely to be against this section of it that he would direct his suspicion. Yet his conduct reveals no sign of any such feeling, for he not only showed marked favour to this class in the magistracies at Rome, but he employed them freely in important positions in the imperial provinces. In the last years of his reign the greater part of the Roman army, including all the legions nearest to Italy, was actually under the command of such men, a circumstance which certainly does not point to any distrust of the old nobility on the emperor's part.[2] It is im-

[1] Homo, 32–3. Baker takes a similar view throughout his book, but makes the senate hostile from the start.

[2] In Lower Germany (four legions) L. Apronius was legate from 28 to 37; he was a new man raised to the consulship in A.D. 8 by Augustus and was the father-in-law of the legate of Upper Germany. In Upper Germany (four legions) Cn. Cornelius Lentulus Gaetulicus was legate from 29 to 39; he was a member of one of the most illustrious families of the republican nobility. In Dalmatia (two legions) L. Volusius Saturninus was legate from 34 or 35 to 41; he belonged to a family which had attained praetorian rank under the republic; his father was consul in 12 B.C. and he himself held the office in A.D. 3. In Pannonia (three legions) C. Calvisius Sabinus was legate shortly before 38; his grandfather was consul in 39 B.C., his father in 4 B.C., and he himself held the office in A.D. 26. In Africa the senatorial proconsul was M. Junius Silanus, a member of an old and distinguished consular family; he assumed command in Africa in 32 or 33 and held it for six years, a proconsulship of unusual length.

possible to show that the death of Germanicus and the trial of Piso had any effect upon the relations between Tiberius and the senate, for the only apparent change in the emperor's policy was that with the death of Germanicus he withdrew the favour which he had for a short time shown to the lesser nobility and new men.

What the facts seem to show is that Tiberius tried in vain to make the senate a serious partner in the government, and that the attempt failed, not because he gave that body too subordinate a role, but because the part he wished the conscript fathers to play demanded a degree of independence of which they were incapable. He constantly consulted them and strove to secure free discussion, restraining the servility into which they were always prone to lapse. He had a downright hatred of flattery and refused to allow any language which was inconsistent with his constitutional position; thus when a speaker addressed him as 'Lord' he treated it as an insult, and when another said that he appeared before the senate by the emperor's 'authority', he compelled him to change the word authority to 'advice'.[1] He was careful to avoid any appearance of dictation, taking part in the debates as a simple senator; on one occasion he begged the pardon of Haterius, if, as a senator, he had spoken too freely in opposition to him, and declared that he looked upon the senators as kind, just, and indulgent masters. A good emperor, he said, ought to be the servant of the conscript fathers.[2] The consuls he treated with marked respect, rising in their presence and making way for them in the streets. Moreover, he studiously refrained from any encroachment on their functions. When envoys were sent to him from the senatorial province of Africa he delayed taking any action, so that they were finally forced to refer their business to the consuls.[3]

At first this attitude of the emperor may have had an appreciable effect, for the senate seems to have acted with some

Syria (four legions) was under L. Vitellius, a new man, from 35 to 39, and Moesia (two legions) under P. Memmius Regulus, also a new man, from 35 to 43. Egypt (two legions) was under a Roman knight, Avillius Flaccus. The legate of Spain (three legions) is unknown. See the *Prosopographia*; Liebenam, *Die Legaten*; Lang, 83–92.   [1] Suet. 27.

[2] Suet. 29. Tacitus in a general way confirms the attitude which the anecdotes of Suetonius imply.

[3] Suet. 31. It is not clear why he did not send them to the consuls at once.

independence; Suetonius and Dio affirm that decrees were passed contrary to the opinions of Tiberius.[1] But such freedom was delusive, and neither the senate nor the emperor could make it real, for the conscript fathers could not forget that Tiberius controlled the patronage of the empire and the monarch could not relax this control, nor could he permit serious interference with his policy in important matters.[2] Apparently this was clearly understood from the first, so that the senate took good care never to oppose the emperor on matters in which he was likely to feel any great interest or concern. Perhaps it was a clear perception of this political timidity which made Tiberius often exclaim when leaving the senate, 'Oh men ready for slavery'.[3]

Although Tiberius was unable to endow the senate with real independence, his reign saw an important extension of its functions in that it became a high court of justice where certain cases and certain classes of persons were regularly tried. This development was probably not the result of any formal law, but rather of a gradual assumption of power in dealing with concrete cases. The beginnings of the process must certainly go back to the time of Augustus, but it was completed under Tiberius, and it is very probable that it had not proceeded far at his accession. As to the legal basis of the senate's jurisdiction we are left entirely to conjecture, but it is not difficult to point out how it may have arisen. Under the republic the conscript fathers were sometimes called on to pronounce as to the interpretation of laws, and one of their essential functions had been to advise the magistrates as to the exercise of the *imperium* in doubtful or important cases. Thus, after the arrest of the Catilinarian conspirators, the senate by its decree practically declared that the conspirators were public enemies and advised Cicero to put them to death by virtue of his authority as consul. Strictly speaking, this decree did not make them outlaws, but asserted that they were such already in the opinion of the senate, a view which was sharply criticized by the popular party. Here, then, what the senate did from the constitutional standpoint was to pronounce

[1] Suet. 31; Dio, 57, 7.
[2] The only concrete instance of resistance on the part of the senate which is recorded is given by Suetonius (31) and is in a matter of purely local importance.
[3] *Ann.* 3, 65.

its opinion on a disputed legal question, whether the conspirators should be considered public enemies or Roman citizens, and to advise the consul to act on their interpretation of the law. When Augustus extended the law of treason to include libel we may safely assume that he secured a decree of the senate interpreting the law in this sense.[1] Thus even under the republic an inquiry in the senate might sometimes take the place of a regular trial, for, if a man were adjudged an outlaw, he would be subject to the summary action of the magistrates. Until the time of the empire, however, such decisions by the senate could be questioned and their validity disputed by its opponents. With the establishment of the principate the possibility of such attacks disappeared and the decrees of the senate became practically final. Under these circumstances it is not surprising that in certain cases the emperor should turn to the senate rather than to the regular courts.

An examination of the first cases brought before the senate in the reign of Tiberius suggests that the development of its jurisdiction was far from complete at his accession. In A.D. 15 we have the charges against Falanius and Rubrius which were lodged with the consuls, who were evidently expected to bring them before the senate, but a letter from Tiberius to the consuls promptly put an end to the matter.[2] Here we might infer that the reference to the senate was due to the fact that it was not clear that the acts alleged against the knights could be considered treason (the emperor's letter plainly asserts the negative), and that the delators hoped to obtain from the senate a decree under which they could bring a prosecution in the regular courts with better chances of success. Soon afterwards Granius Marcellus was brought before the senate charged with treason and extortion. He was acquitted of treason and the charge of extortion was referred to a commission of five senators according to the law. This was the first case of treason to be 'tried' in the senate, and the acquittal may have been merely a decision

---

[1] *Ann.* 1, 72; Dio, 56, 27; Suet., *Gaius*, 16. If Suetonius is right in saying that the writings of Cassius Severus were suppressed by a decree of the senate, it is highly probable that the senate played some part in his banishment, as we know that it did in the punishment of Valerius Messalla Volesus for maladministration in Asia (*Ann.* 3, 68). Both events occurred in the last three years of the reign of Augustus.　　　　[2] *Ann.* 1, 73.

that nothing of which he was accused came within the scope of the law.[1] Moreover, in this same year one of the praetors addressed a question to Tiberius which proves that prosecutions for treason were still brought in the praetorian courts.[2]

In the next year we have the case of Libo Drusus. An information against him was lodged with the consuls and an investigation by the senate demanded. The conscript fathers were summoned 'for consultation concerning an important and atrocious matter'. The senate began an investigation of the charges and continued it in spite of Libo's suicide. In the end decrees were passed against his memory and his property was divided among the accusers. We may reasonably surmise, therefore, that he was declared a public enemy and that, if he had not anticipated his fate, the consuls might have been advised to execute him as in the case of the Catilinarian conspirators.

In A.D. 17 Appuleia Varilla was 'tried' for treason and adultery. Tiberius himself interposed to prevent the extension of the law of treason to cover her offences, and she was acquitted on this count. On the charge of adultery the emperor again intervened, and her punishment was left to her family. Her lover was banished, however, perhaps by a decree of the senate. It is possible that in his case, as in that of D. Silanus,[3] the 'banishment' was not a legal sentence but rather a solemn warning which he was wise enough to heed. At any rate, in dealing with Appuleia the senate seems to have shown a disposition to take on itself the powers of a court, for Tacitus tells us that it was due to the emperor's intervention that she was not punished under the Julian law, but was left to be dealt with by her relatives. Whatever the reason for the attitude of Tiberius on this occasion, it seems clear that the senate would soon assume the functions of a court if cases continued to be brought before it. The right to advise the magistrates that a certain person was outside the protection of the law and that some specific action should be

---

[1] Tacitus (1, 74) says that the senators believed the truth of the charges but that Tiberius permitted them to acquit Marcellus. This seems somewhat strange, but if Tacitus did not realize that the senate was not yet a court of justice the apparent contradiction is easily explained; the senate might decide that the charges against Marcellus did not constitute treason, even if convinced that he was guilty.   [2] *Ann.* I, 74.   [3] *Ann.* 3, 24.

taken against him, could be distinguished from the right to pass a formal sentence only by legal pedantry, on which there was no one with the will and power to insist. If the assumption of a definite jurisdiction over certain cases and over certain persons was agreeable to both the emperor and the senate, nothing was easier than to extend the advisory and interpretative powers of the senate till they grew into such a jurisdiction.

Yet even as late as A.D. 20 the senate's jurisdiction over its own members was so far from being established that it was still regarded as somewhat exceptional. In his speech at the opening of Piso's trial Tiberius declared that he placed Germanicus above the law in only one respect, namely that his death should be investigated in the senate rather than in the ordinary courts. Nor did the senate as yet have exclusive jurisdiction in cases of treason, for in that same year we hear of a provincial who was tried and condemned on this charge in the regular courts.[1] After this time, however, the senate apparently became the regular, if not at first the exclusive, court for the trial of all cases of treason, and it exercised a general criminal jurisdiction over its own members and, to some extent at least, over the knights as well.

While the exact status of the senate's jurisdiction under Augustus cannot be determined owing to the scantiness of our information, several facts in the cases cited above seem to show that its complete development dates from the reign of Tiberius,[2] and that he was in large part responsible for it. His motives in encouraging its growth are not difficult to guess. To magnify the power of the conscript fathers wherever this was possible without materially hampering the imperial government would be in harmony with all that we know of his policy in the first years of his reign. The jurisdiction of the senate could hardly be considered dangerous, since the senate was more readily influenced by the emperor than the ordinary courts, and in some cases it might well seem a better tribunal. An offender of high

[1] *Ann.* 3, 38.
[2] In this connexion the text of a decree of the senate of 4 B.C. recorded in an inscription in Cyrene is of significance. I agree with Anderson (47) and von Premerstein (527) that it marks a stage in the development of the senate's judicial power, the beginnings of which would thus fall within the reign of Augustus.

rank would be less able to overawe or corrupt his peers than the jury of a praetorian court, and thus the trial by the senate of governors accused of extortion might appear to offer a better guarantee of justice. It must also have appeared a logical development in that it gave the senate a new means of control over the administration of those provinces for whose good government that body was in theory responsible. Interference by the princeps in this field by the prosecution of a governor would, moreover, be less likely to cause resentment if the decision of the matter was, nominally at least, left to the senate, since under these circumstances the emperor would hardly appear to be encroaching on the authority of the conscript fathers, but simply assisting them in the exercise of that authority by giving them the benefit of such special information as he might obtain through his fiscal agents in their provinces (the procurators), and hence strengthening rather than weakening their control. A further advantage was to be found in the fact that, as the senate gradually assumed its jurisdiction by virtue of precedents rather than formal law, it was not fettered by strict rules of procedure, and in its decisions it could give more weight to equity than to the letter of some statute. Thus the senate could punish a governor who had oppressed the provincials even if he had refrained from doing anything which was explicitly forbidden, and in cases of treason it was possible to deal with conduct which in any given circumstances might seem to the senate dangerous even if the illegality of such conduct was more or less doubtful.

That the senate would welcome such an extension of its functions seems highly probable, since, in appearance at least, its powers were increased, and an added dignity was given to the nobility by making them more than ever a privileged class whose offences were only subject to the judgement of their peers. The chief objection to the new system was one which it is unlikely that either the senate or the emperor perceived clearly at first. This objection was that in view of the servility of the senate the emperor came to have a much more arbitrary power over the lives and fortunes of the nobles than would have been the case had they remained subject to the ordinary courts. It may be doubted whether this consequence made itself seriously

felt in the reign of Tiberius, since, in spite of the rhetoric of
Tacitus, who was probably misled by his own experience of
senatorial subservience under Domitian, the conscript fathers
down to the death of Tiberius seem from the record to have
remained capable of independent verdicts, and, even in the
panic after the fall of Sejanus, we have instances of acquittals
which cannot be attributed to the interference of the emperor.

A word seems necessary in regard to the jurisdiction commonly ascribed to the emperor himself. It is generally held that
the princeps was invested with a judicial power co-ordinate
with that of the senate and the regular courts, so that any case
might be brought before him in preference to any other tribunal.
It has, I think, been shown[1] that this view is a mistake in so far
as the early empire is concerned. Certainly there is no sufficient
evidence that either Augustus or Tiberius ever exercised any
jurisdiction over Rome or Italy.[2] Not only would a power of
such vast extent have been inconsistent with the theory of the
principate, but, if it was held by Tiberius, it seems incredible
that we should find no clear trace of it. As proconsul of a number
of provinces governed by his deputies the emperor could
obviously allow appeals to himself in certain cases, and he thus
placed himself at the head of a court with appellate jurisdiction
over those provinces,[3] but it cannot be shown that the authority
of his court extended further than this in the reign of Tiberius.
Only two instances can be cited where he even appears to possess
a wider jurisdiction. The accusers of Piso requested him to
undertake the *cognitio* of the case, to which Piso readily agreed.
This does not necessarily mean that the emperor was asked to
conduct a formal trial, since a *cognitio* might be merely an investigation to determine whether a prosecution was justified.
Both sides might expect that a definite decision of the emperor
pronounced after such an investigation would amount in fact to
a final judgement; if Piso was declared innocent, his accusers
would probably abandon the prosecution, while a judgement
against him would render his chances so desperate that he

[1] By McFayden, though I am unable to accept his views in regard to the
jurisdiction of the senate.
[2] Dio (58, 16) is evidently puzzled by the failure of Tiberius to do so and tries
to explain it.
[3] Probably Dio, 57, 7 refers to this court

would probably accept the emperor's verdict and either retire into exile or commit suicide at once. As we have seen, however, Tiberius refused to pronounce a definite opinion and referred the matter to the senate. The second instance occurred towards the end of the reign when we are told that the emperor put to death two of his companions at Capri, but the words of Tacitus clearly imply a compulsory suicide rather than a legal execution,[1] and this might naturally follow an investigation in which their guilt was fully established. So far, therefore, as our records show, Tiberius never exercised any personal jurisdiction over Rome or Italy, and the authority of the magistrates and the ordinary courts was only abridged by the assumption of judicial powers on the part of the senate.[2] But while Tiberius refrained from encroaching on the courts, he sought to render the administration of justice in them more efficient. We are told that he often assisted the praetors as an adviser,[3] and it is clearly implied that he did this when he thought that there was danger of a miscarriage of justice through bribery or influence. His intervention seems, therefore, to have been prompted by the best intentions, but Tacitus is doubtless right in feeling that the precedent so set endangered the independence of the courts, and that this outweighed any temporary good which might, and as he admits did in fact, result.[4]

From the time when Augustus restored the republic the inadequacy of its machinery made itself constantly felt. The annually changing magistrates, many of them young and inexperienced, were unable to provide the city with an efficient administration, and it became necessary to supplement their activities by the creation of new agencies. This process threw an ever increasing responsibility on the emperor, for men inevitably turned to him in all matters where mismanagement

[1] *apud principem Vescularius Flaccus ac Julius Marinus ad mortem aguntur* (*Ann.* 6, 10).

[2] The institution of the city prefect as a permanent official probably did not at first constitute an encroachment on the courts, for his function was to keep the peace by exercising a summary jurisdiction over the rougher elements in the city. It is unlikely that many of the cases he dealt with would have come before the courts.

[3] *Ann.* 1, 75; Suet. 33; Dio, 57, 7.

[4] I think that is the real meaning of his remark that by such intervention of the emperor *dum veritati consulitur, libertas corrumpebatur* (*Ann.* 1, 75).

was intolerable. Augustus was early forced to take charge of the food-supply of Rome and later of the water-supply as well. To deal with the first he organized a regular service under a *praefectus annonae* of equestrian rank appointed by himself, and the charge of the latter was entrusted to a *curator aquarum* chosen from the consulars. The oversight of temples and public buildings was given to two curators selected from the praetorian senators, *curatores viarum* were put in charge of the roads, and a special force, the *vigiles*, was organized to deal with fires. To safeguard the public order when he was absent from the city Augustus designated a *praefectus urbi*, though this office remained intermittent and exceptional. Tiberius inherited this new administrative machinery and developed it still further in order to deal with matters which Augustus had left to the magistrates or had regulated when necessary by special and temporary means. Thus Tiberius seems to have created a new board of five senators, probably selected by lot, one from each rank of the senate, known as *curatores locorum publicorum iudicandorum*, to reclaim public property which had passed into the possession of private persons. Another similar board of five senators was established to take charge of the banks and bed of the Tiber with a view to minimizing the damage resulting from the recurring floods and droughts.[1] This last *cura* seems to have been instituted after an especially disastrous flood in A.D. 15, which led to a motion in the senate for a consultation of the Sibylline books; the emperor, however, preferred to take steps of a more practical nature. He procured the appointment of the first board of *curatores riparum et alvei Tiberis* and directed their chief, that is the consular member, who in this case was L. Arruntius, to consult with the *curator aquarum* and devise some means of preventing such floods in the future. The result was a plan for regulating the flow of the Tiber by diverting the water of the tributary lakes and streams along its course. Such measures, however, would affect the interests of a number of municipal towns and colonies, which promptly protested, and there were many who feared giving offence to the gods by an interference with their homes and works. These objections

---

[1] Both boards acted under the authority of decrees of the senate as is shown by inscriptions (*C.I.L.*, vi, 1237, 1266; *I.L.S.*, 5925, 5939).

prevailed with the senate and the scheme came to nothing,[1] but the board created on this occasion remained a part of the administrative machinery of the state. We can hardly suppose that the report was presented to the senate without the previous knowledge and consent of Tiberius, and he was evidently prepared to undertake an extensive series of public works for the protection of the capital, but gave way in face of the opposition of the senate.

Of much greater importance was the change in the character of the city prefecture, which Tiberius made a permanent instead of a temporary office in A.D. 17.[2] The three urban cohorts were placed at the disposal of the prefect, and he soon came to exercise a wide jurisdiction over the lower classes in Rome. The result must have been to give greater security to the poor by the better maintenance of order and the more efficient repression of petty crime, and this seems clearly to have been the purpose of Tiberius, though by the creation of a permanent and powerful official under the immediate control of the emperor the authority of the magistrates was still further undermined.

Another change of great significance for the future was the concentration of the praetorian guards in a single camp outside the city.[3] We are told that this measure was suggested by Sejanus, and if the reasons which Tacitus represents him as urging in its favour may be trusted, Tiberius gave his consent in the hope of promoting military efficiency. As long as the guards remained dispersed, discipline was necessarily lax, while prompt action was impossible; from this point of view the concentration was obviously desirable, and the future danger to the throne which it involved was certainly not foreseen.

In the administration of the imperial finances Tiberius made

---

[1] *Ann.* 1, 76 and 79; Dio, 57, 14. Dio is confirmed by the inscription cited above (1237). I have followed the suggestion of the editors of the *C.I.L.* (p. 166), which reconciles the apparently divergent accounts of Tacitus and Dio.

[2] I have accepted the emendation of Nipperdey changing the twenty years in *Ann.* 6, 11 to fifteen, since the absence of the city prefect among the officials swearing allegiance to Tiberius at his accession (*Ann.* 1, 7) seems to show that no prefect held office at that time, although both Tiberius and Augustus had left the city. Probably Augustus intended to return very soon and the appointment of a prefect for so brief a period was not thought necessary.

[3] *Ann.* 4, 2; Dio, 57, 19; Suet. *Aug.* 49.

no serious innovation. Throughout Italy and the provinces the emperor had in various ways, chiefly by confiscations and legacies, become the owner of a vast amount of property from which he drew a considerable part of his revenues. Augustus had managed this property through procurators. These officials were generally taken from the equestrian class, although in some cases they were imperial freedmen.[1] Tiberius seems to have made no change in the system itself, but according to Tacitus he used the greatest care in the selection of his agents, appointing only men of the highest character. Once appointed they were seldom changed, although the emperor evidently made no attempt to shield them if they were guilty of misconduct, for we see him in A.D. 23 allowing the senate to try and condemn Lucilius Capito, procurator of Asia, for offences in that province.[2]

From the provinces, from Italy, and from Rome itself an immense mass of business thus came in one way or another into the hands of the emperor. The theory of his office required that he should deal with it himself, and he was provided with no regular ministers to relieve him of any portion of the burden. Under Claudius the imperial freedmen did much of the work, and as a consequence exercised much of the power, and still later a regular civil service was organized. That we hear nothing of either device under Tiberius[3] shows clearly that he possessed a great capacity for work and laboured diligently in the discharge of his manifold duties. Yet the task must have been so great that he could not fail to welcome the help of a capable and trustworthy subordinate, and the rise of Sejanus may have been due in no small degree to this pressing need. Something of the kind is suggested by the emphasis which Tacitus places upon the industry of the favourite.[4] A competent servant who could look after details must have seemed invaluable to the overburdened emperor, and Sejanus knew how to take full advantage of this to make himself indispensable and gradually to gain the confidence of his master.

---

[1] This is suggested by the case of Licinus (Dio, 54, 21), although he was a freedman of Julius Caesar and not of Augustus.

[2] *Ann.* 4, 15.

[3] Tacitus says that Tiberius had few freedmen (4, 6), and none of them was of sufficient importance to be mentioned by name.   [4] *Ann.* 4, 1.

We have seen strong reasons for thinking that in A.D. 14 the imperial treasury was exhausted by the frontier wars in the last years of Augustus. Since Tiberius was unwilling to increase the taxation of the empire, he had no choice but to adopt a policy of strict economy. He refused to lavish the resources of the state on games and shows for the amusement of the Roman mob,[1] regardless of the unpopularity which was the inevitable result of such a course. Even when he had succeeded in restoring the finances to a condition of prosperity, he remained consistently opposed to useless expenditure and preferred to hoard the surplus in the treasury rather than to purchase the applause of the people by a wasteful liberality. Such hoarding is hardly in accord with modern conceptions of finance, but in ancient times there was much to justify it. The machinery of public credit was still very imperfectly developed, and the government could not meet an emergency by an issue of bonds. If the state had no reserve at hand, a crisis made oppressive taxation necessary. Under these conditions the wisest and most far-sighted of the Roman emperors followed the example of Tiberius in laying by large sums of money against a day of need.

But though Tiberius managed the treasury with strict economy, he had no desire to fill it by confiscation or plunder;[2] even Tacitus admits that avarice was not one of his vices.[3] The historian indeed alleges that one man was put to death on account of his wealth, but this conclusion is based on the fact that the victim's mines in Spain were turned over to the imperial treasury instead of to that of the senate,[4] which seems somewhat unconvincing, since this is the only case in which Tacitus attributes such a motive for a prosecution to Tiberius, and in only one other does he accuse the emperor of dealing harshly with the property of persons who had been condemned.[5] In general, Tiberius carried his disinterestedness in money matters

---

[1] According to Suetonius (34 and 47) he limited the expenditure on private shows and gave no public ones. Tacitus (4, 62) confirms the rarity of shows under Tiberius, but the statement of Suetonius is too sweeping (*Ann.* 1, 76).

[2] Suetonius (49) asserts that he did finally resort to plunder and that he had the leading men of Spain, Gaul, Syria, and Greece prosecuted on trivial charges and their property confiscated. The testimony of Tacitus seems to me a sufficient refutation of this statement. For a fuller discussion see the appendix on 'Tacitus, Suetonius, and Dio'.

[3] *Ann.* 3, 18.   [4] *Ann.* 6, 19.   [5] *Ann.* 4, 20.

so far that he refused to accept legacies from strangers or to the detriment of natural heirs.[1] Moreover, in spite of his economy he was generous upon occasions when expenditure was really justified,[2] and in time of public calamity he threw open the doors of the treasury and granted prompt and liberal relief. He checked a panic by loaning money without interest ;[3] twice after fires he rebuilt parts of the city at public expense ;[4] and he came to the assistance of the provincials when twelve cities of Asia Minor were destroyed by an earthquake.[5]

It might have been expected than an emperor who was frugal and austere in his own life would have tried to check the fashionable luxury of which he disapproved. A section of the senate was strongly in favour of sumptuary legislation in accordance with the old Roman tradition, but Tiberius was too clear-sighted not to recognize its futility. In A.D. 16, however, he permitted the senate to pass a decree forbidding the use of solid gold for dishes and the wearing of silk clothing by men. One of the senators went further, calling for restrictions on silver-plate, furniture, and the number of slaves in a household ; this met with opposition, and Tiberius remarked that it was not the time for a censorship, but if manners deteriorated he would take measures to correct them.[6] Later, in A.D. 22, the aediles complained that the existing sumptuary laws were being disregarded and that banquets were given on a scale more lavish than was permissible. This evil they declared was increasing daily and could not be checked by ordinary means. The senate referred the whole matter to Tiberius, who communicated his views in a letter from which Tacitus quotes at length, and since it must have been on file in the archives of the senate, he has probably reproduced its substance with accuracy. According to his version Tiberius wrote as follows:

In all other matters, Conscript Fathers, it were perhaps better that I should be interrogated in your presence, and tell you what I

---

[1] *Ann.* 2, 48.   [2] *Ann.* 1, 75.   [3] *Ann.* 6, 17; Suet. 48.
[4] *Ann.* 4, 64 and 6, 45. Suetonius (48) mentions only the first.
[5] *Ann.* 2, 47; Suet. 48.
[6] Suetonius (34) says that Tiberius himself proposed the limitation on furniture; this is in conflict with Tacitus, who mentions only one such proposal (2, 33) and attributes it to Octavius Fronto. Tiberius is represented as opposing the proposals of Fronto with the remark cited above.

think the public interest demands. But in regard to this question, it is well that my eyes should be elsewhere; lest if you were to mark out those whose fears or faces betrayed a consciousness of shameful extravagance, I might perceive them myself, and as it were detect them. If, indeed, our excellent Aediles had taken counsel first with me, I might perhaps have advised them to take no notice of failings which have come to a head, and are overmastering us, rather than proclaim the fact that there are scandals with which we are unable to cope. They, however, have done their duty, as I should wish to see all magistrates do theirs; but for me, it is neither seemly to keep silence, nor yet easy to speak out, seeing that I do not hold the office either of Aedile, of Praetor, or of Consul. Some greater and grander utterance is expected from the Princeps; and whereas every one takes credit to himself for his own well-doing, the odium of all men's sins falls upon me alone. And where am I to begin? Which form of extravagance am I to prohibit first, or cut down to the standard of olden times? Is it the vast dimensions of our country houses? the number and varied nationality of our slaves? the weight of our gold and silver plate? our art-marvels, in bronze or painting? the wearing of the same textures by men and women alike? Or that special feminine form of luxury which transports our treasure to foreign and even hostile lands for the purchase of precious stones?

I know that these things are denounced at dinner tables and other gatherings, and that some restriction is called for. But if a law were passed, and penalties proclaimed, these same gentlemen would cry out that everything was being turned upside down; that all outstanding citizens were being threatened with ruin, all citizens alike with prosecution. But just as in the body there are ailments of long standing, come to a head through time, which cannot be arrested but by severe and violent remedies; so when the mind has become corrupt and the breeder of corruption, its distempered and fevered condition can only be assuaged by remedies as potent as the passions which have inflamed it. The many laws devised by our forefathers, and those passed by the Divine Augustus, have but given immunity to extravagance; the former have passed into oblivion: the latter—what is more shameful still—have been contemptuously disregarded. For if a man desires what has not been forbidden, he may be afraid of prohibition; but if he may with impunity do what has been prohibited, neither fear nor shame can restrain him longer. Why, then, was economy the rule of old? Because every one exercised self-restraint; because we were citizens of a single city; our very temptations were not the same so long as our rule was confined to Italy. Foreign conquest has taught us to squander what belongs to others; civil war to be wasteful even of our own.

And how paltry are the matters of which the Aediles warn us! How insignificant, if the whole field be taken into view! Not one of you recalls the fact that Italy cannot live without foreign aid; that the sustenance of the Roman people is day by day being tossed about at the caprice of wave and storm! For were it not that the provinces came to the help of masters, slaves, and lands, with their resources, would our pleasure-groves and country palaces support us? And yet, Conscript Fathers, this is the charge which the Princeps has to undertake; to neglect it would bring the State to ruin. For all else, we must seek a remedy within ourselves. We senators may be turned to better things by shame; the poor by necessity; the wealthy by satiety. Nevertheless, if any of the magistrates will proffer their services to grapple strenuously and strictly with this evil, I will not only commend them, but will acknowledge that they are relieving me of part of my burdens. But if they propose to denounce men's failings, and then, having gained credit for that performance, to leave with me the animosities which they provoke: believe me, Conscript Fathers, I am no more anxious to rouse ill-will than they are. I am ready to face fierce resentments, unjust as they often are, incurred in the public service; but I decline, and rightly decline, to face such as are purposeless and fruitless, and present no prospect of usefulness either to you or to me.[1]

After this plain-speaking the senate determined to leave the matter to the aediles and the existing laws. The candour with which Tiberius expressed himself may have caused some resentment, but he was clearly not disposed to permit new sumptuary regulations, and the lavish banquets continued unchecked.

Though in important matters Tiberius seldom failed to act wisely, in smaller ones he was often lacking in tact and graciousness. Cold and distant in bearing, he had few intimate friends, while his stern expression, frequent silence, and slow speech inspired awe and fear,[2] however little his deeds might justify these feelings. Even when he made concessions to the wishes of the senate he sometimes made them in such a way that they inspired little gratitude. As an example we may take an

[1] *Ann.* 3, 53-4. I quote from Ramsay's translation.
[2] *Ann.* 4, 7; Suet. 68.

incident in A.D. 16. Hortensius Hortalus, the grandson of the celebrated orator of Cicero's time, finding himself in straitened circumstances, placed his four young sons at the door of the senate, and, rising in his place, implored the emperor to take steps to relieve the poverty of the family, declaring that he had only married at the bidding of Augustus; to this plea Tiberius replied:

If every poor man is to come to this House and ask for money for his children, there will be no satisfying the claimants, and the public exchequer will be emptied. When our ancestors permitted senators to pass beyond the limits of a motion, and use their turn of speaking to make suggestions for the public good, it was not to enable us to push our private interests, or advance our family fortunes, bringing odium thereby alike on Senate and on Emperor, whether the bounty were granted or refused. It is no petition, this: it is a demand, a demand as unseasonable as it is unexpected; that a member should get up, when the fathers have been summoned for some other purpose, and by recounting the number and ages of his children put pressure on the Senate, and on me also, and as it were force open the door of the public treasury. That treasury we may exhaust by favouritism: but if we do, we shall have to replenish it by crime. The Divine Augustus did indeed give you money, Hortalus, but he gave it unasked; nor did he bargain that he was to go on giving it for ever. If it be otherwise—if a man is not to rely upon himself in his hopes or fears—all energy will be sapped; a premium will be put on lethargy: men will look calmly for help to others, throwing on me the burden which they have not the spirit to bear themselves.[1]

Perceiving, however, that the senate listened with disapproval and regarded the suppliant with favour, Tiberius after a short silence announced that he would bestow two hundred thousand sesterces on each of the four children. The conscript fathers thanked him, but the gift did not save the family from sinking into abject poverty which Tiberius did nothing further to relieve.

To understand the bearing of Tiberius on this occasion we must take into account what had gone before. In the previous year a senator had asked permission to resign his rank because of poverty and the emperor, finding that his financial difficulties were not due to his own extravagance, presented him with the

[1] *Ann.* 2. 38. I quote from Ramsay's translation.

million sesterces which was the property qualification of a
senator. This generosity led to other applications from senators
in embarrassed circumstances, so that Tiberius laid down the
rule that they must bring their cases before the senate and
show legitimate reasons for their poverty. This measure was
considered unduly harsh,[1] and it is possible that in his desire to
protect the treasury Tiberius required a greater degree of
publicity than was really necessary. The Roman aristocracy
were of course convinced that the old families ought to be preserved as a governing class and the emperor evidently shared
this view to some extent, for he had shown himself ready to
come to their assistance when he thought that the aid so given
would be a permanent relief, but to give the money of the public
to men who had squandered their own doubtless seemed to him
simple waste. Although he was right in principle, it is difficult
to defend his course in the case of Hortensius, for the relief
which he allowed the senate to extort from him was evidently
thrown away, either because the amount was insufficient or
because Hortensius was a hopeless spendthrift. Moreover, the
emperor's bitter speech must have gone far to deprive his
reluctant concession of any value in conciliating the senate.
After such a scene it is easy to believe that the conscript fathers
may have disliked and feared Tiberius in spite of his outward
deference to them; Augustus would have known how to reject
the petition of Hortensius without incurring their ill will, but
Tiberius probably provoked their resentment even in the act of
yielding to their wishes.

[1] *Ann.* I, 75; Suet. 47; Seneca, *de Ben.* 2, 7–8.

VI

TIBERIUS AND THE EMPIRE

IN considering the government of Tiberius in Rome we have been forced to limit ourselves largely to the first part of his reign and to postpone a discussion of its character during his last years because of the general acceptance of the Tacitean view that it underwent a marked degeneration after the death of his son Drusus. In regard to his government of the empire no such limitation is necessary, for it is admitted that in this field his conduct was consistent from the beginning to the end. We have already seen that he was resolved to respect the solemn warning of Augustus against further conquests and to accept the frontiers finally decided on by his predecessor; these, however, he was determined to hold firmly and with the least possible expense of blood and money. This policy may have been congenial to his temperament, but there were strong reasons for it which might well seem conclusive to a far-sighted statesman. The success of Augustus blinded his contemporaries, and has largely blinded posterity, to the narrowness and instability of the foundations on which the empire rested. The circumstances under which he rose to power convinced him that it was necessary to preserve the dominant position of the Italian race, and he had, therefore, abandoned the policy inaugurated by Julius Caesar of bestowing citizenship freely on the provincials. In this he was probably wise, for the facts seem to show that Caesar had been in advance of his time and that the Italians were not yet ready to share their privileges with others, nor the provincials yet prepared for equal rights. The edicts of an autocrat cannot work miracles, and a wholesale creation of citizens who had not been thoroughly Romanized might have proved a dangerous experiment. Augustus and Tiberius were both evidently convinced that the time had not yet come for any considerable extension of citizenship, and until it came the Italians must remain the ruling people of the empire, in spite of the fact that as long as this condition continued the government must rest on too narrow a basis for real security. In the last analysis the supreme power was vested

in the army, and Augustus was determined to keep the army
Roman by recruiting the legions solely from the Roman citizens.
In this there can be little doubt that he was guided by a true
instinct, if not by a profound insight, for to have filled the legions
with Gauls or other provincials still hardly touched with Roman
civilization might easily have wrecked that civilization and
brought about the barbarization of western Europe four hundred
years earlier than it happened. Although it must be granted that
Augustus was right in preserving the Roman character of the
army, yet his policy involved serious difficulties, for the Italian
people were not numerous enough to furnish readily an adequate
supply of soldiers. It was not, perhaps, a matter of population
as measured by a census, and it is very probable that a regular
system of conscription would have supplied an abundance of
men, but such a system the government did not dare to introduce, and it became increasingly difficult to get the troops by
such means as the emperor could venture to employ. Perhaps
the prosperity which Italy enjoyed under Augustus in one way
actually weakened the empire by making men less willing to
enlist. The difficulties in this matter have been sufficiently
emphasized already, and they could only be met by filling the
ranks with provincials or by increasing the pay of the legionaries
to such a point as to render the service attractive to the Italian
peasants. Neither Augustus nor Tiberius cared to adopt either
method, probably because they believed that under existing
conditions both involved too great a risk.

Their wisdom can hardly be questioned when we remember
that the empire included large regions which had only recently
been conquered, and whose Romanization was still in its
initial stages. To destroy the national character of the army
at such a time must have appeared as dangerous as to demand
heavy sacrifices from warlike peoples, still more or less restless
under a foreign yoke. When a new generation had grown up
and the progress of civilization had advanced by so much
further, it might be possible to extend Roman citizenship more
widely and to increase the financial resources of the government
by imposing new burdens on the provinces, but Tiberius
evidently considered that the time when such measures could
be safely adopted was still in the future. He, therefore,

maintained the system of Augustus without change, seeking to make it adequate to the needs of the moment by a policy of peace on the frontiers and of strict economy at home.

From this point of view the importance and significance of his reign may best be seen by a brief examination of the conditions in Gaul.[1] It must always seem a remarkable fact that the people who had fought so valiantly against Caesar should, after his final victory over Vercingetorix, have accepted their fate so quietly. This acceptance of the situation on their part is the most impressive of testimonies to the tact, moderation, and insight displayed by him and by Augustus in the organization of the conquered territory. The information at our disposal, scanty as it is, enables us to see clearly the main outlines of that organization. To its completion Augustus devoted more personal attention than to any other provincial problem,[2] and it bears throughout the stamp of his cautious statesmanship, although there can be little doubt that he followed in the main the lines already laid down by Caesar. No doubt he looked forward to the ultimate transformation of Gaul from a land of warlike and half-barbarous tribes into a land of city-states on the Graeco-Roman model, but such a transformation required time, and for the present Augustus accepted without serious alteration the political divisions which Caesar had found in Gaul when he began his conquest. Each of the old Gallic peoples remained as an autonomous community under the supremacy of Rome, and the government was more or less completely concentrated in their chief town or village. The old institutions of the Gauls here furnished an excellent point of departure, and they were dextrously adapted to the new conditions. Before the time of Caesar the nobles had already to a large degree acquired political control, and the assemblies of the freemen had fallen into a state of decay. It was a comparatively easy matter, therefore, to induce the aristocracy to settle in the local capital and to form from their number a governing body similar to the Roman senate. The old magistracies of the community were not

[1] For the best account of Gaul under the early emperors see the fourth volume of Jullian's history.

[2] He spent a considerable time in Gaul between 26 and 24 B.C. and again from 16 to 13 B.C.

immediately abolished or transformed,[1] but with the passage
of time they were gradually brought more and more into
harmony with those to be found among the Italian municipal
towns and the Roman colonies. The popular assembly, already
weak, tends rapidly to disappear, and the chief town of the
community becomes more and more a city of the familiar type,
whose aristocratic government exercised authority over a wide
stretch of country under the general oversight of a Roman
governor.

In the old province of Transalpine Gaul, where the ground
was well prepared by a long Roman occupation, the transformation was rapid and complete. Caesar had strengthened the
Roman element in this region by planting six or seven colonies,
and Augustus added some twelve others in which a considerable
body of natives was joined with the new settlers. After this he
regarded the province as sufficiently Romanized to warrant him
in transferring it to the senate under the name of Narbonensis.

In the newly conquered territory Augustus refrained from the
establishment of any colonies,[2] evidently feeling that, by disturbing the existing organization, they would be a source of
discontent rather than a support to Rome, and trusting to the
neighbourhood and example of the colonies in Narbonensis for
the spread of Roman ideas among the Gauls. The regions
acquired by Caesar were divided into three provinces under
governors of praetorian rank, but these governors were sometimes subject to a viceroy, closely related to the emperor, who
was given the supreme command over Gaul and the armies on
the Rhine.

If the Romans imposed tribute upon the people of Gaul, they
gave peace and prosperity in return. The internal strife and
confusion ceased with the conquest, and under Augustus the
country was opened up to trade by five great roads designed by
Agrippa. These were extended and supplemented later till they
spread like a net-work over the whole country. With peace and

---

[1] The single annual magistrate of the Gauls, known as a *vergobret*, continues
to be found under both Augustus and Tiberius. Later he is apparently in
some cases replaced by two *vergobrets*, who are finally styled praetors (Jullian,
iv. 337).

[2] Jullian, iv. 76. Lugdunum (Lyons), the one colony in this region, was
founded by Plancus before Augustus gained control of Gaul.

better communications commerce rapidly developed and Gaul soon became prosperous. There seems little reason to doubt that the tribute was light compared with the cost of the old tribal wars with their devastations and mercenaries.[1] No doubt many individuals and classes found the new conditions irksome and disadvantageous to their interests, but the population as a whole must have benefited. With commerce came industry and the gradual growth of the political centres into real cities, and with city life Roman civilization began to take firm root. The process seems to have been slow,[2] but it progressed steadily, and the mass of the population learned to forget the past in the growing prosperity of the present, while the nobles little by little acquired Roman manners and habits of life. There is clear evidence, however, that when Tiberius came to the throne the peace of Gaul still rested on a more or less unstable basis. In A.D. 21 there occurred the first rebellion since the completion of the conquest. The causes of this movement are somewhat obscure; it involved chiefly the Treveri and the Aedui, but Tacitus informs us that a spirit of unrest was general throughout the country.[3] The revolt broke out prematurely among the Andecavi and Turoni, where it was easily suppressed. The rising of the Aedui was more serious, and was only put down by Silius at the head of two legions from the Rhine. The leaders of the revolt were Julius Florus among the Treveri and Julius Sacrovir among the Aedui; both were of noble birth, but they seem to have drawn their supporters chiefly from the lower classes, while the aristocracy stood aloof. Tacitus makes the cause of the discontent the burden of debt and the continuance of the tribute, together with the exactions of the Roman bankers and money-lenders. The Treveri and the Aedui were free or allied peoples, and as such they were supposed to enjoy fiscal immunity;[4] the violation of this immunity was probably the reason for the revolt. The expression of Tacitus as to the continuation of the tribute may perhaps be explained by his statement[5] that after the campaign of Germanicus in A.D. 15 Gaul, Spain, and Italy had offered him arms, horses, and money to

---

[1] Jullian, iv. 83.   [2] Rostovtzeff, 203.
[3] For the rebellion see *Ann.* 3, 40–6.
[4] Jullian, iv. 154–5.   [5] *Ann.* 1, 71.

repair his losses. We may conjecture that many of the *civitates* of Gaul had at this time made voluntary contributions which the government continued to exact afterwards, and we may also conjecture that in many cases they had borrowed from Roman money-lenders and traders in order to make their offering promptly, which obligations they now found difficulty in meeting. It seems hardly likely, however, that such grievances were at all general, and it is possible that they were limited to certain peoples, since aside from the language of Tacitus, who may have been misled to some extent by the exaggerated rumours which were prevalent in Rome, the outbreak seems to have been confined to a part of Gaul, though this may have been due to the prompt action of the Roman officials. In addition to financial causes it is possible that the measures taken by Tiberius in restraint of the Druids[1] played a part, but these measures may equally well have been a result of the revolt, or they may have had no connexion with it. In any case, the movement shows clearly that the Roman peace was still somewhat precarious, and that serious or widespread grievances might easily produce a really formidable uprising.

Tiberius was probably well aware of the conditions in Gaul, for his policy was admirably adapted to them. Under the circumstances the vitally important thing was to preserve peace till Roman civilization had taken firm root, and this could best be accomplished by mild and honest administration. In addition to this the most effective measures were those which would tend to foster trade and so increase the general prosperity. It was probably as a step in this direction that Tiberius suppressed or limited the right hitherto held by the cities to coin silver, since a uniform currency would facilitate business transactions.[2] His most important measures, however, were directed to the improvement of communications, repairing old highways and building new ones in southern Gaul and Spain. This work, of which we learn only from inscriptions, can be traced throughout the reign,[3] but the most important developments seem

---

[1] Pliny, *Nat. Hist.* 30, 13.
[2] Jullian, iv. 286.
[3] The earliest inscription in Tarraconensis dates from 14 or 15 (*C.I.L.*, ii. 4905; *I.L.S.*, 152). The great majority, however, are later than A.D. 31.

to belong to its closing years and will be dealt with in a later chapter.

The problem of the German frontier was closely associated with the protection of Gaul. Here we have already seen something of the policy of Tiberius. He was willing to permit Germanicus to conduct punitive expeditions into Germany, probably because he was convinced that this was necessary to ensure peace along the Rhine for the future. It is possible that, if these campaigns had promised a speedy reconquest of the country, he would have given a somewhat reluctant consent. This, however, in view of what we know of his attitude, must seem very doubtful, and it is much more likely that he never intended a permanent advance beyond the Rhine. As soon as the expeditions of Germanicus had achieved their purpose of restoring Roman prestige, Tiberius put a stop to the war. He did not wish to annex Germany, and he was convinced that the warlike tribes would soon be quarrelling among themselves once the outside pressure was removed.[1] The course of events fully justified this belief, for Germanicus had hardly returned to Rome when war broke out between Arminius and Maroboduus. The latter, being unsuccessful, appealed to Tiberius for help, but the emperor refused to interfere, and replied that as the German had given no aid to the Romans they were under no obligation to come to his assistance.[2] After his failure against Arminius, the downfall of Maroboduus was rapid, and his ill-compacted empire broke up. Tiberius sent his son Drusus to Illyricum, from which point of vantage the prince no doubt did his utmost to assist the internal forces of disruption which were destroying the once powerful kingdom of the Marcomanni. Within two years it had gone entirely to pieces, and the king was forced to seek an asylum in Roman territory. His ruin was speedily followed by the death of his rival Arminius, and with this event Rome no longer had to fear the rise of a strong German state. The various peoples fell apart, occupying themselves with their own disputes and rivalries, and the Romans were left to guard the Rhine in peace. The only incident of importance in this quarter during the remainder of the reign was the revolt of the Frisians in A.D. 28.[3] Their territory was the last fragment which

---

[1] *Ann.* 2, 26. [2] *Ann.* 2, 46. [3] *Ann.* 4, 72–4.

remained to Rome of the Germany that had been lost by Varus, and they were goaded into revolt by an oppressive increase in their taxation which was due to the rapacity of a subordinate official rather than to Tiberius. They inflicted a defeat upon L. Apronius, the legate of Lower Germany, and the emperor apparently accepted the result and made no effort to reconquer them.

Under Augustus, the Raetians and Vindelicians had been subjugated by Tiberius and his brother. This conquest opened a way into southern Germany, and, while the Romans hoped to secure the Elbe frontier, one or two legions were stationed in what is now Bavaria. They were probably withdrawn during the campaign of Tiberius against Maroboduus and the camp which they had occupied destroyed.[1] After the loss of Germany the legions did not return, but the defence of this portion of the frontier was entrusted to auxiliary troops. No attempt seems to have been made to garrison the banks of the Danube, the Romans contenting themselves with keeping a watch on the river from stations in the interior.[2] At first Raetia was governed by a prefect under the commander of the Rhine legions, but later, probably when Germanicus was recalled, this officer was replaced by a procurator directly responsible to the emperor. The complete organization of the province and the construction of a system of roads there would appear to have been the work of Claudius.[3]

From Noricum to the Black Sea Tiberius sought to strengthen and consolidate the frontier already marked out. Augustus had annexed Pannonia, and had established a military station at Siscia on the Save river, but it was Tiberius who completed the conquest of the country by suppressing the great revolt in A.D. 6 to 9, and the final settlement of the province must be attributed to him. He extended the territory effectively occupied by Rome to the Drave, transferring the principal garrison from Siscia to Poetovio, with an outpost at Carnuntum on the Danube.[4] From these points of vantage the legate of

[1] It was near Augsburg though the exact site is unknown (Wagner, 10).
[2] One was at Auerberg to the south of Augsburg (Wagner, 10–11).
[3] Haug, article on Raetia in Pauly-Wissowa; and Wagner, 10.
[4] Mommsen, *The Provinces*, i. 205. For a discussion of the discoveries of Roman remains at Carnuntum see Nowotny in *Die röm. Limes*, xii. 163–75.

Pannonia could doubtless keep the district between the Drave and the Danube quiet and check any serious movement of the barbarians across it, though its thorough occupation seems to have taken place only under Claudius.[1] It was obviously essential that the Roman army should be able to move swiftly and that it should have easy communication with Italy, and Tiberius was fully alive to these considerations. At his accession we find some of the Pannonian army engaged in road work at Nauportus,[2] and we may reasonably guess that they were constructing the highway which led from that point to Poetovio. Though this work was begun under Augustus, it is probable that the design was due to Tiberius, who must have seen its necessity in his Pannonian campaigns. It is certain that during his reign several important roads were constructed in this region, and that towards its close one was built along the Danube in Moesia.[3]

To the south in the province of Dalmatia we have evidence of similar activity on the part of Tiberius. Here inscriptions reveal the fact that five roads were built between A.D. 16 and 20, all leading from Salonae and serving to open the province to Roman influence.[4] No doubt military reasons played a part in this programme, but it seems reasonable to attribute to the emperor the further object of promoting the spread of civilization by facilitating commerce, since such a purpose is clearly discernible in the construction of roads in Gaul and Spain.

The extension of the Roman frontier to the lower Danube by Augustus had resulted in the formation of the province of Moesia, but it seems that the banks of the river were not effectively occupied as far as the Black Sea. For the protection of the country near the mouth of the Danube Augustus would appear to have relied upon the vassal kindom of Thrace,[5] whether or not any territory north of the Haemus was included in its boundaries. The peoples of Moesia and Thrace were of the same race and spoke a language closely related to that of the Dacians, who retained their primitive independence outside the empire.[6] Instead of attempting to conquer the turbulent and

---

[1] Henderson, 156.   [2] *Ann.* I, 20.   [3] Lang, 73–4.
[4] *C.I.L.*, iii. 3198, 3199, 3200, 3201 (*I.L.S.*, 5829, 5829 a). See also Lang, 74.
[5] Mommsen, *The Provinces*, i. 209.   [6] Mommsen, *The Provinces*, i. 207–8.

warlike Thracians, Augustus had preferred to keep them quiet and make them useful by a steady support of the most important of their princely houses. This policy resulted in the formation of a native kingdom in Thrace and in bringing about the outward unification of the country. Yet the unity thus achieved was far from solid, and the kings who had risen by the help of Rome were obliged to lean upon her more or less constantly in order to maintain themselves. In 11 B.C. a revolution broke out which ended in the defeat and death of the reigning king, Rhascuporis I, but his uncle, Rhoemetalces, escaped and with the help of a Roman army succeeded in recovering the throne.[1] He seems to have been a fairly able monarch, for we hear of no further disturbances in Thrace during his life, and he came to the assistance of Tiberius in the great Pannonian uprising.[2] On his death, which occurred between A.D. 9 and 12, Augustus divided the kingdom between his brother Rhascuporis II and his son Cotys, assigning to the latter the more settled and civilized parts which were nearest to Greece, while the former was given the more barbarous and turbulent districts,[3] probably because Rhascuporis was considered better qualified to maintain order among these restless tribes and to guard effectively the Danube frontier. The division, however, proved unsatisfactory to Rhascuporis, who soon became ambitious to acquire the entire kingdom. While Augustus lived he restrained himself, but with the accession of Tiberius he threw caution aside and began to ravage the territories of his nephew. Tiberius, who had no wish to see the arrangements of Augustus overthrown and who was anxious to preserve peace, dispatched an officer to prevent a war between the two kings. Cotys at once disbanded his forces, but Rhascuporis resolved on treachery; he succeeded in luring his nephew to a personal interview, where he made him a prisoner, and after this he was able without difficulty to seize his territories. He then wrote to Tiberius justifying his action by alleging that Cotys had formed a plot against his life, and under cover of a war with the barbarians

---

[1] Dio, 54, 20 and 34.
[2] Dio, 55, 30.
[3] *Ann.* 2, 64. Tacitus spells the name of the brother Rhescuporis, but I have followed the orthography of the *Prosopographia*.

across the Danube[1] he set about gathering an army. To his excuses Tiberius replied quietly that he must submit himself to the judgement of the senate, but that if innocent he had no occasion to fear the result. The emperor's letter was transmitted to Rhascuporis by Latinius Pandusa, then governing Moesia under Poppaeus Sabinus,[2] and this officer, who was accompanied by a body of troops, demanded that Cotys should be surrendered to him. Rhascuporis, much disturbed, murdered his prisoner, pretending that it was a case of suicide. The death of Pandusa, occurring at this moment, made a new agent necessary for the execution of the imperial policy, and Tiberius selected Pomponius Flaccus, a man of consular rank and a friend of Rhascuporis. Tacitus will have it that this friendship was one of the chief reasons for his appointment, since it would render it easier for him to deceive the king. The assumption of treachery is, however, unnecessary; Flaccus was an experienced soldier who had already served in Moesia[3] and his friendship with the king would be of advantage in an entirely legitimate way; both the emperor and the senate would be obliged to judge of events partly by the reports of the Roman officer on the spot, and the attitude of this officer could easily facilitate or hinder the gathering of evidence and its transmission to Rome. Rhascuporis had complained of the hostility of Pandusa, and Tiberius may have wished to give him a pledge of an impartial hearing by appointing an envoy who was well disposed toward him. Certainly Flaccus discharged his mission with success, whatever the methods employed; the king was induced to come within the Roman military posts, where he was promptly made a prisoner and sent to Rome. If he was duped in the matter he can claim little sympathy, for Tiberius had told him frankly from the start that he must submit to an investigation of his conduct.[4] Once in Rome he was tried before the senate on the

[1] The barbarians were the Bastarnae and the Scythians, who inhabited southern Russia. This strongly suggests that Rhascuporis had some authority over the region of the Dobrudja, since under the circumstances he would not have ventured to announce an intention of crossing Roman territory to attack tribes beyond the frontier of the empire.

[2] See Domaszewski, *Röm. Provinzialv.*; and Stout. The events here narrated are taken from Tacitus (2, 64–8).

[3] See the *Prosopographia*, and Domaszewski, *Röm. Provinzialv.*, 5.

[4] Tacitus may have derived his suspicion of treachery from the defence of

accusation of the widow of Cotys. His guilt being established, he was banished from his kingdom and sent to Alexandria, where he was soon after put to death on the charge of attempting to escape.

The disappearance of Rhascuporis from the scene made a new settlement of Thrace necessary. In this Tiberius respected as far as possible the arrangements of Augustus; the division of the kingdom into two parts was continued, the portion which had originally been assigned to Rhascuporis being given to his son, Rhoemetalces II, who was considered innocent of any share in his father's offences, while the part which had belonged to Cotys was restored to his children. These children were for the present too young to be invested with the government, and they were, therefore, kept in Rome, where they were educated in company with Gaius,[1] the future emperor, and in the meantime a Roman official, Trebellenus Rufus, of praetorian rank, was appointed to administer the kingdom.

This new régime, established in A.D. 19, was soon involved in difficulties. Neither Rhoemetalces nor Rufus seems to have been popular, perhaps chiefly because the new arrangements were looked upon as a first step in the direction of annexation by Rome,[2] and in A.D. 21 a revolt broke out against the new rulers. The tribes rose under their local chiefs, but without any general plan or direction; some crossed the Haemus in the hope of finding allies, probably in Moesia or among the Dacians, while others besieged Rhoemetalces in Philippopolis. The siege was promptly raised and the rebels defeated by the officer in immediate command of Moesia, where the nearest army was stationed. After this the country remained quiet for a time, but in A.D. 26 another insurrection occurred, which, though confined to the mountainous part of the district administered by Rufus, was a much more serious affair. The cause of the revolt was partly the demand of the Romans for recruits, and partly a rumour that these recruits were to be sent to remote

Rhascuporis in the senate. It is, of course, quite possible that Tiberius felt justified in securing the person of the king and at the same time avoiding a war by any means that promised success.

[1] See the *Prosopographia*.

[2] Tacitus (3, 39) implies hostility to Roman rule and the exactions of the two rulers as the causes.

G

regions of the empire. Tacitus informs us that hitherto the
people had always stipulated that their young men should be
required to serve only under their own chiefs and against the
neighbouring nations.[1] They now suspected that these conditions
were to be disregarded and accordingly made threatening repre-
sentations to Poppaeus Sabinus, the imperial legate in supreme
command of Moesia, Macedonia, and Achaia. He made soothing
answers to them till he had concentrated an army, including
one legion from Moesia and auxiliaries under Rhoemetalces.
As soon as this was accomplished he took the field against them,
and after a desperate struggle on the part of the rebels he
succeeded in restoring the authority of Rome, for which the
senate rewarded him with the triumphal insignia. After this we
hear nothing more of Thrace, and we may therefore infer that
its unruly people gave the Roman government no further
trouble. In A.D. 35 Trebellenus Rufus committed suicide in
Rome, apparently because accused of treason,[2] but we know
nothing of the nature of the charge and as little as to how the
part of Thrace which he had governed was administered afterwards. Perhaps no new regent was appointed and the country
was practically annexed to Macedonia. Whether Tiberius had
any serious intention of restoring it to the sons of Cotys we have
no means of knowing, but in any case the restoration was not
made during his life, though this may have been due to the
youth of the princes.

The facts which are known to us with certainty are sufficient
to make clear both the character of the emperor's policy and its
complete success. From Noricum to the Black Sea he made no
attempt to extend the boundaries of the empire, but contented
himself with consolidating Rome's hold on her existing possessions and facilitating their gradual Romanization. For both
these objects peace was highly desirable, if not essential, and
he preferred to employ the legions in the building of roads
rather than in campaigns against independent barbarians
without, or half-subdued barbarians within. He got rid of

---

[1] *Ann.* 4, 46–51. I am inclined to think that their suspicions as to the
intentions of the Romans were well founded. Since the tribes involved seem
to have been turbulent and savage, the Romans may have planned to make
it easier to control them by sending many of the young warriors to other
parts of the empire.   [2] *Ann.* 6, 39.

Rhascuporis without a war, and he utilized the opportunity which the king's crimes put in his way to bring the more settled parts of Thrace under direct Roman administration, but he took care to do this in such a fashion as to spare as much as possible the love of freedom which was still felt by the native population. The rule of a Roman regent would be well calculated to pave the way for that of a Roman governor, and in case he should conclude to restore the kingdom to its nominal sovereign, the education of the future king in Rome would serve as a guarantee that the work begun would be continued. In spite of his careful management he encountered resistance, but this was on so small a scale that it could be dealt with by the officers on the spot without the necessity of any reinforcements. We may, however, legitimately conclude that but for his astute handling of the situation a wasteful and difficult war might easily have resulted. If the son of Rhascuporis had been refused his father's share of the kingdom, the rebellion of A.D. 21 might have been headed by a leader whose energy and capacity seem amply attested by the fact that he kept his subjects quiet during a reign of considerable length.[1] Even if Rhoemetalces had been disposed of at the same time and in the same manner as Rhascuporis it seems not unlikely that the second insurrection would have spread to his portion of Thrace, which embraced the least civilized and most turbulent parts of the country. The avowed annexation of the kingdom of Cotys would also doubtless have made both revolts more serious. Altogether we must credit Tiberius with real statesmanship, and admit that he pursued the true interests of Rome in such a way as to secure them at the smallest possible cost both in blood and in money.

We have already seen the policy adopted by Tiberius in regard to Armenia and Parthia and the settlement arranged by Germanicus during his mission to the East. This settlement lasted without serious disturbance till A.D. 34 and does not, therefore, call for further discussion at this point.

In Palestine and Egypt no serious problems presented themselves, and Tiberius simply maintained the arrangements of Augustus. It is true that during the reign there occurred an

[1] He received the throne in A.D. 19, and it seems clear that he was still ruling in A.D. 37 or 38 (see the *Prosopographia*).

event of transcendent importance to the world, but it was one in which the emperor had no part, for it is most unlikely that he even heard of the Crucifixion of Christ.

To the west of Egypt lay two Roman provinces governed by the senate: Cyrene, which was joined with Crete, and Africa. In neither did Tiberius show any desire to interfere, but in Africa the conscript fathers were forced to seek his help by a troublesome rebellion under a chief named Tacfarinas, who contrived to keep the province in a turmoil for a number of years. Of the causes of this revolt we are very imperfectly informed. Numidia, hitherto a client kingdom, had been annexed to Africa by Julius Caesar, and this arrangement had been maintained by Augustus, perhaps at the urging of Roman capitalists eager to acquire estates in this region. It is not unlikely that the unrest which made possible the career of Tacfarinas was caused by the persistent efforts of the Roman government to extend its authority and the lands of its subjects among the semi-nomadic tribes of the interior,[1] of which efforts an example may no doubt be seen in the activity displayed by the proconsuls of the province in the construction of roads during the reign of Tiberius.[2] Unfortunately it is not altogether clear how far the emperor was personally responsible for such a policy. The senatorial governors were probably inclined to serve their fellow nobles, and the protection of the settled region must have called for measures which the turbulent and still but half-subdued tribes regarded as encroachments on their domain. Possibly one such provocation was the building of an important road from the winter camp[3] of the African legion to the coast at Tacape in the first year of the reign. At first Tacfarinas may have been a simple bandit, but he soon managed to secure the support of some powerful tribes[4] and to carry on a war which has much the appearance of a desperate resistance to the extension of Roman control. By A.D. 17 he had become really formidable, but M. Furius Camillus, then proconsul of Africa, defeated him and checked his depredations for the moment.

[1] Rostovtzeff, 281–2; Broughton, 89–90.
[2] C.I.L., viii. 10018, 10023, 10568, 14386 (I.L.S., 151).
[3] The location of this winter camp has given rise to some difference of opinion. The evidence on the point is well summed up by Gsell, i. 286.
[4] Ann. 2, 52.

In A.D. 20, however, he was able to renew the war,[1] plundering the settled districts and putting to flight a small Roman force. L. Apronius, an experienced soldier who had replaced Camillus, took sharp measures to restore the morale of his men and at length drove the rebel back into the interior. The effect of this victory was only temporary, for the next year Tacfarinas was again harassing the Roman possessions. Apronius had been allowed to administer Africa for three years instead of the usual two, and the senate was on the point of sending a successor. Tiberius reminded the conscript fathers that the situation called for a competent general, perhaps merely intending that the province should be assigned without recourse to lot. The senate, however, requested him to name a proconsul, and he suggested two names, at the same time complaining because the choice had been referred to him. Of the two candidates the senate selected Q. Junius Blaesus, whose military ability was beyond question.[2] Reinforced by a second legion, which had already been dispatched from Pannonia to Africa[3] for the purpose of the war, Blaesus carried on an energetic and skilful campaign, which after three years seemed to be crowned with complete success. In A.D. 23 he was superseded by P. Cornelius Dolabella, and Tacfarinas was then able to renew the war, owing to discontent in the neighbouring kingdom of Mauretania and the recall of the extra legion.[4] It was for the last time, however, for Dolabella succeeded in surprising his forces, and the troublesome Numidian fell, fighting bravely to the last.

This long-drawn-out war in Africa certainly reveals no tendency on the part of Tiberius to interfere with the senate's administration any more than he could help. While Tacfarinas was in the field it was clearly absurd to leave the choice of a governor to chance, but the emperor seems to have had no wish to substitute his authority for that of the conscript fathers, and he insisted that they must take a part in the decision. In view of this attitude it seems doubtful if we can attribute to

---

[1] *Ann.* 3, 20–1.

[2] Tacitus (3, 32) will have it that he was chosen simply because he was an uncle of Sejanus. Nevertheless, we may reasonably infer that his obvious fitness had something to do with his selection.

[3] *Ann.* 3, 9.

[4] *Ann.* 4, 23.

him, except indirectly, any share in the internal affairs of the province, such as the road-building already mentioned.

Though Julius Caesar had annexed Numidia to Rome, he had left the territory to the west subject to vassal kings; Augustus had united these kingdoms into one, known as Mauretania, and had bestowed it upon Juba, a son of the last king of Numidia. This monarch had married a daughter of Antony and Cleopatra and reigned in comparative peace till his death, which seems to have occurred about A.D. 23. Tiberius saw no reason to disturb an arrangement which had worked well, and there was no such motive to extend direct Roman rule over Mauretania as existed in the case of the client kingdoms of the East, so he allowed Ptolemy, the son of Juba, to succeed his father. It was partly discontent with the new king's youth and inexperience that enabled Tacfarinas to find support when he renewed his war with Rome for the last time, but this did not lead Tiberius to interfere, and Ptolemy continued as king of Mauretania to the end of the reign.

While Tiberius laboured to maintain peace and to strengthen the frontiers, he strove earnestly to secure good administration for the provinces. This he may have believed to be a matter of the first necessity, since extortion by the provincial governors would have the same effect as oppressive taxes levied by the emperor. Some of the older provinces might be patient under abuses to which they had become accustomed in the days of the republic, but Augustus had incorporated large territories whose inhabitants could not be misgoverned with safety. The great revolt in Pannonia was a warning of what might result from similar causes in Spain, Gaul, and Moesia. Moreover, if the governors, even in the senatorial provinces, were allowed to enrich themselves by plunder, the future revenues would be imperilled, and financial necessity might force the emperor to resort to new and possibly dangerous exactions, since a serious deficit in the *aerarium* would in the end have to be made good out of the *fiscus*. The establishment of the empire had unquestionably been an immense boon to the provinces in general and especially to those which were placed under the direct rule of Augustus. We have, however, strong reason to conclude that although the founder of the principate strove with much success to restrain abuses and secure for the entire empire a just and honest administration, yet in spite of his efforts much still remained to be done, for we find Tiberius resorting to stern measures, the necessity of which would seem to prove that the old evils of republican days had been alleviated rather than cured. The facts as they are known to us point to Tiberius as the great reformer of the provincial administration, and his strenuous efforts in this direction are admitted to have conferred great benefits on the world even by those who cling to the Tacitean view of his character. We have already seen something of his policy in this respect, but it seems desirable in this connexion to review the facts briefly and to enter upon some further details.

Although the imperial finances were embarrassed when he mounted the throne, probably as a result of the costly wars in the last years of Augustus, Tiberius refrained from any increase in the taxation and sought to balance the budget by strict economy, even reducing the existing taxes when possible.[1] He did not hesitate to sacrifice his own popularity by curtailing the public shows with which Augustus had kept the mob of Rome in a good humour, preferring discontent in the capital, where it could hardly become dangerous with the praetorian guards at hand, to possible insurrection in the provinces. In the collection of the existing revenues he tried to secure strict honesty by the care with which he selected his procurators,[2] who were the officials responsible for the management of the imperial estates. When Aemilius Rectus, prefect of Egypt, sent him a larger sum of money than the regular tribute, the result was a curt message in which the emperor declared that he wished his sheep sheared but not shaved.[3] He not only restrained the avarice of his officials, whether for themselves or the state, but he refused to allow harsh measures to be employed and would not permit the use of flogging or confiscation of property.[4]

---

[1] On the annexation of Cappadocia in A.D. 17 he reduced the tax on goods sold at auction by one-half (*Ann.* 2, 42). Dio's statement that he afterwards increased it to the old figure (58, 16 and 59, 9) is certainly wrong, as is shown by Humbert, article *Centesima* in Daremberg-Saglio.

[2] *Ann.* 4, 6.   [3] Dio, 57, 10; Suet. 32.

[4] *Ann.* 4, 6. Tacitus plainly implies that such humanity was unusual on the part of an emperor.

When in spite of the care with which they were selected his procurators went wrong, he seems to have made no attempt to shield them. The doings of these officials, who were never above equestrian rank, are seldom noticed by our literary sources, yet we learn that one procurator was left to the judgement of the senate,[1] and that another was believed to have killed himself rather than face the emperor.[2]

Of the dealings of Tiberius with the provincial governors we have more evidence. In his own provinces he selected his governors carefully and they gave him little trouble. Since all except those in charge of unimportant provinces were taken from the ranks of the consular and praetorian senators, they would in most cases have already served an apprenticeship in one of the public provinces. This had two consequences; it enabled the emperor to form some estimate of a man's character and capacity, and it also gave to the senatorial governors a powerful incentive to show themselves honest and efficient in the hope of earning further employment in the imperial service. The establishment of this system by Augustus must have been of great advantage to the people of the senatorial provinces, and other measures of his tended in the same direction, such as giving to the governors a fixed salary.[3] Yet the old republican tradition by which the provinces were expected to repair the fortunes of bankrupt nobles appears to have retained its hold, and the events of the reign of Tiberius would point to the conclusion that Augustus had been inclined to overlook senatorial abuses of the milder sort. At any rate we are told that Quinctilius Varus succeeded in amassing a large fortune in Syria,[4] and so far from being punished he was afterward entrusted with the government of Germany. It is hardly possible to doubt that his rapacity in the East has been exaggerated, but it is unlikely that the picture drawn for us by Velleius was wholly without foundation, and his retention of imperial favour seems to show a certain laxity in dealing with senators of high rank on the part of Augustus, which would be in keeping with his general policy of maintaining cordial relations with the aristocracy. It

---

[1] *Ann.* 4, 15; Dio, 57, 23.   [2] Pliny, *Nat. Hist.*, 19, 110.
[3] Dio, 53, 15; Marquardt, *Röm. Staatsverwaltung*, i. 557–8.
[4] Vell., 2, 117.

is also significant that the only instance known to us where severe penalties were inflicted on a provincial governor occurred after Tiberius had returned to Rome from the frontier and had become largely responsible for the policy of the old and failing emperor.[1]

Whatever the attitude of Augustus may have been, the acts of Tiberius afford sufficient evidence that he was resolved to take drastic measures to root out all abuses. For some years after his accession he took no important steps, perhaps because the warning already given had had a considerable effect, perhaps because at first he felt the need of caution and was reluctant to increase his own unpopularity. In any case we hear of only one charge of maladministration in the provinces before the death of Germanicus,[2] and the offences alleged were not of a serious character. In A.D. 21, however, he seems to have taken the matter resolutely in hand, for in the next four years occur all the other prosecutions of governors of senatorial provinces which are recorded during the reign.[3] In this brief period there were four prosecutions, of which the first three resulted in verdicts of guilty and the punishment of the offenders, while the last ended in an acquittal. This series of prosecutions certainly suggests an attempt to enforce higher standards of conduct on the part of the senate's governors by the systematic indictment of all those who had abused their powers, and the absence of further cases of this kind in the following twelve years must be taken as evidence of reasonably complete success. It is impossible to believe that Tiberius grew lax or careless, for he continued to feel a strong interest in the welfare of the provinces down to the end of his life. This is attested by the extensive programme of road-building carried out in Gaul and Spain in his last years, and by the fact that in A.D. 36 he intervened to prevent a bankrupt noble from drawing lots for one of the senate's consular provinces.[4] In the case of his own

[1] The case is that of Valerius Messalla Volesus, who was condemned about A.D. 13 (*Ann.* 3, 68. For the date see the *Prosopographia*).
[2] That against Granius Marcellus in A.D. 15 (*Ann.* 1, 74).
[3] That of Caesius Cordus in 21 and 22 (*Ann.* 3, 38, 70), that of Junius Silanus in 22 (*Ann.* 3, 66–8), that of Vibius Serenus in 23 (*Ann.* 4, 3), and that of Fonteius Capito in 25 (*Ann.* 4, 36).
[4] C. Sulpicius Galba (*Ann.* 6, 40; Suet. *Galba*, 3).

legates the care with which they were selected made the danger
of misconduct less serious, but from his general record we cannot
doubt that Tiberius insisted on the strictest integrity. Lapses
on their part were certainly not condoned or treated leniently,
as is shown by the prosecutions of C. Silius in 24 and of Pomponius Labeo in 34.[1] We have further evidence of the care
taken by the imperial legates to avoid any suspicion of corruption in the story told by Josephus of Pomponius Flaccus,[2] who,
while governor of Syria, instantly broke off all friendship with
the Jewish prince Agrippa on discovering that the latter had
been promised money for the use of his influence.

In his war upon abuses in the provinces Tiberius made use
to a considerable extent of the provincial assemblies. These
assemblies were gatherings for religious purposes of delegates
from a number of different communities; sometimes the union
thus formed was limited to one province or part of a province,
and sometimes it was so extensive as to include several provinces. Such associations for a common worship were not
uncommon, especially in Greece and the East, before the
Roman conquest. When Rome established her predominance
she seems to have dissolved all leagues which had a political
character, though it is probable that those which were purely
religious were permitted to continue or were soon revived.[3] So
far from trying to suppress the assemblies of this sort which he
found, Augustus encouraged their formation, especially in the
western part of the empire. It was he who, through his stepson
Drusus, built the altar to Rome and himself at the confluence
of the Rhone and Saone near Lyons where the assembly of the
three imperial provinces of Gaul had its meeting-place. By the
time of his death such assemblies had become common in both
West and East, though there were still provinces in which
they did not yet exist.[4] At what time they began to assume a
political role in addition to their religious functions the scanty
information at our disposal does not enable us to determine,
but they unquestionably played such a role under Tiberius, and

[1] *Ann.* 4, 18–19 and 6, 29.
[2] *Antiquities*, 18, 6, 3.   [3] Guiraud, 39–45.
[4] For example, Tiberius authorized the establishment of one for Tarraconensis in A.D. 15 (*Ann.* 1, 78). In a few provinces there is no evidence that
such assemblies ever existed.

it is not improbable that it was he who first allowed them to send envoys to Rome for the purpose of laying their petitions and complaints before the emperor and senate.[1] Even if this practice had already begun at the time of his accession, the evidence available proves that he encouraged them to make known their grievances and to express freely their opinions as to the conduct of the Roman officials, both imperial and senatorial. The first certain instance of their activity in political matters is in A.D. 22,[2] when envoys were sent from the province of Asia to assist in the prosecution of the senatorial governor, C. Junius Silanus,[3] and in the next year the same province secured the condemnation of the imperial procurator.[4] In these cases the attitude of Tiberius is unmistakable, and in view of it we cannot doubt that under him the power and influence of the provincial assemblies were greatly extended, and that he deliberately employed them as a means of checking abuses and of imparting a better tone to the provincial administration.

But while Tiberius welcomed the co-operation of the provinces in his efforts to secure good government, he was by no means prepared to tolerate licence or disorder. When the cities of the East began to multiply sanctuaries with the right of asylum to such a point as to endanger the public order, they were directed to send envoys to Rome to justify the claims of their temples, and the decision of all the cases was left to the senate. After a

---

[1] Schiller (i. 286–7) gives Tiberius credit for this development, and Marquardt (i. 509) half inclines to the same view.

[2] Guiraud finds three earlier instances. Suetonius (8) mentions the fact that Tiberius began his civil career by defending the Thessalians before Augustus, but it seems to me very doubtful whether we are justified in assuming with Guiraud (56) that the case involved the Thessalian assembly. If it did, the matter may have had a religious character, and the assembly was clearly answering complaints rather than making them. The other two instances are prosecutions which Guiraud (173) attributes to the assemblies. The first is that of Valerius Messalla Volesus about A.D. 13, but the evidence concerning this case in no way suggests action by an assembly, and the prosecution occurred after Tiberius had practically assumed control of the government. The remaining case is that of Caesius Cordus in A.D. 21, in regard to which the language of Tacitus is vague; he says that Cordus was condemned after the Cyreneans had been heard. Here it seems probable that the Cyreneans in question were private complainants or witnesses, especially as we have no evidence that an assembly ever existed in Cyrene (Guiraud, 55). About this case Guiraud seems oddly confused; he substitutes the delator's name for that of Cordus, gives a wrong date, and contradicts himself (compare 55 with 173).

[3] *Ann.* 3, 67.   [4] *Ann.* 4, 15.

prolonged inquiry decrees were passed by which some of the sanctuaries were recognized and the rest suppressed, and in this way a limit was set to a growing nuisance without unduly disturbing old and deeply-rooted superstitions.[1]

Tiberius also seems to have sought to remove a cause of perennial abuses by restricting the activities of the knights. Under the republic the collection of a large part of the taxes had been farmed to companies of Roman capitalists, a pernicious system which inevitably resulted in the pillage and oppression of the taxpayers. The operations of these companies had been much curtailed by Caesar and Augustus, but some of the revenues were still handled in this fashion when Tiberius ascended the throne.[2] In his later years there is reason to believe that he largely did away with these equestrian companies, except for the collection of the custom dues, in favour of the direct action of the state.[3]

In another important respect Tiberius made a new departure in dealing with the provinces. By strict economy he succeeded in accumulating a considerable surplus, and in spite of his habitual frugality he came to the relief of those communities which were overtaken by sudden calamity with a generosity which was without precedent in Roman history. In A.D. 17 an earthquake inflicted serious damage on twelve cities in Asia. Not only were all taxes remitted for five years, a step in no wise new, for the Romans had often remitted taxes which it was clearly impossible to collect, but Tiberius gave a large sum of money to Sardis and smaller sums to the other cities, a senator being sent to Asia to estimate the damage and the amount of help required.[4] This act amounted to a somewhat revolutionary recognition that empire brought responsibilities as well as privileges, and that, if the provinces paid tribute in time of prosperity, they were entitled to assistance in the hour of misfortune. In this conception of Rome's duty to her subjects, as

---

[1] *Ann.* 3, 60–3.   [2] *Ann.* 4, 6.

[3] Mommsen, *Staatsrecht*, ii. 1017. That the *portoria* were still collected by equestrian companies in the time of Nero is evident from Tacitus (13, 50).

[4] *Ann.* 2, 47. In A.D. 24 two other cities suffered from an earthquake and their tribute was remitted for three years (*Ann.* 4, 13), and there is evidence that Ephesus also had reason to be grateful for help in time of need, probably in 29 or 30 (Lang, 70–1).

in his refusal to permit the use of flogging to collect taxes from provincials, the 'cruel tyrant' showed a humanity little known before his time.

To secure good government in the provinces, however, it was not enough to remedy crying abuses or to punish positive misconduct on the part of the officials, since their inefficiency and incompetence might be the cause of manifold evils to the empire. In his own provinces the emperor could guard against these evils by the careful selection of his legates, but even honest and capable men could not do their best unless they were given a sufficiently long term of office. If the governors were frequently changed the results could not fail to be bad in one of several ways. In the first place a governor would have too little time to become really acquainted with his province and its needs before a successor arrived who was likely to combine eagerness for distinction with jealousy of his predecessor, and who inevitably began his administration ignorant of local conditions. It would often happen, therefore, that each governor would abandon the designs of his predecessor and seek to signalize his tenure of office by some new departure, since it could not be expected that many would be content simply to carry out plans of which a large part of the glory might be claimed by others. Under such conditions anything like continuity of policy was possible only if that policy was more or less specifically laid down by the emperor, but such a course involved the sacrifice of the flexibility which enabled Rome to adapt her administration to the varying conditions in all parts of her immense empire. Her various provinces differed so widely one from another that rigid rules were highly undesirable, and any attempt at uniformity might prove disastrous. The best results were obviously not to be attained by placing the entire direction of affairs in the hands of an autocrat in Rome who must necessarily be ill-informed because he was remote from the scene and overwhelmed with work. It was far better to leave a large discretion to the governors who were upon the spot and in close personal touch with every phase of the problems with which they were called upon to deal. The emperor must of course exercise a general supervision, prescribing the broad outlines of the policy to be pursued, and, above all, he must

see to it that the officers in charge were honest and capable men
and that they were given a fair chance to learn their duties and
to carry out their measures. The policy of constantly changing
the imperial officials had the further disadvantage of removing
one of the chief incentives to efficient work. A governor who
knew that, no matter what his record, his recall would come in
a year or two had little motive for strenuous exertion in comparison with one who knew that good service was likely to be
rewarded by a long lease of power.

These considerations are too obvious to have escaped the
attention of Tiberius, and we cannot be surprised that with his
keen interest in the welfare of his subjects he should have made
it his policy to leave a thoroughly competent and satisfactory
official at his post for many years. This policy the Roman
nobles neither liked nor understood, for they were still under
the influence of the old republican tradition which regarded
public office as something that ought to be passed around among
the families belonging to a narrow oligarchy. Whether they
viewed it as an honour or as an opportunity for plunder, they
were equally sure that each one of their class was entitled to
his share, and no more than his share, of the dignity or of the
spoils. From this point of view one set of men could retain their
posts for any length of time only by defrauding others of their
just chance of distinction and the perquisites which went with
it. It may have been this limitation in the outlook of the
aristocracy which deterred Augustus from adopting the same
policy as Tiberius. He was too able a statesman to be blind to
the advantages of long tenures for his governors, and we may
reasonably assume that, if he did not act accordingly, it was
because he felt that it was more important to keep on cordial
terms with the nobility than to reap those advantages. In some
degree no doubt he was able to secure them by employing
members of his own family as viceroys with general charge of
large portions of the empire, but there is little evidence that
the ordinary legates during his reign often enjoyed more than
two or three years of office. Moreover, the very comments
which Tacitus has reproduced [1] imply that the policy of Tiberius
was something new and in contrast with that of his predecessor.

[1] *Ann.* I, 80.

Certainly under Tiberius we find a number of instances to which we know of nothing comparable in the reign of Augustus. Two governors originally appointed by the latter may be noted at the start; Q. Metellus Creticus Silanus ruled Syria for six years (11–17), and C. Poppaeus Sabinus remained governor of Moesia from A.D. 11 till his death in 35. In addition to these, C. Silius was legate of Upper Germany for eight years (14–22), and Cn. Cornelius Lentulus Gaetulicus held the same province from A.D. 29 to the end of the reign, while L. Apronius was in command in Lower Germany for at least ten years (27–37).[1] We can hardly doubt that if we had fuller information for the other provinces we should be able to extend the list.[2]

It was natural enough that the nobles should be irritated at this policy, but there is something much more significant than irritation in their attitude; they were completely bewildered by the conduct of Tiberius and wholly unable to comprehend his motives. They could not find an explanation in those bad qualities which they so readily attributed to him, for in this matter they could not say that he was cruel, vindictive, or hypocritical. According to Tacitus some believed that he did not wish to see too many people happy, some that he hated the trouble of thinking, others that he thought so much that he could not make up his mind, and that, fearing good men and detesting bad, he found himself unable to arrive at a decision. If Tacitus has here reproduced with any accuracy the comments of the emperor's contemporaries, a flood of light is thrown upon their state of mind; obviously it never occurred to them to consider the interests of the provincials, and their attention was so entirely concentrated on themselves that they could not understand an emperor who cared more for the good government of the world than for the feelings of the Roman aristocracy.

---

[1] Apronius was legate of Lower Germany in A.D. 28 and there is no hint in Tacitus that he had just arrived (*Ann.* 4, 73); I have therefore assumed that his command began not later than 27. He was certainly still in charge in 34 (*Ann.* 6, 30) and probably retained his position till the end of the reign. His legateship cannot have begun earlier than 24, when he is known to have been in Rome (*Ann.* 4, 22).

[2] It will be noticed that the long tenure of their posts by equestrian officials seems to have aroused no opposition. Tacitus (4, 6) mentions it as a good thing and one that calls for no particular comment.

VII

THE STRUGGLE FOR THE SUCCESSION

IN view of the admittedly excellent government of Tiberius in the first nine years of his reign, it seems clear that, if he could have freed himself from the fatal question of the succession to the throne, he would have left behind him the reputation of a just and able ruler, not indeed gracious or popular, but respected by his subjects. Even the suspicion aroused by the untimely death of Germanicus would probably have passed away if it had not been for the tragedies which clouded the last years of the reign. The question of the succession, however, was an incubus which he could not shake off, and in the end it produced tragic consequences which blasted his reputation.

It has already been pointed out that Tiberius came to the throne as a sort of emperor-regent for Germanicus, the plan of Augustus being that his stepson should govern until Germanicus had gained sufficient experience to enable him to discharge with success the heavy duties of an emperor. As Tiberius was about twenty-seven years older than Germanicus it was to be expected that the latter would succeed to the principate in the full prime of life, and would transmit it to his sons, the direct descendants of Augustus himself. But although in many ways such an arrangement seemed admirable, it ignored altogether the natural feelings of Tiberius by requiring him to act as a mere *locum tenens* for another and to set aside his own son in favour of his nephew. There can be no doubt that Tiberius agreed to it, but there seems as little doubt that men believed, rightly or wrongly, that he did so reluctantly. There is, however, nothing in the record as it has come down to us to warrant the suspicion that he had any intention of breaking faith, and the very fact that Augustus trusted him is strong evidence that he was worthy of the trust, for no one was in a better position to know him intimately than his stepfather. The difficulty of his position lay not so much in Tiberius himself as in the world about him. Very soon after his accession we find a party rallying round Drusus, which seems hardly credible if it was believed that the succession

of Germanicus was certain. Under such conditions the sudden
death of Germanicus could hardly fail to turn suspicion on the
emperor: aside from all suspicious circumstances in the trial of
Piso, there remained the great presumptive suspicion that Tiberius must in his heart have been pleased to see the way cleared
for Drusus. Thus the death of Germanicus left the emperor,
who had always been unpopular, surrounded by a cloud of
unjustified, but more or less inevitable, suspicion. If the prince
had lived it is not unlikely that Tiberius would have retired
in due time to Capri, leaving Germanicus to rule in Rome; but
the latter's death led to a long train of disasters.

On the surface the elimination of Germanicus removed all
question as to the succession, but in reality it rendered the
question even more acute. The children of Germanicus were too
young for immediate consideration, and Drusus became inevitably the heir apparent, but it was far from clear whether he
would reign as emperor, or hold a position similar to that of
Tiberius. Augustus had undoubtedly intended that the principate
should ultimately pass to his direct descendants. Would Tiberius
hold himself bound to maintain this arrangement and to exact
from Drusus a pledge to disinherit his children in favour of
those of Germanicus? This must have seemed doubtful to
contemporaries, and even if Tiberius exacted such a pledge,
it must have been still more doubtful if Drusus would keep it.
Yet apparently Tiberius did take the course indicated.[1] He
soon associated Drusus with himself by conferring on him the
tribunician power, while on his side Drusus treated the children
of Germanicus with marked kindness[2] and seemed ready to
accept the situation. Such a supposition, at least, offers the
most plausible explanation of the tragedy which followed.

In his position as heir apparent and co-emperor Drusus
became popular[3]; he seemed a welcome contrast to his father,
being frank and outspoken, and men were willing to pardon his
somewhat dissipated and luxurious life as a relief from the
emperor's puritanical austerity. But though, viewed from without, all appeared to go well with the imperial house, it was torn
by internal dissensions. Agrippina could not easily reconcile

---

[1] Willenbücher, p. xiv.   [2] *Ann.* 4, 4.
[3] *Ann.* 3, 37; see also, however, 3, 59.

herself to her diminished importance, and her relations with Livia can hardly have been improved by the latter's protection of Plancina.[1] Moreover, a new and sinister figure came upon the scene in the person of L. Aelius Sejanus.

Sejanus, who henceforth plays a prominent part in the story of Tiberius, was by birth a knight, although on his mother's side he was connected with some of the noble Roman families. His father, Seius Strabo, was a native of one of the municipal towns of Italy; entering the imperial service, he married into the Cornelii Lentuli,[2] one of the oldest houses of the Roman aristocracy, and reached the highest offices open to a man of equestrian rank; by the time of Augustus' death he had become prefect of the praetorian guard, and under Tiberius he was made governor of Egypt, where he died, apparently in A.D. 20 or 21. One of his sons, L. Seius Tubero, was an officer of Germanicus in A.D. 16, and was raised to the consulship in 18. Another and probably younger son was adopted by a knight named Aelius Gallus and after this adoption was styled L. Aelius Sejanus. Instead of entering on an official career, where his aristocratic connexions would have given him excellent prospects, Sejanus remained in the equestrian order. Tiberius in the first year of his reign appointed him a colleague of his father in command of the praetorians, and when his father went to Egypt in A.D. 16 or 17, he became sole prefect of the guards. Little by little he gained the confidence of Tiberius and gradually became his trusted minister.

Drusus soon began to resent the influence which Sejanus had acquired over his father, and on one occasion he so far forgot himself as to strike the prefect in the heat of his anger.[3] Such

[1] Tacitus (1, 33) says that Livia regarded Agrippina with a stepmother's hatred. It may be, however, that the hatred was mainly on the side of Agrippina, and that Tacitus saw the matter through the eyes of her friends or of her daughter. It is very probable that Agrippina inherited her feud with Livia from her mother Julia.

[2] Cichorius, *Zur Familiengeschichte*. The relationship between the various branches of the Cornelii Lentuli is obscure, and the family tree drawn up by Cichorius seems to me very doubtful. Through his mother Sejanus was certainly related to Ser. Cornelius Lentulus Maluginensis and Q. Junius Blaesus, consuls in A.D. 10. His relationship to any other distinguished Romans seems to me uncertain.

[3] *Ann.* 4, 3. Dio (57, 22) makes Sejanus strike Drusus. Not only is Tacitus more reliable than Dio, but his version is much more plausible. The incident

a manifestation of hostility was a thing that Sejanus could not forget, since it revealed clearly the danger of his position. He might well doubt whether he could long maintain himself against Drusus, and, even if he held the confidence of the emperor, the future was very uncertain, for Tiberius was in the sixties, and, when Drusus succeeded him, Sejanus would have little to hope for. The safety of the minister seemed, therefore, to require the removal of the prince, and the dissensions in the imperial house opened the way for schemes of far-reaching ambition. The marriage of Drusus with Livilla, the sister of Germanicus, was probably not a very happy one, for the vices of Drusus exasperated his father[1] and may easily have alienated his wife. Any friendship between Agrippina and Livilla seems unlikely, and the latter must have resented the arrangement for the succession, to which her husband had apparently consented, by which her children were to be set aside in favour of those of Agrippina. The situation inevitably made the two women rivals, and, knowing the passionate and vindictive character of Agrippina, Livilla may have had real fears for her own safety and that of her children if one of her rival's sons became emperor. For her children's sake, and perhaps to avenge her own wrongs, Livilla was prepared to dare all things, and Sejanus was at hand to play the tempter. Though the prefect was no longer young,[2] his personality was highly attractive to women,[3] and he succeeded in fascinating Livilla so completely that she became his mistress and a confederate in his plots.

To understand the conspiracy of Sejanus and Livilla we need only to keep the actual situation clearly before us. Tiberius was then sixty-five years old and Nero, the eldest son of Germanicus,

may not have occurred at all, but the credit given the story shows that the enmity between Drusus and Sejanus was more or less open and well known.

[1] Suet. 52. Tacitus makes his vices well known (3, 37). What the vices were is not wholly clear. Tacitus suggests cruelty (1, 29 and 76), extravagance in building, convivial banquets (3, 37), arrogance (3, 59), and hints at darker things (4, 10); Suetonius says he was somewhat dissolute, Dio (57, 13) that he was very licentious and cruel.

[2] Tiberius would hardly have made a youth joint prefect of the guards in A.D. 14, and nine years had passed since then.

[3] He is represented as a very successful seducer; exaggeration is probable, but he must have been attractive to women or the stories would not have arisen (Dio, 58, 3).

was about seventeen, while the twin sons of Livilla were only about four.[1] Whether Roman sentiment would accept an untried youth as emperor was very doubtful,[2] and in any case Tiberius was most unlikely to depart so far from the example of Augustus as to try such an experiment; neither Nero nor one of the sons of Livilla could, therefore, be considered as the immediate successor of the aging monarch. Another emperor-regent was necessary, and Drusus had been formally designated for this position, but was pledged to transmit the principate to one of the sons of Germanicus rather than to one of his own. If Drusus should die it would be necessary to select a new emperor-regent, and it did not seem impossible that Sejanus, who stood high in the confidence of Tiberius, might secure the nomination for himself. The fact that Sejanus was only a knight might be a recommendation, since he would be less likely to entertain any hopes of bequeathing the empire to his own children and would be more likely to keep whatever pledges Tiberius might exact. To Livilla Sejanus promised that if he became emperor he would make her his empress and one of her sons his heir. It is highly probable that it was this hope for her children which induced her to become an accomplice in the murder of her husband.[3] There was, of course, the danger that Tiberius would exact the same pledges from Sejanus that he had exacted from Drusus, but Livilla doubtless knew her lover well enough to feel sure that he would disregard them, and, if they were partners in crime, she would have a hold upon him to keep him loyal to her. Whatever her motives and calculations, she entered into the plot, and through her physician and one of her husband's favourite slaves she succeeded in poisoning him. So

[1] They were born in A.D. 19, and one of them died in 23 shortly after his father; the other lived to be murdered by Gaius, the youngest son of Germanicus.

[2] The Romans did accept Gaius at twenty-five and Nero at sixteen; however, much had happened between A.D. 23 and 54, and, moreover, Nero's advisers were in great fear lest his youth should prove a fatal disqualification.

[3] The complicity of Livilla has been doubted by many historians. Dessau (ii. pt. i. 32) is inclined to reject it because she would be empress in any case when Drusus became emperor. I have followed Willenbücher (p. xiv), who suggests anxiety for her children as her chief motive. The evidence of the murder was thoroughly sifted, and all ancient writers accept it and make Livilla an accomplice. I can see no grounds for rejecting their testimony, and the theory of Willenbücher seems the one that makes her guilt most credible.

well was the murder managed that at the time no suspicion was aroused. Perhaps this was in part due to the fact that some two years before Drusus had been dangerously ill,[1] which may have made a new and fatal illness seem more natural.

Whatever differences may have existed between them, the sudden death of his only son in A.D. 23 must have been a great shock to Tiberius. There is no reason to doubt that he was deeply grieved,[2] but he bore himself with stoical fortitude, attending to public business as usual. Aside from any natural feeling at the loss, he could not fail to perceive that it must have serious political consequences, for he was growing old and it deprived him of the support and protection which the presence of an acknowledged heir to the throne afforded. The party strife, which had subsided while the succession of Drusus seemed inevitable, at once revived; even at the funeral Tacitus tells us that beneath the outward show of mourning the senate and people secretly rejoiced at the brightening prospects of the house of Germanicus. We can hardly suppose that the partisans of Drusus shared this feeling, which must have been confined largely to the former faction of Germanicus. The marked favour which Tiberius had shown to the consular families in the last few years must have been seen with bitter feelings by the lesser nobility. While Drusus lived they were restrained by the fear of antagonizing the future emperor, but now they hastened to rally about Agrippina and her sons. Possibly some already dreamed of overthrowing Tiberius and replacing him by an emperor-regent devoted to Agrippina and the Julian line, though probably the majority merely hoped that a strong party supporting Agrippina would be able to extort concessions from Tiberius in the matter of patronage, and perhaps also in the designation of an immediate successor if one should be named. The emperor's attitude after the loss of his son may have encouraged them to believe that such a course could be pursued with safety and with fair prospects of success.

[1] *Ann.* 3, 49.
[2] Suetonius (52) says that Tiberius lacked natural affection, but Dio (57, 22) asserts that he was greatly attached to Drusus. The fact that Tacitus fails to side with Suetonius seems to me decisive against his view. Had Tacitus discovered any reason to believe that Tiberius was destitute of love for his own son, it would certainly not have been omitted from his pages.

Immediately after the death of Drusus, Tiberius presented the two eldest sons of Germanicus to the senate with these words:

When these youths lost their father, I committed them to their uncle's charge; and I implored him, although he had off-spring of his own, to rear and cherish them as his own blood, and to fashion them for himself and for posterity. And now that Drusus has been taken away, I turn my prayers to you, Conscript Fathers; and I beseech you, before our country and our country's Gods, to take under your charge and guidance these great-grandchildren of Augustus, sprung from ancestors so illustrious, and to fulfil towards them my part as well as yours. To you, Nero and Drusus, these Senators will take the place of fathers. Born as you have been born, your good and your ill alike are matters which concern the State.[1]

The audience was deeply moved by this speech, which plainly indicated the two princes as probable successors to the throne. Of a new emperor-regent there was no definite suggestion, but Tiberius spoke of a restoration of the republic and of asking the consuls to undertake the government unless the senate chose to designate some one else.[2]

It is not likely that Sejanus was either surprised or disappointed at this step, since he must have realized that time was necessary for the attainment of his ambitions; he can hardly have expected that Tiberius would forthwith repudiate the Julian line in favour of the Claudian, or that he himself would be immediately designated as the emperor's successor. Both things might be brought about, but patience and astute management would be required. Perhaps, if he gained the principate, he cared little for what prince he acted as emperor-regent. If he could have reached a friendly understanding with Agrippina it is conceivable that he might have been willing to accept her son Nero as the ultimate heir, trusting to promises or to her own guilt to keep Livilla quiet; but he probably knew Agrippina too well to cherish any such ideas. If he had any illusions at first, he must soon have seen that she would never submit to his ascendancy, and that her ruin was essential to his own success.

[1] *Ann.* 4, 8. I quote from Ramsay's translation.
[2] *Ann.* 4, 9. Tacitus treats the suggestion of restoring the republic as ridiculous. On the face of it this seems true enough, but I take the intimation of Tiberius that the consuls or some one else might take charge, to mean that he would leave the choice of an emperor-regent to the senate.

If Agrippina had possessed a little discretion and self-control, she might, perhaps, have thwarted the designs of Sejanus, but, as it was, he found in her an unconscious ally. She took no trouble to placate those whom she disliked, and she seems further to have been obsessed by the suspicion that Tiberius and Livia had somehow contrived to have her husband poisoned. If she really believed this, common sense should have taught her to avoid a collision with them, but her head was turned by the sight of the partisans who were gathering around her, and she appears to have persuaded herself that the emperor would not dare to touch her or her friends. In her folly she gave every provocation to Tiberius and invaluable assistance to Sejanus.

It was obviously not to the interest of the prefect to permit a strong party to rally round Agrippina. If her sons were to gain the throne at all, it must be through his support rather than that of their own partisans, since otherwise he could not hope to maintain himself in power. His ambition and safety alike required that prompt steps should be taken to check the growth of the Julian faction before it became dangerously powerful. In this his interests coincided with those of the emperor himself, who had been greatly weakened by the death of Drusus, which left him in a position of real peril. While Drusus was the acknowledged heir to the throne conspiracies against the emperor were futile, since his death would be promptly avenged by his son, and a revolt was hardly to be feared since there was no commander who could hope to prevail against them both. Under these conditions slander of Tiberius had little political importance, since the heir apparent could not be included in the same charges; no one could plausibly accuse Drusus of hypocrisy, austerity, secret vices,[1] or of poisoning Germanicus. As long, therefore, as his son lived, Tiberius was reasonably secure and could afford to look with contempt on the spiteful gossip of Rome, confident that those who uttered it would not go beyond mere words and that serious treason was extremely improbable. The situation was now profoundly changed; Tiberius stood alone, and, if he were assassinated or overthrown by a sedition of the praetorian guards, confusion must result. Nero, the

---

[1] His vices seem to have been notorious (*Ann.* 3, 37), and Tacitus calls him frank and open (3, 8).

eldest son of Agrippina, was not yet old enough to succeed him immediately, but there was more than one eminent Roman who might hope to seize power as emperor-regent in the young prince's name. Even if Tiberius was not actually deposed, disaffection among the guards or a formidable revolt in the provinces might force him to place the partisans of the Julian house in such commanding positions that he would be left with little but the name of emperor. In such a situation he must have viewed the formation of a strong Julian party as a danger to himself, and Sejanus could easily make use of this feeling.

The plan of the powerful minister was simple enough in its broad outlines. He aimed to increase the enmity between Tiberius and Agrippina and to arouse the emperor's suspicion of her party in the hope that, when this was accomplished, the emperor could be persuaded to set aside the Julian line in favour of the Claudian, represented by his own grandson, and to designate him as the next princeps. The bitterer the feud with Agrippina, the more Tiberius would wish her out of the way; and the more thoroughly he was convinced of the danger of his position, the readier he would be to strengthen it by associating with himself an heir apparent on whose fidelity he could rely. Thus a violent quarrel between Agrippina and the emperor might easily pave the way for the marriage of Sejanus to Livilla, and the succession of the minister as emperor-regent for Livilla's surviving son.

For the first part of this programme Agrippina, by her violent temper and her sinister suspicions, had already laid the foundation, and Livilla could be trusted to use all her influence at court to increase the existing discord. While the court intrigues were being pushed, Sejanus laboured to persuade his master that the growing Julian party was a real menace to the throne. Tacitus tells us that the minister was continually repeating to Tiberius that Rome was divided into rival factions, that the partisans of Agrippina would increase unless checked, and that the only way to stop the growth of disaffection was to strike at one or two of its most active promoters.[1] Whether because of such considerations or not, a series of prosecutions was soon launched against Agrippina's supporters.

[1] *Ann.* 4, 17.

The account which Tacitus gives of the next few years is somewhat obscure in places; in his pages there appears little connexion between the different prosecutions, but this cannot be regarded as decisive. His sources were in the main favourable to the family of Germanicus, and the official records may not have revealed the whole truth, since to bring out the underlying connexion between the various cases would have exhibited Agrippina and Nero as the figure-heads, at least, of a widespread movement of sedition, and Tiberius would naturally be reluctant to throw suspicion of treason upon them until he had fully resolved to set the Julian line aside altogether. Tacitus may, therefore, have followed the official records closely in treating the prosecutions of the years A.D. 24 and 25 as so many isolated cases. Nevertheless there are some facts which suggest that there was more beneath than appears on the surface, and that some at least of the Julian party were actively conspiring, though the precise purpose of the plotters remains uncertain.

The first blow was directed against C. Silius, who seemed the most formidable of Agrippina's friends. The family of Silius had gained the praetorship under the republic and had been consular since 20 B.C. He himself and his two brothers had all held the consulship, and at the death of Augustus he was the legate of Upper Germany. During the mutinies he kept his army quiet, and he took an active part in the campaigns of Germanicus. After the prince's return to Rome he remained at his post and was only recalled in A.D. 21, after having crushed the revolt of Sacrovir in Gaul. His long connexion with one of the most powerful armies of the empire marked him out as a man who might be dangerous; moreover, his wife Sosia was closely connected with Agrippina, and he was now one of the most active leaders of her party. The fall of such a man would make a great impression, and it could easily be brought about with the appearance of justice, for Silius had been guilty of extortion, a crime which Tiberius was not disposed to overlook or to treat lightly.

Silius was indicted before the senate not only for extortion, of which Tacitus admits that both he and his wife were guilty, but for treason as well.[1] In the trial the charge of treason was

---

[1] The nature of the charge is not very clear. Tacitus says that he was accused of connivance in the rebellion of Sacrovir, but Velleius (2, 130) speaks

pressed and Silius, making little or no attempt at defence,
ended the proceedings by suicide. His bearing and death
strongly suggest that he was either guilty, or so involved in
intrigues that he could not clear himself without compromising
others. Probably he saw that his own ruin was inevitable, and,
like Piso, hoped that his suicide would save his family. His
wife Sosia was banished for her share in his guilt, but Tiberius
permitted the children to receive part of the family property.

The death of Silius was soon followed by a curious and spec-
tacular trial. Vibius Serenus, one of the delators who had
appeared against Libo, had been rewarded with the praetorship
and in due course had served as governor of the senatorial
province of Further Spain. In A.D. 23 he had been convicted of
maladministration and banished to the island of Amorgos. His
own son now charged him with having dispatched agents to
stir up sedition in Gaul with the connivance and financial aid
of a praetorian senator named Caecilius Cornutus, so he was
dragged back to Rome to face his son before the senate. At the
very outset of the case, Cornutus committed suicide, but
Serenus defended himself boldly and pointed out that from his
island he could not have engaged in such an enterprise with the
help of a single accomplice. The son then accused two other
persons, Cn. Lentulus and Seius Tubero. These new charges
were not very plausible, since both men were friends of Tiberius
and Tubero was a brother of Sejanus. Accordingly they were
immediately acquitted, and the case against Serenus broke
down in face of the testimony of his slaves. The younger
Serenus, overcome with fear at these developments, fled from
Rome, but was stopped at Ravenna and brought back to the
city where he was compelled to continue his prosecution. New
charges were now produced against the elder Serenus,[1] and in
the end the senate voted in favour of his execution, but Tiberius

of Silius as an enemy of Tiberius. Velleius has probably followed the official
version, and if so, we may conjecture that the charge included some design of
stirring up a revolt of the legions in Upper Germany, perhaps with the hope
that Tiberius would be obliged to replace him in command and thus give the
Julian party the control of an army.

[1] Tacitus says that Tiberius produced a letter sent to him by Serenus eight
years before, and made other charges against him which the testimony of his
slaves failed to sustain. Why the senate should have condemned him to death
is wholly obscure.

opposed this and contented himself with sending him back to
his island. It seems probable that the emperor persisted in the
prosecution because he thought that the accused was guilty,
despite the evidence of his slaves.[1] The prompt suicide of Cornutus was somewhat suspicious, and it is possible that the case
had some connexion with that against Silius, for the charges
seemed to point to a plot to stir up sedition in Gaul and in the
army of Upper Germany; if so, Cornutus and Silius may have
been in league with each other and may have had allies in Gaul.
The charge against Tubero, a former lieutenant of Germanicus
on the Rhine, strengthens this impression, and the failure of the
prosecution may have been due to the desire of the government
not to involve Agrippina in the matter. Altogether the course
of events suggests that Tiberius may have had evidence which
he did not wish to bring forward, and that he finally protected
Serenus because he saw that to condemn him without producing it would appear flagrantly unjust. This is of course
conjectural, and it is also possible that the younger Serenus
lost his head in accusing Lentulus and Tubero. If this were all,
however, it seems strange that he escaped the punishment
which he obviously feared when his charges broke down, for,
if they had no foundation at all, one would naturally expect
that Sejanus would have induced the emperor to punish a false
accusation against his brother.

With Serenus out of the way there remained the case of
Cornutus to consider. A motion was offered in the senate that,
if the accused committed suicide, the informer should receive
no reward. Tiberius opposed this motion on the ground that
it would be better to abolish the laws than to remove their
guardians. This argument is unanswerable, for such a measure,
while it might have put an end to delation, would have effectually prevented the enforcement of the criminal law except
in such cases as involved its perversion for the destruction of the
innocent. The clearer the proof of a man's guilt, the more
likely he was to seek escape by suicide, so that the stronger the
evidence, the less the motive for a prosecution.

---

[1] The explanation of Tacitus, that Tiberius had cherished a grudge against
Serenus for eight years, but, after displaying his rancour in the trial, gave up
his vengeance because of popular feeling, seems very unconvincing.

Apart from such considerations the motion was inopportune, for, at a time when Tiberius had become suspicious of the Julian party, he could hardly be expected to throw away his chief means of detecting their intrigues. In addition to the cases of Silius and Serenus there are other facts which suggest that some of the partisans of Agrippina were engaged in an active campaign against the emperor, for in A.D. 24 and 25 two other persons who had been associated with Germanicus were brought to trial, namely P. Suillius, who had been his quaestor, and Fonteius Capito, who had been his colleague in the consulship. Suillius was convicted of judicial corruption and it was proposed that he should be banished from Italy, but Tiberius insisted on the severer penalty of relegation to an island. In all previous cases where the emperor had interfered it had been in favour of leniency, and his conduct on this occasion aroused much resentment.[1] Fonteius Capito, who had just returned from his proconsulship in Asia, was prosecuted on some unknown charge by the younger Serenus, but was acquitted. Thus in two years four persons previously connected with Germanicus (Silius, Tubero, Suillius, and Capito) were accused and two of them convicted. It is also significant that the charge of slandering the emperor is suddenly revived. Until this time we know of but two instances of such an accusation, the first of which was brought against Granius Marcellus in A.D. 15, and the second against Appuleia Varilla in 17.[2] Both were acquitted on this count, and during the trial of Appuleia Tiberius expressly instructed the senate to disregard any words of the accused reflecting on himself or his mother. After this we hear no more of the charge for some seven years, but in A.D. 24 L. Calpurnius Piso was indicted for numerous offences, among them private talk against the emperor.[3] He died a natural death, however, before his trial took place. Since he was a brother of the enemy

---

[1] Tacitus says that afterwards, when Suillius was pardoned and returned to Rome, men admitted the correctness of the emperor's judgement, but if the penalty was unduly harsh the later misconduct of Suillius cannot serve as an excuse for Tiberius.

[2] *Ann.* 1, 74 and 2, 50.

[3] Tacitus attributes the prosecution to a long-cherished grudge of Tiberius, but it is obvious that Piso had given more recent provocation. None of the cases where Tacitus makes an old hatred on the part of Tiberius the motive for his action seems to me at all plausible.

of Germanicus, it is most improbable that he was a friend of Agrippina, but resentment at his brother's fate may have led him to use bitter language which was now taken more seriously than before.[1] In the same year a knight named Cominius was convicted of writing scurrilous verses against Tiberius, but was pardoned at the intercession of his brother, who was a member of the senate.[2] In A.D. 25 Votienus Montanus, a distinguished orator from Gaul, was accused of slandering Tiberius, and the witness against him, a soldier, persisting in repeating the slanders at length in spite of the clamorous interruptions of the senators. Tiberius, stung to the quick, cried out that he would vindicate himself, but his friends persuaded him to abandon this intention; on second thought he must have seen the difficulty of proving his innocence and must have realized that any action on his part would only lend importance to the slanders. Votienus was convicted and banished[3]; he was the first, and so far as we can determine with certainty, the only man who was punished for defaming the emperor during the entire reign. The fact that the witness against him was a soldier suggests that his offence was not simply libel, but spreading slanderous stories in the army with a seditious intent. The further fact that he was a native of Gaul seems to link his case with those of Silius and Serenus. At any rate this sudden severity, coming after so long a tolerance, points to the conclusion that slander of Tiberius had now assumed a much more serious character than formerly, and that under the existing circumstances it was felt to be dangerous.

At the same time that prosecutions for vilifying the emperor are revived, we find the Julian party attempting to push forward the sons of Germanicus. At the beginning of A.D. 24, when vows were offered for the safety of the emperor, the names of Nero and Drusus were added to his by the pontiffs; an act which Tacitus expressly says was intended to flatter the Julian house. Tiberius not unnaturally resented it, and sharply cautioned the senate against turning the heads of the

[1] Perhaps he repeated the story told by Tacitus in 3, 16. If so, he was unintentionally playing the game of the Julian party by discrediting Tiberius.

[2] *Ann.* 4, 31. Cominius seems to have been the first man who was prosecuted solely for slander of the emperor.

[3] *Ann.* 4, 42. For the penalty see the *Prosopographia*.

young princes by giving them a too exalted notion of their own importance.[1] In the next year, when Drusus was prefect of the city during the Latin Festival, an informer lodged an accusation with him. This was contrary to all custom, for no important business was ever undertaken while the magistrates were absent from Rome attending the festival. The office of prefect of the city during the holiday was, therefore, commonly given to some noble youth below senatorial age, and was considered a purely honorary distinction. The action of the delator was clearly intended to show that a son of Germanicus was different from other such officials, and Tiberius dismissed the accusation and banished the obsequious delator.

All these cases taken together seem to show that the revival of the Julian party was accompanied by a campaign of calumny, mixed with more serious plots, and that Tiberius had determined to stop it. Naturally the partisans of Agrippina censured him for his harshness,[2] although they apparently could not claim that any of the sufferers were innocent.[3] Tacitus says that the complaints of his severity irritated the emperor, so that, when Aquilia and Varius Ligur were accused of adultery, he insisted on a harsher penalty than was at first proposed.[4] It is impossible to determine whether they were friends of Agrippina, for we know nothing more of them except that Ligur was afterwards found to have bribed two delators to suppress a charge against him.[5]

The bitterness felt by the Julian party at this series of prosecutions may, perhaps, be seen from the comments which Tacitus has recorded in connexion with another matter. The

[1] Tacitus attributes this to the enmity of Tiberius towards the family of Germanicus. The warning, however, seems wise and was certainly natural, since, though he might be willing to recognize them as his probable heirs, he could hardly wish it to appear that such recognition was forced upon him.

[2] The only instances of harshness seem to be in the cases of Suillius, Votienus, and Aquilia. Tacitus says that the severe treatment of Suillius provoked indignation, and he mentions the complaints of harshness immediately after the account of the trial of Votienus.

[3] Tacitus would surely represent them as innocent victims if he could, but the only criticism he makes is that of harsh treatment.

[4] Aquilia was banished, but Ligur apparently escaped (*Ann.* 6, 30).

[5] I have omitted four trials during the two years 24 and 25; two of these were non-political in character. One of the others, that of Firmius Catus, will be mentioned a little later, and the fourth, that of Cremutius Cordus, is discussed in the appendix on 'The Law of Treason under Tiberius'.

province of Further Spain asked permission to erect a temple to
Tiberius and his mother, but the emperor declined to permit it.
In this connexion he addressed the senate as follows:

I am aware, Conscript Fathers, that my consistency is challenged
by some, in that lately I did not refuse a like request from the cities
of Asia. I will explain, therefore, my acquiescence upon that occasion,
and announce, at the same time, my purpose for the future. The
Divine Augustus did not forbid the erection of a temple to himself and
to the Roman people at Pergamum. Observing, as I do, everything
that he said or did as a law unto myself, I followed the example
thus approved, and with all the greater readiness that veneration
of the Senate was conjoined with worship of myself. To have accepted
such an honour once, may be excused; but to permit my statue to
be worshipped as divine in all the provinces, would be arrogant and
vain-glorious. And the homage to Augustus will be gone, if it be
made common by undiscriminating adulation.

I call you to witness, Conscript Fathers, and I desire posterity
to remember, that I am but a mortal, discharging the duties of a
man: content if I may fill the highest place worthily. Enough, and
more than enough, will men render to my memory, if they shall
believe me worthy of my ancestors, thoughtful for your interests,
unflinching in danger, undaunted by the enmities which I encounter
in the public service. These shall be my temples in your hearts, my
fairest and most enduring images. For stone-built monuments, if
posterity turn her judgement into hate, are but dishonoured sepul-
chres. I pray therefore to our allies and fellow citizens, I pray the Gods
themselves: these last, to grant me unto the end a tranquil spirit, alive
to the rights of Gods and men; the former, that when I pass away, they
may honour my life and name with praise and kindly recollection.[1]

At first sight it would seem difficult for any one to find fault with
such a speech, but the Romans managed to do so; some attributed the attitude of Tiberius to modesty, many to lack of self-
confidence, and others to a degenerate mind. These last said
that: 'The noblest of mankind had ever the loftiest hopes; it
was thus that Hercules and Liber among the Greeks, Quirinus
among ourselves, had been ranked among the Gods. Augustus
had done better in not putting the hope away. All else Princes
had ready to their hand; but there was one end which they
should pursue unfalteringly: to leave a fair name behind them.

[1] *Ann.* 4, 37–8. I quote from Ramsay's translation.

For to despise Fame is to despise Virtue.'[1] If these comments are not an invention of Tacitus, they show clearly how impossible it was for Tiberius to conciliate the malcontents. If some members of the Julian party were in such a frame of mind the emperor had good reason to regard their activities with suspicion, and could hardly be expected to turn a deaf ear to informers who supported their assertions of conspiracy with what appeared to be strong evidence. Under such conditions he might well agree with Sejanus that stern measures were necessary to keep disaffection within safe bounds.

Under the sharp blows of the emperor and his minister the gathering opposition apparently collapsed, since the campaign of prosecutions was suspended after A.D. 25, and during the next three years only three offenders were brought before the senate. From this we can only conclude that the severity of the government had achieved its purpose, and that the policy which Sejanus had urged upon the emperor had been justified by success. Had that success been purchased by the sacrifice of the innocent or by cruelty toward the guilty? There is little in the record to sustain such a charge against Tiberius, since none of those for whose fate he can be held responsible appears to merit sympathy. He was not to blame because Silius and Cornutus committed suicide; what he would have done to them if they had awaited the verdict of the senate we can only guess, but Silius was admittedly guilty of extortion, and Tacitus does not assert the innocence of Cornutus[2]; neither is the guilt of any of the other sufferers denied, although Tacitus implies that they were harshly dealt with. The presumption seems to be that Tiberius kept his campaign against the Julian party within the limits of strict justice. In two cases the charge was dropped, apparently without serious investigation; one of the accused was acquitted; one who was already in exile suffered no additional penalty; one offender was pardoned after conviction; and one man, Firmius Catus, was punished for having brought a false charge of treason against his own sister. The senate wished to banish

---

[1] *Ann.* 4, 38. I quote from Ramsay's translation.
[2] Tacitus merely says that Cornutus thought himself in danger and committed suicide. The elder Serenus, on trial for the same plot, asserted that Cornutus was innocent; but Tacitus himself expresses no opinion.

him, but Tiberius interfered and would permit nothing more
than his expulsion from the senate. Tacitus does not tell us
what reason the emperor gave for this leniency, but says that
the real motive was gratitude to Catus for his part in detecting
the conspiracy of Libo. It is possible that some charges were
trumped up by Sejanus,[1] but in the main Tiberius seems to have
struck only at real offenders, and the record furnishes no ground
for accusing him of undue severity.

While Sejanus was urging on the war of prosecutions against
the Julian party he was actively intriguing to increase the
dissensions in the imperial family. In the course of A.D. 25 he
felt strong enough to ask for the sanction of Tiberius to a
marriage between Livilla and himself. The emperor clearly
perceived that such an alliance would drive Agrippina to
frenzy and destroy the last hope of peace with her or her sons.
In a long letter to Sejanus Tiberius pointed out these obvious
consequences and, without positively forbidding the marriage,
made his disapproval of it sufficiently plain. He closed, however,
with assurances of greater favours to come:

What projects I have turned over in my mind; by what further
ties I am preparing to bind you to myself, I will forbear for
the present to disclose. This only will I permit myself to say, that
there is no place too high for your merits, and your devotion to
myself; and when the proper time shall come, whether in the
Senate, or before the public, I shall not fail to speak.[2]

The significance of this letter could hardly be mistaken:
Tiberius clearly intended that Sejanus should succeed him as

[1] Perhaps those against Cremutius Cordus, for which he is represented as
responsible (see the appendix on 'The Law of Treason under Tiberius'),
possibly also those against Fonteius Capito, which Tacitus (4, 36) says were
trumped up by the younger Serenus. Fonteius was acquitted, but Serenus was
not punished.

[2] *Ann.* 4, 40. I quote from Ramsay's translation. It is not easy to see how
Tacitus or any preceding historian could have had access to such a letter.
Nevertheless, it may have become known in some way. After the fall of
Sejanus his papers were doubtless seized and sent to Tiberius; in this process
the letter may have been seen by some one. It is also possible that Tiberius
sent it to the senate in connexion with some prosecution, perhaps one of those
in which the name of Livilla was involved: or it is conceivable that Caligula
made it public. If invented by Tacitus it merely shows what he thought
Tiberius likely to write, and in this case I believe that he hit very near the
mark. I cannot agree with Baring-Gould (314) that the request and its refusal
were known at the time.

H

emperor-regent with Nero as the ultimate heir to the throne.
It seems evident from this plan that, however much Tiberius
disliked Agrippina, he did not believe that she had gone far
enough in the direction of treason to justify him in setting aside
her son. The prospect in regard to the principate was doubtless
highly satisfactory to Sejanus, but the conditions indicated
were far less so, for he must have realized, even if Tiberius did
not, that as emperor-regent his position would be extremely
precarious unless he was on friendly terms with his heir. Nero
was completely under his mother's influence, and after what had
passed any reconciliation between her and Sejanus was impossible. His own safety required that the Julian line should be
replaced by the Claudian, and that this should be done by
Tiberius. Probably when he sought the emperor's consent to
his marriage with Livilla he thought that Tiberius was ready for
this step, but the imperial reply showed that this was a mistake
and that it would be necessary to convince Tiberius that Agrippina
and her sons were actively conniving in plots against him before
he would feel himself absolved from his pledges to Augustus.

For the next few years Sejanus concentrated his energies upon
this task. He had for some time been at work with the double
purpose of breaking up the Julian party and of organizing one of
his own in the senate. It might have been expected that this
last undertaking would prove difficult, for the higher nobility was
not likely to favour as a candidate for the principate a man who
was by birth a mere knight, and the lesser had hitherto supported
Agrippina. Her followers had, however, been intimidated by
the prosecutions of the last two years, and, while striking down
their leaders, Sejanus had sought by the use of the imperial
patronage[1] to convince the lesser nobles that he was as friendly
to their interests as the Julian line could be. In this way he hoped
by a mixture of threats and bribes to secure their support when
he could induce Tiberius to designate him as the heir to the
principate. Such hopes were not entirely vain, for several of the
former friends of Germanicus came over to him[2] and he was
able to form a strong Sejanian party. With such aims in view

[1] *Ann.* 4, 2 and 68.
[2] Fulcinius Trio, Q. Servaeus, and P. Vitellius took part in the prosecution
of Piso and were involved in the fall of Sejanus.

he naturally refrained from attacking Agrippina's subordinate followers, who had probably abandoned active propaganda or conspiracy after the sharp lessons which they had received. He now directed his blows at those whose condemnation would serve to throw suspicion directly on Agrippina herself.[1]

In A.D. 27 Claudia Pulchra, a second cousin of Agrippina and her intimate friend, was accused of adultery and of seeking the life of the emperor by poison and magic. The attack on her relative roused Agrippina to fury, and she rushed at once to Tiberius and assailed him with violent reproaches; the only crime of Claudia, she declared, was her foolish love of Agrippina, though the fate of Sosia should have been a warning to her. Tiberius was stung into retorting with a Greek quotation: 'Do you think that you suffer a wrong, little daughter, if you do not reign?'[2] The scene did nothing to save Claudia, who was condemned, probably to banishment.

The anger of Agrippina was, of course, in no wise appeased, and when, apparently soon afterwards,[3] Tiberius visited her during an illness, she suddenly asked permission to marry again, saying that many eminent men would be proud to receive the widow of Germanicus and his children. The emperor could hardly fail to perceive that a marriage would dangerously strengthen the party of Agrippina, since her husband must almost of necessity be recognized, even if unofficially, as the future regent. Nero was reaching an age when he might, nominally at least, become emperor, but he would be too young and inexperienced to undertake the real government, which his stepfather would in all probability direct. With Agrippina in her present mood Tiberius could not safely consent; neither did he wish a prolonged scene with her, and he accordingly departed without a word.[4]

---

[1] Tacitus (4, 52) says that the prosecution of Claudia Pulchra paved the way for that of Agrippina, though precisely how he does not inform us.

[2] *Ann.* 4, 52; Suet. 53.

[3] I have followed the order of events in Tacitus. Suetonius (53) says that after this scene Tiberius refused to see Agrippina, so that the apple incident would come earlier.

[4] Tacitus states that he gets this story from the memoirs of the younger Agrippina, mother of the emperor Nero. Probably Tiberius suspected that the husband she had in mind was Asinius Gallus, whom he afterward accused of adulterous relations with her (*Ann.* 6, 25).

Sejanus must have smiled grimly at seeing Agrippina thus labouring as if of set purpose to assist him in bringing about her destruction. One last incident and her personal clashes with Tiberius were over. Having invited her to dinner, he placed her next to himself. Tacitus says that Sejanus under the guise of friendship had warned her that the emperor intended to poison her,[1] but it seems hardly likely that she needed such a warning from such a source. At any rate, she came with her mind full of this idea, which she made no attempt to conceal; she reclined beside Tiberius, neither eating nor speaking, until he determined to bring the matter to an issue. Praising some apples, he passed them to her just as they had been brought in, before any had been eaten; more than ever suspicious, Agrippina handed them to the slaves in attendance without tasting them. Turning to his mother, Tiberius quietly remarked that it would not be surprising if he should treat with severity one who implied that he was a poisoner. Yet for a time he refrained from following up his threat and merely gave her no more invitations to his table.[2] After such a scene the emperor must have abandoned any lingering hope of reconciliation and have counted Agrippina as a mortal enemy, though he does not yet seem to have regarded her as dangerous.

One cannot wonder that Tiberius grew weary of the feuds that raged around him and that he made up his mind to leave Rome and seek a refuge in the country. As long as he remained in the city he could not avoid being involved in the perpetual quarrels, and whatever he did he gave offence to some one. Probably many other motives influenced him in his decision. He was approaching seventy, and may well have longed for peace and quiet. Moreover his mother seems to have been growing more and more difficult to deal with, for she was determined to interfere in politics, and this Tiberius was equally determined to prevent, though he shrank from an open breach with her.[3] He may also have entertained some hope that in his absence Agrippina would become more rational, and that her son Nero

---

[1] *Ann.* 4, 54. The warning sounds like a clumsy excuse for Agrippina. Perhaps Tacitus found it in her daughter's memoirs.

[2] Suet. 53.

[3] Dio (57, 12) makes his differences with his mother his chief reason. See also *Ann.* 4, 57 and Suet. 51.

would develop enough independence and character to be trusted.[1]
In addition to this, like all Romans, Tiberius was sensitive in
regard to his personal appearance; in his younger days he had
been handsome, but now his face was often disfigured by blotches
due to some skin-disease. Finally, if he feared conspiracies
against his life, he could guard himself more effectively in the
country than at Rome, where he had always been easily
accessible. Whatever his reasons may have been, he took
advantage of the pretext of dedicating two temples in Campania, one to Jupiter at Capua and one to Augustus at Nola,
and left Rome in A.D. 26. He was attended by a small retinue
chiefly composed of Greek men of letters, but including one
eminent jurist, Cocceius Nerva, who was a senator of consular
rank, and one distinguished knight besides Sejanus. In Campania an incident occurred which strengthened the confidence
of the emperor in his minister. It happened that Tiberius was
dining in a natural cave when part of the roof near its mouth
fell in and stones poured down upon the party, crushing some of
the servants and causing a panic among the guests. Sejanus,
instead of fleeing like the rest, threw himself above the emperor's person so as to shield his master from the falling rocks
with his own body.[2] Such devotion made a deep impression on
Tiberius, and henceforth the influence of the prefect seemed to
the Romans to have become unlimited. Probably that influence
was never as great in reality as it appeared to contemporaries,
and the emperor followed the advice of Sejanus because the
minister took care to adapt it to his inclinations. But though
those inclinations could not safely be ignored, they might to
some extent be modified and directed, for most of the emperor's
information concerning public affairs came through Sejanus or
his creatures and hence could be artfully coloured to suit the
interests of the favourite.

The retirement of Tiberius, first to Campania and afterwards
to the island of Capri, left Sejanus a much freer hand than he
would otherwise have had, and he pursued his plans for the ruin
of the Julian line steadily if not rapidly. In A.D. 27 the son of

[1] Schiller (i. 297) thinks he intended to give Nero a chance to take such a
position as he had himself held in the last years of Augustus.
[2] Ann. 4, 59.

Claudia Pulchra was accused, probably of treason, but the senate deferred the trial until the emperor could be present and the matter was allowed to drop. Most of the intrigues of Sejanus were directed against Nero, the probable heir to the throne, who was reaching an age where an emperor-regent might seem no longer necessary, so that, unless he were removed, Sejanus might find his hopes forever dashed. The young prince, surrounded by indiscreet friends and by the spies of his enemy, had a difficult part to play, and, perhaps largely because of his mother's influence, he proved incapable of playing it successfully. His freedmen and clients urged him to take a firm and bold attitude, saying that it would please the army and the people and that Sejanus would be easily abased. Thus urged, the young man sometimes used rash and inconsiderate language, which was reported, doubtless with exaggeration, to Tiberius. Sejanus found an ally, conscious or unconscious, in Nero's wife, who was a daughter of Livilla; she reported to her mother everything her husband said or did, and Livilla promptly transmitted it to Sejanus. Another ally was discovered in the person of Nero's younger brother Drusus. Drusus was not the favourite of Agrippina, whose violent temper he inherited, and he resented her partiality for Nero; Sejanus won his help by the promise of the throne if his brother could be got rid of, and thus stirred up dissensions in the Julian house itself.[1] In spite of these advantages, however, he seemed for a time to make little progress; Tiberius was not to be moved by mere words, and something more was necessary to make Nero appear really dangerous and induce the emperor to take action. Under such circumstances, a plot was certain soon to be discovered or invented.

While Tiberius lingered on the mainland, Sejanus felt the need of caution and assumed an outwardly judicial attitude towards the family of Germanicus, but, when the emperor retired to Capri, he grew more confident, for the island possessed few landing places and the minister doubtless took care to control all communications with Italy. He now ventured to drop the mask in Rome, though probably still retaining it for the emperor's benefit, and no longer made a secret of his

[1] *Ann.* 4, 60.

hostility to Agrippina and Nero. He had them closely watched, and received full reports of their visitors and correspondence. Among the visitors was a knight named Titius Sabinus, who two years earlier had been one of the leaders of the Julian party and was now one of its last important members.[1] He was thus marked out as a probable conspirator or a plausible victim, and four senators of praetorian rank, ambitious for the consulship and hoping to gain it through the favour of Sejanus, set to work to entrap him. One of them succeeded in winning his confidence by professing hatred for Sejanus and sympathy for Agrippina, and lured him into a room especially prepared for the purpose where the other three were lying concealed between the ceiling and the roof. While they listened Sabinus was induced to talk with great freedom, and the four promptly wrote to Tiberius acquainting him with all that was said. The result was that on Jan. 1, A.D. 28 a letter from the emperor was read to the senate denouncing Sabinus as a formidable conspirator and demanding his punishment. With this demand the conscript fathers hastened to comply, and Sabinus was hurried away to immediate execution. Tacitus gives the impression that the unfortunate knight was guilty only of wild talk, but the circumstances make this seem somewhat doubtful. The care taken to secure witnesses suggests that the charges had some real foundation. Those charges were serious enough to justify stern measures, for Sabinus was accused of plotting to murder the emperor in order to raise Nero to the throne.[2] The testimony of the four senators could not be lightly set aside, and there is no reason to doubt that Tiberius was thoroughly convinced of his danger. If the whole conspiracy was invented by Sejanus,[3] it must be admitted that he took care to make the evidence appear conclusive. Such a conspiracy, if the emperor believed in it, could not fail to make a great impression on his mind. Although there may have been nothing to show that Agrippina and Nero had been accomplices, it was clear that their friends were ready to

---

[1] *Ann.* 4, 18 and 68.

[2] Tacitus (4, 70) admits that Sabinus was charged with plotting to murder Tiberius, and from Pliny (*Nat. Hist.*, 8, 145) we learn that it was in the interest of Nero.

[3] Tacitus does not accuse Sejanus of instigating the informers, but says that they acted as they did to gain his favour, with which Dio (58, 1) agrees.

plot for them and had little fear of punishment if the plot succeeded. Even at Capri Tiberius was no longer safe, for Sabinus was accused of tampering with the imperial freedmen. It was impossible to avoid the conclusion that Agrippina and Nero would only cease to be dangerous if they were placed in such a situation that it would be impossible for them to profit by the emperor's death or to stir up a seditious movement against him. Those about them were urging them to flee to the armies on the Rhine, where it was believed that the memory of Germanicus was still fondly cherished, or to make a dramatic appeal to the senate and the people. Tacitus asserts that those who offered this advice were the agents of Sejanus and that Agrippina and Nero rejected it, although they were represented to the emperor as contemplating such a course.[1]

Yet Tiberius still hesitated. After the death of Sabinus he wrote to the senate thanking the conscript fathers for their zeal, but adding that he trembled for his life because of the plots of his enemies; though no names were mentioned, every one knew that Agrippina and Nero were intended.[2] For over a year, however, he took no further step, perhaps hoping that the fate of Sabinus and the ominous hint which he had given would be sufficient, perhaps restrained by his mother, as was later believed. In any case the end was now only a question of time, for Livia was very old and could not live much longer, while, with Sejanus in control of all the reports which reached Capri, nothing that Agrippina or Nero could do would avail to save them.

At length in A.D. 29 Tiberius struck. In that year his mother died at the age of eighty-six, but he did not leave his island to attend her funeral[3]; the estrangement between them, beginning

---

[1] *Ann.* 4, 67. From the fact that Tiberius himself declared that he overthrew Sejanus because of his persecution of the house of Germanicus (Suet. 61), I am inclined to think that Tacitus may be right in denying any serious intention of treason.

[2] *Ann.* 4, 70–1. The anger of Tiberius at a motion made in the senate at this time by Asinius Gallus was probably due to the fact that it seemed like a challenge, daring the emperor to name Agrippina and Nero openly, and not to the reasons given by Tacitus.

[3] Tacitus says (5, 2) that he alleged public business as an excuse. Suetonius states (51) that he intimated his intention of coming but did not do so. The two statements seem hardly likely to have both been true, and that of Suetonius is probably mere gossip. It would be in keeping with the character of Tiberius to shun a public ceremony of this kind.

at his accession and having its origin in his firm determination to prevent her interference in politics, seems finally to have become complete.[1] No sooner was she dead than a letter from Tiberius was produced in the senate,[2] in which he bitterly denounced the conduct of Agrippina and Nero, but without any direct charge of treason; the son was accused merely of vice and the mother of arrogance and pride. This would suggest that, even now, he did not wish to push matters to extremes against them, and it may be that he had resolved only on their removal from Rome, and that he looked forward to a possible reconciliation with Nero when the young prince should have learned his lesson through an exile which would separate him from Agrippina. Such a course would certainly seem unsatisfactory to Sejanus, who might be expected to create or use every possible opportunity to make their ruin complete.

The accusing letter was received by the senate in terrified silence. Its very inconclusiveness created a dilemma: to act was to offend mortally one who, as it seemed, might yet mount the throne, and to refuse to act was to risk offending its present occupant. While the senators hesitated, one of them, Junius Rusticus, who as the custodian of the senate's archives was supposed to enjoy the emperor's confidence, earnestly advised the adjournment of the debate, since perhaps, when the house of Germanicus had perished, the aged emperor might regret their fate. During the debate the populace surrounded the senate-house, bearing aloft the images of Nero and Agrippina, and joining prayers for the safety of Tiberius with clamours that the letter was a forgery. This demonstration doubtless increased the hesitation of the conscript fathers, who dispersed without passing any decree. The tumult in the streets continued and

---

[1] The case of Fufius Geminus seems in point. Tacitus says (5, 2) that Fufius owed the consulship which he held in A.D. 29 to the patronage of Livia, although he did not hesitate to utter bitter jests against Tiberius. Tacitus further implies that these sharp speeches caused his ruin after Livia's death.

[2] Tacitus says that it was commonly believed that the letter was sent to Rome before Livia's death, but that she prevented its production. Modern scholars have treated this as absurd, but I fail to see why. It is of course incredible that Tiberius addressed his orders to Sejanus through Livia, but he might have sent the letter, authorizing his minister to produce it, if and when he thought fit. In that case it is not impossible that Sejanus, knowing that Livia was dying, refrained from action till after her death.

forged speeches, denouncing Sejanus and purporting to have
been delivered by some of the leading senators, were circulated
among the populace.

The suddenness of the riot, which broke out before there was
time for the letter of Tiberius to become widely known, the
images which were apparently ready to hand as ensigns for the
mob, the promptness with which the forged speeches were
distributed, all point to careful preparation and an efficient
organization ready for instant action. The most obvious inference is that the remaining partisans of Agrippina, driven to
desperation by the course of events, had been planning some
seditious movement in Rome and that Sejanus, knowing this,
struck before they were quite ready. It is possible, however,
that he himself was the instigator of the demonstration[1] and
that he intended it to convince his master of the necessity
of stern action against the house of Germanicus; in this case
Junius Rusticus was probably his tool, and he was confident
that with his guards he could suppress the outbreak as soon as
it had served his purpose. Whoever may have started the riot,
Sejanus made prompt and effective use of it. 'The senate', he
informed Tiberius, 'had treated the complaints of the Princeps
with contempt; the people were in revolt, reading and listening
to seditious speeches, and fictitious decrees of the Senate: what
remained for them but to draw the sword, and choose for their
leaders and Imperators those whose images they had followed
as their standards?'[2]

Under the circumstances Tiberius could no longer temporize.
He repeated his denunciation of Agrippina and Nero, issued an
edict rebuking the people, and complained to the senate that by
the disloyalty of one senator the majesty of the emperor had
been insulted; he concluded by demanding that the whole matter
should be referred to him. The conscript fathers passed the
decrees required of them with humble apologies for their
hesitation.[3] The mob, lately so noisy, apparently subsided

[1] Willenbücher, xv and 33. I am rather inclined to accept his theory. Such
a riot seems a very natural step for Sejanus to take in order to complete the
ruin of the Julian line, and I feel somewhat doubtful whether the partisans of
Agrippina were numerous enough.

[2] *Ann.* 5, 4. I quote from Ramsay's translation.

[3] Agrippina and Nero were declared public enemies (Suet. 54). The senate

immediately, leaving Tiberius and Sejanus masters of the situation.

Agrippina and Nero were promptly banished to islands off the Italian coast; from them Sejanus now had little to fear. A reconciliation between Tiberius and Agrippina was too improbable to be considered, but the case of Nero was somewhat different, for the emperor had originally alleged against him only personal vices which he might abandon under the sharp discipline of exile, and his part in the recent outbreak, whatever it may have been, might be attributed rather to his mother's influence than to his own initiative. His recall, therefore, did not seem entirely impossible, but Sejanus doubtless felt confident that he could prevent it if it ever became likely. There remained, however, two younger sons of Germanicus, Drusus and Gaius, who had still to be disposed of. The latter was not dangerous for the present, but Drusus must be dealt with immediately lest Tiberius should put him in Nero's place in the succession. His ruin was not a difficult matter, for his temper and character combined to render him an easy victim. Tiberius was induced to send him from Capri to Rome where Sejanus had him charged with some offence and imprisoned in the palace.[1]

With this event the success of Sejanus seemed certain. Although he had not yet been formally designated as heir to the throne, Tiberius practically treated him as such; all that he lacked was the proconsular *imperium*[2] and the tribunician power, but such honours were showered upon him that none doubted that these would soon follow. The ruin of the Julian line, however, was not yet complete, for Gaius, the third son of Germanicus, had not been involved in the downfall of his kindred owing to his youth and to the fact that he was living with Tiberius at Capri. If the emperor still felt himself bound by his engagements to Augustus, the young prince might even

thus pronounced judgement (*Ann.* 5, 5), but left the punishment to the emperor.

[1] What the offence was we do not know; Dio (58, 3) says that Sejanus induced one of the consuls to bring an accusation against him, and Suetonius (54 and *Gaius*, 7) that both he and Nero were declared public enemies by the senate on the accusation of Tiberius. Tacitus gives us no light on the matter owing to the loss of the fifth book of the Annals.

[2] According to Dio (58, 7) the proconsular *imperium* was conferred on him in A.D. 31.

yet be designated as the ultimate heir. His youth would render
an imperial regency necessary, and Sejanus now felt confident
that he would be chosen for this position. But his breach with
the Julian house was irreparable, and the prospect of reigning
with a member of that house as his heir involved such obvious
danger that he determined to adhere to his original plan by
sending Gaius the way of his two brothers and persuading
Tiberius to transfer the succession to the young son of Livilla.
This might require time, and the first business of Sejanus was to
make his own position as the immediate successor entirely secure.

One of the chief obstacles in the path of the minister was his
equestrian birth,[1] for in a highly aristocratic society like that
of Rome the accession of a new man, whatever his personal
rank, was certain to be resented by the old nobility. While
Tiberius lived there was no fear of open opposition, but his
death might transform the entire situation. The prejudices of
the consular families would have mattered little if many others
had not shared them. Sejanus was well aware that he must
reckon not merely with the feeling of the nobles, but with the
sentiment of the common soldiers and of the people of Italy. He
could hope to retain power only if his legal title to it was
beyond dispute and if the sullen resentment which was certain to
be very widely felt could find no leaders in a position to arouse and
direct it. With the praetorian guards at his back Sejanus might
overawe the capital in any case, but the frontier armies must in
some way be secured; perhaps even the support of the guards
could not be relied on if the senate and the people should unite
against him with strong support from the provinces. These
considerations had not escaped the astute favourite, and he had
been working for some time to create a party of his own which
might dominate the senate and furnish him with adherents
whom he could place in the strategic posts. To overcome, as far
as possible, the disadvantage of his birth he saw no better means
than a marriage with Livilla, and, though he had failed to
secure the emperor's approval of such a marriage some years
before, he had not abandoned hope of ultimate success.

[1] According to Dio (57, 19) he had been given the rank of a praetorian senator
in A.D. 20. How the Romans felt towards a man who was by birth a mere
knight is shown by some of the gossip reported by Tacitus (2, 43).

We have seen how by a combination of menace and seduction he had destroyed the Julian party and attached some of its members to himself. Probably the lesser nobility were not unwilling to accept him as their leader, since their main object was to break down the haughty exclusiveness of the great consular families. This very exclusiveness, by making it impossible for Sejanus, if emperor, to trust them, would compel him to favour the new men and the praetorian families; from their point of view he might, therefore, make a better sovereign than a prince of the Julian line. As the breach between Tiberius and Agrippina widened we may surmise that it was not very difficult to induce a large section of her partisans to abandon her and to turn their faces to the rising sun. We can hardly believe that the higher nobility felt any enthusiasm for Agrippina in view of her violent temper and fierce resentments; all who had been friends of Tiberius or his son Drusus must have feared her vengeance, if Nero, who seemed entirely subservient to her, should come to power. Yet the prospect of Sejanus as emperor cannot have been welcome, and while they paid outward court to him they probably raged in secret at the thought of abasing themselves before an upstart, and looked forward to his accession as a calamity which there seemed no way of averting. If, when the time came, there was any prospect of successful resistance, Sejanus must have felt that they would take prompt advantage of it.

It was on the great frontier armies that everything seemed to depend. Sejanus was probably confident of his ability to manage Tiberius and the senate, while if the mob of Rome proved hostile it could be controlled by the guards; but all this might avail nothing if the legions in the imperial provinces refused to accept him. It was essential that he should place men on whose support he could rely in command of these provinces, but to do so presented many difficulties. While the Romans, judging by external appearances, believed that Tiberius was a mere tool in the hands of his favourite, the minister himself knew better. He dared not press Tiberius beyond a certain point [1] or urge upon him measures which ran counter

---

[1] That Agrippina, Nero, and Drusus still lived, while Gaius was not only alive and undisgraced, seems to me clear evidence of this.

to his deeply rooted prejudices, for, if he did so, his advice was likely to be rejected, and such a rejection might pave the way to his downfall. There must have been many among his enemies who suspected his intrigues, but as long as they believed him to be all-powerful he could terrify them into a conspiracy of silence. If this belief were shaken, however, they might make a desperate effort to open the old emperor's eyes. Moreover, if Tiberius was a man of suspicious temper (something of which there is no evidence except the rhetoric of Tacitus)[1] it was obviously unwise to arouse his suspicion. It was, therefore, no easy matter to secure control of the frontier armies, for the nominees of Sejanus must be men whom Tiberius would readily appoint, and such men seem to have been far from numerous among the partisans of the minister. The emperor had always shown a marked preference for the great aristocratic families, and he would be reluctant to fill the highest positions in his service with new men destitute of conspicuous merit whose only recommendation was their devotion to his favourite.

Yet the skill and patience of the minister seemed finally to triumph over all difficulties. Though he could hope for little from the higher aristocracy as a whole, he was able to bind at least a few of the great nobles more or less closely to himself and to place them at the points where the presence of friends was most vitally necessary, while in less essential posts he was forced to content himself with excluding his enemies. The most important armies were those along the Rhine, four legions in Upper and four in Lower Germany. In A.D. 29 Lentulus Gaetulicus was appointed legate of Upper Germany, and his daughter was betrothed to a son of Sejanus, probably before the appointment. A short time previously the command in Lower Germany had been entrusted to the father-in-law of Gaetulicus, L. Apronius, whose son was a friend of the minister. It was, therefore, probable that both men would accept Sejanus for family reasons. Across the Adriatic was the province of Dalmatia with two legions, and along the Danube were Pannonia with three and Moesia with two. If united, these seven legions

---

[1] I cannot regard the loose assertions of Dio and Suetonius as adding any weight to the testimony of Tacitus (see the appendix on 'Tacitus, Suetonius, and Dio').

would form a powerful army, but of such a union there was little
chance, for Moesia, at least, was in safe hands; the supreme
command over Moesia, Macedonia, and Achaia had long been
held by Poppaeus Sabinus,[1] whose daughter, and so far as we
know his only child, had married T. Ollius, a friend of Sejanus.
What arrangements were made in Dalmatia and Pannonia it is
impossible to say, since we are ignorant of the names of their
governors,[2] but it is unlikely that Sejanus failed to take precautions against serious opposition from their armies. The two
legions of Egypt, commanded by a knight and far removed from
Italy, could hardly be considered dangerous, and the one in
Africa might safely be ignored, so that there remained only
three legions in Spain and four in Syria to deal with. During
the ascendancy of Sejanus both provinces were held by ab-
sentee governors,[3] a circumstance of which no certain explanation can be given.[4] The most probable conjecture seems to be
that in providing for the Rhine and Danube armies Sejanus had
exhausted the supply of available consulars on whom he could
in any degree rely and whose appointment he could venture to
urge, and that, unable to place friends in charge of Spain, and
Syria, he induced Tiberius to detain these legates in Rome.

[1] Liebenam (*Die Legaten*) believes that at this time Sabinus held only
Macedonia and Achaia, and that Pomponius Labeo was in full control of
Moesia. It seems to me, however, that Domaszewski (*Röm. Provinzialv.*) has
practically proved that Labeo was subordinate to Sabinus; this view is also
maintained by Stout in a monograph on Moesia. In this case Sejanus secured
the support of a governor already appointed and had merely to prevent his
recall.

[2] Liebenam (*op. cit.*) makes A. Plautius governor of Dalmatia about 44,
or of Pannonia about 30. I should be glad to put him in either at the earlier
date, but the only authority cited (*C.I.L.* v. 688) describes him as a legate of
Claudius.

[3] L. Arruntius was legate of Spain for ten years (from 24 or 25), and the
legate of Syria in question was L. Aelius Lamia. The date of Lamia's appointment is uncertain (Liebenam, *op. cit.*, and the articles on Lamia and Sentius
Saturninus in the *Prosopographia*), but he was removed in 32.

[4] Tarver (318) suggests that Tiberius intended to keep his legates in Rome
and have them act as secretaries of state for their provinces. If, as I believe,
the detention of these two legates was instigated by Sejanus, it is not impossible
that he advocated some such general scheme and, to prevent Spain and Syria
falling into hostile hands, urged its trial in those provinces, but it is also possible
that he resorted to various temporary pretexts for postponing their departure.
The explanation of Suetonius (63) that Tiberius feared the men he had appointed seems absurd, for there is no apparent reason why he should choose
such men in the first place or why he should retain them afterwards.

They were thus obliged to manage their provinces through deputies of lower rank whose selection could be more easily manipulated to the advantage of the minister, and who, even if hostile to him, would be less able to take the lead in resistance.

It must, therefore, have seemed to Sejanus that, if he became the legal successor to Tiberius, he would be peacefully accepted by the entire Roman world. All that remained was to secure the formal designation as heir to the throne, and at the beginning of A.D. 31 this seemed practically assured. Ever since the fall of Nero, if not earlier, Tiberius had clearly indicated his intention that Sejanus should succeed him, and all Rome was expecting the final step towards which the emperor appeared to be advancing day by day. The betrothal of Sejanus to Livilla was now at length sanctioned,[1] and he was chosen consul with the emperor as his colleague. The significance of this last honour could hardly be mistaken, since Tiberius had held the consulship but twice during his reign, and both times with the acknowledged heir to the throne.[2] A further step was taken when the proconsular *imperium* was bestowed upon Sejanus,[3] and he now lacked only the tribunician power to make him joint emperor with Tiberius. But the end of his career was now at hand, and from the height to which he had risen he was hurled down with dramatic suddenness.

It is impossible to say at what moment Tiberius began to turn against his favourite and to perceive the real character of the man whom he had trusted so implicitly. According to Josephus[4] it was Antonia, the mother of Germanicus, who first opened his eyes. She had lived quietly in Rome, taking no part in politics, although she must have seen the ruin of her grandsons with profound emotion. She may have suspected that they had fallen victims to the intrigues of Sejanus, but recognized that it was useless to accuse him without some definite and positive proof. Such proof she at length secured and hastened to place it in the hands of Tiberius. To reach the emperor was no easy matter, since all communication with Capri passed through the hands

---

[1] In spite of Dio (58, 3), I believe that it was Livilla and not her daughter Julia to whom Sejanus was betrothed. This passage is from the epitome of Zonaras, Dio's text at this point being lost.

[2] In 18 with Germanicus and in 21 with Drusus.

[3] Dio, 58, 7.   [4] *Antiquities*, 18, 6, 6.

of the agents of Sejanus, but Antonia contrived to overcome the difficulty. Whatever the nature of her message, it suddenly awakened Tiberius to a knowledge of some part of the truth.[1] For several years he had seen only through the eyes of Sejanus, and he now realized that the man whom he had trusted so blindly had betrayed his confidence. His friendship for Sejanus turned to deadly hatred, and the more he regretted the past the more fiercely he determined to avenge it.

But to determine on the destruction of the great minister was much easier than to bring it about, for Tiberius had allowed Sejanus to become so powerful that any attempt to overthrow him might cost the emperor both his throne and his life. Even at Capri Tiberius was surrounded by the tools and agents of Sejanus, while at Rome the minister had command of the praetorian guards, and the nearest provincial armies were under men whom he had carefully selected. By every outward sign the senate and the people were devoted to him, and Tiberius seemed utterly isolated and helpless. Nevertheless, imposing as the minister's position seemed, it was in many respects weak, and Tiberius still had some weapons at his disposal if he could use them without allowing Sejanus to suspect his purpose too soon. For the moment it was necessary for the emperor to conceal his wrath and to proceed with caution: in this crisis, at least, he was constrained to play the hypocrite and to pretend friendship for his former favourite while preparing his ruin.

The emperor's first move was to let men see that Sejanus was not quite as powerful as they had hitherto believed.[2] The letters from Capri to the senate, while still breathing affection for him, began to contain criticism as well. While some of the minister's friends were promoted in ostentatious deference to his wishes,

---

[1] Most historians have held that Antonia warned Tiberius that Sejanus was plotting to murder him and seize the throne. This is not only unsupported by adequate evidence but is highly improbable, for Sejanus could not wish the death of Tiberius until his own nomination as heir to the throne was complete. The key to the nature of Antonia's information seems to me to be given by Suetonius (61), who says that in a brief autobiography Tiberius asserted that he had punished Sejanus because he discovered his hatred of the children of Germanicus. For a fuller discussion see the appendix on 'The Conspiracy of Sejanus'.

[2] Owing to the loss of the text of Tacitus for these years we are forced to rely on Dio (58, 4–11) for an account of the downfall of Sejanus.

others were suddenly struck down.[1] The emperor's intentions were left wholly uncertain; one day he was almost at the point of death, another he was well and planning to come to Rome in the near future. In this way the influence of Sejanus was gradually undermined, yet without frightening him too much.

As the belief in the favourite's omnipotence weakened, his foes began to pick up hope and his control was shaken. The young Gaius was cautiously put forward to ascertain if any sentiment still lingered in favour of the Julian line; he was invested with a priesthood, and this move was so well received that Tiberius began to hint that he intended to make the prince, then about nineteen, his successor. This revival of the prospects of the house of Germanicus so alarmed Sejanus that he determined to destroy it for ever. He began an intrigue for the purpose of ruining Gaius[2] and took steps to bring about the death of Nero. It is very likely that when Nero was first banished to an island Tiberius had left to his minister, who then enjoyed his full confidence, the selection of the custodians of the exiled prince; even if this were not the case, Sejanus had since then had ample opportunity to secure control of them. It was now announced that Nero had committed suicide, and it was believed, then or later, that he had been frightened into this act by being falsely told that he had been condemned to death by the senate.[3] The event fitted so well into the designs of Sejanus that there can be little doubt that the minister rather than the emperor was responsible. In the letter announcing the death of Nero to the senate Tiberius referred to Sejanus simply by his name, omitting

[1] Fufius Geminus may have been an instance in point. He had indulged in bitter jests at the expense of Tiberius, and was prosecuted for treason in A.D. 30. Both he and his wife committed suicide. He had been a friend of Livia and his wife an accomplice of Sejanus (*Ann.* 4, 12 and 5, 2; Dio, 58, 4). Perhaps Sejanus willingly sacrificed tools that were no longer useful, or perhaps he was unable to protect them. Since the emperor had grounds for resentment against Fufius his fate would not alarm Sejanus too much, but it might serve to let people see that he was not all-powerful. Possibly Asinius Gallus was another example (Dio, 58, 3).

[2] We know from Tacitus (6, 3) that there was a plot against Gaius, and it seems likely that it was contrived at this time.

[3] Suet. 54. Later Suetonius says (61) that Tiberius put Nero to death. I think the belief mentioned in the earlier chapter is probably close to the truth. Even if Tiberius wished Nero out of the way, it seems most unlikely that he would have had him killed at this time, for Nero alive would have been one more card in his hand against Sejanus.

the customary titles. The minister felt the ground slipping from under him and might have risked a *coup d'état*, but he was unnerved by the enthusiasm displayed by the populace for Gaius. Hitherto he had believed that they were on his side, and the discovery of their real sentiments dismayed him and he let the occasion slip. Tiberius continued to undermine him, but slowly and with caution. An indictment which he had instigated against L. Arruntius was quashed and the informers punished.[1] As the senate was still voting honours to Sejanus, Tiberius forbade the consideration of any measures proposing honours to himself, and so indirectly prevented any for his minister; sacrifices to a living man were also forbidden, and thus those which were being offered to Sejanus were stopped. Yet none of these blows, however much they weakened the influence of the minister, seemed aimed directly at him, and all could be explained by reference to the known characteristics of the emperor.

At length Tiberius resolved to bring matters to a crisis. In order that Sejanus might be taken completely by surprise, the emperor spread a report that he was about to confer the tribunician power on his minister. Tiberius had resigned the consulship early in the year, and Sejanus had of necessity followed his example. Of the consuls then in office one, Fulcinius Trio, was a friend of Sejanus, but the other, Memmius Regulus, was an enemy, though probably his hostility was more or less secret. Tiberius dispatched a long letter to the senate by a trusted agent named Macro, who, entering Rome at night, consulted with Regulus. Besides this letter Macro brought with him a commission from the emperor appointing him commander of the praetorian guard. Laco, the chief of the night-watch, who was also a foe of Sejanus, was taken into the conspiracy, and all the arrangements for the next day were speedily completed.

In the morning Sejanus, uneasy because of his uncertainty as to the contents of the emperor's letter, was hastening to the senate attended by his guards when Macro met him, and drawing him aside, informed him confidentially that the letter brought the coveted tribunician power. Sejanus entered the senate joyfully, leaving Macro and the guards outside. Macro

[1] Dio, 58, 8; *Ann.* 6, 7.

at once produced his commission, and promising the men a donative in the name of Tiberius, he ordered them to return to their camp. The order was quietly obeyed, and, when the guards had withdrawn, their place was promptly taken by Laco and his men. Macro then entered the senate and formally delivered the letter of Tiberius to the consuls. Before a word had been read, however, he left the house and hastened to the camp of the praetorians in order take over the command before Sejanus, as yet wholly unconscious of his danger, could make any appeal to the soldiers who had so long obeyed him.

While Macro was thus occupied, the letter of Tiberius was being read to the conscript fathers. It had been purposely made very long and discursive, so that as much time as possible would be given Macro to complete his preparations before the storm broke. From one topic to another the verbose epistle wandered on, censuring Sejanus here and there, but with no clear indication of the ultimate intention. The senators listened perplexed and uncertain, waiting for a conclusion at the nature of which they could not guess. During the reading Sejanus remained quietly in his place. As the matters for which he was blamed were, taken separately, somewhat unimportant, and as the criticism of his conduct was expressed in mild terms, his apprehensions were not aroused and he waited till the end, perhaps still trusting to Macro's confidential assurances and expecting, in spite of the letter's length and inauspicious passages, that it would close with a request that the tribunician power should be conferred upon him. But when the end was finally reached it proved to be an order that the senate should punish two of his friends, and that he himself should be kept under guard until the emperor could come to Rome. Tiberius further directed that one of the consuls should act as his escort on the journey, declaring that he was a lonely old man in peril of his life.

The suddenness of the blow completely stunned Sejanus. The senators who sat near him shrank away, but he remained passive in his place. When the consul Regulus ordered him to come forward, he still sat bewildered, unable to believe that the consul's words could be addressed to him. The order had to be repeated three times before he comprehended, and then, saying blankly, 'Are you calling *me*?' he rose to find Laco at his side. Probably the conscript fathers guessed from Laco's presence that they were no longer surrounded by the praetorians of Sejanus, for their hatred, long repressed by fear, now broke forth in a tumultuous clamour, even the friends of the minister joining in the outcry to conceal their dismay. Regulus, however, did not dare trust the senate to debate or vote, since a delay might give the partisans of Sejanus a chance to recover from their first consternation. Accordingly he asked the opinion of a single senator on whom he could rely,[1] and receiving a favourable response, he cut short all discussion and ordered Sejanus off to prison. The fallen minister having been led away by Laco and the magistrates, the senate immediately dispersed.

By the populace the fall of Sejanus was hailed with frantic joy, his statues were overthrown wherever they were found, and when it was seen that the guards remained quietly in the camp, the doom of the minister was sealed. Later in the day the senate was again convened; sentence of death was at once pronounced upon him, and in open disregard of the law the penalty was immediately inflicted. The morning of that eventful day had seen Sejanus confident of receiving formal recognition as the heir to the imperial crown, the evening saw his body outraged and insulted by the rabble, and his friends in panic terror of their lives.

While these events were taking place in Rome, Tiberius at Capri waited in intense anxiety, for he feared that the guards might support Sejanus; as a last resort he had instructed Macro to free Drusus and proclaim him emperor.[2] If the blow against Sejanus failed, Tiberius had ships in readiness for flight, and to have a better chance of reaching the armies in the provinces he wished to start at the earliest possible moment; dispatches borne by messengers were too slow, so he had arranged a system of signals by which the news of the result could be conveyed to him with the utmost speed.[3] Even when he knew that his

---

[1] This seems obvious from his asking only one opinion, and Dio says that he feared opposition which might lead to a disturbance from the friends of Sejanus.

[2] Suetonius (65) states this as a fact, but Dio (58, 13) and Tacitus (6, 23) give it as a report. It seems to me very probable. If the measure had been carried out Drusus would have become joint emperor with Tiberius.

[3] Suet. 65.

minister had fallen he still trembled for his own safety, for there were agents of Sejanus among his attendants, and the disillusioned old man no longer felt confidence in any one. Nevertheless since he had triumphed, he must rule, and shutting himself up in one of his villas, he sought to control and direct the course of public affairs from his seclusion.

In Rome the death of Sejanus was followed by a period of riot and disorder. The praetorian guards were furious at the greater confidence that had been shown in the night-watch, and perhaps some of them resented the fall of Sejanus. Their new commander probably could not at first enforce discipline or restrain the rabble. The populace was, therefore, left free to vent its feelings by the prompt murder of any well-known friends of Sejanus on whom it could lay its hands, while the senate exterminated his family. Thus the fall of the great minister was attended by a more or less extensive massacre of his partisans.[1] As soon as possible, however, order was restored and vengeance was once more clothed in legal forms.

As the rioting began to subside another cruel blow fell on Tiberius. Apicata, the divorced wife of Sejanus, when her children were put to death by the senate, no longer wished to live, and committed suicide. She contrived, however, to revenge herself on the imperial princess who had robbed her of her husband, for on the brink of the grave she addressed a letter to the emperor in which she revealed the fact, probably only guessed or suspected by her, that his son Drusus had been murdered by Livilla and Sejanus. Tiberius was aghast at such a revelation. Although the source from which it came was open to suspicion, he could not rest till he had probed the matter to the bottom, and the testimony of the slaves and attendants of Drusus soon removed all doubt, making clear the hideous treachery of the man whom he had so long cherished as a friend and trusted as an adviser. No wonder that in his secluded villa the old emperor was overwhelmed with anguish and with suspicions of all the world, so that he began one of his letters to the senate with the words: 'If I know what to write to you, Conscript Fathers, or

---

[1] We have no means of knowing how many were killed. We can gather a few names of friends of Sejanus who were probably slain in these disorders, in particular Bruttedius Niger, M. Ollius, and possibly Junius Blaesus.

how to write, or what not to write at this time, may gods and goddesses condemn me to worse than I suffer every day'.[1]

From his gloomy despair he soon roused himself to undertake the work before him. He realized that for years he had lived in the midst of plots and intrigues of which he had known nothing. He had been deceived by false evidence and exaggerated reports, with the result that one tragedy had followed another. The murder of his son, the quarrels in the imperial family, the banishment of Agrippina and Nero, the imprisonment of Drusus, the suicide of Nero, the intrigue against Gaius, might all be parts of one immense conspiracy in which he had been made the dupe and tool of Sejanus. He resolved to discover how far the plots had extended, how much injustice they had caused him to commit, and who had been the chief accomplices of the arch-conspirator. The death of his former favourite was not enough, a tardy retribution should overtake his guilty agents; their offences could neither be pardoned nor ignored, for duty demanded a thorough house-cleaning to avenge the past and to safeguard the future, and this task Tiberius grimly took in hand.

[1] It is strange but true that the animus of both Suetonius (67) and Tacitus (6, 6) is such that it enables them to construe these pathetic words as a confession of guilt on the part of Tiberius.

VIII

THE CLOSE OF THE REIGN

IT is generally held that after the fall of Sejanus a reign of terror was inaugurated in Rome and continued till the emperor's death. Some modern historians have sought to relieve Tiberius of most of the responsibility by the suggestion that in his absence from the city 'those elements of envy, rancour, avarice, which he had held in check, broke loose',[1] while others have sought to explain the psychological process which led the old emperor, betrayed by his trusted friend and embittered with the world, to turn savagely at bay and to strike ruthlessly at all who had incurred his resentment or suspicion.[2] Before seeking explanations it is obviously desirable to ascertain as nearly as possible what actually happened. The idea of a reign of terror is supported by the loose general statements of Dio and Suetonius, but it is derived mainly from the much more circumstantial narrative of Tacitus, who employs all his literary skill to cast an atmosphere of gloom and horror over the last years of Tiberius. If, however, we examine the facts recorded apart from the rhetorical setting in which they are presented,[3] we shall find that they give a very different impression. What the facts, taken by themselves, establish, is merely that after the fall of Sejanus a number of persons were prosecuted for complicity in his plots; some of the accused were punished and others committed suicide, but apparently few who did not deserve their fate, while some were spared or acquitted. The number of the prosecutions is much smaller than might have been expected after what had passed, and the proceedings seem to show that a real attempt was made to secure justice; in short the whole picture of the Tiberian Terror is a product of imagination and rhetoric quite unsupported by the evidence.

The fall of Sejanus and the violent lawlessness which followed it doubtless produced a genuine panic in Rome; the enemies of

---

[1] Baring-Gould, 667–8. His eulogy of the praetorian courts as contrasted with the senate which follows is absurd, for we know little of these courts under Tiberius except that Tacitus had no high opinion of them (1, 75).

[2] Baker, 270–4.

[3] See the appendix on 'Tacitus and the Tiberian Terror'.

the favourite sought vengeance by accusing his friends, who tried to escape by bringing accusations in their turn. For a time, therefore, charges were hurled recklessly about in something like an orgy of delation.[1] When order was restored and the law resumed its regular course [2] most of these charges seem to have been dropped, for apparently only those persons against whom there was serious evidence were ever brought to trial. Although the panic was soon checked, we may surmise that confidence was not immediately restored. Hitherto the danger had been confined to the more or less prominent Sejanians, but, since both senators and knights had paid servile court to him in the hour of his greatness, the deliberate probing of his intrigues might well occasion widespread dismay. There must have been many with uneasy consciences, and others who realized that, however innocent of criminal intent, they might readily be confounded with the guilty, or that they might have been the unconscious tools in some of his misdeeds. In this sense, but in this sense only, we may accept the existence of a prolonged reign of terror in Rome.

In his determination to punish the guilty Tiberius began with one of the last plots of Sejanus, perhaps the plot whose discovery had led to that minister's overthrow. In A.D. 32 the emperor sent a letter to the senate revealing an intrigue designed to ruin Gaius and accusing Sextius Paconianus of participation in it. This accusation was eagerly welcomed,[3] for Paconianus was

[1] Tacitus (6, 7) draws a lurid picture of the senators hastening to turn informers against their nearest kindred, but we find no instances of this in his subsequent narrative. Seneca (de Ben. 3, 26) also describes a panic accompanied by wholesale denunciations, and probably something of the kind really occurred, but the failure of Tacitus' narrative to support either his or Seneca's description and the fact that the consuls, after indulging in bitter recriminations (Ann. 5, 11 and 6, 4), did nothing to carry out their mutual threats would seem to show that many charges brought in the first violence of the panic were allowed to drop.

[2] Dio (58, 16) seems to have forgotten that the senate was now the regular court for treason trials and to have felt it necessary to explain why the prosecutions were brought before that body.

[3] I am inclined to think that Tacitus had some authority, perhaps in the works of those historians who were senators at the time (Ann. 2, 88), for his statements about the feeling aroused by a prosecution. It seems probable, however, that in some cases he supplied the reason for this feeling himself. Thus the rejoicing at the death of Vescularius Flaccus (Ann. 6, 10) can hardly have been due simply to his part in the ruin of Libo Drusus (Ann. 2, 28), since his role appears to have been wholly passive, but Tacitus, convinced that

hated as a daring and unscrupulous informer, and the conscript fathers would have condemned him to death if he had not turned state's evidence in order to save himself.[1] If the senators regretted his escape, they were much gratified when in his new role he denounced Latinius Latiaris, who was odious for the part he had taken in the destruction of Titius Sabinus. From their gratification we may infer that, like Paconianus, he was a more or less obnoxious informer, and the senate condemned him to death[2] without reluctance.

Another informer now came forward to accuse Cotta Messalinus, apparently of participation in this same plot, but nothing seems to have been alleged against him except more or less private remarks reflecting on Gaius, Livia, and Tiberius himself. Messalinus had powerful enemies in the senate and would have been condemned if he had not invoked the protection of the emperor, to whose friendship he appealed. Tiberius at once wrote to the conscript fathers,[3] citing the services of Messalinus to himself, and insisting that careless words should not be considered as a crime. In consequence of this letter the senate acquitted Messalinus and punished his accuser.

Q. Servaeus and Minucius Thermus were then brought to trial at the express command of Tiberius, though the exact charge against them is unrecorded. Servaeus was an ex-praetor who had served on the staff of Germanicus,[4] while Thermus was a man of equestrian rank who had enjoyed the friendship of Sejanus but who had, nevertheless, borne himself with modesty. For these reasons much sympathy was felt for them both,[5] but

Libo was innocent of any real crime, might assume such a reason for the rejoicing if his source gave no explanation of it.

[1] His life was spared, but he seems to have been kept in prison, for we find him there in A.D. 36 and there is no record of any other proceedings against him (*Ann.* 6, 39).

[2] This is implied, though not expressly stated, by Tacitus. The fact that Tiberius did nothing to save him would support the view of Tacitus that the offence of Sabinus had been much exaggerated, for the emperor intervened to mitigate the sentence of Firmius Catus, the betrayer of Libo (*Ann.* 4, 31).

[3] It was this letter which began with the pathetic words cited on page 198.

[4] He had also assisted in the prosecution of Piso (*Ann.* 3, 13).

[5] Nipperdey thinks the reference to the connexion of Servaeus with Germanicus is intended to remind the reader who Servaeus was, not to explain the sympathy felt for him. The reference seems, however, to be clearly explanatory (for another explanation of the sort see note 3, page 201).

in spite of this they were condemned, and only saved themselves by turning state's evidence. Their testimony led to the condemnation of Julius Africanus and Seius Quadratus.[1]

Charges were next brought against a knight named M. Terentius, Tiberius apparently having no hand in the prosecution. Terentius defended himself boldly, avowing his friendship with Sejanus and justifying it by the emperor's own example, but denying that he was involved in the recent plots of the minister. The senate not only acquitted Terentius but banished or put to death his accusers, and this without rebuke from Tiberius.[2] These verdicts show clearly that the senate was not so cowed that independent action was impossible, at least in cases where the emperor did not take an active part.

After the acquittal of Terentius, Tiberius wrote in regard to Sextus Vistilius, a senator of praetorian rank who had just committed suicide. He had been accused of being the author of certain writings in which scandalous imputations were thrown on Gaius.[3] Tiberius, evidently convinced of Vistilius' guilt, had forbidden him to present himself at court. Thereupon he opened his veins, then bound them up and wrote a letter of supplication to the emperor; receiving a stern answer to this, he opened his veins again, and this time in earnest. There is nothing to show that Tiberius intended any further action, although, since the circumstances strongly suggest that Vistilius was suspected of an active part in the plot against Gaius, it is not unlikely that he feared, rightly or wrongly, that a prosecution would follow.

Next five members of the higher nobility were indicted at once, but, when they were brought to trial, the charges against two of them broke down, and Tiberius postponed the trial of

[1] The language of Tacitus is obscure. After telling how Servaeus and Thermus were condemned, and turned informers, he says that Africanus and Quadratus *tractique sunt in casum eundem.* This may mean merely that they were also condemned, but more probably the meaning intended is that Servaeus and Thermus denounced them as accomplices in the offence for which they themselves had just been condemned. It is unlikely that Africanus and Quadratus were put to death, for in that case Tacitus would probably have mentioned their fate explicitly.

[2] *Ann.* 6, 9; Dio, 58, 19.

[3] Tacitus, trying hard to present Vistilius in a pathetic light, throws some doubt on his guilt but does not assert his innocence. Evidently there was at least good ground for suspicion.

the other three until he could be present. Since he never returned to the city the matter was dropped, and one wonders why the cases were not dismissed outright. Perhaps the explanation is to be found in the fact that the emperor let fall some ominous words in regard to Mamercus Scaurus, one of the defendants, who was a man of infamous character and had been a friend of Sejanus.[1] In his case Tiberius may have felt that there was some foundation for the charge, whatever it was, and so have wished to leave a possibility of renewing the prosecution.

So far the attempt to detect and punish the accomplices of Sejanus had been attended by little loss of life, but towards the end of the year the tragedies multiplied. At Capri the investigations of Tiberius drove two of his old friends to suicide, a result which occasioned much rejoicing; at Rome three knights were convicted of conspiracy, and Tacitus, by saying that one of them was innocent of anything serious, implies that the other two were guilty. In addition an officer of the praetorian guard killed himself, apparently in prison, and Vitia, an elderly lady whose son had been driven to suicide in the lifetime of Sejanus, was put to death.[2] Last of all a terrified senator fled from Italy, but was arrested and brought back; being unable to explain his flight, he was placed in custody and forgotten.

The known events of this year (32) when candidly considered are far from horrifying. It is true that some nine persons whose names are known perished, but the fate of three of them was regarded with satisfaction; two killed themselves, one without waiting for an indictment; two are by implication admitted to have been guilty of some serious offence; and there are only two who appear from the account of Tacitus to have suffered unjustly, one of whom was Vitia and the other a dissipated spendthrift who had been a friend of Sejanus.[3] Two innocent victims and four executions which were not greeted with applause are hardly sufficient for a reign of terror. On the contrary the number of victims is surprisingly small when we recall the long series of plots and intrigues which had at last been uncovered.

---

[1] *Ann.* 6, 29.

[2] For a fuller discussion of her case see the appendix on 'The Law of Treason under Tiberius'.

[3] This is Tacitus' own description of the innocent knight (6, 14).

There is, moreover, another difficulty in the way of a belief in any reign of terror. If nine persons perished during the year, sèven others who were prosecuted escaped; the emperor intervened to save one, the senate acquitted three, and three cases were indefinitely postponed. From these facts it does not appear that justice was entirely ignored. We should also note that in two instances the informers were punished, one at least being put to death. Nor does the terror gain much if we add the other cases to the list. It is true that there were five more condemnations, but three of the condemned saved their lives at any rate by turning state's evidence, and what happened to the other two is uncertain, and finally two senators were placed in custody.

It is evident that Tiberius took a large part in directing the proceedings: charges are brought at his order, men are protected, and cases are postponed by him, but so far as the facts show he appears to have striven simply for justice. He shielded an unpopular senator[1] who was accused on trivial grounds, ignoring language disrespectful to himself, and he acquiesced when the senate acquitted defendants and punished informers. For that year at any rate he was satisfied with a very moderate number of executions. It is true that in the last months of the preceding year, after the fall of Sejanus, an unknown number of the latter's friends had been illegally put to death by the senate and the mob. For this Tiberius cannot justly be held responsible, but he must answer for what was done once order had been restored and the law could take its course. Although we can determine only very imperfectly what happened in the interval of confusion at the close of A.D. 31, it may be worth while to summarize what we know or can conjecture with some confidence. The actual poisoners of Drusus, a Greek physician and a slave (or freedman), were executed or forced to kill themselves by Tiberius[2]; Livilla died of starvation, either voluntarily or under compulsion[3]; the eldest son of Sejanus, his uncle, and two of his friends were slain,[4] though whether at the order of the emperor or by the mob or the senate is wholly uncertain;

---

[1] Tacitus (6, 5) says that Cotta Messalinus was hated.
[2] *Ann.* 4, 3 and 8; Suet. 62.   [3] *Ann.* 6, 2; Dio, 58, 11.
[4] *Ann.* 5, 7 and 13, 45; Juvenal, 10, 83.

a senator whose name is lost committed suicide,[1] and two others were imprisoned in their houses, one of whom took his own life while the other remained in confinement for the rest of the reign without being brought to trial.[2] Lastly Tacitus says that, although the popular rage was subsiding and most people were satisfied with the punishments already inflicted, it was resolved to execute the two younger children of Sejanus.[3] In this case it is probable that the senate acted without instructions from Tiberius, for if he had been responsible for the fate of the young daughter of the fallen minister, Tacitus would almost certainly have mentioned it. Such a list is very brief, but, though it is obviously incomplete, we have no reason to think that any large number perished.

The task of punishing the accomplices of Sejanus seems to have been almost finished by the end of A.D. 32, for, while the next year was marked by tragic events, there were few trials for treason and the informers devoted themselves chiefly to the prosecution of violators of an old law of Julius Caesar concerning the investment of capital. The result of their sudden activity in this direction was a financial panic which Tiberius was finally forced to relieve by advancing a large sum of money to be loaned on landed security for three years without interest.[4]

In regard to the political cases of the year A.D. 33 we have very meagre information. Considius Proculus was convicted of treason and immediately executed. Such haste suggests some new conspiracy rather than guilt in connexion with old intrigues, nor does this seem at all improbable. The events of the preceding year must have left many of the former Sejanian party in a mood of gloomy apprehension, and some of the more desperate among them may have seen in a new plot, perhaps for the murder of Tiberius, their only hope of safety. It is, however, quite possible that Considius was an informer[5] who was so hated by the senate that the conscript fathers disregarded the law requiring an interval of ten days between a sentence and its execution in their eagerness to get rid of him when an oppor-

---

[1] *Ann.* 5, 6 and 7.   [2] *Ann.* 5, 8; Dio, 59, 6.
[3] *Ann.* 5, 9; Dio, 58, 11.
[4] *Ann.* 6, 16–17; Dio, 58, 21. Dio is almost certainly wrong in some details.
[5] He is probably the same man as the Considius who is mentioned as the accuser of Pomponius Secundus in A.D. 31 (*Ann.* 5, 8).

tunity occurred. The senate also condemned his sister to banishment. Then Pompeius Macer, a knight, and his son, a senator of praetorian rank, were prosecuted and both committed suicide. The daughter of the knight, Pompeia Macrina, whose husband and father-in-law, both influential Greeks, had previously been punished by Tiberius,[1] was exiled. All three are represented as suffering on a frivolous charge, but there is reason to suspect that more serious matters were involved than appear on the record.[2] One other death should be noted at this point, namely that of Asinius Gallus. He had been arrested in A.D. 30, though why it is impossible to determine,[3] and had ever since been kept in close confinement under the guard of the consuls. His death occurred in this year, but whether it was voluntary or not remains uncertain.

If there was a new conspiracy of which Considius was the head and in which Pompeius Macer and his family were involved, its discovery may have convinced Tiberius of the danger of prolonging his investigations and the consequent suspense, or he may simply have decided that the principal offenders had now been brought to justice. At any rate he determined to make an end of the whole matter and issued orders that the friends of Sejanus then in prison should be put to death, with the result that some twenty of them were executed on the same day.[4] Since no names have been recorded, it is most unlikely that any persons of high rank were included in the number, and the victims were probably slaves, freedmen, and clients of Sejanus or his chief accomplices, together with some informers who had been his tools but who are not mentioned in our sources. A

[1] As to when, why, or how we know nothing. Greece was an imperial province under Tiberius so that there was probably no record of the matter in the senate's archives.

[2] See the appendix on 'The Law of Treason under Tiberius'. Tacitus tries to give a political colour to the execution of Sextus Marius for incest by attributing his ruin to the avarice of the emperor. The only reason given for this suspicion is that his mines were seized by the imperial treasury instead of being turned over to the *aerarium*, which was controlled by the senate. Such a reason is unconvincing, especially since this is the only instance where Tacitus ascribes a prosecution to such a motive on the part of Tiberius.

[3] Tacitus (4, 71) intimates that both Tiberius and Sejanus hated him; Dio (58, 3) represents him as paying court to Sejanus and attributes his ruin to Tiberius, leaving it uncertain whether he was arrested as a friend or as an enemy of the favourite.

[4] See the appendix on 'Tacitus and the Tiberian Terror'.

wholesale execution seems horrible at first, though it is difficult
to see how protracting such a business would have made it less
cruel. After all, the really vital question is whether the sufferers
deserved their fate, at least according to Roman ideas; and in
this case it is probable not only that they did but that they had
been legally tried and sentenced.[1] The way having been thus
cleared, Tiberius granted a sort of amnesty by allowing all who
chose, to mourn for Sejanus,[2] thus signifying that friendship for
him should no longer be regarded with suspicion.

Although many must have breathed more freely after this
amnesty, partial as it was, for no security was promised to those
guilty of actual crimes in behalf of Sejanus, the year was
darkened by other tragedies. Drusus, the second son of Germanicus, had been imprisoned in the palace through the
machinations of the fallen minister and had since remained
there in close custody. He was now starved to death[3] and a
record of everything he had said or done in his captivity was
read to the senate by the order of Tiberius. There can be no
doubt of the emperor's responsibility and his motives are not
difficult to guess, for Drusus was clearly unfit to mount the
throne and he was obviously a highly dangerous prisoner. Already
in A.D. 31 a young man had impersonated him and had been received in the East with some enthusiasm.[4] It seems extremely
probable that during his imprisonment the prince became
actually insane, and that Tiberius at length concluded that his
death was a grim necessity of state.[5] The reading in the senate

[1] Tacitus does not even imply that any of the victims were innocent, though
there were children among them. If the children were slaves their execution
might seem justified to the Romans in view of their laws in regard to slaves.
Neither does Tacitus suggest that any one suffered without due process of law,
and one man, Sextius Paconianus, who was almost certainly in prison at this
time but who was not under sentence of death, survived till A.D. 36 (*Ann.* 6, 39).

[2] Dio, 58, 16. Dio asserts that the amnesty was not observed, but his loose
general statements are unreliable and on such a matter the silence of Tacitus
is impressive, for he would almost certainly have mentioned a direct breach of
faith on the part of Tiberius.

[3] Starvation was not regarded by the Romans as a cruel death, for they often
chose this method of committing suicide.

[4] *Ann.* 5, 10. According to Dio (58, 25) the impersonation took place in
A.D. 34.

[5] Tacitus (6, 24) says that Drusus at first pretended madness and uttered
imprecations against Tiberius as if demented. Apparently he continued this
course to the end, making his curses more studied and elaborate as he aban-

of the dying man's frantic curses was certainly meant to make a new impersonation impossible by establishing the fact of his death beyond question, and it may also have been intended by Tiberius to prove his insanity so as to justify an apparently harsh action.

Gallus and Drusus were soon followed by Agrippina and Plancina. When Sejanus was overthrown Agrippina may have hoped that his fall would improve her position, but it had now become evident that, even if Tiberius had been deceived by his favourite when he banished her, he had no intention of granting any relaxation of her exile. She starved herself to death,[1] and Tiberius declared that her suicide was due to grief at the death of her lover Asinius Gallus. Whatever her relations with Gallus may have been, and Tacitus emphatically asserts her chastity, it is to the discredit of the emperor that he heaped abuse upon her in the grave. The fact that he did so shows the bitterness of his feeling towards her, a bitterness she had certainly done much to provoke. Her extravagant pride, her restless ambition, her ungovernable temper, and her baseless suspicions had been the source of much trouble to him and to the empire. Her death was followed by that of her old enemy Plancina. It is alleged that Tiberius had hitherto spared her, partly to please his mother and partly to spite Agrippina; now that both these motives were removed she was prosecuted and took her own life.[2]

But while Rome was filled with prosecutions and trials,

doned hope. The expression that he pretended madness has been considered an interpolation, but without it the assertion remains that his curses resembled the ravings of a madman.

[1] Tacitus suggests a doubt as to whether her death was voluntary; Suetonius (53) had evidently no doubt, for he says that Tiberius had her fed by force; Dio (58, 22) represents Tiberius as her murderer. I think that Tacitus had found no reputable writers who did not accept the theory of suicide, or he would have cited their version, at least in such general terms as 'some writers report'.

[2] *Ann.* 6, 26. Dio (58, 22) agrees with Tacitus that she was spared to spite Agrippina; he adds that Tiberius hated her for a reason quite apart from Germanicus, but unfortunately he does not give this reason. As to the charges against her Tacitus merely says that she was prosecuted for crimes which were not at all secret. The expression suggests immorality, though his remark that her fate seemed late rather than undeserved might be taken as referring to her rejoicing at the death of Germanicus. However, I believe that Tacitus would have been more explicit if he had had this last in mind.

I

Tiberius did not forget the provinces for whose good government and prosperity he felt himself responsible. Our literary sources throw little light on this side of his activity, and we are forced to rely on occasional inscriptions for most of our information. We have already seen that from the beginning of his reign he had interested himself in the improvement of the means of communication throughout the empire. Nor were the roads which he constructed intended wholly for military purposes, since it seems evident that he was well aware of the fact that the opening up of backward districts not only facilitated commerce, but promoted the growth of towns and the spread of Roman civilization. Nowhere were such developments more to be desired than in the most recently conquered parts of Spain and Gaul, and during his last years Tiberius pushed forward to completion an extensive system of roads in those regions. Though something had already been accomplished,[1] the inscriptions so far discovered would indicate that the most important part of this work was only undertaken after A.D. 31. From that time on, however, we have ample evidence[2] of the active prosecution of a well-conceived plan such as could have been executed only with the approval and under the direction of the emperor himself.[3] The roads then constructed not only did for Spain something of what the roads of Agrippa had done for Gaul, but they had their value for the latter country as well, for one of them traversed the Pyrenees, connecting Burdigala with northern Spain, and the repair of the old highway through Narbonensis was of obvious importance. Thus by the end of the reign Gaul, Spain, and Italy were linked together and trade was able to develop freely between them. The building of these roads served to consolidate the empire within, but there were

---

[1] This is shown by an inscription found in Tarraconensis dated A.D. 14/15 (*C.I.L.* ii. 4905; *I.L.S.* 152).

[2] The road through Narbonensis was repaired in 31/32 (*C.I.L.* xii. 5445, 5449, 5557, 5588, 5600, 5619, 5665, and others where the date is defaced or missing; *I.L.S.* 5818). Most of the inscriptions in Tarraconensis date, either certainly or probably, from 32/33 (*C.I.L.* ii. 4778, 4904, 4945, 4947, and others where the date is defaced); one falls in 33/34 (4883). In Baetica there are two inscriptions dated 35/36 (4712, 4715).

[3] Lang, 74–5. That the work was designed by Tiberius is shown by the fact that it required the collaboration of several governors, imperial and senatorial.

others which were intended primarily for the defence of the frontiers. Such work had been in progress at the accession of Tiberius, and he did not allow the tragic events in Rome to interrupt it, for in A.D. 33 or 34 we find the Moesian legions busy on a road along the Danube, the construction of which involved serious difficulties, since in places it had to be cut in the face of the cliffs overhanging the river.[1] It is very probable that the chief highways in both Pannonia and Moesia, namely those from Nauportus to Poetovio, from Aemona down the Save to the Danube, and along the Danube,[2] were largely built by Tiberius, though the first at least was begun under Augustus. The carrying out of such extensive works in the last years of his reign is conclusive evidence that to the end of his life Tiberius continued to take a keen interest in the provinces and never relaxed his attention to their welfare.

The emperor's firm grasp of imperial affairs is also shown by his handling of the Eastern problem which again became acute in the last years of his reign. The settlement which had been arranged by Germanicus endured without disturbance till the death of Zeno, whom he had set up as king of Armenia. This event took place about A.D. 34 and at once precipitated a new crisis. During the long peace Artabanus had consolidated his position in Parthia, and had adopted the oriental precaution against possible rivals of putting to death all the adult princes of the royal family who were within his reach. He had, moreover, been successful in wars against the neighbouring peoples, and his success had served to make him arrogant and cruel. As a result his hold upon his magnates and people grew weaker without his perceiving it, and in his pride he determined that he would no longer submit to Roman dominance in Armenia. The death of Zeno gave him an opportunity to interfere, and he succeeded in placing one of his sons, named Arsaces, on the Armenian throne. With this accomplished he felt that he was strong enough to challenge the power of Rome, especially as Tiberius, old and unpopular, was now living in seclusion. Assuming an aggressive attitude, he put forward a preposterous claim to all the territories formerly held by the Persian kings and by Alexander the Great, but he soon discovered that he

[1] Lang, 73-4; *C.I.L.* iii. 1698 (*I.L.S.* 2281).   [2] Charlesworth, 174-7.

had misjudged the situation. Tiberius had withdrawn from society, but he continued to give vigilant attention to the interests of the empire. No sooner had Armenia been lost than he took measures to regain it. For this purpose he began negotiations with the king of the Iberians (the modern Georgians), and having reconciled him with his brother Mithridates, he drew them both into an alliance with Rome by the offer of the Armenian throne to the latter.[1] Tacitus mentions these arrangements with the Iberians as if the whole matter was concluded in A.D. 35,[2] but since the negotiations must have taken a considerable time, it seems fairly certain that they were begun immediately after the loss of Armenia. While they were in progress another opening for an attack on Artabanus appeared. A party among the Parthian magnates, wearying of his tyranny, sent a secret embassy to Rome to ask that one of the sons of the former king Phraates should be sent to them,[3] promising to support him against Artabanus. From Tacitus we should gather that this movement was wholly spontaneous on the part of the Parthians, yet it is difficult to avoid a suspicion that the suggestion may have come from Tiberius, and that as soon as he had seen Arsaces established in Armenia he had begun to undermine the Parthian king in his own country. In any case the emperor lost no time in taking advantage of the opportunity which the discontent of the magnates presented, and he promptly sent a prince, named after his father, to Syria. The young Phraates died almost as soon as he arrived in the East, but Tiberius quickly found a new pretender in the person of Tiridates, a grandson of king Phraates.[4] At the same time he dispatched L. Vitellius as governor of Syria to carry out the imperial policy on the spot.

Artabanus discovered his danger before the Romans were ready to place their pretender in the field, and took prompt measures to defend himself. These measures were directed, however, not toward Syria but toward Armenia. This was probably due to the fact that Tiberius had secured such prompt

---

[1] I infer this from the fact that Mithridates received it afterwards.

[2] *Ann.* 6, 32. The silk trade along the northern trade route had probably led to more or less close relations between Rome and the Iberians long before this crisis.   [3] *Ann.* 6, 31.   [4] *Ann.* 6, 37.

success in that quarter as to remove all chance of an attack on the actual possessions of Rome. His Iberian allies had contrived to have Arsaces murdered and to seize the Armenian capital. With that kingdom in hostile hands Artabanus dared not risk any action on the Roman frontier; instead he dispatched another son to recover Armenia, and, when this expedition failed, he marched with his whole force against the Iberians. Before he had accomplished anything of importance it was rumoured that Vitellius was about to invade Mesopotamia. In view of the disaffection of his subjects Artabanus was afraid to continue his campaign, and realizing that he could not fight Rome and her new allies at the same time, he retreated to his own dominions. All the actual fighting had been done by the Iberians, who had wrested Armenia from the Parthians, and Vitellius had done nothing except to march with his army to the Roman frontier and to circulate reports as to his intentions.

The retreat from Armenia proved ruinous to Artabanus. If Vitellius had done no fighting, he had been active in other ways, corresponding with the leading Parthian magnates and inciting them to desert their king. The Armenian fiasco had, temporarily at least, destroyed his prestige, and the Roman intrigues were so successful that the discredited monarch, finding himself generally deserted, fled to Scythia. The triumph of Tiridates seemed assured, and in A.D. 36 Vitellius at the head of the legions escorted him across the Euphrates into Mesopotamia, where a number of powerful Parthian magnates joined him with large bodies of troops. The legate, doubtless guided by the instructions of Tiberius, now thought that he had done enough, and accordingly retired again to Roman territory, leaving Tiridates to make what he could of the opportunity presented to him. At first all went well, and he was solemnly crowned king of Parthia at Ctesiphon, but he showed himself completely under the influence of one faction among the magnates, with the result that another turned again to Artabanus, who was soon able to advance against his rival at the head of an army. Thus threatened, Tiridates fell back towards the Roman frontier, and the retreat became a flight which terminated the brief reign of the new king, who took refuge in Syria with a few followers. So far as we can learn Rome

made no effort to support her protégé and offered no opposition
to the restoration of Artabanus. Tiberius might reasonably
hope that the recently arrogant Parthian had been made
wiser by experience, and in fact he gave no further trouble.

In Rome after the wholesale execution of A.D. 33 there was
little further pursuit of the partisans of Sejanus, perhaps indeed
no one else suffered for complicity in his intrigues, since there is
only one subsequent case which was certainly based on an
alleged friendship for the fallen minister. This occurred in
A.D. 34 when an informer brought charges (undoubtedly of
treason) against Lentulus Gaetulicus for having betrothed his
daughter to a son of Sejanus. The result, however, was that
the accuser was banished from Rome while Gaetulicus remained
undisturbed at the head of the legions in Upper Germany.
For the three years from A.D. 34 to 36 the pages of Tacitus
record the suicide or punishment of some eighteen persons,
but an examination of the cases will show that very few of
them can be regarded as victims of the tyranny of Tiberius.
One woman, Aemilia Lepida, was accused of adultery with a
slave, and, since there was no doubt of her guilt, she preferred
suicide to a public trial[3]; three informers were banished, but
they seem to have little claim upon our sympathy[4]; a provincial
governor, Pomponius Labeo, killed himself, and his wife followed
his example, when he was charged with maladministration[5]

---

[1] Tacitus reports a story, based merely on popular rumour, that Gaetulicus
wrote to Tiberius explaining his consent to the proposed marriage as due to
the emperor's own advice and threatening to revolt if he were recalled to Rome.
Tacitus finds this story almost incredible but thinks that it derives some
support from the fact that Gaetulicus was the only person related to Sejanus
who escaped uninjured. This support seems weak, and, in view of the fact that
no previous historian had thought the story worth recording, we need attach no
weight to it. According to Dio (58, 19) Tiberius also ignored an insult to himself
on the part of Caesianus, a friend of Sejanus and the son of Apronius, who was
the father-in-law of Gaetulicus and the legate of Lower Germany. Tiberius may
have hesitated to attack two commanders so powerful and so closely related,
but he was always reluctant to remove capable governors, and it seems more
likely that he saw no reason to suspect these two of anything beyond a willing-
ness to accept Sejanus if he were declared the legal heir to the throne. Such an
attitude the emperor obviously could not regard as criminal.

[2] There seems to be a gap in the *Annals* (6, 40) by which we have lost one
or more names.

[3] *Ann.* 6, 40. This is the only case where Tacitus makes guilt the reason for
suicide. It must, however, have been a common motive.

[4] *Ann.* 6, 30.   [5] *Ann.* 6, 29. His wife was involved in the charges

and another imperial official, Trebellenus Rufus, also took his own life. The exact charge against Rufus is unknown, but, since he had long acted as regent in Thrace for the children of Cotys, it seems very probable that it was maladministration.[1] A knight, on trial for some offence whose nature is not recorded, swallowed poison in the senate house, after the informers had finished presenting the evidence against him,[2] evidently because he saw that he could make no defence. Furthermore there are four suicides which seem to have been entirely unnecessary, since no prosecution had been begun or even threatened. One of these was the wife of Mamercus Scaurus, who killed herself with her husband; two others were cousins of Sejanus, who, having been promised priesthoods while he was still a favourite, took their own lives when these were given to others; the fourth was a consular, C. Galba, who made an end of himself when Tiberius forbade him to draw lots for a province.[3] In the case of Galba we discover the real motive behind his act when Suetonius informs us that he was a ruined spendthrift,[4] who evidently hoped to restore his fortunes by plundering the provincials, and when he was rightly denied an opportunity preferred death to the poverty which was the result of his past extravagance. It seems highly probable that a few more details concerning the cousins of Sejanus would reveal a better reason for their suicide than the one suggested by Tacitus, namely that they construed the appointment of others to the promised priesthoods as a hint that it was time for them to die. It is hard to see that any blame attaches to Tiberius in any of the twelve cases so far considered, and we are left with but six possible 'victims' in the course of these three years. In three of these six cases our information is extremely meagre. Tigranes, formerly king of Armenia, was probably put to death for treason,[5] and two senators were certainly charged with this offence, one of whom killed himself and the other was executed.[6] One of the remaining three was Mamercus Scaurus, who was accused of adultery and practising magic arts. Like so many others he committed suicide, and Tacitus expressly attributes

[1] *Ann.* 2, 67; 3, 38; 6, 39.   [2] *Ann.* 6, 40.
[3] *Ann.* 6, 29 and 40.   [4] Suet., *Galba*, 3.
[5] *Ann.* 6, 40.   [6] *Ann.* 6, 38.

his ruin to Macro rather than Tiberius.[1] Fulcinius Trio, finding
himself beset with informers, likewise took his own life without
waiting for a trial,[2] and Sextius Paconianus, who had saved
himself in A.D. 32 by turning state's evidence, was now executed
because he had amused himself in prison by writing songs
reflecting on Tiberius.[3] Scaurus, Trio, and Paconianus had all
been friends of Sejanus, but Tacitus declares that this had
nothing to do with the fate of Scaurus, and the offence of
Paconianus was obviously committed after the death of the
minister. It is, therefore, not unlikely that Trio was involved
in some new intrigue. In this connexion it should be borne in
mind that four of the six cases of treason, namely those of Trio,
Paconianus, and the two senators, occurred in A.D. 35 when
Tiberius had left Capri and was staying in country villas near
Rome.[4] Under these circumstances a plot might have much
better chances of success and new conspiracies would seem
probable.

In the events of these three years (A.D. 34 to 36) there is
nothing, apart from Tacitean rhetoric, which suggests a reign
of terror or continued persecution of the former adherents of
Sejanus. The actual prosecutions seem somewhat few in number
and we have no reason to suppose that any of the sufferers were
innocent or were punished on frivolous charges, since Tacitus
does not venture such assertions in regard to any of them. The
common impression that in his last years Tiberius became
pitiless, if not a bloodthirsty, tyrant, is entirely unsupported by
the recorded facts, and since Tacitus strives throughout his
narrative to picture him in this light, we can hardly suppose
that he has failed to make the most of all the material he could
find.

With A.D. 37 we come to the last year of the reign. Tiberius
was in his seventy-eighth year, his health was failing, and in the
last months of his life his grasp of public affairs seems to have
weakened. The question of the succession still haunted him
and embittered his last days. Of the Claudian house there were
left his own grandson, who was only about seventeen, and his
nephew, the future emperor Claudius, who was considered of

[1] *Ann.* 6, 29.   [2] *Ann.* 6, 38; Dio, 58, 25.
[3] *Ann.* 6, 3 and 39.   [4] *Ann.* 6, 39.

weak mind; of the family of Germanicus only the youngest son, Gaius Caesar, survived, and he was approaching twenty-five. None of them seemed fit for the position, but Tiberius, perhaps still feeling himself bound by his promise to Augustus, or perhaps seeing no better arrangement, left the path clear for Gaius. It is true that he did not formally designate Gaius as his successor, but he must have known that the prince was almost certain to mount the throne if no steps were taken to prevent it, and he took none. Probably he accepted this solution, but, in view of the prince's youth and inexperience, refused to assume the responsibility of forcing him upon the Roman world.[1]

The dying emperor spent his last days in Italy, dragging himself from one villa to another. Meanwhile the prosecutions still went on in Rome. Acutia, formerly the wife of a man who had committed suicide under suspicious circumstances after the fall of Sejanus, was convicted of treason, but the silence of Tacitus as to her fate makes it seem probable that her life was spared. Then a woman by the name of Albucilla was accused of disloyalty[2] and adultery; among her accomplices and lovers were named three men of the highest rank along with some of lesser degree. The important personages were Cn. Domitius, the husband of one of Agrippina's daughters and by her the father of the future emperor Nero, Vibius Marsus, and L. Arruntius. The silence of the emperor's letters in regard to these three gave rise to the suspicion that he knew nothing of the case and that the charges were trumped up by Macro, who was an enemy of Arruntius. Knowing that Tiberius was near his end, Domitius and Marsus saved themselves by delaying their trials till after the emperor's death, but Arruntius preferred suicide, and according to Tacitus justified his choice to his friends by pointing out the evils which he foresaw under Gaius, saying that, if Tiberius had been transformed under the burden of the

[1] Tacitus (6, 46) tells us that Tiberius clearly discerned the real character of Gaius. This is possible, but what was that character? Gaius began his reign well, but became a tyrant later. The generally received opinion is that he became insane. If so, it would seem that we should judge his character by his acts while he possessed his reason rather by than what he did when he was mentally deranged.

[2] *impietas in principem.* Probably some kind of conspiracy was alleged.

empire in spite of his age and experience,[1] nothing good could be expected of a mere youth like Gaius with such a minister as Macro. Albucilla herself was flung into prison after a futile attempt at suicide,[2] one of her less important lovers was banished to an island, and another was expelled from the senate. Still another man, an informer, was banished, though whether as a lover and accomplice of Albucilla or on other grounds is not clear.

These were the last public events of the reign of Tiberius, who died on the 16th of March, A.D. 37, at the villa of Lucullus near Misenum. His death was declared natural, but a story circulated and came to be generally believed that his end was hastened by violence. According to this story Tiberius fainted, and his courtiers, believing him dead, saluted Gaius as emperor; but when it was suddenly announced that Tiberius had revived Macro saved the situation by smothering him. There were other rumours, however; some thought that he was poisoned by Gaius, others that he was refused food after an attack of fever.[3] Perhaps after all the official version was correct and he died naturally at the age of seventy-eight in the twenty-third year of his reign.

As to the character of Tiberius judgements will always differ to some extent. That he was not the monster depicted by Tacitus is now fully admitted, and the stories of his wild debaucheries at Capri are generally rejected. For most of the other evil qualities attributed to him, whether by Tacitus or others, there is no serious evidence. There is nothing in the recorded facts to suggest that he was an astute hypocrite; if he sometimes expressed himself ambiguously in the senate, and if he dissembled when he resolved to destroy Sejanus, these traits were but the necessary consequences of his position. It is beyond question that he was an able soldier and administrator and that he laboured strenuously and successfully to govern the provinces with humanity and justice. Even Tacitus admits that in Rome for the first nine years of his reign he ruled with moderation

---

[1] Since Tacitus admired Arruntius and since this view was in conflict with his conception of the character of Tiberius, I believe that he had some authority for the substance of this speech. For this case see also Dio, 58, 27.

[2] According to Dio (58, 27) she died there.

[3] For the death of Tiberius see the appendix on 'The Sources of Tacitus'.

He inherited the constitution of Augustus and strove to maintain it intact, respecting the republican forms and giving the senate as much independence and as large a share in the government as possible. He sought to restrain flattery and was patient of slander and abuse. If his government deteriorated, it was only under the influence of a treacherous but trusted minister, the stress of continual intrigues provoked by the fatal question of the succession, and the consciousness of the growing hatred of his subjects. He was unpopular from the beginning because of his cold and reserved manners, and because he would not squander the public revenues to amuse the Roman mob. Lacking in tact and in geniality, he may have made a blunder by too strict an economy in the matter of games and shows, in allowing his contempt for the populace to be too plainly perceived, and in showing too marked a preference for the old nobility. At any rate he soon came to stand out in marked contrast to Germanicus, his peculiar relation to whom laid him open to suspicion. The sudden death of Germanicus was a blow from which he never recovered; he was no longer merely unpopular, but the darkest suspicions gathered round him and steadily deepened. The rise of Sejanus was probably in some degree due to the reflex action on the emperor's mind of the growing hate and suspicion: the more he knew himself detested, the more he clung to the man whom he believed to be his loyal friend. Under such conditions a gradual degeneration in his character would be intelligible, but there is nothing to show that it took place. He long endured the reckless provocations of Agrippina and only banished her when he became convinced that she was really dangerous. The ruin of the house of Germanicus was a tragedy which threw a sombre shadow over the last years of his reign. The blame for this disaster seems to lie partly with Agrippina and her friends, and partly with Sejanus, who took prompt advantage of her foolish violence to fill his master's mind with suspicions which were probably not wholly justified. When at last Tiberius awakened to the deceptions which had been practised upon him, the punishment of the guilty was an obvious duty. Even then the recorded facts furnish no evidence that he was either cruel or unjust. When we remember all that had passed, the number of those who suffered does not seem excessive. Among them there was only one whom Tacitus ventures to pronounce innocent, and he seems to have been involved with others whose guilt the historian plainly implies.[1] The acquittals and the punishment of informers seem to point clearly to an attempt, at least, to secure justice.

Even so, we must admit that the fall of Sejanus was followed by a period of gloom. Tiberius was old, isolated, and detested; the higher nobility could not forgive the rise of the favourite, the lesser were completely alienated by his overthrow. The former partisans of Germanicus who had deserted Agrippina must have looked with painful misgivings to the accession of her surviving son, while the old aristocracy which had opposed Germanicus can likewise have felt little confidence in Gaius. Thus all parties and all classes were sullen and resentful in the present and faced the future with anxiety. Under such circumstances it would not be surprising if new plots and intrigues were formed, and if both the emperor and his subjects viewed each other with suspicion. The principate of Augustus was dead and despotism stood forth undisguised. It is true that the theory of the constitution remained the same and that the change was psychological rather than legal, but it was none the less real and significant. When Tiberius left Rome and secluded himself at Capri a profound change took place in his relations with the senate and the nobility. Hitherto, following the example of his predecessor, he had been readily accessible to the conscript fathers and had taken an active part in their proceedings; he had carefully avoided the appearance of dictation, and had at times yielded to their manifest wishes, thus allowing them to feel that their views were an important factor in shaping the policy of the government. While he was present at their debates they could defer to him as the most eminent of their number without feeing any deep humiliation, but, when they were forced to bow to the upstart favourite of an absent monarch, the fact that their opinions no longer mattered was too plain to be disguised, so that in their submission to Sejanus they first realized that they were the helpless

---

[1] In this case, that of the three knights of whom Tacitus calls one innocent the combination of the three may have been due to their common rank, though a common charge against them is suggested.

subjects of an autocrat. The yoke may have been no heavier than in the past, but they became acutely conscious of it and hated Tiberius as though he had invented it and imposed it upon them. A constitution has its true existence in the minds of men rather than in laws, and a profound change of sentiment may make a new form of government without the alteration of a word in any document. In the last years of Tiberius the principate seemed to the Roman nobles to have been transformed into something new and odious, and it was inevitable that they should lay the blame upon the emperor. The ancient world had little perception of political or economic causes, and events were generally explained by the personalities of their chief actors. It was natural, therefore, to attribute to the wickedness of Tiberius the disastrous results of his reign, even if those results were mainly lost illusions. To suppose, as some have done,[1] that he left behind him the reputation of a just and able ruler, and that Tacitus first persuaded men to regard him as a tyrant, seems patently absurd. A rhetorician, setting out to reverse the views of his contemporaries as to the character of an emperor who occupied a prominent place in history, would have smoothed out inconsistencies, and omitted such details as did not fit his general design whenever their omission was possible. Tacitus has done neither of these things with the care and efficiency which come of deliberate dishonesty, and hence we must conclude that he simply accepted the conception of Tiberius which he found prevalent.[2] He told the truth as he saw it and was scrupulous in matters of detail. He would not make a positive assertion without what he considered adequate evidence, nor suppress what he believed was proved even though it seemed out of harmony with his picture, but he did, more or less unconsciously, present recalcitrant facts in such a way that they would make upon the reader what he regarded as the right impression. Thus in the end, while, on the one hand, by his literary genius he was able to stamp his portrait of Tiberius on the minds of men for centuries, on the other, he supplied the materials for a more impartial and sober judgement.

But if the picture of Tiberius which lived in men's memories was strangely distorted, we need to consider its development a

---

[1] Jerome, for instance.　　　　[2] Boissier, 114–27.

little more fully. As has just been said, the fact that under him the way was prepared for the later tyranny was enough to create a Tiberian legend. We may, however, surmise that it was not until the reign of Domitian that this legend was completely elaborated. At any rate there is little trace of it in those writers who were contemporaries of Tiberius or who grew up while many who had known him were still living. There is no suggestion of a tyrant in Philo, and neither Seneca nor the elder Pliny in referring to Tiberius gives any hint of the worst features of his character as drawn by Suetonius and Tacitus.[1] For this final development Domitian was probably in large part responsible. He was a constant reader of the memoirs and writings of Tiberius,[2] and this fact was not likely to be overlooked when in the latter part of his reign he aroused the deadly fear and hatred of the aristocracy. It would then be natural enough for the cowering nobility to picture the recluse of Capri as bearing a close resemblance to his admirer, and to ascribe to Tiberius the same suspicious cruelty and the same vices with which they were familiar in Domitian. Moreover, there were circumstances which rendered such a transfer of qualities singularly easy. The real tragedies of the reign of Tiberius furnished a basis for wild exaggeration, and the seclusion of his last years gave free play to imaginations inspired by hatred. In addition to this there was no longer a living tradition handed down from those who had known Tiberius personally. The great houses of his time which had enjoyed his favour had almost all become extinct. The Flavian senate was largely composed of men whose ancestors had occupied a comparatively humble station in the days of the early Caesars. The old families which survived were too few to influence the hostile tide of opinion in the new aristocracy or to check its extravagances, and some of them cherished grievances of their own against Tiberius. Thus the legend readily gained complete credence and so impressed itself upon the mind of Tacitus that the study of the records failed to change his preconceived ideas.

[1] Martial does not attack Tiberius, probably because of Domitian's attitude, and Juvenal likewise spares him, perhaps because the poet belonged to the lower middle class rather than the aristocracy.

[2] Suet., *Domitian*, 20. The writings (*acta*) would be his speeches, letters, decrees, &c.

Whether such a man as Tacitus has pictured could exist at all we need not discuss.[1] That Tiberius was not such a man the record seems to prove beyond reasonable doubt. Most of the charges against him are refuted by the facts: he did not nurse the law of treason, but struggled steadily against its extension; he did not encourage delation, but punished false accusers to the last; he was not cruel or bent upon a stern severity. For years his government was singularly lenient, and even in his last years the number of his victims seems very small when we consider what had passed and the real danger of his isolated position. Tacitus will have it that his gloomy temper led him to brood over his resentments for years and then break out in sudden vengeance, yet in every case where this charge is made, the supposed victim of these old grudges had been guilty of some fresh offence. That he forgave his enemies cannot be asserted, but there is nothing in the record to prove that he was implacable or vindictive. That he was suspicious there is exceedingly little to show. Augustus in his last days warned Tiberius of several possible pretenders to the throne; one of these, Cn. Piso, was trusted in an important post; another, Manius Lepidus, was honoured and respected till his death; a third, L. Arruntius, was allowed to live unmolested until the emperor himself was dying, and the Romans believed that the 'suspicious tyrant' was ignorant of his fate.[2] Asinius Gallus it is true was imprisoned by Tiberius, but only after many years of immunity and for reasons which remain obscure. Nor is the charge of hypocrisy any better sustained. It seems to have been based chiefly on the emperor's bearing in the senate, which was misunderstood by a later generation, and perhaps in some degree by contemporaries as well. At the accession of Tiberius the republican forms still possessed some vitality and he was sincerely anxious to preserve the independence of the senate. With this object in view he was forced on many occasions to hide his real feelings and opinions under ambiguous phrases for fear of influencing unduly the decisions of the conscript fathers.

[1] It is difficult to believe that a man who has kept up the appearance of virtue till he was nearly seventy would then drop the mask. If he did, we can only suppose that in his last days his mind to some extent gave way.

[2] *Ann.* 6, 47.

Tacitus tells us that while his language was usually guarded even to hesitation so that his words seemed to struggle forth with difficulty, yet when he acted mercifully he spoke with readiness and fluency.[1] The historian is somewhat puzzled by the contrast and fails to see the obvious explanation, namely that, when Tiberius intervened in the proceedings by virtue of his imperial prerogatives, he bore himself naturally, since it was impossible to disguise his interference. By the time of Tacitus the senate had become accustomed to the open and constant assertion of the imperial authority, and it was easy for those who disliked the memory of Tiberius to construe his attempts to respect the freedom of that body as evidence of hypocrisy.

The real faults of Tiberius seem to have been quite different. A Roman of the old school, he had little sympathy with the prevailing tendencies of the generation in which he lived, and ignored too much the smaller arts of popularity. A blunt soldier, he found the part of princeps as designed by Augustus an irksome and difficult one to play. He lacked the genial tact which had enabled his predecessor to smooth over and disguise unpleasant realities and to keep up agreeable fictions. He hated flattery and strove to maintain the independence of the senate, but disposing as he did of the patronage of the empire, he could accomplish little. In his heart he despised his contemporaries, and took too little pains to conceal his feelings. On several occasions he failed to realize, or wilfully ignored, the effect of his conduct on the public mind, as, for example, when he absented himself from the funeral of Germanicus. Whatever his reasons for leaving Rome, his long seclusion at Capri was a serious blunder, since it destroyed the illusion on which the principate was based. His blind confidence in Sejanus seems to show a real lack of discernment; perhaps it indicates that, although Tiberius was a shrewd judge of ability, he had little insight into character.[2] But the most formidable obstacle to a successful reign was the fatal question of the succession. It is true that the arrangements of Augustus placed Tiberius in a

---

[1] *Ann.* 4, 31.

[2] None of his appointees seem to have lacked intellectual capacity. Piso, however, was temperamentally unfit for the role assigned him, and, if we may accept Tacitus' judgement, Macro was morally unworthy.

very difficult position, but it is hard to escape the impression
that the problem might have been more skilfully handled.
After the death of Germanicus and Drusus the situation was
undoubtedly delicate: a loyal heir apparent was an invaluable
support, and a disloyal one a real danger to the emperor. Perhaps
no one could have avoided a quarrel with Agrippina; certainly
Tiberius was not the man to do it. After it came, however, the
emperor seemed unable to grasp the realities of the situation
and drifted to a disaster which a man of clearer insight or fewer
scruples would have prevented or minimized. His apparent
plan to make Sejanus emperor-regent for Nero might have been
possible if Agrippina had been promptly banished as soon as
the breach between her and Tiberius became irreconcilable,
for left to himself Nero might have proved pliable, and in that
case Sejanus might have been willing to accept him as the
ultimate heir. But such an arrangement was hopeless if Agrippina remained in Rome and was a bitter enemy of the minister.
It is no credit to the judgement of Tiberius that he failed to
realize this even when Sejanus, by seeking to marry Livilla,
had clearly shown his hand. After that, if the emperor still
wished his minister to follow him, he should have seen that he
must set aside the Julian line in favour of the Claudian; on the
other hand, if he still felt bound by his pledges to Augustus, he
should have sought a successor friendly to Agrippina. As it was,
he hesitated and would come to no decision; he clung to Sejanus,
without repudiating Nero or banishing Agrippina, and a tragedy
was the inevitable result. It seems almost incredible that so
astute a man as Tiberius entirely overlooked conditions and
consequences so obvious. Probably he foresaw that Agrippina
would ruin herself and her son, and merely waited until he felt
that they had so completely forfeited all claim on his for-
bearance that none could question the justice of their fall.[1] He
allowed Nero's younger brother Drusus to be imprisoned in the
palace, and the way seemed clear for the substitution of the
Claudian line. Yet it may be doubted if Tiberius ever really
contemplated such a step, for the only thing which points in

[1] Gaius, when emperor, produced the charges sent to Tiberius against his
mother and brothers, and defended the emperor on the ground that he could
not reject such a mass of testimony (Suet., *Gaius*, 30).

this direction is his tardy sanction of the betrothal of Sejanus and Livilla.[1] If Tiberius really intended to permit the marriage, which is somewhat doubtful, he must have foreseen that Livilla would make a desperate effort to secure the throne for her own son. Perhaps Sejanus had succeeded in sowing distrust of Gaius in the emperor's mind, but, if so, the distrust was of short duration. It may have been these machinations against Gaius which Antonia revealed to the old and secluded monarch. Whatever the nature of her revelation, it convinced Tiberius that he had been deceived by his trusted minister, and the fall of Sejanus was the consequence. This event saved Gaius, and the emperor gave up any plan he may have had of changing the succession. For the deaths of Agrippina and Nero Tiberius was probably not responsible. If Nero had lived he might have been restored to his former place, since it is not unlikely that the charges against him had been greatly exaggerated and that Tiberius finally realized this. For the death of Drusus the plea of state necessity can be made, whatever such a plea is worth. Certainly the emperor cannot reasonably be blamed for punishing those who had been guilty of real crimes in connexion with the long series of intrigues of which Sejanus was the instigator. The record seems to prove that Tiberius tried to secure justice and did not intentionally oppress the innocent. There is nothing to show that there was any fundamental change in either his character or his conduct; if in the last years of his reign there were more suicides and executions, the most simple and natural explanation is that many crimes had come to light, and that the isolated position of the emperor led to more frequent conspiracies. Yet the number who suffered was small, and if there was terror in Rome it was due rather to the guilty consciences of those who escaped than to the cruelty of Tiberius.

Yet it cannot be denied that, in spite of his ability and his good intentions, Tiberius failed in his role of princeps, and that the constitution of Augustus broke down in his hands. For this failure he was not wholly or even chiefly responsible, but it is impossible not to feel that a man of greater tact and more

---

[1] It is possible that this was sanctioned only after the overthrow of Sejanus was determined on, and that it was intended merely to lull the minister into a false sense of security.

winning manners might have reconciled the feuds in the imperial family, or at least have kept them within bounds, and that Tiberius committed a grave blunder in not dealing more promptly and firmly with the question of the succession. Sejanus was certainly the evil genius of the emperor, and but for him the reign might have had a happier ending, for it is at least possible that the tragic ruin of the house of Germanicus might have been averted it if had not been for the sinister influence of the favourite. As a result of his blind confidence in an unscrupulous minister, Tiberius, as princeps, was defeated in most of his aims. He tried to maintain the independence of the senate, but he left it more subservient than ever; he sought to restrain delation, but it steadily developed, and even if he was not himself a tyrant, it was under him that the apparatus of the later tyranny took shape; he made a sincere effort to preserve the republican monarchy of Augustus, but it was transformed into the despotism of the later Caesars, and it was this last fact which, perhaps, contributed most to blast his memory.

It only remains to attempt some general estimate of Tiberius as a ruler of the empire, and of the permanent value of his work. We may do this with some confidence because, in spite of the scantiness of our information, we know enough to discern clearly and unmistakably the broad outlines of his policy. In foreign affairs he abandoned all thought of expansion and sought to maintain peace without in any degree sacrificing the security of the frontiers; at home he preferred to meet the financial difficulties of the government by rigid economy rather than by an increase in taxation, and he was so successful that he was able to accumulate a large reserve from which he could meet emergencies without the sudden imposition of new burdens; he fostered commerce and the general prosperity, not only by keeping down taxation, but also by improving the existing means of communication, and there can be no doubt that in this way he hoped to hasten the spread of civilization and the Romanization of the newly acquired provinces; he laboured earnestly and intelligently to give the empire a just, honest, and efficient administration and to root out the abuses which still lingered as an inheritance from republican times; in addition to all this he put the relations between Rome and her subject

peoples on a new and better footing by his generous recognition
of her obligation to assist them when they were overtaken by
calamity, and by the encouragement which he gave to the
provincial assemblies to make known the wishes, and voice the
complaints, of the provinces. In the pursuit of these aims he
did not hesitate to face misunderstanding and unpopularity.
His economy displeased the rabble of the capital, and perhaps
many of the higher classes as well; his peaceful policy abroad
was certainly offensive to a large and influential section of the
aristocracy; the long tenure of office which he accorded to
competent and successful governors was viewed with profound
disfavour by the senate; and the political role assumed by the
provincial assemblies must have been a source of irritation to
the nobles, who would naturally resent the criticism of their
conduct by those whom they regarded as inferiors. At a later
time we have evidence of how keenly the conscript fathers felt
the necessity, which the activity of these assemblies imposed
upon them, of stooping to conciliate the provincials,[1] and we
cannot doubt that Tiberius provoked much ill-will and aroused
many painful misgivings by his course. Nevertheless, although
he was well aware that in nearly every phase of his policy he
was antagonizing some more or less powerful group in Rome,
he resolutely adhered to it in spite of the steadily growing
opposition. On one occasion he declared that he was ready to
face resentment, no matter how bitter or unjust, in the interest
of the commonwealth,[2] and his conduct fully demonstrated that
this declaration was no idle boast. In justice to him we are
forced to recognize that he gave the empire over twenty years
of peaceful prosperity, that he introduced drastic reforms into
the provincial administration, and that in doing so he deliberately
sacrificed his own popularity.

In viewing the policy of Tiberius as a whole we cannot avoid
the conviction that it was based upon a far-sighted statesmanship and a clear perception of the crying needs of the empire.
Under Caesar and Augustus such extensive annexations had
taken place that Rome imperatively required a period of peace
during which she could assimilate her new possessions, and to

---

[1] See the speech of Thrasea Paetus, in A.D. 62 (*Ann.* 15, 20–2).
[2] *Ann.* 3, 54.

attempt new conquests before this had been accomplished might easily have overtaxed her strength and endangered the very foundations of her power. Whatever his motives may have been, Tiberius served his country well in putting aside all thought of military glory and devoting his energies to the consolidation of her hold upon what his predecessors had won. As a result he left the empire immensely strengthened, for civilization made steady progress and a new generation grew up which associated the dominion of Rome with peace, prosperity, and good government. He found a Gaul where a rising against Rome was still a possibility, and he left one which was ready for a large extension of Roman citizenship by Claudius. In his efforts to reform the provincial administration he also accomplished durable results. He succeeded in impressing a new standard of integrity and moderation on a reluctant official class, and the tradition which he did so much to establish survived him. This may have been due in large part to the fact that in the provincial assemblies he developed an efficient check upon official abuses, and at the same time, by bringing the provincials into close touch with the emperor, he inspired a new loyalty on the one side and a new interest on the other. The provincial administration continued for many years to move along the lines which he had determined, regardless of the personality of the ruling prince, and it was largely because of this that the world suffered so little serious damage from Caligula or Nero. If we look at Tiberius as he appeared to all the world except the conscript fathers and the populace of Rome, it will be difficult, if not impossible, to deny his claim to a place among the best and greatest of the emperors.

APPENDIXES

I. THE SOURCES OF TACITUS

A READING of the historical works of. Tacitus leaves the impression that they are the result of considerable research and a careful comparison of the writings of his predecessors in the field. The accuracy of this impression has, however, been seriously challenged, and against it has been set up what may be termed the single source theory. As the controversy has been carried on almost entirely in French and German, it may be worth while to examine briefly the questions at issue. The scholar who has given the fullest exposition of the single source theory is Fabia,[1] and we may confine our attention chiefly to a consideration of some of his principal arguments.

Briefly stated, Fabia's theory is that Tacitus in composing both the *Histories* and the *Annals* simply rewrote with more or less condensation the work of some earlier author, and that he made scarcely any use of any other writers. It is admitted that Tacitus sometimes consulted other works and compared their version of events with that given in his main source, but Fabia contends that he did this only occasionally. The greater part, enormously the greater part, of his material was taken bodily from a single work, and nearly all his references to other accounts or to different opinions were simply copied from it. Thus, when Tacitus tells us that most writers give a certain version of Galba's last words, he has merely transcribed this statement from his single source, and we have no right to conclude that he had ever read more than one account of the death of Galba. Fabia holds that Tacitus used the work of Aufidius Bassus as his *source principale* for the first books of the *Annals* and that of Cluvius Rufus for the last, while for all the extant portion of the *Histories* he based his narrative on the history of the elder Pliny. In the *Histories* Fabia contends not only that he used Pliny, but that he hardly looked at any other work; in the *Annals* he made a slightly greater use of secondary sources, yet here too their part is really insignificant and Tacitus only consulted them when he found his chief source unsatisfactory upon some point.

If we ask for the evidence on which these conclusions rest, we

---

[1] His book on the sources of Tacitus was published in 1893 and has met with a varied reception. Andresen in his edition of *Nipperdey's Tacitus* calls it the 'grundlegende Werk auf diesem Gebiete' (i. 27, note 1); Rosenberg accepts the conclusions as to the *Histories*, but finds the treatment of the *Annals* less convincing (258); and Groag sharply criticizes the entire theory. All references to Fabia in this appendix are to *Les Sources de Tacite*.

find that it is of two kinds. In the first place we are informed that this was the universal method of writing history among the Romans and that they never dreamed that any other was possible. As proof of this assertion we are told that Nissen has shown that Livy employed this method and that the younger Pliny in his letters assumed it to be the only one. The case of Livy need not detain us here, for, even granting that he followed a single source (which is not what Nissen maintains),[1] his practice would not justify a universal statement about all Roman historians. The methods of H. G. Wells are not those of all English historians, and whatever Livy may have done in a history covering some 750 years, it would by no means prove that Tacitus must have written his works, whose scope is very much more restricted, in the same way.[2] The citation from the letters of Pliny is more significant. The success attending the publication by Tacitus of the first books of the *Histories* moved Pliny to consider seriously undertaking some similar work. But there were difficulties in the way, for if he took a recent subject never before treated, he ran the risk of giving offence and could expect little thanks, while if he chose one already handled by others, though their investigations would save him much trouble, the work of comparing their accounts would be laborious. The Latin is here worth citing verbatim and not merely in paraphrase. Asking what subject to choose, Pliny continues: *vetera et scripta aliis? parata inquisitio sed onerosa collatio: intacta et nova? graves offensae, levis gratia* (*Epist.* 5, 8). From this Nissen draws the conclusion that it never occurred to Pliny that it was necessary to go back to the primary sources if these had been already examined; all that needed to be done was to compare the secondary accounts based upon them.[3] Fabia reiterates this conclusion,[4] but it seems to me rather too sweeping. We are hardly warranted in saying that Pliny regarded reference to the archives as unnecessary, but only that he thought that a previous investigation of them would save a great deal of trouble. He would not be obliged to read through the entire mass of the *acta senatus*, for example, since the works of his predecessors would furnish him a guide as to where to look and what to look for. Thus if Tacitus found in previous writers no mention of any proceedings in the senate during a given year which he cared to record it was unnecessary for him to examine the *acta senatus* for that year. If he did find three or four

---

[1] Nissen, *Kritische Untersuchungen*, 340–1. A glance at this table makes it clear that Nissen did not maintain that Livy followed a single source in the fashion that Fabia contends that Tacitus did.

[2] Furneaux (i. 24, note 9) raises this point.

[3] Nissen, *Die Historien*, 501.   [4] Fabia, 117.

debates or trials of which he wished to give an account,[1] he could restrict his inspection to the documents relating to those proceedings. But even if we assume that Pliny meant what Nissen construes him to mean, Fabia has gone a step further. He repeatedly informs us that the ideas of Pliny were the same as those of Tacitus, and then attempts to prove that Tacitus made no *onerosa collatio* at all. Yet surely Pliny cannot have meant that all that was necessary was to take a single book and rewrite it. It seems clear from this passage that it never occurred to Pliny that history could be written in the way in which, according to Fabia, his intimate friend was writing it. In the first two books of the *Histories* Fabia thinks that there are no traces that Tacitus ever consulted any other work than that of the elder Pliny. There are, it is true, two short passages in these books which Tacitus added to his *source principale* (1, 11 on the administration of Egypt, and 2, 38 on the progress of ambition at Rome), but they were added from his own general knowledge and not as a result of the consultation of other works while writing his own. In Book III Tacitus has made some slight use of Messalla, but has taken very little from him and has added one anecdote of the civil war between Pompey and Caesar from Sisenna (51). For the rest of the book he has added one or two details from his personal knowledge or from oral tradition (38–9, 71, 74, 75). In Book IV he has added a digression on the Batavians from Pliny's German Wars (12) and one on Serapis from a Greek source (83–4) and one or two details from personal knowledge or oral tradition (5–6, 48, 50, 67, 81). In the part of the fifth book that has survived he has added two details from oral tradition (5, 13).[2] In sum, besides a few details from his own personal knowledge or oral tradition, he has glanced at Messalla and at Pliny's work on the German wars.[3] Certainly by no stretch of language can this be called a laborious comparison. The younger Pliny must have been exceptionally indolent to have been deterred by this. If his testimony proves anything as to the methods of his friend, it is that Tacitus did not write his history according to the single source method.

But such general arguments have comparatively little weight. If Fabia can prove that Tacitus *did* follow this method, it matters little what Livy did or what the younger Pliny thought, so it is to Fabia's

[1] In A.D. 18 Tacitus has actually recorded nothing which took place in the senate; in A.D. 16 he has given an account of one trial and four debates.

[2] Fabia, 259–61.

[3] Neither the anecdote from Sisenna nor the digression on Serapis can be said to involve any comparison, as they are from works treating of different subjects.

supposed proof that Tacitus actually followed the single source
method that our main attention must be devoted. This proof is
found chiefly in a comparison of Tacitus, Plutarch, and Suetonius
for the reigns of Galba and Otho. To me, at any rate, it seems that
this comparison leads to results very different from the conclusions
which Fabia draws from it. On one point, however, I can heartily
agree: Fabia's arguments seem to show conclusively that all three
writers made extensive use of a common source, and that they did
not use each other. If this were the point at issue, I should be quite
ready to admit that Fabia had settled it, but he has attempted to
prove much more than this. His theory requires not only that
Tacitus and Plutarch should have used a common source extensively,
but that this source should have been practically their only source.[1]
He declares explicitly that in the first two books of the *Histories* he
can find no evidence that Tacitus consulted any work except the
common source. The comparison with Plutarch having shown, as
Fabia thinks, that in the *Histories* Tacitus followed the single source
method, it remains to consider the *Annals*. Here we have no material
for a comparison, so another sort of proof must be devised. This is
found in the two different accounts which Tacitus has given, in the
Histories and in the *Annals*, of the relations between Nero, Otho, and
Poppaea. From the fact that their relations are given differently in
the two works Fabia concludes that Tacitus has followed his single
source unquestioningly in both cases, but that he did not follow the
same source in the *Annals* and in the *Histories*. If then, he argues, we
find Tacitus using a single source at the beginning and at the end of
his career as a historian, we are justified in assuming that he followed
one throughout. It is evident that the whole force of the argument
depends upon the demonstration that Tacitus did use the single
source method in the *Histories*. If that has not been proved, even
Fabia would, I should imagine, be forced to admit that the reasonable explanation of the discrepancy between the *Annals* and the
Histories is that in the interval between the two works Tacitus
had changed his mind on the matter in question. Personally I think
this the reasonable explanation in any case, but it would surely
seem so unless the single source method is demonstrated for the
Histories.

As so much hinges on this particular matter, it will be well to
begin with a comparison of the various accounts of the relations
between Nero, Otho, and Poppaea. Of the five that have been preserved we may ignore that of Dio, since we have only the epitome and

[1] Fabia, 144–5, admits the use of other sources by Suetonius.

since Dio may have used the others. The four remaining accounts are as follows:[1]

Tacitus, *Histories*, 1, 13.

'For Otho, after a neglected boyhood, and an ill-regulated youth, had won Nero's favour by emulating his vices. Thus it was that Nero had left his favourite mistress, Poppaea Sabina, with Otho, as a confidant in his love affairs, until such time as he could put his wife Octavia out of the way. After a time, however, becoming suspicious of Otho's relations with that same lady, he secluded him, under pretence of a Legateship, in Lusitania.'

Tacitus, *Annals*, 13, 45–6.

'Thus while still the wife of Rufrius Crispinus, a Roman Knight, to whom she (Poppaea) had borne a son, she was won over by the youth and fervour of Otho, knowing also that he stood high in Nero's favour; nor was it long before marriage followed on the adultery. Otho was for ever boasting to Nero of his wife's charms and beauty; whether out of mere lover's thoughtlessness, or because he wished to kindle his desires in the hope that the joint possession of Poppaea might be a bond to strengthen his influence with the young prince. He was often heard to say, on quitting the Emperor's table that, *He was going to Poppaea—a woman who had brought to him birth and beauty ; what all men pray for, and only the fortunate enjoy.* Under incitements such as these, delay was short. Admitted to the Emperor's presence, Poppaea made her way at first by artful blandishments, affecting inability to withstand his love, and to be enamoured of his beauty . . . Otho's former intimacy with the Emperor was now broken off. Before long he was excluded from his company and his suite; and in the end, to prevent his remaining in Rome as a rival, he was appointed to the province of Lusitania.'

Suetonius, *Otho*, 3.

'He (Otho) was privy to all the emperor's plans and secrets . . . Also when Poppaea Sabina, who up to that time had been Nero's mistress, was separated from her husband and turned over for the time being to Otho, he pretended marriage with her; but not content with seducing her he became so devoted that he could not endure the thought of having Nero even as a rival. At all events it is believed that he not only would not admit those whom Nero sent to fetch her, but that on one occasion he even shut out the emperor himself, who

---

[1] In the translations which follow I have quoted the versions of Tacitus from Ramsay, that of Suetonius from Rolfe, and that of Plutarch from Perrin.

stood before his door, vainly mingling threats and entreaties and demanding the return of his trust. Therefore Nero annulled the marriage and under colour of an appointment as governor banished Otho to Lusitania, contenting himself with this through fear that by inflicting a severer punishment he would make the whole farce public; but even as it was, it was published abroad in this couplet:

> Why, do you ask, in feigned honour does Otho in banishment
> languish?
> With his own wedded wife he had begun an intrigue.'

Plutarch, Galba, 19–20.

'Marcus Otho, now, was a man of good lineage, but from his very childhood corrupted by luxury and the pursuit of pleasure as few Romans were. And as Homer often calls Paris 'the husband of fair-haired Helen', giving him a dignity borrowed from his wife, since he had no other title to fame, so Otho was celebrated at Rome for his marriage with Poppaea. With Poppaea Nero was enamoured while she was the wife of Crispinus, but since he respected his own wife still and feared his mother, he put Otho up to soliciting her favours for him. For because of Otho's lavish prodigality Nero made an intimate friend of him, and was well pleased to be rallied by him often for parsimony and meanness . . . But as for Poppaea, Otho corrupted her with hopes of Nero's favour and seduced her first himself, and persuaded her to leave her husband. However, after she had come to live with him as his wife, he was not content to have only a share in her favours, and was loth to give Nero a share, while Poppaea herself, as we are told ,was not displeased at the rivalry between them. For it is said that she would shut out Nero although Otho was not at home; whether it was that she sought to keep his pleasure in her from cloying, or whether, as some say, she recoiled from a marriage with the emperor, but was not averse to having him as a lover, out of mere wantonness. Otho, accordingly, came into peril of his life; and it was strange that although his own wife and sister were put to death by Nero on account of his marriage with Poppaea, Otho himself was spared. But Otho had the good will of Seneca, by whose advice and persuasion Nero sent him out as governor of Lusitania to the shores of the western ocean.'

A comparison of these four accounts will show that we have here three quite different versions of the affair. Plutarch and Suetonius are clearly in conflict with each other; Plutarch indeed makes Nero fall in love with Poppaea before her marriage with Otho, but yet makes her the mistress of Otho before she is that of Nero, while Suetonius states that she was the mistress of Nero first. The explanations which they furnish of the marriage are also different; according to Suetonius Nero contrives the marriage, which is intended as a mere form and is designed to provide for Poppaea till he can get rid of his own wife; while according to Plutarch the marriage is contrived by Otho in the hope of gaining the favour of Nero through a woman with whom he knows that the emperor is in love. Now it seems clear that in the *Histories* Tacitus agrees not with Plutarch but with Suetonius; he makes Poppaea the mistress of Nero before her marriage with Otho, and implies clearly that the marriage was at Nero's instigation and was intended as a mere form. Fabia thinks that when Tacitus says that Nero became suspicious of the relations of Otho with Poppaea and banished him, he is alluding to the story of Plutarch.[1] With this I cannot agree. There is indeed a *sous entendu* in the words, but they refer plainly to the story as given by Suetonius. To say that Nero grew suspicious of the relations of Otho with Poppaea is quite intelligible if Nero had contrived the marriage intending it as a mere form, but it is meaningless if Otho had contrived the marriage in the fashion that Plutarch says. There is no hint in Plutarch that Nero was responsible for the marriage or that he had any reason to think that it was a mere form. What cause then did he have for suspicion? To me it seems clear that when he wrote the *Histories* Tacitus accepted a version of the story substantially like that given in much greater detail by Suetonius. Moreover, on the point of the danger to Otho Tacitus again agrees with Suetonius and not with Plutarch. Plutarch distinctly asserts that Otho was in peril of his life but was saved by the intervention of Seneca. Suetonius denies any real danger and gives an excellent reason why Nero could not treat him with severity. In this passage Tacitus ignores the danger altogether. This might be explained as due to brevity were it not that in another passage he ignores it a second time. Otho was urged to conspire against Galba by various soothsayers, prominent among whom was a certain Ptolemy. This astrologer had already gained credit with Otho by a successful prophecy which is given by Plutarch as a prediction that Nero would not kill him. This is a clear reference to his danger, but this reference Tacitus eliminates entirely, saying that the prophecy was merely that Otho would survive Nero.[2] If Fabia is right both writers took their account from the same source, but if so, Tacitus has first left out any hint of danger to Otho and has then altered the prophecy of Ptolemy to accord with his omission. The two changes

[1] Fabia, 13.
[2] *Hist.*, 1, 22, and Plut., *Galba*, 23.

taken together can hardly have been other than intentional, and suggest the use by Tacitus of other works.

My own conclusion is that Plutarch and Tacitus (in the *Histories*) cannot both have drawn their accounts from the same source, but that Tacitus and Suetonius may have done so. In that case either Tacitus or Plutarch has substituted another version of the story for that given in their common source. Later, when he wrote the *Annals*, Tacitus had seen reason to change his mind, but did not think it necessary to comment on the discrepancy, which he may have forgotten.

In this comparison no reason has appeared for concluding that Tacitus followed the single source method even in the *Histories*. If we extend the comparison other differences of the same sort appear. As might be expected *a priori*, such a comparison is only productive of definite results at a few points. The common source, whatever it was, has perished. Both Tacitus and Plutarch presumably chose it because they thought it generally reliable, and they are naturally in frequent agreement with each other. Differences there are, but they are not all of such a sort as to justify any conclusion. Tacitus was writing a general history, while Plutarch was composing a biography, and as a natural consequence one has given many incidents which the other has omitted. Even where they both recount the same incident, one might easily omit details which the other preserved. Thus, when they both describe how Galba offered sacrifice on the last morning of his life and reign, the difference in the audiences for which they wrote would adequately account for certain differences in the details. Tacitus, writing for Romans, did not think it worth while to state that the sacrifice was in the morning, but does give the name of the temple. Plutarch, writing for Greeks, is more precise as to the time but less so as to the place. Such differences would only show that neither felt bound to reproduce every detail in the common source, but each made a selection according to his own taste or the supposed interest of his readers.

There are, however, some differences which seem to me to prove that, while both writers used a common source, they compared this source with other accounts and made additions and corrections freely as a result of this comparison. A brief consideration of two episodes will make this clear and will be sufficient for the present purpose.

In their accounts of the adoption of Piso,[1] Plutarch and Tacitus differ markedly in the following particulars:

1. Tacitus gives the promise of Otho to marry the daughter of Vinius as a mere piece of gossip which he evidently thinks unworthy

---

[1] Plut., *Galba*, 21 and 23; *Hist.*, i, 13–19.

of credit, while Plutarch gives it as a fact about which there was no doubt. Did the common source express a doubt which Plutarch has suppressed? Or did Tacitus add the doubt, and if so, why? Fabia can hardly admit that Tacitus added the doubt, because this would imply that he had examined other accounts and found the story to have little or no foundation, and an examination of other works is precisely the thing of which Fabia can find no evidence in this book of the *Histories*.[1] We seem forced to conclude, then, that Plutarch has given as solid fact what his only source of information gave as worthless gossip. That Plutarch was careless and inaccurate may be admitted, but this seems rather an extreme instance.

2. Tacitus says that Galba adopted Piso before anything definite was known about Vitellius. Plutarch says it was the news of the proclamation of Vitellius as emperor that decided Galba to make the adoption. This might pass as a mere slip of the pen on the part of Plutarch if this difference stood alone; however, it does not stand alone.

3. Plutarch states that some of Galba's friends favoured Dolabella, of whose candidacy Tacitus says not one word. Here again if this were the only difference, we might explain it as a detail omitted by Tacitus.[2]

4. Plutarch says that Galba selected Piso without consulting any one. Tacitus says that Galba did so either of his own initiative, or as some believed (*ut quidam crediderunt*) at the suggestion of Laco, who, though an old friend of Piso, falsely pretended not to know him. Here the explanation of Fabia that Plutarch simplified and exaggerated[3] seems wholly inadmissible. Plutarch had the common source before him as he wrote, and if it contained the statement about Laco it seems incredible that Plutarch could have said what he did. To me there seems but one reasonable conclusion in the matter, namely that Tacitus has added to the common source at this point.

5. Tacitus gives a considerable number of details about the proceedings in the senate relative to the adoption, all of which are omitted by Plutarch.

The omissions noted above under 3 and 5 would by themselves prove nothing, but they are not without force when taken in connexion with the positive discrepancies. There are, however, such differences in the accounts of the adoption of Piso and of the relations

---

[1] Fabia (15) passes this point over very lightly, merely saying that Tacitus is less positive than Plutarch. It seems to me to merit more attention.

[2] Fabia, 20, seems to regard it in this light.   [3] Fabia, 20.

K

of Nero, Otho, and Poppaea as make it impossible for me to believe
that both the accounts of Tacitus and Plutarch can have been taken
from a single source. It seems clear that one or both of them
modified and added freely to the common source as a result of a more
or less extensive comparison with other works. If we assume that
Plutarch has reproduced the common source accurately, then it
seems clear that Tacitus has substituted a different version of the
relations between Nero, Otho, and Poppaea, and has modified the
prophecy of Ptolemy to fit; that he has been led to regard the story
of Otho's promise to marry the daughter of Vinius as a mere bit of
idle gossip and says so, and that he has added the statement about
Laco. As to the candidacy of Dolabella, Tacitus may have omitted
it as unimportant, while the details about the senate may have been
left out by Plutarch because he had little interest in that body.

Another episode in the reign of Galba which is worth examination
is its closing scene.[1] When the emperor began the day with the usual
sacrifices, the omens were unfavourable and pointed to conspiracies
against him. So far Plutarch and Tacitus agree so closely that we
cannot doubt that they were following a common source. But how
was Otho, who was near Galba at the time, affected by the omens?
Plutarch says that he changed colour with fear, while Tacitus
affirms that he was pleased at what he considered prophecies of his
success. Fabia's attempt to reconcile the two statements by saying
that Otho may have felt both emotions at once and that the common
source may have said so, seems to me, as it does to Groag,[2] singularly
unconvincing.

In the accounts of the murder of Galba there are likewise some
striking differences. Tacitus mentions only horsemen as being sent
to kill the emperor, while Plutarch affirms that there were both
cavalry and infantry. Tacitus gives two versions of Galba's last
words, while Plutarch gives only one. Plutarch says that Galba was
wounded in the arms and legs *before* he was killed, while Tacitus says
that it was after his death that these wounds were inflicted. Both
mention three men as having been named as the actual murderer, and
both agree that the most common account credited the deed to a
certain Camurius, but Plutarch adds a fourth name, that of Fabius
Fabulus, who cut off the head of Galba and carried it to Otho on a
spear. Tacitus does not mention Fabulus and is silent as to how the
head was taken to Otho, but he does say that it was afterwards
carried through the streets on a pole. Fabia explains the omission

---

[1] Plut., *Galba*, 24–7, and *Hist.*, 1, 27–44.
[2] Groag, 742–3, and Fabia, 25.

of Fabulus and how he brought the head to Otho by saying that
Tacitus has not described the horrible scene.[1] Tacitus has, however,
given enough details here and elsewhere to make it clear that the
omission is not due to any wish to spare himself or his readers
gruesome details, and it seems strange that he should have copied
three names and omitted the fourth. It can hardly have been merely
an accidental oversight on the part of Tacitus, because while in
Plutarch two of the other names are bare names and nothing more,
Fabulus is not only mentioned but a story of some length is told
concerning him. The simplest explanation is that the common source
gave only the three names which Tacitus has reproduced and that
Plutarch has added Fabulus to the list on the authority of some
other writer or writers.[2] Another difference is that Plutarch makes
Sempronius Densus defend Galba, while Tacitus says that he defended Piso. That there was a foundation for the version of Tacitus
is shown by Suetonius, who says explicitly that no one defended
Galba. In this case Fabia thinks that Plutarch was deceived by his
memory, but this explanation can hardly be accepted, since it seems
clear that Plutarch had the common source before him as he wrote;
the verbal similarities on which Fabia insists throughout the passage
show this if they show anything. Moreover, the order of events is
different in the two accounts: Tacitus places the incident of Densus
after the death of Vinius, while in Plutarch it comes just before the
death of Galba. Among other differences we may note that the
death of Laco is given differently as to both place and time, the
rumour of the death of Otho which induced Galba to leave the palace
is given without comment by Plutarch, while Tacitus says that
many thought it a ruse of the conspirators to lure the emperor out
of the palace,[3] and finally Plutarch gives the last words of Vinius as
certain, while Tacitus gives them as doubtful.

It would appear then that in the account of the death of Galba
there are such close resemblances between Plutarch and Tacitus as
to force us to conclude that they both used a common source as the
basis of their works, but at the same time there are such differences
as to show clearly that they compared this common source with
other accounts and modified it as a result. Here again as in the case

[1] Fabia, 32.
[2] I agree with Groag (744) that it is very strange that Plutarch can find
space for the names of all who were suspected of killing Galba but not for both
versions of his last words. I am inclined to think with him that the common
source gave only one version. Suetonius (*Galba*, 20) gives different details as
to the treatment of Galba's head.
[3] Suetonius says the rumour *was* a ruse of the Othonians.

of the account of the adoption of Piso and that of the relations between Nero, Otho, and Poppaea we have plain traces of such a
collatio as Pliny thought necessary for the writing of history. But
these are just the places in the first book of the *Histories* where we
have the best opportunity for making a comparison, and where
Fabia thinks the evidence for the single source theory is strongest.
If the theory fails here, it is unnecessary to carry the comparison
further. If Tacitus did not follow this method at the beginning of
his career as a historian, then there is no evidence that he ever
adopted it.

If it be accepted that Tacitus did make some sort of a *collatio* in
writing his *Histories*, we have still to ask how careful and how extensive it was. This is the more necessary because some scholars
who reject the single source theory have found grounds for thinking
that the study on which Tacitus based his works was somewhat
narrow and limited. On examination these grounds will, I think, be
found very inadequate.

As a first point in such an examination we must consider briefly
the general citations which are so common in Tacitus. Fabia holds
that most of them were taken at second-hand by the historian from
his main source. The argument for this view is based on two com-
parisons. Plutarch tells us that Otho wrote letters to the provincial
governors under the name of Nero Otho. As his authority for this
statement he cites Cluvius Rufus, who was governor of Spain at the
time.[1] Suetonius makes the same statement but gives his authority
in general terms, *ut quidam tradiderunt*[2]; from which Fabia concludes
that in such general citations in Roman writers the plural often
stands for a singular. It seems a little sweeping to say, as Fabia does,
that this conclusion is proved, but it is not at all impossible. It
seems too sweeping, since we have no evidence that other writers had
not made the same statement as well as Cluvius, and that Suetonius
had not seen it in other works. Nevertheless it does look as if both
Plutarch and Suetonius might here be citing the same authority, the
one by name and the other in a vague phrase. We may reasonably
conclude that we cannot in all cases feel entirely sure of the genuine
plurality of a vague plural citation.[3] It is very possible that Tacitus
may at times have written some expression like *ut quidam tradiderunt*
when he had in mind only a single author. More than this it would
seem rash to conclude.

[1] Plut., *Otho*, 3.   [2] Suet., *Otho*, 7.

[3] Suetonius was undoubtedly careless in his use of plurals (see appendix on
'Tacitus, Suetonius, and Dio'). Nevertheless, the clearest proof that Suetonius
did something is no evidence that Tacitus did the same.

Having used this first comparison to prove that in general citations the plural often stands for the singular, Fabia brings forward the last words of Galba to prove that such general citations were often copied second-hand from another author. The account of Tacitus is as follows: *extremam eius vocem, ut cuique odium aut admiratio fuit, varie prodidere. Alii suppliciter interrogasse, quid mali meruisset, et paucos dies exsolvendo donativo deprecatum: plures obtulisse ultro percussoribus iugulum: agerent ac ferirent, si ita e re publica videretur.* (*Hist.*, i. 41). Suetonius reports the matter in these words: *Sunt qui tradant, ad primum tumultum proclamasse eum: 'Quid agitis, commilitones? Ego vester sum et vos mei', donativum etiam pollicitum. Plures autem prodiderunt obtulisse ultro iugulum et ut hoc agerent ac ferirent, quando ita videretur, hortatum* (*Galba*, 20).

Here Fabia insists that the verbal similarities are so close that both writers must have copied almost verbatim from a common source. If this be so, he reasons that the *plures* (*prodiderunt*) was contained in that source and was simply transcribed from it by both writers, so that we have no reason to assume that either Tacitus or Suetonius had ever read any of these writers or knew anything about them except what was stated in their common source.[1] We may readily agree that this particular passage would not justify us in asserting that they *had* read the works which give the favourable version of Galba's last words, but does it warrant us in *denying* that they had? Granted that they did find the statement as to what most writers said in their common source, may they not have copied it precisely because they knew, from their reading, that it was true? It is clear that they did not hesitate to alter the common source and that they had read some other accounts at least, for they give the unfavourable version of Galba's last words differently. Moreover, either Suetonius has left out the *e re publica* and so quite spoiled the point of the favourable version, or else Tacitus has inserted these words from some other source. In view of these differences I do not see how we can conclude that neither had read any other account of the death of Galba than that in their common source, and unless we can reach that conclusion I do not see that the fact that they both copied the words *plures* (*prodiderunt*) proves anything of importance.

But though something must be conceded to Fabia in these two cases, it seems that he goes much too far when he assumes that all the general citations in Tacitus may safely be ignored. That they did sometimes represent a real comparison of several writers by the historian Fabia admits. Why one instance of copying such a reference

[1] Fabia, 149-50.

second-hand should reveal the habitual practice of Tacitus better than several instances where similar references were the result of real research on his part, I am unable to understand.

But Fabia has some grounds for thinking that even where Tacitus did compare various works the comparison was very much less extensive than we might at first glance imagine. In his account of the sack of Cremona Tacitus mentions only two authorities, Messalla and Pliny, from which Fabia argues that he had no others, and that neither Cluvius Rufus nor Fabius Rusticus had treated of this event.[1] The theory that there were but two authorities for this portion of the *Histories* has had considerable currency and is still regarded with favour.[2] The passage on which it is based reads as follows: 'Whether it was Hormus who made this suggestion (the offer to the Flavian soldiers of the plunder of the city of Cremona), as Messalla relates, or whether we should prefer the testimony of Gaius Plinius, who throws the blame on Antonius, I cannot readily determine; except that no act of infamy, however gross, would have been foreign to the life and character of either'.[3] The uncertainty of Tacitus is limited to one point, the name of the Flavian officer who made the infamous suggestion. The fact that Tacitus cites only two authorities may mean merely that but two writers had attempted to fix the responsibility.[4] To some it may have seemed unimportant what individual made the offer, while others may have thought it dangerous to discuss it; it was enough that the offer was made and acted upon. If other writers had passed the matter over in this way there was no reason for Tacitus to refer to them on this subject.

It seems to me, then, that in the first books of the *Histories* there is clear evidence that while Tacitus followed one writer[5] as his chief source and the basis for much of his narrative, he compared this account with those of other writers and made additions or modifications as a result. How many other writers Tacitus examined we have no means of knowing, but there is certainly no just ground for concluding that for the sack of Cremona he was using only two. Even if for this event Tacitus did consult two writers only, this may have

---

[1] Fabia, 177–8 and 211.   [2] Rosenberg, 258.

[3] *Hormine id ingenium, ut Messalla tradit, an potior auctor sit C. Plinius, qui Antonium incusat, haud facile discreverim, nisi quod neque Antonius neque Hormus a fama vitaque sua quamvis pessimo flagitio degeneravere (Hist.*, 3, 28) I quote from Ramsay's translation.   [4] Groag, 777.

[5] Who this writer was I shall not attempt to discuss. Mommsen proposed Cluvius Rufus; Nissen insisted strongly on the elder Pliny, and Fabia adopts this view with some new arguments; Groag rejects Pliny and decides for Fabius Rusticus or some unknown writer. I cannot feel that any of the arguments are conclusive.

been (as Fabia seems to hold) because there were no others who were worthy of serious attention. We have no right to limit the comparison elsewhere to two, since other portions of the period, short as it was, may have been described by a larger number of writers whose works were of real value.

Groag goes further and maintains that Tacitus made an extensive use of the archives of the senate as well as of previous writers,[1] basing his opinion on the fact that he gives rather full details of the senate whereas such details are almost entirely lacking in Plutarch. From this circumstance Groag infers that they were not found in the common source but were added by Tacitus. This seems to me very probable, but by no means certain, for Plutarch may have omitted these details because he was not particularly interested in the senate. Even if Tacitus did add them to what he found in the common source, there is no actual proof that he took them directly from the *acta senatus* rather than from some other writer who had used the *acta*. Still, there is nothing to show that Tacitus did not consult the archives, and these details certainly suggest that he may have done so. There are reasons apart from the account of the siege of Cremona to raise a doubt as to whether the history of Cluvius went beyond the death of Otho at the farthest,[2] and Messalla seems to have written memoirs rather than a history,[3] yet so far as we know Cluvius and Messalla were the only writers who were senators, and hence had access to the archives of the senate, which were not open to the public. We have no reason to suppose that either Fabius Rusticus or the elder Pliny could have used the *acta senatus* if they desired to do so.[4] From what we know of the writers of the time it would, therefore, appear that Tacitus must have obtained his information

[1] Groag, 711–29.

[2] Tacitus gives the secret negotiations between Vitellius and Sabinus according to rumour (*Hist.*, 3, 65), yet he expressly says that Cluvius was present at them. It seems clear, therefore, that Cluvius did not give an account of these negotiations, and if he went beyond the death of Otho, it seems probable that he would continue to the death of Vitellius.

[3] Fabia's arguments on this point (231–6) seem to me to establish a strong probability.

[4] Fabia seems to overlook the fact that Pliny was not a senator, and that this constitutes a difficulty in the way of accepting his work as the common source of Plutarch and Tacitus. If, however, the common source was almost the only source of both, it is a serious objection. Groag's further objection (782) that the author of the common source was not a military man, while Pliny was an experienced soldier, seems to me of less weight, since there is no doubt that Tacitus used Pliny. We must, therefore, assume either that Pliny was a poor judge of strategy in spite of his experience, or that Tacitus could misunderstand it.

about the proceedings in the senate by personal research in the archives. Yet we can hardly draw such a conclusion with much confidence when we recall how limited is our knowledge of the Roman writers of this period.

Whatever method Tacitus may have used in composing the first books of his *Histories*, even Fabia admits that in the books which are lost he must have gathered his material largely from the sources, and that they represented a work of real scholarly research.[1] This was not a matter of choice but of necessity, since as no previous writer had written the life of Domitian, it was impossible for Tacitus to follow the single source method in dealing with that emperor's reign. When he came to treat of the earlier empire, however, he was again upon ground that had been worked over, and Fabia contends that he at once reverted to his former method. In the case of the *Annals* we have no material for a comparison such as that between Tacitus and Plutarch, so we are obliged to judge Tacitus very largely by himself. Fabia's main argument, which is based on the difference between the account of the relations of Nero, Otho, and Poppaea in the *Annals* from that given in the *Histories*, we have already examined and found weak; he advances other arguments, however, that are worthy of attention, especially since some scholars who reject his general theory have been impressed by these same points.

In the *Annals* (13, 20) Tacitus mentions the views of three writers, Cluvius Rufus, Fabius Rusticus, and the elder Pliny, adding that he intends to follow the authorities when they agree and to record their differences under their names.[2] It is clear, however, that this formal promise has not been literally kept. Fabia holds that it was broken almost at once, since Tacitus (13, 45–6) makes no reference to the divergent version of Pliny as to the relations of Nero, Otho, and Poppaea.[3] The conclusiveness of this argument rests in part on the theory of Fabia that Plutarch and Tacitus in the *Histories* have both followed Pliny in this matter. As we have seen that they did not both follow the same author and as it is not certain that either followed Pliny, the argument is much less strong than Fabia believes. Still it does seem unlikely that all three of the historians mentioned by Tacitus should have agreed on a matter of which we know that there were other versions. The impression that Tacitus has failed to keep his promise is strengthened by the fact that if we examine the

---

[1] Fabia, 311.

[2] *Nos consensum auctorum secuturi, quae diversa prodiderint sub nominibus ipsorum trademus.* The *quae* is doubtful, some editors preferring *si qui*, but the sense is the same.

[3] Fabia, 405.

Annals from the point where Tacitus makes it to the end, we find
that his practice is quite obviously at variance with his words, for
he continues to refer to different versions of events without giving
the names of his authorities. The context, however, seems to make it
clear that he did not intend to note all differences in all writers, but
only the differences in the three historians whom he names, that is to
say Pliny, Cluvius, and Fabius. Even as thus limited, the promise
evidently was not kept, for although Tacitus twice mentions some
detail given by one of the three but not by the other two, he notes
only one conflict between them. It is incredible that any three historians, even if drawing from a common source, which was not the
case with these three, could have displayed such close and complete
agreement in narrating the events of eleven years. Yet it seems
hardly likely that Tacitus would formally announce what is evidently
a new policy, and then make no effort whatever to carry it out. A
more reasonable conclusion seems to be that he did not mean his
statement literally. He can hardly have intended to pledge himself
to mention every minute difference between the three writers, but
only such differences as he considered important. The principle of
following the most reliable authors when they were in harmony was
not an innovation, but had been his method throughout his work.
What then was it that he now announced that he would henceforth
do?[1] Not that he would mention different versions of events, for he
had been doing that all along. Hitherto, however, he has referred
to contradictory statements without naming the authors, giving his
own account and merely adding a vague phrase to the effect that
some writers report the matter otherwise. From now on he announces
that he will give the name of any of these three authors who may
give a different version of any event, in case the particular point in
dispute is mentioned. Whether he lived up to his promise even as
thus understood can only be determined by a brief examination of his
citations of authority from the point in the *Annals* where he announces his new policy. These citations are as follows:

13, 20. Fabius gives certain details which are contradicted by

---

[1] Clason argued that Tacitus has up to this point based his work on the use
of one main authority (not as a single source, however), and that the new
policy is that he will henceforth use three. Here I cannot follow him. If
Tacitus was in the habit of following one writer as a sort of rough outline for
his own work, I can see no reason why he should change at this point, since a
careful comparison would be all that was necessary. Moreover the careful
analysis which Marx has made of the arrangement of the events of each year,
which is the same throughout the *Annals*, does not suggest that Tacitus ever
followed one writer closely as a main authority, but rather that he gathered
his material from various sources and then organized it for himself.

Pliny and Cluvius.[1] Tacitus seems to accept part of the story of Fabius, gives a reason for not accepting all of it, notes the conflict between his authorities, and announces his new policy.

14, 2. Fabius gives one account of the relations between Nero and his mother, while Cluvius and all other writers (undoubtedly including Pliny) give another. Tacitus clearly prefers that of Cluvius, but adds that of Fabius, concluding with a reason why the others might have made a mistake.

14, 9. Tacitus gives the incidents of Agrippina's murder about which there was no disagreement, then adds certain details reported by some but denied by others. The three may have been silent as to these details, or reported them doubtfully, or differed about them.

14, 51. Tacitus considers it uncertain whether or not Burrus died a natural death. After describing his malady, Tacitus adds that many (*plures*) assert that Nero had him poisoned. Whether any of the three were among the *plures* is doubtful.

14, 59. Tacitus says that some report certain additional details (*sunt qui . . . ferant*). Probably none of the three is here intended.

15, 16. An incident is taken from the memoirs of Corbulo. There is here no conflict, merely an addition of a rather striking character for which Tacitus gives his authority. This is no new departure, for he has done the same in the earlier books of the *Annals* (1, 69 and 4, 53).

15, 38. Tacitus is uncertain as to the cause of the Great Fire, whether it started by chance or was started by Nero *nam utrumque auctores prodidere*. It seems highly probable that the three took different sides in the matter, but the uncertainty was so great that Tacitus refused to enter upon any discussion. At any rate Pliny in his *Natural History* (17, 1) attributes the Fire to Nero.

15, 45. Tacitus says that some report (*tradidere quidam*) that Nero tried to poison Seneca. Apparently Tacitus does not believe the story and probably none of the three gave it.

15, 53. A detail is added from Pliny. Tacitus is evidently sceptical, for he says that it seems absurd, but coming from Pliny ought not to be concealed; he closes with a reason why it may be regarded as at least possible. It is obvious that neither Cluvius nor Fabius mentioned the story.

---

[1] Furneaux and Nipperdey take the clause *Plinius et Cluvius nihil dubitatum de fide praefecti referunt* to mean that they did not mention any doubt as to the loyalty of Burrus. Gerber and Greef, however, seem clearly right in construing *nihil* with *dubitatum*, which would make Pliny and Cluvius definitely assert that there was no doubt of his fidelity. Even if we accept the first construction, it seems clear that Tacitus regarded the silence of Pliny and Cluvius as an implied contradiction of the statement of Fabius.

15, 54. Tacitus says that Milichus, who betrayed the Pisonian conspiracy, may have been an accomplice who had been loyal to his associates up to this time, or, as a great many have thought from what followed (*ut plerique tradidere de consequentibus*), he may have been ignorant of it hitherto. Here possibly the three were among the *plerique*, but, in spite of their agreement, the other view seemed quite as probable to Tacitus.

15, 61. Tacitus gives some details as to the death of Seneca taken from Fabius. Evidently they were mentioned only by him.

15, 74. Tacitus records a motion in the senate which he says he found in the *acta senatus*. Probably it was not mentioned by the three, or, if any of them referred to it, Tacitus for some reason thought it worth while to consult the archives.

16, 3. Tacitus tells his story and adds that some report certain details differently. Probably none of the three was among those referred to by the phrase *quidam tradidere*.

16, 6. Tacitus contemptuously rejects the story told by some writers that Poppaea was poisoned. Here the three are almost certainly excluded, for Tacitus pronounces the story absurd and only mentions it because it was rather widely believed.

From this enumeration it will be seen that Tacitus never names an author whose testimony he entirely rejects. Are we then to assume that he never felt certain that one of his three main authorities was wrong, or that in such a case he refrained from mentioning the erroneous view at all? To me the latter supposition seems the more probable. If we adopt it, for the moment at least, we have to ask ourselves how Tacitus could decide between them when their accounts were in conflict. In the first place, Tacitus was not wholly destitute of the critical faculty in dealing with his predecessors. In 13, 20 he hesitates to accept part of the story told by Fabius, not only because the others deny it, but also because he considers that Fabius was inclined to be unduly partial to his patron Seneca. Here Tacitus has clearly shown both independence and discernment. Fabius was intimate with Seneca and in a position to know much that went on in the palace which might not reach the ears of Cluvius or Pliny; hence up to a certain point his positive assertion should have as much weight as their denials, but he was likely to exaggerate the part played by his patron, and this should be carefully allowed for. This is sound enough procedure, and if Tacitus dealt with the other two in the same manner he might see reasons on which to base a decision in some cases where they differed. It is not unlikely that he did so, for the three must rather obviously have derived their information from different sources. So far as we know Fabius never entered the senate, and Pliny certainly did not; but Fabius could draw upon Seneca and other friends, while Pliny would have his special intimates. As a senator and member of Nero's court Cluvius must have been an eye-witness of many events, and he could consult the senate's archives freely, while it is doubtful if the other two could gain access to them. Their authority on different points would thus be somewhat variable, and Tacitus appears to have appreciated this fact. If he understood how to evaluate testimony, there must have been other writers, treating limited subjects, who would have special weight on certain matters, and Tacitus may have allowed for this also. Moreover, if neither Fabius nor Pliny used the *acta senatus*, an examination of the archives[1] would often prove them to be wrong and Cluvius right. Altogether it seems probable that Tacitus could often decide a disputed point to his own complete satisfaction. When this happened it seems clear from his practice that he did not think it worth while to repeat the version which he had definitely rejected[2] unless it was so commonly believed as to require mention, in which case (as in 16, 6) he records it but refrains from citing any names.

If his promise is interpreted in this sense, Tacitus may have fulfilled it fairly well. His three main authorities probably agreed rather closely as to the general course of events, and their differences were often on details in which Tacitus had little interest and which he did not care to mention in his work.[3] In addition he did not think it worth while to refer to actual errors by any of the three. The result was that he found so few differences to note that we may legitimately wonder why he took the trouble to make a formal announcement of his intention to record them. The explanation is probably to be found in his method of composition; he seems to have worked on the *Annals* book by book without an initial survey of the whole period,[4] so that when he was writing the thirteenth book he

---

[1] That Tacitus sometimes used the archives is shown by 15, 74. He may have found this motion by accident while investigating something else, or by checking his authorities on this particular point.

[2] Thus he does not mention Seneca's version of the death of Tiberius (*Ann.* 6, 50, and Suet. 73).

[3] Pliny's history in thirty-one books covered only part of the period dealt with by Tacitus in sixteen. Pliny went beyond the *Annals*, it is true, and may have gone to the death of Vespasian, but he did not treat the reigns of Tiberius or Caligula and covered little, if any, of that of Claudius, so that his work must have been much more detailed than that of Tacitus. Probably Fabius and Cluvius were also longer and fuller. Moreover, Tacitus himself suggests omissions, as in 13, 31 and 15, 37.

[4] See my article on 'The Composition of the Annals'.

imagined that he would find a much larger number of insoluble contradictions among his authorities than he actually did find. Had he realized how rarely he would wish to record their differences under their names he would probably not have made his promise.

It remains to consider his failure to notice the discordant accounts of the affairs of Nero, Otho, and Poppaea. Tacitus in the *Histories* and in the *Annals* tells the story quite differently, but in neither case does he mention any other version than the one he gives. Fabia holds that he simply copied from his single source in each case, but used different sources for the two works. There is, however, another possible explanation. When he wrote the *Histories* Tacitus was just beginning his career as an historian, and his critical method may not yet have been fully developed. Beginning his work with the year A.D.69, it is quite possible that it did not occur to him to check his account by a reference to authors who did not treat of this period, so that he did not consult those histories which stopped with the death of Nero or extended very little beyond it. Probably Cluvius stopped with Nero's death, and it is not unlikely that Fabius did the same,[1] since if he had covered the period dealt with in the *Histories* it is rather surprising that Tacitus, who already knew and esteemed his work,[2] should not have cited it as he does in the *Annals*. It seems a reasonable assumption that neither Cluvius nor Fabius went beyond A.D. 68 and that Tacitus did not consult them when he began writing his *Histories*, but confined his comparison to works dealing with the period he meant to treat. This reduced his list of authorities to Pliny, Messalla, and an unknown number of other writers whose names have perished. On the relations of Nero, Otho, and Poppaea he may have found Pliny at variance with the majority. Later in a similar case he would have investigated or hesitated, having found that the majority might be wrong, and having learned to weigh evidence more critically. If Plutarch followed Pliny this would explain the difference between them. Later, when he came to write the *Annals*, Tacitus may have read the account given by Fabius of this matter for the first time and accepted it without hesitation, since, as the friend of Seneca, Fabius might be supposed to be well informed on such a subject, while Cluvius and Pliny would have had only rumour and gossip to guide them, and Tacitus had now come to estimate the value of testimony with more discrimination than he had done when he began to write. Such a theory is of course

[1] See Fabia, 169–83, 210–11, 380–2. I cannot accept his argument from the fact that Tacitus cites only Messalla and Pliny on the sack of Cremona as having much weight, but his other arguments seem sound.

[2] *Agricola*, 10.

conjectural, but it appears to me more plausible in itself and more in accord with such facts as are known than the single source theory of Fabia. What seems certain is that between writing the *Histories* and the *Annals* Tacitus became acquainted with some new evidence which led him to change his mind as to the relations of Nero, Otho, and Poppaea, and that this new evidence was so conclusive that he did not think it worth while to mention any other version.

In the first six books of the *Annals* Tacitus does not cite any of his main authorities by name, but Fabia admits that here too he had three authors whom he used in much the same way that he did Cluvius, Fabius, and Pliny in the last books. These three were Aufidius Bassus, Servilius Nonianus, and perhaps the elder Seneca. Fabia goes even further and concedes that there was a fourth writer whose name is unknown, but the grounds for this supposition do not appear very substantial.[1] Although it is thus conceded that throughout the *Annals* Tacitus referred to several writers, Fabia maintains that he made no *onerosa collatio*, but followed one main source with no more than an occasional glance at the others. We have already examined some of Fabia's grounds for this belief in regard to the books dealing with the reign of Nero, so it only remains to consider his arguments against a real *collatio* in the first six. Here Fabia admits that Tacitus has consulted other works than his main source on a few special points. A list of the instances where such consultation seems to Fabia most probable will be of interest. They are as follows:[2]

1, 69. An incident is here taken from Pliny's history of the German wars. Pliny may also have been consulted in 1, 29 and 2, 17.

1, 81. Here a consultation of various works is admitted.

2, 88. Here Tacitus may have compared Servilius at least with his principal source.

4, 10–11. On the death of Drusus Tacitus has compared several accounts.

4, 53. An incident is here taken from the memoirs of the younger Agrippina.

4, 57. Tacitus has compared a number of writers as to the reasons for the retirement to Capri.

5, 9. A detail is here given on the authority of writers of the time. Fabia, however, thinks that the plural may be emphatic, and that Tacitus may not have looked beyond the pages of his main source, which was by a contemporary of Tiberius.

5, 10. Tacitus has examined all his authorities as to the false Drusus.

---

[1] Fabia, 353–4.   [2] Fabia, 404–11.

6, 7. Tacitus has completed his account of the trials which followed the fall of Sejanus from other writers.

6, 20. The prophecy that Galba would become emperor has been added by Tacitus from a writer of the Flavian period or from oral tradition.

This is not a very long list, and if even approximately complete it reveals nothing approaching a serious comparison. Fabia contends that Tacitus merely condensed and rewrote the work of Aufidius Bassus, looking at any other history of the period only when something in Aufidius aroused his doubts or provoked his curiosity. We must also conclude from the infrequency of such occasions that Tacitus was neither very sceptical nor very curious. The evidence which Fabia offers in favour of this view, aside from repeating that this was the method of Tacitus in his *Histories*, seems to me very inconclusive, but his main arguments are worth a brief discussion.

Although in 1, 69 an incident is taken from Pliny's history of the German wars, Fabia contends that Tacitus cannot have compared this work carefully with the account in his main source because he describes the coast of the North Sea where Germanicus was shipwrecked as having cliffs (*scopuli*) and rocky islands (2, 23-4), while Pliny, who had seen the country, gives a more accurate description of it in his *Natural History* (16, 1-2). If Tacitus had read Pliny, Fabia argues that he would have followed his description, since Pliny was an eye-witness as to the character of the coast.[1] Here are several unfounded assumptions. Pliny's description in the *Natural History* is a general one of a considerable district, and we do not know that he ever saw the particular place where the fleet was wrecked. If he did, we have no means of knowing how clearly or fully he described it in his work on the German wars. Even granting that he gave a clear description of it, we can hardly conclude that Tacitus had not read it because he did not follow it. He has evidently followed a source which used, or professed to use, the testimony of eye-witnesses, for he reports some of the strange tales told by the survivors of the wreck. He could not quite swallow these stories, but he may have thought that such survivors could be trusted as to the character of the coast where the wreck occurred, and he might believe their report of rocky islands, even if he doubted their assertions about sea-monsters. Moreover, Fabia's geography has been sharply questioned; he asserts that the coast where the wreck took place is flat, but Kessler declares that it has sand dunes some sixty feet in height,[2] which from a distance might look like cliffs. Kessler

[1] Fabia, 406-8.   [2] Kessler, 60-2.

further points out that the Romans were but slightly acquainted with sand dunes, and had perhaps no better word for describing them than *scopuli*, even if they knew that they were sand rather than stone. Finally he asserts that some of the islands off the coast do have rocky cliffs. In view of all the circumstances it seems to me that we have here no serious ground for concluding that Tacitus had not compared the accounts of all his various authorities; taking things at their worst, he merely made a mistake as to which was the most reliable.

In 4, 53 Tacitus cites the memoirs of the younger Agrippina, but Fabia contends that he can have made little use of them because in 2, 54 he is uncertain whether or not an oracle prophesied the early death of Germanicus. If Tacitus had troubled to look into the memoirs, Fabia argues that he would have been certain.[1] We may pass over the assumption that Agrippina must have mentioned this particular point, since it is not at all clear that Tacitus had any doubts in the matter; what he says is *ferebatur Germanico per ambages, ut mos oraculis, maturum exitium cecinisse,* and in such a connexion *ferebatur* may mean nothing more than that the fact is recorded, whether in the memoirs of Agrippina or elsewhere. If we assume that the word necessarily implies doubt, is not the doubt natural? The oracle gave out an ambiguous response which was afterwards construed to predict an early death to the prince. Why should anything which Agrippina might say convince Tacitus that it was a real prophecy? Surely his scepticism only proves that he possessed more common sense in such matters than most Romans of his day.

The last argument which requires consideration is based on the fact that Tacitus narrates the death of Tiberius as though the circumstances were not open to dispute. We know, however, that there were several different versions of that event, and from this fact Fabia draws the conclusion that Tacitus paid very little attention to any writer but Aufidius Bassus, since it is certain that he occasionally consulted several sources and it is impossible that they all gave the same account of the emperor's death without mentioning any other version than the one on which they agreed.[2] This sounds

---

[1] Fabia, 332.

[2] 'Sur la mort de Tibère il ne donne qu'une version. Suétone en donne plusieurs, dont une de Sénèque le Rhéteur. Même en admettant que Sénèque le Rhéteur ne fût pas au nombre des sources de Tacite, la différence ne pourrait s'expliquer que par le peu d'attention qu'il a accordé aux sources secondaires: car il est certain qu'il en a eu plusieurs et il est impossible que, toutes, elles aient donné, et donné uniquement, sans la moindre mention de versions divergentes, la même version.' Fabia, 411-2.

plausible until we examine closely what the other versions were. According to Suetonius there were five, as follows:

1. Gaius poisoned Tiberius (73, and *Gaius*, 12).

2. Tiberius was refused food when he was recovering from a fever (73).

3. Tiberius was smothered (73, and *Gaius*, 12). This version is adopted by both Dio (58, 28) and Tacitus (6, 50), though with some differences of detail.

4. Gaius strangled Tiberius (*Gaius*, 12).

5. Tiberius died a natural death (73).

The stories of poisoning, starvation, and strangling may, I think, be set aside as mere rumours (such as Suetonius not infrequently retails) which probably were not accepted by any reputable historians. The story of a natural death seems from Suetonius to have been given only by Seneca, so we may leave it out of account for the moment. There remains then only the third version to consider. As Dio and Tacitus agree on this it seems reasonable to conclude that it was the one which was most widely believed, and we can readily conjecture why this should be the case. The circumstances of the murder as given by Tacitus make it obvious that there were a number of persons about the emperor who might have strong suspicions, if not actual knowledge, of the truth. Their reports of what happened could readily become known later on and reach the ears of writers connected with court circles in any intimate way. There might be discrepancies in some details, but there might also be a very general agreement on the main facts. These facts, according to Tacitus, were that Tiberius lapsed into unconsciousness and was believed to be dead. The courtiers saluted Gaius as emperor, but while they were congratulating him word was brought that Tiberius had recovered and was asking for something. In the midst of the general dismay Macro hastened to the chamber of Tiberius, where he ordered the attendants to pile bed-clothes on the old man and then to leave the room. Later it was found that Tiberius was certainly dead. It will be seen that there were a number of witnesses to these events; what happened after the slaves withdrew would not of course be known, but it might be conjectured. If Tacitus has described the course of events correctly, it is not in the least impossible that all the best-informed historians reported the story substantially as above. On what points then was there disagreement? We may leave Dio out of the discussion, since it is clear that in his account of the reign of Tiberius his main sources were not the same as those used by Tacitus.[1]

---

[1] See the appendix on 'Tacitus, Suetonius, and Dio'.

We have thus to examine only the points on which Suetonius and Tacitus differ. Suetonius records several improbable versions which seem unlikely to have any serious basis, such as that Gaius himself strangled Tiberius. If we ignore these versions and confine our attention to the account which Suetonius says was given by several writers, there are only two differences: Suetonius makes Tiberius ask for a ring which had been taken from him while he was unconscious, and says that he was smothered by a pillow, while Tacitus states that Tiberius asked for food and that Macro *comprimi senem iniectu multae vestis iubet*. The *vestis* here obviously refers to the bed-clothes, among which the pillows would naturally be included. As to what Tiberius asked for, the testimony might easily be conflicting, since the news of his recovery created a panic in which such a detail might not be clearly understood or accurately remembered. If this point was differently reported, Tacitus may have followed the majority of his sources and may not have thought a discrepancy on this matter worth mentioning, while Suetonius may have favoured the less general account because it fitted the rumours he had heard about the ring, and in his turn he may not have considered divergencies on this detail important enough to record. It seems, therefore, entirely possible, in spite of Fabia, that Tacitus followed a general agreement of authorities in this case. It remains to ask why, if Seneca was among the authors used by Tacitus, his version was completely ignored. It is not difficult to suggest a reason for this. Seneca almost certainly wrote his account of the death of Tiberius during the reign of Gaius, and so naturally repeated the official story; since Tacitus did not believe this story, he saw no reason for mentioning Seneca's account, even if he took the trouble to consult it on a point where he knew in advance that he should attach little importance to it.

There is, however, one difference in the account of the last days of Tiberius given by Suetonius and that given by Tacitus which calls for notice. Suetonius says that Tiberius was angry because, on reading the proceedings of the senate, he learned that some persons concerning whom he had written to the conscript fathers had been discharged without a trial. Tacitus omits this altogether, although the close similarity between him and Suetonius in what immediately precedes suggests that they were using the same source. The particular statement was one which could be readily verified or disproved by a consultation of the archives of the senate, and this circumstance may explain the omission.

To sum up the results of this brief review of Fabia's chief argu-

ments, it seems to me that he has entirely failed to prove his case.
It is not improbable that Tacitus relied chiefly on some earlier
history which furnished him with a convenient and generally reliable
outline, but there is no substantial reason to doubt that he carefully
compared this account with other trustworthy authorities. We have
no grounds for thinking that when he says in general terms that some
writers report an event differently he copied this statement from his
main source, as Fabia maintains was often the case, and that he had
not himself read those other writers. Such evidence as there is points
in the opposite direction, and we have no real ground for doubting
the truth of the impression which is made by a reading of the *Annals*,
namely that Tacitus based his work upon a real and conscientious
study of his predecessors in the field.

It remains, however, to consider the question whether Tacitus
made use of primary sources in the composition of the *Annals*.
Fabia holds that it was an accepted principle of ancient historians
that when the archives had been once examined subsequent
writers did not need to refer to them, and many [1] who are not
advocates of the single source theory have held that Tacitus made
little or no use of them, at least for the reign of Tiberius. Now a
large part of the material of the *Annals* must have come originally
from the *acta senatus*, so the question is really this: did Tacitus
himself consult the *acta*, or did he simply take over this material
from his predecessors? As we have seen, his main secondary authorities for the reign of Nero were the elder Pliny, Fabius, and Cluvius,
while for the reign of Tiberius they were Aufidius, Servilius Nonianus,
and possibly the elder Seneca and an unknown writer. Of the six
whose names we know Cluvius and Servilius were certainly senators
and had access to the senate's archives, Pliny and Seneca were not
senators, nor, so far as we know, was Aufidius. In contending that
Aufidius and Pliny were the main sources of Tacitus, Fabia must
assume that they both were somehow in a position to consult the
acta senatus, an assumption which is quite possible but for which he
produces no evidence whatever.[2]

The actual facts of the case are, however, more important than
any speculations: twice in the *Annals* we have the positive statement
of Tacitus that he had consulted the archives. In his account of the
funeral of Germanicus he tells us (3, 3) that he had found no mention
of the prince's mother in any historian or in the *acta diurna*. Later,

---

[1] For example Furneaux, i. 18.

[2] Aufidius *may* have been a senator, and it is quite conceivable that a
distinguished non-senator like Pliny *might* obtain permission to consult the *acta
senatus* as a special favour.

in describing the honours voted to Nero after the discovery of the Pisonian conspiracy, Tacitus records a motion by the consul designate and expressly states (15, 74) that he found it in the *acta senatus*. We have no grounds for assuming that these were the only cases in which he consulted the archives, since there is an obvious and special reason why he should mention the fact of such consultation in these two instances. The absence of Antonia from the funeral of her son seemed to him very strange, and he evidently thought that it would seem so to his readers; he, therefore, took the trouble to give them a definite assurance that the fact was beyond question. The motion in honour of Nero was that a temple should be erected to him as a god, and Nero vetoed it, fearing that it might be construed as an omen of his death. Tacitus, being somewhat sceptical of omens, took pains to verify this one and to give his readers an assurance of its authenticity. On other occasions when he consulted the archives he may have seen no reason to mention the fact.

Although we have thus clear evidence that Tacitus made some use of the archives, several scholars have found instances where he failed to consult them when we might have expected him to do so. Nipperdey is so much impressed by two of these instances that he concludes that Tacitus did not refer to the *acta senatus* in writing the first books of the *Annals*.[1] The first of them is when, in speaking of the consular elections under Tiberius, Tacitus declares (1, 81) that he can make no general statement concerning them, because the manner in which they were conducted is variously reported by the historians and in the speeches of Tiberius himself. Nipperdey apparently holds that if Tacitus had consulted the *acta senatus* he could have settled the question. Here I agree with Fabia that Nipperdey misses the point about which Tacitus was uncertain.[2] The context shows that what he could not determine was the part played by the emperor, a subject on which the *acta senatus* would contain only such information as could be derived from the speech of the emperor on each separate occasion.[3] If, as Fabia holds, the speeches of Tiberius had been collected and published, Tacitus took the very natural course of referring to this collection instead of looking up each speech in the archives. Consequently no conclusion can be drawn from his failure to use the *acta senatus* in this instance.

---

[1] Nipperdey, i. 28.   [2] Fabia, 316–17.

[3] For a fuller discussion see the appendix on 'The Elections under Tiberius'. Rietra (22–3) questions the existence of a published collection of the speeches of Tiberius, which Fabia regards as certain. Personally I share Rietra's doubts, but I have accepted Fabia's view in the text. If there was no such collection, this passage shows a consultation of the archives by Tacitus.

The second instance of Nipperdey is rather stronger. In 2, 88 Tacitus says he found in writers who were senators at the time that letters were read in the senate from a chief of the Chatti offering to poison Arminius, which offer was scornfully rejected by Tiberius. For this reply the emperor is warmly praised and Tacitus is evidently very proud of it.[1] Nipperdey's comment is worth quoting: 'Es ist klar', he says, 'dass Tacitus sich hier nicht auf Schriftsteller, die zu der Zeit Senatoren waren, sondern auf die offiziellen Protokolle berufen haben würde, wenn sie ihm zur Hand gewesen wären'.[2] This reasoning, however, involves a fallacy; of course a modern historian would cite the archives instead of the writers, but Tacitus was a Roman. His only reason for mentioning his authority at all was to assure his readers of the truth of what he said, and it is quite possible that for this purpose he thought a reference to writers who were also senators was better than one to the *acta senatus*. Such a reference had at least one obvious advantage in that it could be verified in any library, while the archives were closed to all except the conscript fathers. It is of course quite possible that the testimony of the writers seemed so convincing to Tacitus that he did not take the trouble to look farther. At the utmost, the only conclusion which we can draw is that he did not consult the *acta senatus* when the evidence on any point seemed to him so satisfactory as to leave no doubt concerning the matter. In other words, when all his authorities—all at least whom he thought likely to be well informed on a given subject—were in agreement he followed them without question.

To these arguments of Nipperdey, intended to prove that Tacitus did not use the archives in writing the first books of the *Annals*, Fabia has added several others with the same purpose.[3] Thus in 1, 41 Tacitus says that Caligula was born in camp, while Suetonius (*Gaius*, 8) proves conclusively that he was born at Antium. It is obvious at once that on this point Tacitus did not consult the *acta diurna*, but we have no right to draw any further conclusion. We know from Suetonius that Pliny asserted that Caligula's birthplace was a village among the Treveri, a statement which harmonizes well enough with that of Tacitus if the expression *in castris* is not taken too literally. Further than this, Suetonius cites some verses which were circulated after Caligula became emperor which seem to show that the story that he was born in camp was widely accepted. In the

---

[1] Stein (31) explains the reference to the writers instead of the *acta senatus* by the theory that Tacitus wished to show his readers that the senators felt the same pride as himself in the answer of Tiberius. This explanation seems to me somewhat far-fetched.

[2] Nipperdey, i. 28.   [3] Fabia, 321.

passage in question Tacitus is describing the effect produced on the mutinous legions by the departure of Agrippina and her son from their winter quarters. Now the important matter in this connexion was simply the belief of the soldiers. If the authorities whom Tacitus followed in his account of the mutiny agreed that one cause of their sudden change of heart was their belief that Caligula was born in the midst of the army, there was no reason why Tacitus should stop to investigate the archives to determine where the child was actually born.

In 2, 63 Fabia believes that Tacitus used the speeches of Tiberius but did not consult the *acta senatus*.[1] If we look at the passage it will be apparent that there was no reason why he should, and no evidence whatever that he did not. Maroboduus, a German king who had lost his throne, wrote to Tiberius asking for an asylum within the empire, and Tiberius granted his request. The fallen king wrote proudly and Tiberius replied courteously, but there is nothing in the least remarkable about the letters, and there was no occasion for Tacitus to say that he had read them, if he had, or to inform his reader that they were in the archives. But Tacitus goes on to tell us that Tiberius in the senate described Maroboduus as an enemy as dangerous to Rome as Philip of Macedon had been to Athens. Such language is extraordinary, for there is nothing in the account which Tacitus has given of the German to suggest such a comparison, and his readers might, therefore, wonder whether Tiberius really said anything of the kind, so Tacitus gives an assurance on this point by stating that the oration is extant. This statement has two distinct implications: first, that Tacitus has read it, and second, that if the reader still doubts he can look it up for himself in the collected speeches of Tiberius. The failure to cite an authority for the letters proves nothing, because there was no reason for doing so. The conclusion of Fabia, therefore, that Tacitus had not seen the correspondence is quite unjustified.

In 3, 13, Tacitus tells us that Vitellius made an eloquent speech at the trial of Piso. Now we know from Pliny that in his day this speech was still extant, and that in it Vitellius argued that Germanicus must have been poisoned because his heart would not burn, while Piso replied that this was also true in some kinds of disease.[2] Tacitus makes no allusion to this argument of Vitellius, and Fabia concludes that this shows that he drew his entire account of the trial from a

---

[1] Fabia, 327. It will be recalled that it is very doubtful if the speeches of Tiberius had been collected and published as Fabia supposes (see note 3, page 260). If there was no collection of them, Tacitus here practically asserts that he has seen the speech in the archives. [2] *Nat. Hist.*, 11, 187.

single source and took no trouble to verify it.[1] But why should
Tacitus refer to the matter? He expressly tells us that the charge of
poisoning broke down, and there was, therefore, not the slightest
reason for repeating the futile arguments of the prosecution. His
silence affords no evidence whatever that he had not consulted the
acta senatus on the subject of the trial, or that he had not read the
speech of Vitellius in some published collection.

With one more instance we may close our examination of Fabia's
arguments. In 6, 7 Tacitus says: 'Minucius and Servaeus, having
been condemned, turned informers. In the same fate were involved
Julius Africanus, who came from the district of Saintonge in Gaul,
and Seius Quadratus, whose origin I have not found.'[2] The reasoning
of Fabia on this passage is worth quoting in his own words: Tacitus,
he says, 'n'a pas trouvé, nous dit-il, la patrie de Seius Quadratus:
"Originem non repperi". Il l'a donc cherchée; il l'a cherchée dans
tous les documents qu'il avait sous la main. Or, à propos du procès
de Quadratus, ce détail devait figurer dans les actes du sénat, comme
il figure aujourd'hui dans nos comptes rendus des débats judiciaires.
Puisque Tacite ne l'a pas trouvé, c'est que les actes du sénat n'étaient
pas ici au nombre de ses sources.'[3] With all due respect to the eminent
scholars who have accepted this argument, it seems to me to involve
two obvious fallacies. In the first place it is patently absurd to
assume that because a modern European court would record something, a Roman court must have done likewise. We have no means of
knowing whether a provincial on trial before the senate would be
asked where he was born,[4] or, if so, whether the answer would be
recorded in the minutes of the session. We have no reason to believe
that the Romans had as efficient a system of stenography as we have
to-day, and it is almost certain that the proceedings of the senate
were not fully reported except when set speeches were read or

---

[1] Fabia, 340.

[2] *Sed Minucius et Servaeus damnati indicibus accessere. Tractique sunt in
casum eundem Iulius Africanus e Santonis, Gallica civitate, Seius Quadratus:
originem non repperi.*

[3] Fabia, 314. Clason (107–8) advanced the same argument earlier.

[4] The information would be of value only as a means of identification, and
in many cases it is merely a piece of legal formalism. It is a wholly gratuitous
assumption that the Romans paid any particular attention to the matter in
the case of provincials resident in Rome. If Quadratus was a Roman citizen
of provincial origin the tribe in which he was registered might be recorded
while the place of his birth might be considered quite irrelevant. If inferences
are to be drawn from modern practice, then the example of America should
have as much force as that of France: a naturalized citizen of the United
States, if brought to trial, might or might not be asked in what country he
was born.

communications made in writing. We have no right to take it for granted that if Tacitus had consulted the *acta senatus* he would have found any record of the birthplace of Quadratus. If the passage warrants any conclusion as to the use of the archives by Tacitus, it seems to me that we must infer that he had consulted them in vain. In the second place we have no right to assume that Tacitus made any extensive search for the information. All he says is that he has not found it, and while this clearly implies that he has looked for it, it implies nothing as to the extent of his investigation. He may merely have examined the book under his hand and have taken no further trouble, since Quadratus was a person of little consequence and his birthplace was a matter of no importance. Tacitus confessed his ignorance for a very simple reason. He has mentioned two men and recorded the nationality of one of them, so that to say nothing about the nationality of the other might appear to the reader as a careless oversight; to remove this impression Tacitus explains that he has not found any information on this point in his source or sources. It is not at all unlikely that Tacitus drew his account of this case from a special work, and that it was not alluded to at all by the writers whom he usually followed. Immediately after his confession of ignorance he says that he is aware that most historians have omitted many trials, some of which he thinks worthy of being known, and he then gives a rather full account of the acquittal of M. Terentius. It may be that the remarks with which he prefaces the case of Terentius are intended to explain his mention of Africanus and Quadratus as well as that of Terentius. Now Tacitus had a special reason for being interested in the fate of Africanus. The son of this native of Gaul was a distinguished orator in the reign of Nero, and his biography was written by Julius Secundus. Tacitus was a pupil of Julius Secundus [1] and would therefore be likely to have read the biography, so that it is not improbable that he got his information about the elder Africanus and Quadratus from this work of his former teacher, and that their trial was not mentioned by most of the historians of Tiberius. In that case the search of Tacitus may have been on a very limited scale, and perhaps extended no further than the pages of the biography. On the other hand it is entirely possible that he investigated the matter thoroughly, looked carefully in all the histories at hand, consulted the senate's archives, and found nothing. From this passage it seems to me that we can draw no conclusion whatever except that Tacitus made some effort to clear up the point, but how much effort we have no means of determining.

[1] For references see the *Prosopographia*.

We have now examined what seem to me the strongest arguments by which Fabia and others have attempted to prove that Tacitus made very little use of primary sources and made no serious comparison of the works of previous historians. It appears to me that these arguments derive almost all their plausibility from the unconscious assumption that the ancient historians followed the same methods in citing their authorites that a modern historian would. If Tacitus does not refer to the archives where we think that he should have done so, it is taken for granted that he had not consulted the archives on that point, and if he did not consult the archives where a scholar to-day would feel such consultation necessary, then we are to conclude that he made practically no use of them. Now an ancient historian never gave his authority for a statement without a special reason for doing so, and when he did, he cited only such authority as seemed necessary for his purpose and best adapted to it. That Tacitus sometimes mentions only a secondary source does not, therefore, prove that he had not consulted the archives on the matter in question. Neither does the fact, if established, that he did not consult the archives on some occasion where we think that he should have done so, prove that he did not make a very considerable use of them. He has himself given us an indication of his standards and methods, and we have no sufficient evidence that he did not apply them with reasonable care and honesty. We have not the slightest grounds for concluding that when he tells us that some writers gave a different account of an event, he had not read the writers in question but merely copied the statement from his main source.

From what Tacitus has told us of his methods and from what we have seen of them, we may draw some tentative conclusions. It seems clear that he based his historical writings on a comparison of such of the works of his predecessors as he considered most trustworthy. How careful this comparison was we have no means of determining, but there is nothing to indicate that he did not examine all the works from which he thought that any information of value could be derived on every topic he discussed. We have some evidence that he not only compared his authorities but weighed their testimony as well. If he made allowances for the prejudices of a writer, as we know he did, it seems reasonable to infer that he took into account any special sources of information which he knew that such a writer possessed. When his authorities agreed, he generally followed them without question, and when they disagreed, he investigated the point in dispute and tried to settle it if he thought it important enough to deserve mention. In such an investigation he would often consult the archives, and the documents which they contained would sometimes enable him to reach a decision. When there was nothing in the archives of any real value, he might turn to special works whose authors had personal knowledge on the point at issue or had been acquainted with eye-witnesses to the events. When Tacitus reached a definite decision on any matter, he seldom referred to any divergent accounts unless some erroneous version was so generally believed that he felt obliged to mention it, if only to show that he had not set it aside through ignorance. In case the result of his investigation was not entirely decisive, he frequently recorded the different versions, though in the early books of the *Annals* he did not give the names of the authorities on each side. How frequently Tacitus consulted the archives we have no means of knowing. I think it likely, though I would not undertake to prove, that he made a rather extensive use of them and that he examined the documents which were preserved there relating to all the important trials of which he has given an account. If, in spite of the unanimous silence of his authorities, he took pains to verify the absence of Antonia from the funeral of Germanicus, it seems to me improbable that he would have made such positive statements about the failure of the prose-cution to establish the charge of poisoning against Piso without consulting the records of the trial, since he must have been aware that the charge was widely believed, even if his main authorities agreed in rejecting it. On the whole I can see no serious reason for doubting that the historical works of Tacitus were based, as they profess to be, on a real and serious study of the sources, both second-ary and primary, and that they are the most reliable authority that we possess for the period covered. We should, therefore, accept his statements of fact in all cases except the few where we have strong grounds for questioning his accuracy.

II. KESSLER'S THEORY

IT may be well to consider very briefly a theory advanced by
Kessler[1] as to the sources followed by Tacitus for the career of
Germanicus. Kessler holds that some friend and companion of the
prince wrote a biography of him, and that this biography was used by
both Tacitus and Dio. We may limit our discussion to the story of
the mutiny, where it seems to me that Kessler has made out the best
case. For this episode he believes that Dio has reproduced the common source briefly, but without alterations or additions, while
Tacitus has substituted another account in regard to the departure
of Agrippina and Gaius. For the first part of the mutiny both
historians have, in Kessler's view, based their narratives upon the
biography, the evidence for this supposition being found in the close
similarity of the two accounts. In this conclusion I find myself
unable to concur, for the similarities seem to me only such as were
bound to occur if the facts and the chronological order of events
were not utterly disregarded; Dio and Tacitus differ wherever
differences are possible throughout.[2] It is not merely that one gives
details which the other omits, for this we might expect, but that in
these details they contradict each other. The causes of the mutiny
are given in much the same way by both, but Dio implies that the
whole army on the Rhine mutinied, while Tacitus says that the
outbreak was limited to the army in Lower Germany. Both tell us
that the soldiers offered the principate to Germanicus, but Dio makes
the offer come from *all* the troops,[3] while Tacitus says that it was
made by *some* of them only. What follows is quite different in the
two authors. According to Dio, on hearing the offer Germanicus
pleaded with the men for a long time, and being unable to move
them, finally drew his sword as if he were about to kill himself; the
soldiers only jeered at him, and seeing that his suicide would have
no effect Germanicus did not persist. Tacitus represents Germanicus
as leaping down from the tribunal when he heard the offer; the
soldiers tried to force him to remount it, whereupon he drew his
sword and attempted to kill himself but was stopped by those near
him; some of the men jeered at him, and his friends hurried him

---

[1] In his monograph on Germanicus.

[2] The account of the mutiny is given in Tacitus, 1, 31–49 and in Dio,
57, 5–6.

[3] That this is not merely careless writing on Dio's part is shown by his
emphatic statement later (57, 6).

away. In both Tacitus and Dio we are told that Germanicus then forged a letter purporting to come from Tiberius, but as to what followed the two accounts diverge rather widely. The men were given their discharges and rewards at once; Dio implies that this was voluntary on the part of Germanicus, while Tacitus says that the men suspected the forgery and compelled the prince to redeem the alleged promises of Tiberius immediately. Before long envoys arrived from Rome; Dio says that they came from Tiberius, while Tacitus says they came from the senate. Moreover, Dio states that the emperor had given them only such instructions as he wished Germanicus to know and had as far as possible concealed his own plans; Tacitus is entirely silent as to this reticence on the part of the emperor, although it is hard to understand why an act so characteristic of the devious methods constantly attributed to Tiberius by Tacitus should have been deliberately omitted. Both Tacitus and Dio agree that on the arrival of the envoys there was a new outbreak of disorder, because the men feared that they would cancel the concessions which had been granted. Tacitus says that the soldiers feared this because they were conscience-stricken, while Dio attributes their fear to the fact that they learned 'the stratagem of Germanicus', namely that the letter was a forgery. Both, it is true, tell the story of how, when Germanicus attempted to kill himself, one of the soldiers offered him a sharper sword, but little weight can be given to this similarity, since we have no means of knowing how wide a circulation this particular anecdote had. These differences might be explained if we knew that Dio and Tacitus had based their accounts upon a common source, but they certainly do not help to establish such a theory.

As to the end of the mutiny, Kessler thinks that Tacitus abandoned the biography, which Dio continued to follow. Undoubtedly Tacitus and Dio disagree, and Kessler contends that Dio's account is the only one worthy of credit. The reasons for this conclusion may be briefly stated. In the first place, Kessler holds that Tacitus contradicts himself: in I, 39 the first and twentieth legions occupy separate camps and Germanicus lives in a house outside the camps, while in I, 40-1 the legions occupy one camp and Germanicus lives inside it. This contradiction is due to Kessler, however, and not to Tacitus; Nipperdey has satisfactorily explained the expressions on which Kessler bases his view by the supposition that the two legions had separate camps within the same walls. In the second place, Kessler insists that the version of the departure of Agrippina and Gaius given by Tacitus is absurd on the face of it, for Germanicus, believing his family to be in serious danger, allowed them to go on foot and without escort through the camp of the mutinous soldiers. But there is not the slightest intimation in Tacitus that Germanicus thought that there was any immediate peril. It is true that his staff urged him to send his wife and child away for safety, but the danger which they feared seems to have been future rather than present; no one could tell what the disaffected legions might do, though at the moment they were quiet. After the outbreak against the envoys Germanicus had made a speech to them which Tacitus says intimidated rather than quieted them. As Germanicus had already tried to work upon their feelings by his attempt at suicide, it seems very possible that he would seize this occasion to do the same thing by so arranging the departure of Agrippina and Gaius that it would make a dramatic emotional appeal. So far as we can see there was no reason to fear that any harm would be done to them at that moment, whatever dangers might develop if they remained in the camp and the rioting broke out again. Kessler complains that Germanicus promised that Gaius should return when he was still in the camp, where he and his mother had been detained by the soldiers. But Tacitus does not say that Agrippina and Gaius were stopped, and his narrative implies that they had left the camp. Kessler also emphasizes the point that Tacitus says that the soldiers were moved by the fact that Gaius had been born in camp, whereas he was really born in Antium. This is true, but we know that it was popularly believed that Gaius was born in camp, and that Pliny fixed his birthplace among the Treveri.[1] Kessler holds that Dio copied a biography written by an eye-witness, and Dio says that he was brought up in the camp. If such an expression occurred in the source used by Tacitus and if Tacitus was persuaded that Pliny was correct as to the birthplace of Gaius, he might easily turn the accurate expression into an inaccurate one.

On the whole I can see no reason to prefer the account of Dio to that of Tacitus as to the end of the mutiny. The butchery of the ringleaders seems to fit much better with the picture of a sudden revulsion of feeling than with a gradual change of mood, and the departure of Agrippina and Gaius seems a possible cause for such a revulsion. If Kessler's theory is adopted it makes little difference on any point of real importance. In any case the conduct of Germanicus is not altered greatly and our judgement of him must remain much the same.

There is, however, one other point in connexion with Kessler's

[1] Suet., *Gaius*, 8. See pages 261–2.

theory which deserves a moment's attention. He maintains that the
source used by Tacitus for a part of his narrative of the life of Germanicus was a biography of the prince written by a friend and
companion who was an eye-witness of many of the events both in
the West and in the East. The proof of the existence of such a work
is found in the numerous details which are given by Tacitus and
which would hardly be known to any one who was not present on
the occasion. This is distinctly true in the account of the mutiny,
where we find such details as that the soldiers put the hand of
Germanicus in their mouths so that he might feel their toothless
gums, and bared their bodies to show the marks of their floggings,
that the name of the man who offered Germanicus his sword was
Calusidius, that the name of the standard-bearer who protected
Plancus was Calpurnius, &c. In fact the whole account of the mutiny
on the Rhine in Tacitus reads as if it had been taken from the report
of an eye-witness, but did it therefore come from a biography of
Germanicus? Against this we have to set the fact that Tacitus is
equally copious of detail and of the names of unimportant persons
in his account of the mutiny in Pannonia, and the further fact that
after Germanicus goes to the East we find little or nothing in Tacitus
which was not likely to have been brought out in the testimony given
at the trial of Piso. It seems to me, therefore, that the theory of a
biography by a friend and companion is hardly sustained by the
evidence. A more probable conjecture would be that Tacitus has
used some historian whose work was based, in part at least, on the
recollections of eye-witnesses. Such a supposition offers no difficulties. We know, for example, that Caecina Severus was present at
the mutiny on the Rhine and that he served in the German expeditions. He afterwards returned to Rome and made a speech in the
senate in A.D. 21. How much longer he lived we cannot ascertain,
but it may have been some years. Junius Blaesus, who was in
command of the Pannonian army at the time of the mutiny, perished
at the downfall of Sejanus in A.D. 31.[1] It would have been an easy
matter for a historian in Rome to have obtained details from these
two officers, and they were certainly not the only ones who could
have furnished such details. As to who the historian was it is hardly
worth while to speculate, but that some writer acquainted himself
with the recollections of officers who had been present at the mutinies
and had served in the German campaigns seems to me very probable.

---

[1] For references see the *Prosopographia*. Apronius was another officer of
Germanicus who may have survived Tiberius, but it is uncertain whether he
was present at the mutiny.

The details given by Tacitus were, I believe, drawn from this source either directly or through Pliny, and they are entitled to some weight as being in all likelihood derived from the testimony of eye-witnesses. I can see no good evidence that Tacitus changed his authority in the course of his narrative, and I do not think that Dio used the same sources as Tacitus.

A COMPARISON of the accounts of Tiberius in the *Annals* of Tacitus, the *Lives* of Suetonius, and the *Roman History* of Dio Cassius will show that Tacitus was much more careful and accurate than either of the others. In the main the three certainly followed different sources, and those of Tacitus were decidedly the most trustworthy. While neither Dio nor Suetonius should be ignored, their statements can only be accepted with caution and their loose generalizations can be given very little weight. A brief critical examination will suffice to make these points clear.

Taking Suetonius first, we may begin by comparing his account of certain events with that which Tacitus has given of the same incidents. Suetonius asserts that Tiberius was parsimonious (46) and that, having helped a few needy senators, he refused to give assistance to any others unless they proved to the senate that there were good reasons for their poverty. As a result, modesty and shame prevented applications from many, 'among them Hortalus, a grandson of Quintus Hortensius the orator, who, though his family fortune was small, had begotten four children with the encouragement of Augustus' (47). Certainly from this no one would suspect that this same Hortalus appealed for help in the senate and succeeded in getting it without, apparently, showing the causes of his poverty (*Ann.* 2, 37–8); either these two chapters of Tacitus are simply fiction, or Suetonius is in error. Tacitus tells us that the family of Hortalus sank into poverty in spite of the help given them, and Suetonius was probably misled by this fact and assumed that they had not applied for relief.

From economy Suetonius asserts that Tiberius went on to plunder, and gives instances of the crimes which he committed to get money (49). We are told that he condemned Lepida for trying to poison her husband Quirinius, who had divorced her, and that Tiberius did this to gratify Quirinius, a very rich and childless consular; the implication is clear that the emperor acted thus with a view to inheriting the fortune of Quirinius. Now Tacitus has given a full account of this case (3, 22–3), and according to his version Lepida was not charged with trying to poison her husband, but with pretending to bear a son to Quirinius, and afterwards with adultery, poisoning, and treason. Tacitus says that she was infamous and guilty, but that the animosity of Quirinius aroused some sympathy for her. She was banished, but her property was not confiscated, and it was only after the sentence had been pronounced that Tiberius made it known that the examination of the slaves had revealed the fact that she had tried to poison Quirinius. Either the entire account of Tacitus is wrong, or Suetonius in collecting examples of imperial avarice has used a case about which he was not well informed.

In this same connexion Suetonius (49) tells us how Vonones, driven from the throne of Parthia, sought refuge in Syria with a large treasure; here he was treacherously robbed and murdered, presumably from the context by order of Tiberius. Tacitus has given us a full account of the death of Vonones (2, 58 and 68), in which he does not mention the treasure as a motive and in which he excludes all agency on the part of Tiberius. To the treasure we have only casual references: we are first told that Vonones had won the favour of Piso by giving presents to his wife (2, 58), and in another connexion that later the Parthian king claimed the treasure which Vonones had brought with him (6, 31). Either Tacitus was completely misinformed, or Suetonius has illustrated the emperor's avarice with another instance about which he knew little.

There is a further point to be noted in connexion with these two cases. The death of Vonones occurred in A.D. 19, and the trial of Lepida in 20. If Tiberius began plundering thus early in his reign, it is difficult to see how Tacitus can have remained entirely ignorant of the fact, and ignorant of it he unquestionably was. In his account of A.D. 15 he says that Tiberius liked to be liberal on proper occasions, and that he retained this virtue longer than any other (1, 75); under A.D. 17 we are told of the emperor's reluctance to accept bequests where there was any better heir (2, 48); under A.D. 20 it is expressly stated that avarice was not one of his vices (3, 18); last of all we are positively informed that in A.D. 24 Tiberius for the *first time* showed any desire for property not his own (4, 20). It is evident that if we accept the authority of Suetonius as to Lepida and Vonones we must conclude that Tacitus has contrived to form a wholly false conception of the emperor's conduct during the first ten years of his reign. The only alternative is to suppose that Suetonius took little or no trouble to verify details, and that he had only a vague notion of the chronology of events.

The second alternative is proved to be the true one by an anecdote related by Suetonius (42) to illustrate the vices of Tiberius and the unworthy motives which led him to advance men to important offices. The story is that Tiberius, after he became emperor, and while he was correcting the public morals,[1] spent two days and

---

[1] There is nothing in Tacitus to show that Tiberius ever did this.

L

a night feasting and drinking with Pomponius Flaccus and L. Piso, and that he *forthwith* appointed one of them governor of Syria and the other prefect of the city, describing them in their commissions as the pleasantest of friends. This anecdote is chronologically impossible. Two men named L. Piso seem to have held the office of prefect of the city under Tiberius. The first died in A.D. 32 (*Ann.* 6, 10–11, and Dio, 58, 19), after serving for twenty years according to Tacitus. Nipperdey alters the twenty to fifteen, and one of his reasons seems sound, namely that the account which Tacitus gives (1, 7) of the oath taken at the accession of Tiberius by the high officials clearly shows by omission that the city prefecture was vacant at that time. In any case, whether Piso was appointed in A.D. 12 or 17, Pomponius Flaccus was not sent to Syria till A.D. 32.[1] The second L. Piso was prefect of the city in A.D. 37 according to Josephus (*Antiquities*, 18, 6, 5, 10) and cannot have been appointed till some time after A.D. 33.[2] Thus the appointment of Flaccus cannot be made to coincide, even approximately, with that of either Piso, and Suetonius is clearly guilty of a blunder. In this instance we are able to trace the growth of the story. Seneca (*Epist.* 83, 14), without mentioning Tiberius, describes the first Piso as a heavy drinker, but adds that he discharged his duties as prefect efficiently in spite of this; the elder Pliny tells us (*Nat. Hist.* 14, 144–5) that Tiberius was fond of wine in his youth, though in later life he became abstemious, and says that it was believed that he had appointed the first Piso after a drinking bout of two nights and two days; Pliny does not mention Flaccus and implies that the appointment of Piso occurred early in the reign. In this form the story is not altogether impossible, but Pliny is careful not to assert its truth; by the time of Suetonius, however, it had grown into absurdity through the addition of Flaccus. Tacitus makes no reference whatever to the incident; he was too well informed to pay any attention to it in the form in which it is given by Suetonius, and he has likewise ignored the earlier and more credible version of Pliny. This omission was certainly not due to any wish to conceal the vices of Tiberius, and we must suppose that he either found no serious authority for the story, or else that he did not care to allude to the faults of Piso, whose general character he admires. What seems clearly established is that Suetonius has repeated an anecdote without making the least effort to determine its truth or even its possibility, since the dates at which

---

[1] *Ann.* 6, 27, and Dio, 58, 19. For further references see the *Prosopographia*.
[2] Lamia, who succeeded the first Piso, died in 33 and must have been followed by Cossus Lentulus (Seneca, *Epist.* 83, 14).

important officials were appointed could easily have been ascertained by any one who cared to take the trouble.

If Suetonius is thus careless and inaccurate in regard to prominent men and women, we can feel little confidence in his vague general statements; when not unfounded they are often wildly exaggerated, and they are sometimes wholly false. To see this we may check chapter 61 of Suetonius with the data furnished by Tacitus. Suetonius begins by saying that he will give examples of the various forms of the emperor's cruelty. He continues that not a day passed without the punishment of some one, not even sacred days, for some suffered on New Year's day. The general statement is obviously absurd; Tacitus gives the case of one man executed on New Year's day, namely Titius Sabinus (4, 70), though Pliny (*Nat. Hist.* 8, 145) shows that his slaves suffered with him. Next it is asserted that 'many were accused and condemned with their children and even by their children'. In Tacitus we find only one instance of a man's children being condemned, namely those of Sejanus (5, 9), and the only case where a son accused his father was that of Vibius Serenus (4, 28). Perhaps we should add the case of Vitia, who was put to death not with, but sometime after, her son (6, 10). Suetonius then states that relatives of those condemned to death were forbidden to mourn for them. Tacitus (6, 19) says that the relatives of the victims of the massacre of A.D. 33 did not dare to mourn, and Dio (58, 16) says decrees were passed, though not observed, permitting mourning for Sejanus. Special rewards, Suetonius declares, were decreed to informers and even witnesses. Tacitus mentions special rewards only in the case of Libo (2, 32). Next we are told that no delator's word was doubted. If this be true, how are we to explain the acquittal of Terentius and the punishment of his accusers (6, 8–9), as well as other cases of the same sort? Suetonius affirms that all crimes, even a few words, were treated as capital. But Tacitus tells us that Tiberius intervened to prevent careless talk from being punished in the case of Cotta Messalinus (6, 5), and that two women (6, 18), three informers (6, 30), and two senators were banished, and another senator was deprived of his rank (6, 48). Next we have what is obviously an account of the cases of Mamercus Scaurus and Cremutius Cordus. Suetonius says that a poet was punished for slandering Agamemnon, and an historian for calling Brutus and Cassius the last of the Romans; their works were also suppressed, and all this in spite of the fact that the writings in question had been read in the presence of Augustus some years before. But according to Dio (57, 24 and 58, 24) and Tacitus (4, 34–5 and 6, 29) both of these men committed suicide, and the charge against Scaurus was not his tragedy, though this had angered Tiberius. Both Tacitus and Dio give the impression that the tragedy was recent; if so, it could not have been read before Augustus, though Dio says that Augustus had read the history. Both Dio and Tacitus agree that the history was suppressed, but neither says anything of the sort in regard to the tragedy, which according to them was not openly brought into the case against Scaurus. Suetonius further informs us that those in custody were not allowed to read or converse. Dio asserts (58, 3) that one such person, Asinius Gallus, was not allowed to talk to any one and was given only enough food to keep him alive; Tacitus is completely silent on the matter. If Tacitus had known of this practice or had believed such a story, it seems very strange that he has made no allusion to it even in the case of Gallus (6, 23), on whose death he comments in such a way that his failure to refer to the harsh conditions of his imprisonment seems highly significant. We are next told that some who were accused opened their veins at home and some took poison in the midst of the senate, but the wounds were bound up and they were dragged half-dead to prison. Tacitus narrates the case of one knight who took poison in the senate house and who was carried dying to prison, where the executioner pretended to strangle his dead body (6, 40, and Dio, 58, 21), but we hear nothing of any one who tried to commit suicide at home being dragged to prison. Suetonius continues that all who were punished were cast out on the Stairs of Groaning and dragged with hooks (to the Tiber), and that as many as twenty, among them women and children, were thus treated on a single day. The close of this sentence refers to the massacre of A.D. 33, and here Suetonius is more restrained than Tacitus (6, 19), who speaks of an immense number of victims slaughtered at one time. As to the first part of the sentence, Dio (58, 15) confirms Suetonius, and as this was the usual practice there is no reason to doubt the substantial accuracy of the statement. The next assertion of Suetonius, however, cannot be so readily accepted; he says that 'immature girls were ravished by the executioner before being strangled, since by old custom it was contrary to divine law to strangle virgins'. Dio informs us (58, 11) that the daughter of Sejanus was treated in this barbarous fashion, and Tacitus merely reports (5, 9) that he has found such a story in her case in writers of the time. Suetonius concludes the chapter under consideration with three anecdotes which we have no means of checking.

Other instances might easily be cited, both of inaccurate statements as to prominent persons, and of loose general statements which are either exaggerated or without any foundation at all so far as we can discover. Enough evidence has, however, been given to show the general character of the work of Suetonius. The life of Tiberius seems to have been composed somewhat after this fashion: Suetonius read a number of works dealing with the period and made somewhat careless notes on them; these he arranged in a more or less logical order, paying no attention to chronology, and he added by way of summary a considerable number of general statements for which he trusted to his memory. The biography reflects the general tradition as to the character of Tiberius and his reign, and contains a number of anecdotes, some of which are worthless, while others probably rested upon good authority. For any serious study of the period we can neither trust Suetonius nor ignore him. He is a good witness as to the view of Tiberius prevalent among the Romans after the emperor's death, and we may accept, though with some caution, such of his stories as fit into the framework of facts furnished by Tacitus. General statements which are not sustained by Tacitus must be disregarded entirely, and, where Tacitus and Suetonius differ, we should follow Tacitus unless there are good reasons for thinking that on the particular point in question Suetonius happens to have reproduced a more reliable authority.

It remains now to consider the comparative reliability of Dio and Tacitus. It is easily apparent that Dio did not follow the same sources as Tacitus, and his work is thus valuable as bringing us into touch, to some extent at least, with a Roman historical tradition [1] which was used by Tacitus but which he often set aside in favour of other authorities. In the case of Dio it would seem not improbable that he took some rather full and detailed history as his main source, although his language clearly asserts that he read more or less widely and made some comparison of the various versions of events. Unfortunately his account of Tiberius is comparatively brief, filling only two books, while Tacitus devoted six to the same period. Moreover even these two books of Dio have reached us in a somewhat fragmentary condition, though we are able to fill some of the gaps after a fashion by the help of epitomes of Dio's work, chiefly those of Xiphilinus and Zonaras. The result is that there are only a few of the events of the reign upon which we can make a detailed comparison between Dio and Tacitus. For our immediate purpose, however,

[1] I say historical tradition because the chief work used by Dio may not have been written till after the time of Tacitus, though on the other hand it may have been one of his three or four chief authorities.

enough material is ready to hand. A brief comparison of their treatment of a few incidents will suffice to show that they followed different authorities.

Both Tacitus (1, 6) and Dio (57, 3) agree that the murder of Agrippa Postumus occurred immediately after the death of Augustus and before the formal accession of Tiberius. Both writers also agree as to such facts in connexion with this crime as might be more or less publicly known, namely that Agrippa was killed, that Tiberius denied having given any order for his death and threatened to have the matter investigated or to punish the person responsible, but that the matter was allowed to drop. However, Tacitus and Dio accept different theories of the murder, Dio holding Tiberius responsible and Tacitus laying the blame equally on Tiberius and Livia. Tacitus says that Tiberius pretended that Augustus had left orders with the officer in charge of Agrippa to kill the prisoner as soon as he heard of the emperor's own death. Dio says nothing of this, but tells us that some people thought that Augustus had Agrippa killed before his own death. Tacitus informs us that Tiberius threatened to bring the matter before the senate, while Dio makes no mention of the senate. Dio gives several stories which he tells us were believed: one just mentioned that Augustus killed Agrippa, another that the centurion who was guarding him detected the prisoner in some plot and killed him without orders from any one, and still another that Livia and not Tiberius was responsible.[1] Of these Tacitus says nothing at all. Lastly Tacitus gives some details of the actual murder and tells us that Sallustius Crispus sent the order and that it was he who persuaded Tiberius to drop the matter, all of which is omitted by Dio. It seems clear that the two writers did not use the same source and that Tacitus probably drew upon some authority whom he regarded as reliable for what went on behind the scenes in the palace. This last point is suggested by the positive way in which Tacitus refers to the part played by Sallustius Crispus in the affair.

As to the funeral of Augustus there are also considerable differences. Dio (57, 2) states that Tiberius asked the senate to help him maintain order at the funeral, pretending to fear a popular disturbance. Tacitus says nothing of any such request to the senate, though he tells us that Tiberius issued a proclamation urging the people to refrain from any disturbance. As to the honours accorded to Augustus, Dio (56, 47) says that the senate resolved that its members should submit their proposals in writing to Tiberius, who should choose such of them as he pleased; Dio adds that Livia took

---

[1] Compare Suet. 22.

part in the matter as if she were a ruler herself. Tacitus (1, 8) makes no mention of any such procedure, but gives some of the honours in question as voted by the senate itself. The part ascribed to Livia is in line with another assertion of Dio (57, 12) that for a time the letters of Tiberius bore her name as well as his own, a statement which is not confirmed by the inscriptions found at Gythium (Seyrig) and which Tacitus (1, 14) denies by implication in what he says of the attitude of Tiberius toward his mother.

In regard to the formal accession of Tiberius, Tacitus and Dio differ irreconcilably on some points. Dio (57, 7) asserts that Tiberius consented to become emperor only when the entire Roman world had acquiesced in his rule; this would make him continue his pretence of reluctance until he learned that the mutinies had been suppressed.[1] On the other hand Tacitus (1, 13) evidently believed that he accepted the principate as definitely as he ever did accept it at the session of the senate on September 17. Lastly Dio (57, 14) tells us that Tiberius delayed the payment of the bequests made by Augustus in his will until the next year, and even then paid them only when a man had pretended to send a message to Augustus by a corpse which was being carried through the Forum; Tiberius had the man executed, bidding him give Augustus the message himself,[2] but afterwards paid the legacies. Tacitus makes no mention of any delay in carrying out the provisions of the will and does not allude to this story. It is very difficult to see why he should have omitted any allusion to it unless he was either ignorant of it or convinced that it was false.

The two accounts of the mutiny on the Rhine have already been compared[3] and found to present important differences. It will suffice now to call attention to the fact that in his narrative of the Pannonian mutiny Dio (57, 4) informs us that the soldiers thought of setting up another emperor, while Tacitus is silent as to any such idea on their part. Dio's version of the Libo Drusus affair is also at variance with that of Tacitus, but this has been discussed elsewhere and we need not consider it here.[4]

For the trial of Piso we have only the epitomes of Dio, but they seem to show that his version of that event was sharply at variance

---

[1] Augustus died on August 19 and the eclipse of the moon which played so striking a part in the Pannonian mutiny occurred on the morning of September 27 according to civil reckoning (September 26 by astronomical time). The news of the suppression of the mutiny could not have reached Rome before the beginning of October. The mutiny on the Rhine apparently lasted somewhat longer.　　　[2] Suetonius (57) gives the story with some differences of detail.

[3] See the appendix on 'Kessler's Theory'.

[4] See my article on 'Tacitus and Aristocratic Tradition'.

with that of Tacitus. Dio affirms (57, 18) that Germanicus was poisoned by the agency of Piso and Plancina, that Tiberius himself accused Piso of murder before the senate, and that Piso secured some delay and killed himself. With all this Tacitus is wholly out of harmony.

One more brief comparison will be enough for the present purpose. Both Tacitus (6, 47–8) and Dio (58, 27) have given an account of the case of Albucilla and others, which occurred at the very end of the reign. Both agree that Macro trumped up the charges, that Albucilla wounded herself and was sent to prison, where Dio says that she died, and that Arruntius committed suicide. There are, however, important differences. Dio attributes the escape of some of the accused to the astrologer Thrasyllus, who led the dying emperor to believe that he would live ten years longer; thus deluded, Tiberius was not enraged when the senate postponed judgement upon those of the accused who denied the testimony which had been procured by the use of torture. Others who were condemned to death were saved because they could not be executed for ten days and Tiberius died in the interval. In contrast with this, Tacitus makes no mention of any one who was condemned to death; he tells us that three persons were punished, two being banished and one expelled from the senate. He makes no allusion to any postponement of judgement by the senate, but says that Domitius and Marsus, who with Arruntius were the most prominent of those implicated, saved themselves by postponing their trials, Domitius preparing his defence and Marsus pretending that he meant to starve himself to death. Of Thrasyllus and his deception of Tiberius there is not a word in Tacitus.

From this brief comparison it is clear that Tacitus and Dio have not followed the same authorities, and we have next to consider which had the most trustworthy sources. In general it seems to me that the advantage is decidedly with Tacitus, except in the case of Libo and perhaps that of Agrippa Postumus. In regard to Libo, I believe that Tacitus was somewhat too credulous of aristocratic tradition, and the account of the part played by Sallustius Crispus in the death of Agrippa, a part which must have been very carefully concealed, is certainly open to some legitimate scepticism. For the rest, the version of Tacitus is obviously the more credible one. It is very difficult to believe that Tiberius kept up his show of reluctance to accept the principate for about a month, or that he ever wrote letters, of an official character at least, in the name of Livia as well as his own. Surely no one would be inclined to adopt Dio's account of the trial of Piso or the case of Albucilla in place of that of Tacitus.

The case against Dio is strengthened by a number of other inaccuracies. The story of how Tiberius was finally induced to pay the bequests of Augustus needs no comment, and the same may be said of the stories told of Sex. Marius (58, 22). If Zonaras has correctly represented Dio (57, 22), we find that Sejanus hoped to gain the throne by marrying Livilla because Tiberius detested his grandson as not being the child of Drusus. Apparently Dio did not know or forgot that Livilla was the mother of this grandson.

There are a number of other incidents mentioned by Dio where the silence of Tacitus, dangerous as this argument always is, seems decisive. We are told (57, 15) that in A.D. 16 Cn. Piso induced the senate to pass a decree against the wishes of Tiberius and Drusus, which decree was vetoed by a tribune. Dio says (57, 22) that in A.D. 23 Tiberius had Aelius Saturninus tried by the senate and hurled down from the Capitol on the charge of having recited some verses reflecting on him. We are also informed (57, 24) that in A.D. 25 a man charged with having sold the emperor's statue along with a house was only saved because the consul called upon Tiberius to give the first vote.[1]

To such instances we may add the cases of manifest exaggeration in the loose general statements which make up a large part of Dio's narrative. We are told (57, 9) that Tiberius, at the beginning of his reign, released some who were accused of taking a false oath by the fortune of Augustus, but that later he put to death a very large number, apparently on this charge. Tacitus mentions one man who was so released (1, 73), and none who were punished for this offence. Dio states (57, 10) that Tiberius enriched many senators who wished to resign their rank on account of poverty. Tacitus (1, 73) gives one such case and says that when other senators asked aid they were required to justify their claims before the senate. Dio tells us (58, 16) that Tiberius, after a long time, granted a sort of amnesty by permitting mourning for Sejanus, but that after a little he punished many for this or on other lawless charges, such as having dishonoured and killed their nearest female relatives. Tacitus mentions no case of any one being punished on the first count and only the case of Sex. Marius that comes under the second. In his account of A.D. 33 Dio asserts (58, 23) that so large a number of senators had perished that there were not enough governors for the senate's provinces, so that the praetorian provinces were held for three and the consular for six years because of the lack of successors to relieve their governors. For the consular provinces at least we are able to check this

---

[1] We get this incident from the epitome of Xiphilinus.

statement. It is true that P. Petronius was governor of Asia from 29 to 35 and M. Junius Silanus of Africa from 32 to 38,[1] but were they left in these provinces for such long terms because so many consulars had been slain that successors could not be found? If any such massacre took place it must have been between 29 and 31, for which period the text of Tacitus is lost. Between 25 and the end of 35 we know of only two eligible senators who had lost their lives,[2] and the failure of Tacitus to allude to such a butchery of the highest nobles in the sixth book is difficult to explain except by entire ignorance of it on his part. We have, however, positive as well as negative evidence; if Tiberius had wished to recall Petronius in 32 there would have been available all the senators who had held the consulship in A.D. 22 or earlier[3] and who had not already governed Asia or Africa, unless they happened to be holding commands in the imperial provinces. We know of two men who were certainly qualified in 32, namely D. Haterius Agrippa and C. Sulpicius Galba, and of two others who were certainly alive and in Rome and who probably fulfilled the other condition as well.[4] In A.D. 35 there were also several senators who could have drawn lots for Asia, certainly Galba, probably Cotta Messalinus and Haterius Agrippa,[5] and in addition the consuls for 23, 24, and 25, of whom four are known to have been alive, namely C. Asinius Pollio, Q. Sanquinius Maximus, C. Calpurnius Aviola, and P. Cornelius Lentulus Scipio. From what we know of the

[1] For references see the *Prosopographia*.

[2] They were M. Cocceius Nerva and Mamercus Scaurus. For Scaurus see note 4. Nerva was consul before 24 and killed himself in 33. So far as is known he never held a province. Sejanus, Fufius Geminus, Asinius Gallus, and Fulcinius Trio were not eligible.

[3] The normal interval between the consulship and the proconsulship was ten years or more.

[4] They were Mamercus Aemilius Scaurus and M. Aurelius Cotta Messalinus. Dio asserts (58, 24) that Scaurus never held a province, but the date of his consulship has given rise to some controversy.. Liebenam (*Fasti*) places it in 16, while the *Prosopographia* assigns it to 21. If Liebenam's date is correct he should have had an opportunity to draw lots for a province before 32, and if he waived his claim it is not certain whether he would have a second chance. It is possible that Messalinus held Africa between 30 and 32, when there is an apparent gap in the list of governors. However, when he was indicted in 32 he was accused of remarks reflecting on Gaius; this looks very much like an attempt on the part of the prosecution to connect him with the plot of Sejanus against that prince. Such an attempt suggests that he had been in Rome during 30 and 31. Moreover, we should expect that if he had been in Africa charges relating to his proconsulship there would have been brought among the others and that Tacitus would have made some allusion to his recent return.

[5] Unless Messalinus had been proconsul of Africa and unless Agrippa had died in the interval. This last seems improbable, since as Tacitus had mentioned him a reference to his death might be expected.

imperial legates of consular rank in 35 we may conclude that while
the emperor might have needed one or two of these last four in his
provinces he could hardly have required the services of them all.[1]
There may have been good reasons why some of the men eligible
should not be permitted to govern provinces,[2] and some of them
may not have wished to leave Rome[3]; nevertheless, it is certain that
the long proconsulships of Petronius and Silanus were not due to
the lack of senators legally qualified to succeed them. Probably the
statement of Dio is an attempt on his part to account for these unusual terms of office, which struck him as strange and so appeared
to require some sort of explanation.

How many of these loose generalizations are really due to Dio and
how many he may have copied from his sources we have no means
of determining.[4] Whoever was responsible, it seems clear that little
or no weight should be given to any vague general statement found
in Dio. In his case, as in that of Suetonius, we can regard such statements as entitled to serious attention only when they are supported
by definite facts, and those facts must come mainly from Tacitus.
Nevertheless Dio must be taken into account; as has been said, the
authorities he followed were not those chiefly relied upon by Tacitus,
so that he represents a different historical tradition. Although it is
necessary to use his work with caution, his pages nevertheless
furnish some valuable material. If it be assumed that Dio based
his history in the main upon one chief source, we may conjecture
with some certainty from his constant unreliability as to the proceedings in the senate that the author of this principal source was not
a senator. This, of course, in no wise implies that the author in
question was not well informed as to all matters of general notoriety.
Dio records a number of details which fit in so well with the statements of Tacitus that it seems reasonable to accept them as authentic.
The importance of Dio is thus very considerable, and in particular we
owe to him our only connected account of the downfall of Sejanus.

---

[1] There were seven imperial legates of consular rank. The positions and the
men holding them in 35 were as follows: Moesia, held by C. Poppaeus Sabinus
till the end of 35, when he died and was succeeded by P. Memmius Regulus;
Dalmatia, probably held by L. Volusius Saturninus from 34 or 35 to 41;
Lower Germany, held by L. Apronius from 28 to 37; Upper Germany, held by
Cn. Cornelius Lentulus Gaetulicus from 29 to 39; Spain, held nominally by
L. Arruntius from 25 to 35; Syria, held by L. Pomponius Flaccus or L. Vitellius
who succeeded him; and Pannonia, perhaps held by C. Calvisius Sabinus.
See Lang, *Beiträge*, Liebenam, *Die Legaten*, and the *Prosopographia*.
[2] Tiberius evidently thought so in the case of Galba (Suet., *Galba*, 8).
[3] Tiberius complained of such reluctance (*Ann.* 6, 27).
[4] I have given none which may be due to the epitomators.

IV. TACITUS AND THE TIBERIAN TERROR

IT seems desirable to devote some space to a consideration of the reasons why Tacitus held so firmly to the view that the last years of Tiberius were a reign of terror, and of the literary devices by which he has impressed this picture on his readers.

It is probable that he originally derived his conception of a terror from the tradition concerning Tiberius which was current in his day, since both Dio and Suetonius hold the same general view. A number of reasons have been suggested in the text to account for the development of a Tiberian legend, and the problem here is not why Tacitus accepted it at the start, but why he clung to it after he had become familiar with the facts. This may have been due in part to his method of composition. I have elsewhere [1] pointed out some reasons for thinking that Tacitus, instead of making a careful study of the whole reign before beginning his work, examined and compared his various sources for the two or three years which he intended to treat in a single book, and that, as soon as this study was completed, he forthwith wrote the book, and then took up the investigations preliminary to the next. Thus, when he began, he had only a vague and general knowledge of the events of the reign, and he assumed that they would be found to harmonize with the legendary character of Tiberius. What he learned in gathering material for the first books of the *Annals* compelled him to admit that for some years Tiberius had shown himself a wise and able ruler, but this difficulty was easily overcome by the help of that hypocrisy which seems to have been attributed to Tiberius by tradition. There was, therefore, nothing in the early part of the reign which could force Tacitus to modify his preconceived ideas, and all that was necessary was to let the reader see through the mask worn by the emperor. This Tacitus accomplished by numerous comments, innuendoes, and anticipations, and, as he wrote, the picture which he was drawing became so vivid in his mind that it completely dominated his imagination. When finally he reached the sixth book and with it the dreadful climax for which he had from the first been preparing his reader and himself, he was no longer capable of weighing evidence fairly. Since a reign of terror was a logical necessity if his portrait was to stand, it only remained for him to present the facts in such a way that they would make what he thoroughly believed to be the right impression on the reader. If enough victims could not be found, he (6, 7) explained the

---

[1] In my article on 'Tiberius and the Development of the Early Empire'.

deficiency by the assumption that previous historians had wearied of the monotonous catalogue of executions and suicides, and exerted himself the more to make up for the inadequacy of his material by the dexterous use of rhetoric.

To examine all the devices which he has employed even in the sixth book would be a laborious and unprofitable enterprise. It will be sufficient to analyse his narrative for two or three years and to point out the more obvious of the rhetorical touches. In the text the events of A.D. 32 have been somewhat fully discussed and no evidence found of a reign of terror. In the next year Tacitus could discover few victims whose names he cared to mention, but the deaths of Drusus and Agrippina and the wholesale execution furnished material admirably adapted to his purpose. His description of the execution is worth quoting because it requires a brief discussion. 'At last', he writes, 'excited to madness by all these executions, Tiberius ordered that every one who was in custody [prison] on the charge of complicity with Sejanus should be put to death. There lay the victims, in untold number; of both sexes, of every age, high and low, singly or huddled together: no relative or friend might stand by, or shed a tear over them, or even cast a look at them for more than a moment. Guards were set round to watch for every sign of grief, and to follow the rotting bodies until they were dragged into the Tiber, there to float down the stream, or ground upon the bank: none might burn them, none touch them. Terror had cut them off from all commerce with their kind; and cruelty, waxed wanton, closed the door of pity on them.' [1]

This is a powerful and vivid description, but Tacitus himself supplies the proof that strict accuracy has been sacrificed to effect. He asserts that all who were in prison as accomplices of Sejanus were put to death and we are, therefore, surprised to learn of the execution in prison of Sextius Paconianus in 35.[2] He had been condemned to death in 32 but had saved himself by turning state's evidence and it seems almost certain that, while his life had been spared, he had been imprisoned. The only alternative is to suppose that he was fully pardoned in 32 and afterward thrown in prison for some other offence which Tacitus has not mentioned. Aside from this, it is very strange that such a massacre as is here described should have escaped the

---

[1] *Ann.* 6, 19. I quote from Ramsay's translation. He should have written 'prison' instead of 'custody'. The expression rendered 'high and low' is *inlustres ignobiles*. Ordinarily *inlustres* would mean members of the nobility, but I think that Tacitus would have given the names of any persons of really high rank. Probably the word is here used as a sharp contrast to *ignobiles*, which term would naturally refer to slaves and freedmen. [2] *Ann.* 6, 39.

notice of Dio and Suetonius. The latter (61) merely states incidentally that as many as twenty persons, including women and children,[1]
were put to death on one day. The 'untold number' (*immensa
strages*) of Tacitus thus shrinks very considerably. In Dio (58, 21-2)
we are told that Tiberius had the most notorious informers executed
on one day and that he was praised for it, a piece of information
which, if true, presents the massacre in a new and singular light,
for we should never have expected to find Tacitus pitying the hard
fate of delators. The truth of the matter cannot be determined with
certainty, but perhaps the best guess at what really happened is
that Tiberius ordered the immediate execution of some twenty
persons then in prison under sentence of death. Why they had not
been already executed we do not know, but it is possible that some
of them had been spared in the hope that they could be induced to
give important information to the government. If this was the case,
their execution was a natural prelude to the amnesty which Dio
(58, 16) mentions without assigning it to any definite date. Whatever the facts may have been, it seems clear that Tacitus has made
use of the incident to throw an atmosphere of gloom and horror over
the entire year by exaggerated and inaccurate rhetoric.

In A.D. 34 Tacitus has no such golden opportunity and is compelled
to use considerable ingenuity. He begins with an account of the
Egyptian phoenix and then continues his reign of terror with the
remark that at Rome the slaughter continued and that Pomponius
Labeo opened his veins, his wife following his example. If Tacitus
had at once added that Labeo was accused of maladministration in
Moesia and other crimes, the proper effect would hardly have been
achieved, so he follows the suicide of Labeo and his wife by some
general comments on the motives for suicide; the fear of the executioner drove men to seek a prompt death, since, if they waited to
be condemned, their property was confiscated and they were refused
sepulture, while, if they passed sentence on themselves, their bodies
were buried and their wills respected as a reward for haste. The
proper atmosphere having been now created, the charges against
Labeo may safely be stated. The statement, however, is introduced
by the words, 'But Tiberius declared in letters sent to the senate', as
though the emperor, unsatisfied with the death of his victim, had
maliciously sought to blacken his memory. In this way our sympathy is enlisted for Labeo without any assertion of his innocence
on the part of Tacitus. Then follows a confused account of the pro-

---

[1] If the children were slaves their execution might be in accordance with
Roman law.

secution and suicide of Scaurus,[1] so contrived that, although Tacitus
attributes the responsibility to Macro, we are yet left with the
impression that Scaurus was somehow a victim of Tiberius, whom he
had angered by some lines in a tragedy he had written. Another
touch is added when, having to record the banishment of three
informers, Tacitus begins by saying that even *they* were punished if
an opportunity offered. By these means he has succeeded in placing
the events of the year in a wholly false perspective. The reasons
given for suicide are adequate only if those accused were guilty or
if they had no hope of a fair hearing. But immediately after the fall
of Sejanus several who faced a trial before the senate were acquitted,
and we have no grounds for thinking that an acquittal had become
impossible since that time.[2] If Labeo and Scaurus were guilty there
was nothing horrible in their fate, and in the case of the informers
it is clear that Tacitus is ready for Tiberius whatever he may do;
if he punishes the delators, it shows how bloodthirsty he was, and,
if he spares them, it shows the same thing.

The narrative of Tacitus for the next year (A.D. 35) reveals his
rhetorical method even more plainly. He begins by putting together
the events of two eastern campaigns and apologizes for this violation
of chronology by saying that he has done so to give his readers some
relief from the record of domestic calamities, for, although three
years had passed since the death of Sejanus, neither time nor prayers
nor satiety, which soften other men, had any effect on Tiberius, who
continued to punish old and uncertain offences as if they had been
recent and serious. The suicide of Trio[3] is then briefly told and the
four other cases for the year dismissed in a few lines. This brevity
of treatment robs them of most of their effectiveness, but Tacitus
more than makes up for this by his concluding comment: 'Tiberius',
he says, 'heard of these things, not across a strait of the sea, as

[1] Probably the confusion was not wholly intentional. The tradition seems
to have been that Tiberius drove Scaurus to suicide because of his anger at the
tragedy (Suet. 61; Dio, 58, 24). Tacitus found the facts out of harmony with
this view, but he could not bring himself to discard it altogether.

[2] Tacitus probably omitted later acquittals because they were not adapted
to his purpose and he did not regard them as important in themselves. The
only alternative seems to be the supposition that Tiberius only permitted the
trial of those against whom there was conclusive evidence.

[3] Probably the remark about old and uncertain offences was intended to
apply only to the case of Trio. If, as Tacitus implies, he did not wait for an
indictment, no charge would be on record, and Tacitus might assume that he
feared one based on his old friendship with Sejanus. Dio (58, 25), however,
says that he was actually indicted. In any case he was never tried, and, since
the evidence against him was not made public, his guilt might be considered
uncertain.

formerly,[1] or by the hands of messengers from a distance, but so close to the city that he could answer the dispatches from the Consuls on the same day, or with only a night intervening, and almost see with his own eyes the blood streaming through men's houses, or the hands of the executioner.'[2] The force of this passage is as remarkable as its irrelevance, for the proximity of Tiberius to Rome cannot increase his wickedness if he was guilty of murdering the innocent. However, Tacitus does not say that any of the victims were innocent, and it can hardly be doubted that he would have done so if he could. The rhetorical machinery is very evident at this point. The introductory remarks on the implacability of Tiberius naturally lead us to expect something horrible, we are then hurried past the facts, and by a lurid picture at the close we are left with the impression, if we do not stop to think, that the events so briefly narrated were very horrible indeed.

It is unnecessary to give further examples of the literary devices by which Tacitus has succeeded in persuading the world that during the last years of his reign Tiberius was a ferocious tyrant, wallowing in blood. A careful reading of the sixth book of the *Annals* will show that the whole picture of the Tiberian Terror is derived from the rhetorical setting in which the facts are presented and not from the facts themselves.

---

[1] Tiberius had left Capri and was staying at various country villas on the mainland of Italy.

[2] I quote from Ramsay's translation, but I have omitted two words in the last clause. Tacitus does not say that Tiberius could almost see the blood 'dripping down the hands of the executioner', but that he could almost see it in the houses or the hands of the executioner (as he strangled his victim).

V. THE LAW OF TREASON UNDER TIBERIUS

SINCE the view which I have taken of the law of treason under Tiberius differs from the generally received opinion, a brief discussion of the whole subject seems desirable. It is commonly held that under Tiberius this law was stretched to include trivial acts and careless words if these could be so construed as to imply disrespect for the emperor or his predecessor. This impression is certainly that given by our ancient authorities; Dio and Suetonius distinctly assert that men were put to death on the most frivolous grounds; Seneca makes the same assertion (*de Ben.* 3, 26), but unlike Suetonius and Dio he does not attribute the responsibility to the emperor. Of nearly all the cases of this sort mentioned, though without names, by Suetonius and Dio, Tacitus seems to be entirely ignorant. Thus Suetonius asserts (58) that it was considered a capital offence to criticize anything done or said by Augustus, and that a man was put to death because he allowed his native town to confer an honour upon him on the same day on which it had formerly decreed honours to Augustus. Now Tacitus not only does not mention the case of this anonymous person, but he gives no hint that any one was punished for criticisms of Augustus. That Tacitus should have concealed any cruelties of Tiberius seems incredible, so the only reasonable explanation of his silence is that he had found no evidence which he regarded as trustworthy of any such straining of the law. Tacitus does, however, distinctly tell us that after the fall of Sejanus there was a sort of epidemic of accusations in Rome, and his words on the subject are worth quoting in this connexion. 'Of all the evil features of that time', he says, 'none was more calamitous than this, that the first men in the Senate would practise the vilest delation: some openly, some in secret; not distinguishing between kinsfolk and strangers, between friends and unknown persons, between things of yesterday and things obscured by time. Words uttered in the street, or across the dinner-table, on any subject whatever, were noted for accusation, every man hurrying to be the first to mark down his victim: some few acting in self-defence, the greater number as if infected by some contagious malady.' [1] This agrees very closely with what is said by Seneca, and it will be noted that no blame is thrown upon Tiberius. Perhaps we are justified in concluding that the overthrow of Sejanus was followed by a short period of panic and confusion during which his former friends sought to turn suspicion from themselves by

[1] *Ann.* 6, 7. I quote from Ramsay's translation.

accusing others, and his secret enemies sought revenge by the same means. The attitude of the government, however, brought about a restoration of more normal conditions. The passage quoted from Tacitus is almost immediately followed by the account of the acquittal of Terentius and the punishment of his accusers, which probably did much to relieve the tension in Rome. It is quite probable that while the epidemic lasted many frivolous charges were made, but that the charges were dropped when order was fully restored.[1]

The evidence in favour of the view that the law of treason was extended under Tiberius to include trivial acts and careless words is thus reduced to the general statements of Suetonius and Dio, and such statements by these writers have elsewhere been shown to deserve very little credit.[2] Tacitus makes no such sweeping assertions, but furnishes a number of specific instances of persons prosecuted under Tiberius, and it seems to me that it is upon these that we must base our conclusions. In a number of these cases we have what appears at first sight to be a straining of the law, and the testimony of Tacitus seems to give support to Suetonius and Dio if we make allowance for exaggeration on their part and the omission by Tacitus of the names of many of the less important victims. I believe that a closer examination of the cases given by Tacitus will greatly modify such an impression and will show that there can be found in his pages no real basis for the conclusion that the law of treason was extended or abused by Tiberius.

If we begin with the trial of which we have the fullest account, namely that of Piso, we may gain some idea as to the Roman procedure at this time. Piso was really prosecuted for his actions in Syria and for the murder of Germanicus, yet the prosecution began with an arraignment of his career as governor of Spain a number of years before. Tacitus rightly observes (3, 13) that this had no bearing on the main charge, but he does not suggest any reason for bringing up the matter. It is, however, easy to see why the prosecutors opened their case in this manner. The obvious intent was to prejudice the senate against the accused: if the conscript fathers could be persuaded that Piso was a thoroughly bad man, they would be more ready to believe him guilty on the counts that really were at issue. In this particular case Piso persisted in his defence until all the charges against him had been presented in the senate and until he had answered each as well as he could under the circumstances. It would appear that the trial was drawing to its close before Piso

---

[1] See page 201, note 1.
[2] See the appendix on 'Tacitus, Suetonius, and Dio'.

killed himself. In general we gather from Tacitus that if the accused committed suicide before his trial was begun, or at the very beginning of the proceedings, the matter was allowed to drop at that point. In such a case the archives of the senate would probably contain the indictment, and, if the trial had been begun, the initial proceedings, but nothing else, except perhaps the final verdict in the shape of the rewards voted to the informers. It must, therefore, have sometimes happened that when the accused resorted to suicide the archives contained little or nothing more than the bare charges of the informers, and to these Tacitus seems to have paid little attention. If we assume that the trial of Piso followed the normal course, we must conclude that the prosecution usually began with accusations of little real importance, intended simply to create a prejudice against the accused, and that it was only later that the serious counts of the indictment were taken up. If the accused killed himself very soon after the beginning of the trial, it might, therefore, happen that only trivial matters had as yet been considered. We cannot say whether the indictment gave in detail all the charges which it was proposed to bring forward, or whether it was couched in more or less general terms. In any case if Tacitus attached no credence to the assertions of informers which the accused had not lived to answer, there would be a number of instances where nothing of a serious nature had ever been brought up in the senate and where the accused might seem to him to have suffered on trivial grounds. If Piso had killed himself after the first day or two of his trial the only charge which he had answered would have been that of misgovernment in Spain. The accusations of murder and insubordination in the East might have been vaguely expressed as treason or might have been given in detail in the indictment,[1] but even if the trial was continued and the evidence produced, it would have been only the evidence of informers and it would have been brought forward only after Piso could no longer answer it. Under such circumstances if Tacitus had a fair opinion of the accusers he might record the charges, but if they were the usual type of professional informers, he would probably ignore the evidence which they produced when they were secure against any attempt at a reply.

If we turn to the case of Libo Drusus the force of these considerations will at once appear. The proceedings opened with a number of silly charges based on the dealings of Libo with soothsayers, the purpose

---

[1] Probably in the case of Piso the charges were given in detail, since there was a preliminary hearing before the emperor. If Tacitus has given the opening speech of Tiberius accurately as to its substance, the various accusations were clearly set forth.

of which is obviously the same as that of the initial charge against Piso, namely to prejudice the senate against the accused. From an inscription we know that Libo was convicted of plotting to murder the imperial family and seize the throne, yet the first charges appear to have nothing to do with this. Libo was accused of having asked soothsayers if he would ever be rich enough to cover the Appian Way with money as far as Brundisium. It seems clear that the motive for bringing this matter up was to show that Libo was dreaming of the throne, since it could readily be argued that only the emperor could possess such riches as Libo from his question obviously hoped for. The moment that the proceedings in the senate reached the point of real conspiracy Libo secured an adjournment and killed himself. The proceedings were, indeed, continued after his death and the main charges produced, but Tacitus has completely ignored them. Evidently he had no faith in the informers and attached no importance to what was alleged against Libo when he could no longer answer his accusers.[1]

The cases of Piso and Libo Drusus throw a new light on that of Cremutius Cordus. Tacitus (4, 34–5), Dio (57, 24), and Suetonius (61) all agree that he was prosecuted on account of the terms in which he had referred to Brutus and Cassius in a history which he had written. Both Tacitus and Dio imply that it was Sejanus rather than Tiberius who instigated the prosecution, while Suetonius puts the responsibility upon the emperor. We have, however, in this case testimony from another source which is of exceptional interest. Seneca was acquainted with the daughter of Cremutius Cordus; in his *Consolatio ad Marciam* (1 and 22) he refers to her father's death, and we cannot doubt that he was familiar with her version of it. He does not allude to Tiberius as being in any way to blame, nor to the history of Cordus as the cause of his fate. According to Seneca Sejanus was angered by some bitter remarks of Cordus and as a result instigated an attack upon him. What charges were brought Seneca does not say, but we are told that Cordus starved himself to death as soon as the trial began. Seneca adds that when it became known that he intended suicide by this rather slow method, the informers feared that they might lose their profits and complained to the consuls, evidently desiring to secure a resumption of the trial so that they could produce charges and evidence which had not yet been brought forward. Cordus died, however, in the midst of their efforts. There is certainly something strange in the anxiety of the informers, because in the preceding year it had been proposed in the

---

[1] See my article on 'Tacitus and Aristocratic Tradition'.

senate that if a person accused of treason killed himself before the
end of the trial the informers should receive no reward, and this
motion had been rejected owing to the opposition of Tiberius (4, 30).
Why then should the informers become excited because Cordus chose
to commit suicide rather than attempt a defence? Perhaps the most
plausible conjecture would be that the indictment was drawn in very
general terms and that they wished to present some of their more
serious charges so that they, or their patron, would not be open to
the suspicion of having instituted the prosecution on wholly frivolous
grounds. Either this, or they hoped that if the case were continued
they could give it such a character that they would receive some
addition to the usual reward. Whatever the explanation, it is clear
that they were anxious for some reason that the trial should be
resumed, from which circumstance we are justified in concluding
that they had brought forward only the matter of his history. Cordus
did not care to face further proceedings and took his own life before
the informers had got beyond their opening charge, which was
intended simply to create a prejudice against him and pave the way
for more important matters. Seneca evidently took it for granted
that Marcia did not attach much importance to this charge, but
he did not think it discreet to mention, even if he knew, the real
nature of the case. In the archives of the senate there was no proof
of anything against Cordus, perhaps nothing clearly set down even
as an accusation, except the expressions in his history, and hence
the view of Tacitus, Suetonius, and Dio as to the cause of his fate.

From the examination of these three cases it seems clear that we
are not justified in assuming that when a man committed suicide
early in his trial the trivial charges against him which had so far
been brought forward were the only ones. Unfortunately we cannot
always determine at what point in the proceedings the accused took
his own life, but when we find a frivolous accusation followed by
suicide we have at least good grounds for suspecting that there may
have been more behind. If we examine the facts given by Tacitus in
the light of these conclusions, we shall find that there is reason for
doubt in all the cases mentioned by him where the law of treason
appears at first sight to have been strained. Since these cases are not
very numerous, a brief discussion of each may be worth while.

In A.D. 21 Clutorius Priscus was condemned and executed by the
senate during an absence of the emperor from Rome. The charge
was frivolous, and on his return to the city Tiberius blamed the
senate for its action and took steps to prevent such hasty executions
in the future. According to the account of Tacitus (3, 49–51), which

is confirmed by that of Dio (57, 20), Tiberius was in no way responsible for this straining of the law. In A.D. 32 Vitia was put to death
for bewailing the death of her son Fufius Geminus. The account of
Tacitus (6, 10) is compressed into a few words and we can gather
only that she was put to death after a trial in the senate. Bewailing
her son may have taken the form of violent denunciations of Tiberius
which were believed to have a seditious purpose, or, since the wife of
Fufius had taken part in the intrigues of Sejanus (*Ann.* 4, 12), it is
quite possible that his mother also was involved and that Vitia
committed suicide early in her trial. Tacitus, indeed, says that she
was put to death, but he might refer in this manner to a compulsory
suicide. Suetonius (61) uses such an expression in reference to both
Scaurus and Cremutius Cordus, and it seems somewhat unlikely that
he was ignorant of the fact that both took their own lives. In A.D. 33
Pompeius Macer and his son were prosecuted because an ancestor
had been accorded divine honours by the Greeks. Both killed themselves and the case must, therefore, be regarded with suspicion; the
charge as given seems very like the preliminary charges brought
against Libo and may have been intended to serve the same purpose.
A daughter of Pompeius was banished, but Tacitus does not specify
her offence; perhaps the charges against her were the same as those
which her father and brother had not cared to face. However, since
Tacitus tells us that her husband and her father-in-law had already
suffered through Tiberius, it is possible that there were other grounds
for her exile.

These are the only cases of execution or suicide where the accusations seem trivial, but there are some instances of lighter penalties
being inflicted on such grounds. Pomponius Secundus was imprisoned
in his house from A.D. 31 to the end of the reign, but he was never
brought to trial and so there was no formal indictment against him.
Tacitus gives a somewhat trivial reason for his detention (5, 8), but
the historian may very possibly have accepted Pomponius' own
explanation in the absence of any other information. At any rate
Tacitus was probably in a position to know the version of Pomponius,
who was the teacher of the elder Pliny, the father by adoption of the
younger Pliny, an intimate friend of the historian. There remain
only Calpurnius Salvianus (4, 36) and Junius Gallio (6, 3), who were
banished for apparently trivial acts to which some political significance was attributed.

Against the very few instances where our meagre information
makes it seem that men were punished on trivial grounds must be
set the instances where Tiberius interfered to prevent it. In A.D. 15

he dismissed frivolous charges against Falanius and Rubrius (1, 73), in 22 those against Ennius (3, 70), in 32 those against Cotta Messalinus (6, 5–7), and in 34 those against Lentulus Gaetulicus (6, 30). Instead of trying to stretch and strain the law of treason we thus find Tiberius down to the last opposing such an extension.

It is evident, therefore, that the facts furnished by Tacitus lend no support to the sweeping statements of Suetonius and Dio. To me this seems sufficient ground for refusing to attach any importance to their generalizations. If their assertions are true the silence of Tacitus is beyond explanation. He certainly cannot be accused of concealing anything to shield Tiberius, for he is engaged throughout in drawing up an indictment of him. In doing this he was certainly not so burdened with victims of high rank that he could not allude, at least in general terms, to the many victims who suffered on trivial pretexts. His failure to refer to them can only mean that he did not know of them. He had probably seen such loose phrases as are used by Suetonius and Dio, but he had examined the facts too carefully to believe in them. Tacitus used rhetoric repeatedly to give his facts what he believed was the right colour, but unlike Suetonius and Dio he used rhetoric only in connexion with facts and did not substitute it for them.

VI. THE ELECTIONS UNDER TIBERIUS

THERE are three passages in Tacitus concerning the elections for the republican magistracies, but unfortunately they are far from clear and their interpretation is a matter of considerable difficulty. In the first (1, 14–15) Tacitus says that in A.D. 14 Tiberius 'nominated twelve candidates for the praetorship, the number handed down from Augustus; and being urged by the senate to increase the number, he bound himself by an oath not to exceed it. Then for the first time the elections were transferred from the people to the senators: for until that day, although the most important elections (or matters) had been decided by the will of the princeps, yet some had been left to the votes of the tribes. The people did not complain at their rights being taken away except by idle murmurs, and the senate was pleased at being set free from the necessity of bribes and base supplications. Tiberius restricted himself to commending not more than four candidates who must be chosen without rejection or canvass.'[1] The language of Tacitus seems clear, but it is really somewhat ambiguous, and the interpretation generally accepted raises very serious difficulties. Evidently it was customary for those who desired to stand for the office to give their names to the emperor, who nominated as candidates such of them as he chose to regard as eligible. No doubt it was theoretically possible for a man whom the emperor did not nominate as a candidate to present himself at the election, and Tacitus says that in regard to the consular elections Tiberius frequently gave formal permission for any others than those whose names he had transmitted to the consuls to offer themselves for the office if they had confidence in their popularity or their merits.[2] However, Tacitus regards such a permission as quite without value, and this view seems unquestionably correct. We can hardly believe that any one wishing to become a candidate would fail to present his name to the emperor, and if it was rejected, it is incredible that he should have had any chance of success. We may regard it as certain that only those who were nominated by the emperor were in any sense serious candidates. Now

---

[1] *Candidatos praeturae duodecim nominavit, numerum ab Augusto traditum; et hortante senatu ut augeret, iure iurando obstrinxit se non excessurum. Tum primum e campo comitia ad patres translata sunt: nam ad eam diem, etsi potissima arbitrio principis, quaedam tamen studiis tribuum fiebant. Neque populus ademptum ius questus est nisi inani rumore, et senatus largitionibus ac precibus sordidis exsolutus libens tenuit, moderante Tiberio ne plures quam quattuor candidatos commendaret, sine repulsa et ambitu designandos.*

[2] *Ann.* 1, 81.

in the last years of Augustus and the first part of the reign of Tiberius we know that the number of praetors was fixed at twelve.[1] What, therefore, Tacitus seems to say in this passage is that Augustus had been in the habit of nominating only as many candidates as there were places to be filled, so that the people had no voice at all in the matter, and that Tiberius followed his example, rejecting the request of the senate that they might be allowed some freedom of choice. There are, however, reasons for doubting whether this is what Tacitus meant.

In the first place, what are we to make of the statement that while up to this time the most important elections had been made in accordance with the will of the emperor, nevertheless some had been left to the vote of the people, and the further statement that the senators were glad to be released from the need of distributing money and soliciting votes? We may reasonably infer that Tacitus is here speaking of all the elections and not exclusively of those for the praetorship, and it might be assumed that the canvassing was confined to contests for the lower magistracies; in which case we could reconcile the two passages by the supposition that Augustus had named all the consuls and praetors, but had allowed some choice to the people in the other offices. It is, however, equally possible to construe the passage as meaning that the most important matters had been decided by the will of the princeps, although some had been left to the people.[2] In that case we should conclude that the emperor decided how many consuls and praetors should be elected each year, who should be permitted to offer themselves as candidates, how many and which of the candidates must be elected, and how many and which would have to depend upon the popular vote for success. In favour of this interpretation is the fact that the emperor especially *commended* some candidates to the people and that these *candidati Caesaris* must be elected without the need of canvassing for the office. This practice certainly applied to the praetorship, and if the choice of all the emperor's nominees was practically obligatory, it is not easy to see why it was observed, for the commendation of the emperor would in that case have been merely an honorary distinction. If it was based on the legal fiction that other candidates might present themselves, we could regard it as an empty form kept up simply to preserve the republican tradition, but such an explanation is hardly tenable, since the formal *commendatio* appears to have been a somewhat recent development.

---

[1] Dio, 56, 25.

[2] It is thus construed in Gerber and Greef, *Lexicon Taciteum*, under *potis*.

In the first part of his reign Augustus went about among the people with the candidates whom he favoured and solicited votes for them,[1] exactly as any citizen might do under the republic. In A.D. 8, however, owing to old age and feeble health, he abandoned this practice and simply posted a notice recommending certain candidates.[2] This seems to have been the beginning of the formal *commendatio*, and it is hardly likely that Augustus would have taken the trouble to issue such a notice unless it had some real importance. There seems to have been no fixed limit to the number of candidates whom Augustus could commend, but Tacitus informs us that at the first election of praetors under Tiberius the new emperor made a definite arrangement that for this office the number should not exceed four. Such a limitation is difficult to understand if the *commendatio* was an empty honour and all the imperial nominees were as sure of election as those who received it.

In the second place, the attitude of Tiberius is very singular if Tacitus means precisely what he says. It would, perhaps, be natural that the senators should ask him to nominate more candidates,[3] so that they might have some choice, and it is readily conceivable that, on that particular occasion, he should be unwilling to grant their request, but he does much more than that: he takes an oath that he will never allow the senate any voice in the election of the praetors. This seems a wholly gratuitous affront to the conscript fathers and is irreconcilable with the policy of Tiberius. In the first part of his reign he tried hard to maintain the outward dignity and independence of the senate, and it is incredible that he should have taken pains at the first elections under the new system to make the senate's part in them a mere farce, and should have gone even further and proclaimed his intention that it should always remain a farce.

These difficulties are at once removed if we assume that the candidates who received the emperor's commendation (the *candidati Caesaris*) were not included in the list of twelve whom he nominated. Then, if in A.D. 14 there were four *candidati Caesaris*, the senate would choose eight out of the twelve and would have a real voice in the election. If this was the case, we must suppose that what the

---

[1] Suet., *Aug.* 56. Suetonius is speaking of the reign as a whole, and ignores the new practice after A.D. 8 (Dio, 55, 34).

[2] Dio, 55, 34:

[3] I do not see how in this request the senate can have made any pretence of increasing the emperor's powers, since there is no reason to believe that there was any restriction on the number of candidates he could nominate (see Haverfield, *Four Notes*, 199–200).

senators asked for was that Tiberius should increase the number of the praetors and that this was what he refused to do. We have already seen that on this supposition the attitude of the senators and of Tiberius may be readily understood, but how are we to explain the language of Tacitus? What Tacitus says is simply that Tiberius 'nominated twelve candidates for the praetorship, the number handed down from Augustus'. Now it is not difficult, allowing for a slight carelessness in writing, to construe this to mean, 'the number of praetors handed down from Augustus'. It was probably customary to make public the two lists, that of the nominees and that of the *candidati Caesaris*, at the same time, and the contemporaries of Tacitus may have had no difficulty in understanding him.

The view that the senate had some power of choice is confirmed by the description of the manner of conducting the elections which Dio has left us (58, 20). After noting the irregularities in the consular elections, he says that Tiberius selected as many as he pleased from those seeking the other offices (the praetorship is obviously included) and sent them back to the senate; some, being recommended by him, were elected unanimously, while some were chosen on account of their merits, by agreement, or by lot. He adds that if a violent rivalry arose between any of them, the number of magistrates was reduced, and he makes it clear that he is here thinking of the praetors. From the passage as a whole we may safely conclude that Tiberius submitted the names of more candidates for the praetorship than there were praetors to be chosen and left the senate to reduce the list to the proper number. This was sometimes done by ballot, sometimes by the withdrawal of some of the candidates in accordance with an agreement among themselves or with the other senators,[1] and sometimes by the use of the lot.

There is also reason to think that the senate continued to take a more or less active part in the praetorian elections as late as the time of Trajan. In his *Panegyric* (69), Pliny praises the bearing of Trajan towards the candidates and says that some went away with joy, some with hope, and many were to be congratulated and none consoled. The context makes it clear that Pliny is thinking of the candidates for the praetorship, and there can be little doubt that he refers to the *candidati Caesaris*, who, having received the *commendatio*, were joyful because their election was certain, and to those who, having received only the *nominatio*, were hopeful because they might be

---

[1] The emperor probably commended the new men whom he wished to advance. Of the aristocratic candidates one or two might withdraw because they saw little chance of success, or they might retire in return for promises of support at the next election.

successful. The last phrase suggests that Trajan accepted all names that were presented to him and made no use of his right of rejection.

If Tacitus is obscure in discussing the praetorian elections, he is equally so in regard to the consular. In 1, 81 he says that he hardly dares affirm anything concerning them under Tiberius, 'as such variations are found not only in the historians but in the speeches of Tiberius himself. Sometimes, omitting the names of the candidates, he described their birth, life, and military service so that it was understood who they were; at other times, omitting even this indication, he urged the candidates not to disturb the elections by canvassing, promising that he would take charge of the matter. Very often he declared that he had given to the consuls the names of as many as had offered themselves; others might come forward if they had confidence in their popularity or merits. The words were fair, but the permission was idle and hypocritical, the fatal plunge into slavery was made worse by the semblance of liberty.'[1]

In this passage Tacitus seems to say that at some of the elections the names of the candidates were not announced, but their identity was made known by a description. It is difficult to see any motive for such reticence. Moreover, it would appear from what follows that the consuls presided over the elections and hence must have announced the names of the candidates,[2] so that the emperor's failure to mention them would be quite meaningless, unless we take it as a device for making known the imperial wishes while avoiding any appearance of a formal commendation. We should, I think, interpret the passage in the light of the points about which Tacitus says he can make no general statement because the practice was so variable. These points were apparently two: whether Tiberius allowed all who chose to become candidates, and whether, when there were

[1] *De comitiis consularibus, quae tum primum illo principe ac deinceps fuere, vix quicquam firmare ausim: adeo diversa non modo apud auctores, sed in ipsius orationibus reperiuntur. Modo subtractis candidatorum nominibus originem cuiusque et vitam et stipendia descripsit ut qui forent intellegeretur; aliquando ea quoque significatione subtracta, candidatos hortatus ne ambitu comitia turbarent, suam ad id curam pollicitus est. Plerumque eos tantum apud se professos disseruit, quorum nomina consulibus edidisset; posse et alios profiteri, si gratiae aut meritis confiderent: speciosa verbis, re inania aut subdola, quantoque maiore libertatis imagine tegebantur, tanto eruptura ad infensius servitium.*

[2] This appears from the declaration very often made by Tiberius that he had given to the consuls the names of all who had applied. Evidently, at least on these occasions, it was the duty of one of the consuls to preside and announce the names of the candidates. As Tacitus makes no allusion to any variation in this part of the procedure it seems probable that it was regularly followed.

more candidates than there were places to be filled, Tiberius influenced the choice of the senate. Tacitus finds that very frequently
Tiberius declared that he had permitted all who presented themselves to become candidates. Evidently the emperor did not always
make this declaration, and when he did not, we may infer that he
had rejected the names of some of those who sought the office. It is
probable that in this way he sometimes reduced the number of
candidates to the number of consuls who were to hold office during the
year, as Dio (58, 20) makes it clear that they were all chosen at one
election. When there were more candidates than consulships the
practice of Tiberius was also variable: sometimes without mentioning
names he contrived to indicate to the senate that he wished certain
candidates to be chosen, on other occasions he gave no such indication, leaving the senate free to make its own selection. It was on
these occasions that he warned the candidates not to be too active
in canvassing and promised to attend to it for them. This promise
probably meant that he would see that they had an opportunity to
present their claims to the senate, his action in the matter being
dictated by a desire to prevent the stirring up of factional or party
strife.[1] It is, of course, impossible to determine how much choice
was ordinarily left to the senate. It is clear that Tiberius usually
allowed all who wished to become candidates to present their names
to the senate, and that he occasionally left the senate to elect the
consuls freely, either from all who had come forward or from those
whose names he had given to the consuls. We do not know how
frequently he influenced the election by pointing out the candidates
whom he favoured, nor whether on such occasions he left some places
to be filled at the senate's discretion, although I conjecture that this
last was often the case. The number of consuls during a year varied
from two to six, and even when the emperor indicated his preferences,
he might limit his indication to two or three candidates when there
were three or four consuls to be elected. There was evidently no
formal *commendatio* for the consulship, and since there is no mention
of the assembly in either Tacitus or Dio, we may reasonably conclude
that the people in the case of the consuls as of the other magistrates
merely acclaimed those selected by the emperor and the senate.

There remain for consideration certain differences between Dio
(58, 20) and Tacitus. Dio clearly believes that the emperor appointed

---

[1] Dio's description of the praetorian election shows that Tiberius sought to
prevent factional strife. If the canvass became too bitter he reduced the
number of praetors, probably in order to secure the defeat of the offending
candidates, since the strife was likely to be between the two or three whose
chances of election were least promising.

the consuls outright, and notes certain irregularities in the manner
in which he did so. In making the choice of the consuls depend on
the emperor alone it seems to me that Dio is clearly in the wrong.
His error may be explained by the fact that this was the practice in
his own time; probably the senate ceased to have any active part
in the consular elections under Nero,[1] while it retained a real share in
the praetorian elections even in Dio's day. As a result of this he
grasped the significance of what he found in his authorities as to the
latter, but failed to realize the change which had taken place in the
former. What struck his attention in the case of the consular
elections was the irregularity with which Tiberius made his appointments; sometimes, Dio says, he named a man as consul for a whole
year and then deposed him and set up a second and even a third
consul in his place. There seems no reason to doubt the truth of his
statement, and we can readily suggest a possible reason for the emperor's action. It is most unlikely that he actually deposed a consul,
but he could always persuade him to resign before the end of the term
for which he had been chosen. If this happened, a special election
to fill the vacancy would become necessary, and the emperor may
have felt less scruple in dictating the result on such an occasion than
at the regular elections.[2] On this supposition he usually gave the
senate a fairly free choice in the regular election, and sometimes
secured the advancement of some of those to whom he wished to
give consular rank by using his influence to create vacancies.
Tacitus ignored this practice of Tiberius because he was not greatly
interested in it. Unlike Dio, Tacitus was clearly aware that the
senate had had some share in the elections under Tiberius and he
was concerned with trying to determine how large that share had
been. As a result Tacitus fixed his attention on matters which Dio
misunderstood or of which he was ignorant, and Dio emphasized
matters which Tacitus did not specifically mention.

In the third passage referring to the elections (2, 36) Tacitus tells
us that Asinius Gallus proposed that the magistrates should be elected
for five years in advance, that the emperor should nominate twelve
praetors for each year, and that all *legati legionum* who had not
already held the praetorship should be elected. Tacitus adds that
this motion was an attempt to strike at the secret methods of the
imperial government, but that Tiberius opposed it as though it were
a proposal to increase his power. Yet the arguments which Tiberius

---

[1] Mommsen, *Staatsrecht*, ii. 924–5.

[2] This explanation applies equally well, or ill, to all the irregularities
mentioned by Dio.

is represented as using do not seem to fit this description of his attitude. His objections may be summed up briefly as follows: the responsibility of deciding on so many claims was too great, since it was difficult to avoid giving offence even when the magistrates were chosen each year and any one who was rejected could hope for better success in the near future; it was impossible to foresee what changes might take place in so long a time in a man's mind, family, or fortune; men were already proud of being designated for office a year in advance, and this pride would be increased if they were selected five years before they would hold office; it would upset all the laws which fixed a time for candidates to show their industry, to seek and to enjoy the honours of office. From this it does not seem that Tiberius argued that his power would be increased, but simply that he would be under the necessity of giving greater offence and that the existing system would be destroyed. In spite of Tacitus it would appear not unlikely that these reasons weighed heavily with him. It is, however, somewhat difficult to conjecture the motive which led to the proposal. What were the secret methods of the government at which Tacitus believed that Gallus was aiming a blow? Unfortunately we are not told and can only guess. On the whole it seems probable that the election of the magistrates for five years in advance was intended to restrict the emperor's choice and to make those chosen more independent of him, since once assured of their office men would have less motive for seeking to gain the imperial favour. No doubt too the bitterness of the resentment which the higher aristocracy would feel at being forced to wait so long for the honours which they claimed almost as a right would make the emperor reluctant to reject their claims, and in this way render the promotion of new men more difficult.

VII. THE CONSPIRACY OF SEJANUS

IN the text I have rejected the view commonly accepted by modern historians that Sejanus was engaged in a conspiracy to depose and murder Tiberius in order to seize the throne. It seems desirable, therefore, to examine with some care the evidence in regard to this point, on which the testimony of antiquity is divided.

Josephus in his *Antiquities of the Jews* gives us the fullest account of such a conspiracy. He says (18, 6, 6) that Sejanus was plotting against the emperor and that he would have succeeded but for Antonia, the mother of Germanicus; she had always held aloof from politics, but when she learned of the treasonable designs of Sejanus she contrived to send a letter to Tiberius in which she warned him of his danger. This story derives some confirmation from Dio, who tells us incidentally (65, 14) that Antonia had once employed a certain Caenis, afterward the concubine of Vespasian, to write a secret letter to Tiberius about Sejanus. This statement of course gives no support to the idea of a conspiracy against Tiberius,[1] but it does clearly imply that Antonia supplied the emperor with some sort of information concerning his minister and did so with great secrecy. Suetonius (65) is brief and general, but his view is clear enough when he says that Sejanus was plotting a revolution. But Josephus and Suetonius are the only writers who speak clearly of a conspiracy against Tiberius. Juvenal in his tenth Satire (ll. 56–107) describes the downfall of Sejanus, but gives no hint that he was a traitor to his master. It is doubtful, however, how much importance can be attached to his silence, since his artistic purpose can hardly be said to call for any reference of the sort. Dio, who has left us the only connected account of the actual overthrow of the minister, plainly excludes the idea of any plot against the emperor (58, 5–13). This negative testimony seems to me of very considerable importance, for Dio represents the views held by some Roman historian or historians who were conversant at least with such facts as were widely and generally known.[2] If Sejanus and his friends were charged with a conspiracy against Tiberius it seems incredible that any doubt could exist on the matter. The fact that Dio implies so clearly that Sejanus had not formed any plot against his master seems to mean that no such charge was ever brought, at least officially.

[1] The text of Dio just before the fall of Sejanus is lost and can only be imperfectly reconstructed from the epitomes. These contain no mention of Antonia and give no reason for the change in the attitude of Tiberius toward Sejanus.　　　　　[2] See the appendix on 'Tacitus, Suetonius, and Dio'.

The loss of the fifth book of the *Annals* makes it impossible to determine what view Tacitus held about the conspiracy; all that can be done is to examine such references to it as occur in the surviving portion of the *Annals*, and unfortunately these give us no certain indication. In such an examination we need to keep the general situation in mind. After the fall of Sejanus on 18 October, 31 [1] there was wild confusion for a time; some of his supporters were murdered by the mob and others were put to death by the senate. We recover the guidance of Tacitus at the very end of the year and his text is complete from then on except for a slight break in the account of A.D. 36. It is difficult to believe that all who had been involved in a conspiracy against Tiberius were so easily detected that they were killed in the last months of 31 for which we have no detailed record, especially as the murder of Drusus, the son of Tiberius, came to light at that time. We should, therefore, expect that the year 32 would open with prosecutions directed at those suspected of complicity in the plot to overthrow and murder the emperor if such a plot had existed, but this is not the direction taken by the prosecutions. The first man brought to trial was Sextius Paconianus, who was accused of having been an agent of Sejanus in an intrigue against Gaius. He saved his life by turning informer, and accused Latinius Latiaris, probably of the same offence. Next came the prosecution of Cotta Messalinus, and an obvious attempt was made to connect him with this plot against Gaius. Then at the direct command of Tiberius a senator named Cestius brought charges against Q. Servaeus, an ex-praetor, and Minucius Thermus, a knight, but we are not informed what the charges were. It seems unlikely that they were accused of planning a revolution, for Tiberius had to order their prosecution, and though he denounced them as pre-eminent in crime, much sympathy was felt for them. This sympathy in the case of the knight Tacitus attributes solely to the fact that, though a friend of Sejanus, he had borne himself with modesty. Moreover, it is immediately after telling us how Cestius brought the prosecution that Tacitus refers to the epidemic of delation, speaking bitterly of the way in which even senators of high rank stooped to become informers. All this sounds very much as if the senate thought that Tiberius exaggerated the offences of the two men and felt that they might have been forgiven, which could not have been expected if they were charged with plotting against his life or throne. Tacitus does not suggest the innocence of either Servaeus or Thermus, and it seems probable that they were accused of being accomplices of

[1] For references as to the date see the *Prosopographia*.

M

Sejanus in some of his intrigues. There were doubtless many such intrigues, and we know definitely of two, one intended to ruin Gaius and the other directed against the emperor's friend Curtius Atticus, whose ruin was achieved (6, 10). Then followed the cases of Julius Africanus and Seius Quadratus, who were, perhaps, involved in the same charges as Servaeus and Thermus, both of whom turned informers to save themselves, and the prosecution of a knight, M. Terentius, apparently as a friend of Sejanus. From the description which Tacitus gives of the epidemic of delation—and Seneca confirms his picture (*de Ben.* 3, 26)—we can hardly avoid the conclusion that many wild accusations were brought at this time which were not taken seriously, since we hear of very few trials as compared with the number which the language of Tacitus and Seneca would lead us to expect.

Turning now to the passages in Tacitus which may refer to a revolutionary conspiracy on the part of Sejanus, we find the first in 5, 8, where we are told that P. Vitellius was accused of having offered to use the money in the military chest of which he was custodian to promote a revolution. Whether innocent or guilty, he committed suicide without waiting for his trial. It is possible that the revolution intended was in the interest of Sejanus, but if so, it may have had nothing to do with his overthrow. It would seem very probable that when Sejanus felt the ground slipping from under him in the last months of his life he would have had moments of dejection during which he might have discussed the chances of a revolt against Tiberius with some of his supporters. On the other hand, it is equally possible that some of his friends, terrified by his fall, might have seen in such a revolt their only hope of safety; or again the charge may have been one of the reckless accusations brought during the epidemic of delation, and if so, Vitellius may have killed himself because he feared that a trial would expose his guilt in some other matter.

In 5, 11 Tacitus further says that at the close of A.D. 31 a quarrel broke out between the consuls in which Fulcinius Trio accused Memmius Regulus of slackness in putting down the accomplices of Sejanus, and Regulus retorted by threatening an investigation of Trio's part in the conspiracy. Many of the senators interposed and the quarrel came to nothing, though Trio killed himself four years later in fear of charges of whose nature we are ignorant. The language of Tacitus in this passage clearly implies that Sejanus had been engaged in some sort of a conspiracy at the end of his life, but it gives no clue to the purpose of the conspiracy.

According to the account of Tacitus as we have it the first man to defend himself boldly was M. Terentius. He frankly avowed his friendship with Sejanus but denied that he had had any part in the last designs of the minister. He ended his speech by declaring that while plots against the state or against the life of the emperor should be punished, the conduct of the friends of Sejanus ought to be judged by the same rule as that of the emperor himself. At first glance his peroration seems to imply the existence of a conspiracy to assassinate Tiberius, but if we recall the situation and consider the context, this is by no means clear. The speech of Terentius was delivered in the midst of the epidemic of delation, when all sorts of charges were being made, some of which probably had little or no foundation except a few careless words and some senator's desire to gain credit for loyal zeal by bringing an accusation, and when Terentius argued that mere friendship with Sejanus was not criminal, he was almost obliged to make it clear that he had no intention of excusing those who might have been engaged in really serious plots. If there was no record that he had said any thing of the kind, Tacitus was justified in attributing some such expression to him as natural under the circumstances. His words cannot, therefore, be taken as proof that such plots as he refers to had actually been formed by Sejanus or his friends, and the *novissimi consilii* of the minister with which he professes to have had no connexion may very well have been the intrigue against Gaius.

In 6, 14, at the close of A.D. 32, we are informed that three knights perished on a charge of conspiracy. Here again the nature of the conspiracy is not specified and it may have been that against Gaius or some other of the intrigues of Sejanus. It is also possible, as was suggested in the case of Vitellius, that it was a plot formed in desperation after the death of the favourite by his former partisans.

In 6, 19 we have the description of the 'massacre' of all who were in prison on the charge of being associated with Sejanus. This expression is very vague, and while it certainly implies men accused as accomplices of the minister, it tells us nothing as to the kind of intrigues in which they were, or were supposed to have been, involved.

The last reference in Tacitus is in 6, 47. In the closing days of the reign Macro brought charges of disloyalty (*impietas in principem*) against Albucilla and a number of others. Satrius Secundus, who had been her husband, is described as the informer who revealed the conspiracy. It has hitherto been held that the conspiracy in question was that of Sejanus, but I confess I cannot see why it may not have been that of Albucilla. Tacitus always mentions the fact if any of the accusers were closely connected with the accused, and would naturally do so if a man brought charges against his former wife. If the conspiracy was that of Sejanus the matter is less simple; on that supposition Satrius must have figured more or less prominently in the fifth book, and there seems little reason for referring to him here. But accepting the generally received interpretation and assuming that Satrius did betray the conspiracy of Sejanus, presumably to Antonia, this tells us nothing of what the aim of the conspiracy was, and in fact leaves us exactly where we were before.

From the references in Tacitus it seems clear that following the fall of Sejanus charges were bandied about that he, or some of his friends, had at least considered a revolution against Tiberius, but it is not clear that any one was ever actually prosecuted on such a charge. Some of those who suffered may have been so accused, or they may have been tried as agents and accomplices of the favourite in some of his other intrigues and plots which were now exposed. What Tacitus believed must, therefore, remain uncertain, and his authority cannot be cited on either side.

There is one last piece of testimony to be examined. Suetonius tells us (61) that Tiberius composed a brief account of his own life in which he wrote that he had punished Sejanus because he discovered that the minister was pursuing with hatred the children of Germanicus. Suetonius treats this statement as a daring falsehood, but it is difficult to see any motive for a lie, for if Tiberius detected Sejanus in a plot to murder him there seems no reason why he should refrain from saying so. Moreover, if a number of persons had been accused of being accomplices in such a conspiracy, it seems incredible that Tiberius could have written such a statement. If Suetonius has reported the matter accurately, and I think we are justified in accepting a specific assertion of this sort, the probable assumption seems to be that Tiberius told the truth. In that case the real cause of the downfall of Sejanus was the discovery by the emperor of the intrigues of his favourite against Agrippina and her sons. It was for conspiracies against the house of Germanicus and not against Tiberius that Sejanus was overthrown, and it was as agents and accomplices in these intrigues that his friends were prosecuted and punished. Such a view is in harmony with the account of Dio and is not inconsistent with anything said by Tacitus in reference to the matter.

A serious difficulty in the way of supposing that Sejanus conspired against Tiberius is the lack of any apparent motive. As long as Sejanus hoped to secure the legal designation as heir to the throne he had every reason to wait. The authority of Tiberius would help greatly in keeping the armies quiet, and after they had once accepted Sejanus as heir, they would be less likely to offer any opposition to his actual accession. On the other hand, if he attempted to gain the crown by revolutionary and criminal means, the probability of revolt would be greatly increased; the murder of Tiberius and the proclamation of Sejanus as emperor by the praetorian guards, while it might succeed in Rome, would almost certainly plunge the empire into civil war.[1] It is difficult to believe that Sejanus was blind to such considerations, and it is, therefore, extremely unlikely that he would plan a revolution as long as he had any hope of securing the succession by legal means. This at once places us in a dilemma, since the conduct of Tiberius seems to show clearly that he intended to make Sejanus his immediate heir up to the time when he received the warning letter from Antonia. Until, therefore, his treason was revealed Sejanus had no motive for being a traitor. The only solution of the mystery of why Sejanus should have acted in direct opposition to his own interest is to suppose with Ferrero [2] that Tiberius never dreamed of designating Sejanus as his successor, and that the minister planned a revolution when he became convinced that there was no chance of his legal nomination as heir. To suppose this, however, requires us to set aside the authority of both Dio and Tacitus and to assume that Tiberius was entirely blind to the obvious implication of his own acts. It seems to me that we are justified in accepting such an explanation only if no other can be found, and in this case it is quite unnecessary. If we take the statement of Tiberius recorded by Suetonius at its face value, we can easily harmonize the statements of Dio and Tacitus, and the other evidence is not difficult to explain. We have only to remember that up to the time when Tiberius received the letter of Antonia he regarded Sejanus as his successor. After this time the emperor sought to undermine his minister but without alarming him too much. In spite of all precautions, however, there must have been moments of anxiety when Sejanus considered what course he should pursue under certain circumstances. At such moments he may have discussed the possibility of a *coup de main* with some of his supporters, but the discussion apparently came to nothing, for to the very last Sejanus was hopeful of securing his legal recognition as heir. Nevertheless such discussions may have furnished the basis for exaggerated charges in

---

[1] Dessau (ii. pt. 1, 74–5) has appreciated the force of some of these considerations, but most historians seem to have overlooked them.

[2] Ferrero, *The Women of the Caesars*, 200–1.

the period of panic which followed his fall. It is also possible that some of his partisans who had been deeply involved in his intrigues may have formed revolutionary plots after his death, seeing in the overthrow of Tiberius their only chance of safety. In any case the dramatic suddenness of his ruin would naturally give rise to all sorts of rumours among the ill-informed. It is very likely that he was popularly supposed to have conspired against Tiberius and that this belief was readily accepted by careless writers, like Suetonius, and by provincial historians, like Josephus, neither of whom probably made any serious effort to investigate the matter.

LIST OF WORKS REFERRED TO IN THE NOTES

IN the following list no attempt has been made to compile a complete bibliography or even enumerate all the works consulted in the preparation of this book. It is intended merely to furnish adequate information concerning the works referred to in the notes so as to simplify the references there without inconvenience to the reader who may wish to verify some statement.

THE SOURCES

The chief sources for the reign of Tiberius are the works of Tacitus, Dio Cassius, Suetonius, and Velleius Paterculus. There are also passing references in Josephus, Juvenal, Philo, both the elder and the younger Pliny, and Seneca. Where I have cited any particular edition or translation it is given below under the name of the editor or translator. In addition there are the numerous inscriptions of this period published in the *Corpus Inscriptionum Latinarum* (*C.I.L.*), some of which are also given by Dessau in his *Inscriptiones Latinae Selectae* (*I.L.S.*), and elsewhere; a number of these have been cited directly in the notes and many more may readily be found through the references to other works such as the *Prosopographia*.

MODERN WORKS

Anderson, J. G. C.—*Augustan Edicts from Cyrene* in the *Journal for Roman Studies*, xvii (1927).

Asbach, J.—*Das römisches Kaisertum und Verfassung bis auf Trajan.* Cologne, 1896.

Baker, G. P.—*Tiberius Caesar.* New York, 1928.

Baring-Gould, S.—*The Tragedy of the Caesars. A Study of the Characters of the Caesars of the Julian and Claudian Houses.* 8th edition. London, 1923.

Boissier, G.—*Tacite.* 4th edition. Paris, 1912.

Broughton, T. R. S.—*The Romanization of Africa Proconsularis.* Baltimore and London, 1929.

Charlesworth, M. P.—*Trade-routes and Commerce of the Roman Empire.* 2nd edition. Cambridge, 1926.

Ciaceri, E.—*Processi Politici e Relazioni Internazionali. Studi sulla storia politica e sulla tradizione letteraria della repubblica e dell'impero.* Rome. 1918.

Cichorius, C.—*Römische Studien.* Berlin, 1922.

Cichorius, C.—*Zur Familiengeschichte Seians* in *Hermes*, xxxix (1904).

Clason, O.—*Tacitus und Sueton. Eine vergleichende Untersuchung mit Rücksicht auf die beiderseitigen Quellen.* Breslau, 1870.

Dessau, H.—*Geschichte der römischen Kaiserzeit.* Vol. i and parts 1 and 2 of vol. ii have appeared. Berlin, 1924–30.

Dessau, H.—*Inscriptiones Latinae Selectae.* 3 vols. Berlin, 1892–1916.

Domaszewski, A. von—*Geschichte der römischen Kaiser.* 2 vols. Leipzig, 1909.

Domaszewski, A. von—*Zur Geschichte der römischen Provinzial-verwaltung: I. Moesia und Hispania citerior* in Rheinisches *Museum für Philologie,* xlv (1890).

Duruy, V.—*Histoire des Romains depuis les temps les plus reculés jusqu'à l'invasion des barbares.* New edition. 7 vols. Paris, 1879–85.

Fabia, P.—*Les sources de Tacite dans les Histoires et les Annales.* Paris, 1893.

Fabia, P.—*L'Avènement officiel de Tibère. Examen du récit de Tacite* (*Ann.* 1, 11–13) in the *Revue de Philologie,* xxxiii (1909).

Ferrero, G.—*The Women of the Caesars.* New York, 1912.

Freytag, L.—*Tiberius und Tacitus.* Berlin, 1870.

Friedlaender, L.—*Darstellungen aus der Sittengeschichte Roms in der Zeit von Augustus bis zum Ausgang der Antonine.* 10th edition revised by G. Wissowa. 4 vols. Leipzig, 1922.

Furneaux, H.—*The Annals of Tacitus. Vol 1: Books I–VI.* 2nd edition. Oxford, 1896.

Gelzer, M.—*Die Nobilität der römischen Republik.* Leipzig, 1912.

Gerber, A. and Greef, A.—*Lexicon Taciteum.* Leipzig, 1903.

Groag, E.—*Zur Kritik von Tacitus' Quellen in den Historien* in *Jahrbücher für classische Philologie.* Supplementband xxiii (1897).

Gsell, S.—*Inscriptions latines de l'Algérie.* Paris, vol. i, 1922.

Guiraud, P.—*Les Assemblées provinciales dans l'empire romain.* Paris, 1887.

Haverfield, F.—*Four Notes on Tacitus* in the *Journal of Roman Studies,* ii (1912).

Henderson, B. W.—*Five Roman Emperors: Vespasian, Titus, Domitian, Nerva, Trajan.* A.D. 69–117. Cambridge, 1927.

Homo, L.—*L'Empire romain. Le gouvernement du monde—La défense du monde—L'exploitation du monde.* Paris, 1925.

Humbert, G.—Article *Centesima* in Daremberg-Saglio, *Dictionnaire des antiquités grecques et romaines.*

Ihne, W.—*Zur Ehrenrettung des Kaisers Tiberius.* Originally published in English in the *Proceedings of the Literary and Philosophical Society of Liverpool,* 1856–7. Translated into German by W. Schott. Strassburg, 1892.

Jerome, T. S.—*Aspects of the Study of Roman History*. New York, 1923.

Jullian, C.—*Histoire de la Gaule*. 8 vols. Paris, 1907-26.

Kessler, G.—*Die Tradition über Germanicus*. Berlin, 1905.

Knoke, F.—*Die Kriegzüge des Germanicus in Deutschland*. 2nd revised edition. Berlin, 1922.

Kuntz, O.—*Tiberius Caesar and the Roman Constitution* in *University of Washington Publications in the Social Sciences*, vol. ii, no. 1. Seattle, 1924.

Lang, A.—*Beiträge zur Geschichte des Kaisers Tiberius*. Jena, 1911.

Liebenam, W.—*Fasti Consulares Imperii Romani von 30 v. Chr. bis 565 n. Chr. mit Kaiserliste und Anhang*. Bonn, 1909.

Liebenam, W.—*Forschungen zur Verwaltungsgeschichte des römischen Kaiserreichs. I Band: Die Legaten in den römischen Provinzen von Augustus bis Diocletian*. Leipzig, 1888.

Liebenam, W.—*Bemerkungen zur Tradition über Germanicus* in *Jahrbücher für classische Philologie*, cxliii (1891).

Macé, A.—*Essai sur Suétone*. Paris, 1900.

McFayden, D.—*The Rise of the Princeps' Jurisdiction within the City of Rome* in *Washington University Studies*, Humanistic Series, x (1923).

Marquardt, J.—*Römische Staatsverwaltung*. 2nd edition. 4 vols. Leipzig, 1881-5.

Marsh, F. B.—*The Founding of the Roman Empire*. 2nd revised edition. Oxford, 1927.

Marsh, F. B.—*Roman Parties in the Reign of Tiberius* in *The American Historical Review*, xxxi (1926).

Marsh, F. B.—*Tacitus and Aristocratic Tradition* in *Classical Philology*, xxi (1926).

Marsh, F. B.—*Tiberius and the Development of the Early Empire* in *The Classical Journal*, xxiv (1928).

Marx, F. A.—*Untersuchungen zur Komposition und zu den Quellen von Tacitus' Annalen* in *Hermes*, lx (1925).

Merivale, C.—*History of the Romans under the Empire*. New edition. 8 vols. London, 1881-3.

Meyer, E.—Article on *Parthia* and part of that on *Persia* in the *Encyclopaedia Britannica*. 11th and 14th editions. New York, 1910-11 and 1929.

Mommsen, T.—*The Provinces of the Roman Empire from Caesar to Diocletian*. 2 vols. London, 1886.

Mommsen, T.—*Römisches Staatsrecht*. 3rd edition. 3 vols. Leipzig, 1887-8.

Nipperdey, K.—*P. Cornelius Tacitus erklärt von Karl Nipperdey. Erster Band. Ab Excessu Divi Augusti I–VI.* 11th edition revised by G. Andresen. Berlin, 1915.

Nissen, H.—*Kritische Untersuchungen über die Quellen der vierten und fünften Dekade des Livius.* Berlin, 1863.

Nissen, H.—*Die Historien des Plinius* in *Rheinisches Museum für Philologie,* xxvi (1871).

Nowotny, E.—*Die Grabungen im Standlager zu Carnuntum 1908–11* in *Der römischen Limes in Oesterreich* issued by the Kaiserliche Akademie der Wissenschaften. Heft xii. Vienna, 1914.

Oldfather, W. A. and Canter, H. V.—*The Defeat of Varus and the German Frontier Policy of Augustus* in *University of Illinois Studies in the Social Sciences.* Urbana, 1915.

Pauly-Wissowa,—*Real-Encyclopädie der classischen Altertumswissenschaft.*

Perrin, B.—*Plutarch's Lives.* Vol xi, containing the lives of Galba and Otho. *The Loeb Classical Library.* New York, 1926.

Premerstein, A. von—*Die fünf neugefundenen Edikte des Augustus aus Kyrene* in *Zeitschrift der Savigny-Stiftung für Rechtsgeschichte, Romanistische Abteilung,* xlviii (1928).

Prosopographia Imperii Romani. 3 vols. Vol. i, edited by E. Klebs; vol. ii, edited by H. Dessau; vol. iii, edited by P. de Rohden and H. Dessau. Berlin, 1897–8.

Ramsay, G. G.—*The Annals of Tacitus. An English Translation.* 2 vols. London, 1904–9.

Ramsay, G. G.—*The Histories of Tacitus. An English Translation.* London, 1915.

Riepl, W.—*Das Nachrichtenwesen des Altertums mit besonderer Rücksicht auf die Römer.* Berlin, 1913.

Rietra, J. R.—*C. Suetoni Tranquilli Vita Tiberi, c. 24–c. 40 neu kommentiert.* Amsterdam, 1928.

Ritter, J.—*Die taciteische Charakterzeichnung des Tiberius.* Rudolstadt, 1895.

Rolfe, J. C.—*Suetonius.* 2 vols. *The Loeb Classical Library.* New York, 1914–24.

Rosenberg, A.—*Einleitung und Quellenkunde zur römischen Geschichte.* Berlin, 1921.

Rostovtzeff, M.—*The Social and Economic History of the Roman Empire.* Oxford, 1926.

Schiller, H.—*Geschichte der römischen Kaiserzeit.* 2 vols. Gotha, 1883–7.

Schott, W.—*Die Kriminaljustiz unter dem Kaiser Tiberius.* Erlangen, 1893.

Seyrig, H.—*Inscriptions de Gythion* in the *Revue Archéologique*, xxix (1929).

Sievers, G. R.—*Studien zur Geschichte der römischen Kaiser.* Berlin, 1870.

Stahr, A.—*Tiberius: Leben, Regierung, Charakter.* 2nd edition. Berlin, 1873.

Stein, A.—*Die Protokolle des römischen Senates und ihre Bedeutung als Geschichtsquelle für Tacitus.* Prague, 1904.

Steup, J.—*Eine Umstellung im zweiten Buche der Annalen des Tacitus* in *Rheinisches Museum für Philologie*, xxiv (1869).

Stout, S. E.—*The Governors of Moesia.* Princeton, 1911.

Tarver, J. C.—*Tiberius the Tyrant.* Westminster, 1902.

Wagner, F.—*Die Römer in Bayern.* Munich, 1924.

Warmington, E. H.—*The Commerce between the Roman Empire and India.* Cambridge, 1928.

Wilcken, U.—*Zum Germanicus-Papyrus* in *Hermes*, lxiii (1928).

Willenbücher, H.—*Tiberius und die Verschwörung des Sejan.* Gutersloh, 1896.

THE JULIAN LINE

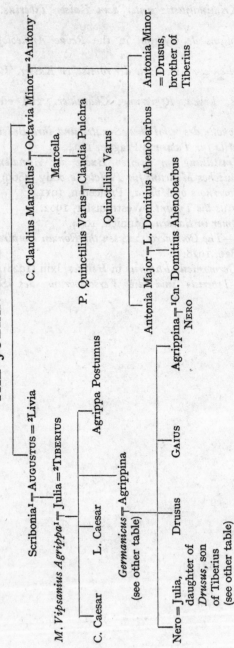

Note.—The names of emperors are printed in small capitals, those of recognized heirs to the principate in italics.

THE CLAUDIANS

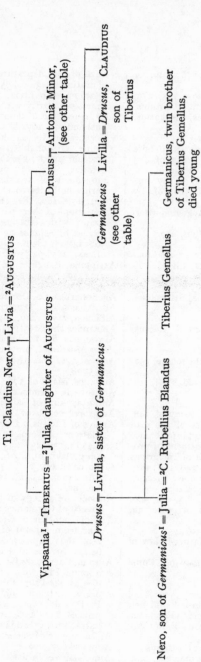

Note.—The names of emperors are printed in small capitals, those of recognized heirs to the principate in italics.

INDEX

Achaia, province of, 29, 146; Sabinus, governor of, 191.

Acquittals, 112, 123, 203, 205, 220, 287; *see also* Capito, Lentulus, Marcellus, Messalinus, Terentius, Tubero, Varilla.

Acta diurna, 5, 259, 261.

Acta senatus, contents of, 3 f., 96 note 2, 291, 293; trustworthiness of, 4 f.; ultimate source of much of the Annals, 6, 259; use of, by historians, 234 f., 247 f.; use of, by Tacitus, *see* Tacitus.

Actium, problems of Augustus after, 16.

Acutia, wife of P. Vitellius, 217.

Adriatic, 33, 190.

Adultery, 111, 115 note 4; *see* Albucilla, Aquilia, Lepida, Ligur, Pulchra, Scaurus, Varilla.

Aedui, people of Gaul, 138.

Aelius, *see* Gallus, Lamia, Saturninus, Sejanus.

Aemilia, *see* Lepida.

Aemilius, *see* Lepidus, Rectus, Scaurus.

Aemona, road from, 211.

Aerarium, treasury of the senate, 150, 207 note 2.

Aerarium militare, 51, 306.

Afghanistan, 82.

Afranius, *see* Burrus.

Africa, province of, 29; army of, 148, 149, 191; gap in list of the proconsuls of, 282 note 4; interference of Tiberius in appointment of proconsul of, 149; revolt of Tacfarinas in, 148 ff.; roads in, 148, 150; proconsuls of, *see* Apronius, Blaesus, Camillus, Dolabella, Silanus.

Africanus, Julius, 203, 263, 264, 306.

Africanus, Julius, son of preceding, 264.

Agamemnon, allusion to, 275.

Agricola, Cn. Julius, father-in-law of Tacitus, 2.

Agricultural crisis following Punic Wars, 21 f.

Agrippa, D. Haterius, 282.

Agrippa, M. Vipsanius, general of Augustus, 33; son-in-law and heir of Augustus, 33; sent to Pannonia, 35; death of, 35; roads of, in Gaul, 137.

Agrippa Postumus, *see* Postumus.

Agrippina, wife of Germanicus, marriage of, 41; departure from camp of mutinous legions, 55, 262, 268 f.; relations with Livia, 77, 86, 162; courts popularity with soldiers, 77, 90; convinced of the murder of her husband, 95, 167; last warnings of Germanicus to, 96; her return to Rome, 96; unable to accept her position, 161 f.; her folly an aid to Sejanus, 167, 168; figure-head in movement of sedition, 169; Tiberius hesitates to strike at, 169, 171, 178, 180, 182, 184, 219, 225; desertion of her partisans, 178; scenes with Tiberius, 179 f.; intrigues of Sejanus against, 181 ff., 308; fall of, 185 ff., 219, 225; death of, 209, 285; party of, *see* Party.

Agrippina, daughter of Germanicus, 217, 250; memoirs of, 5, 179 note 4, 254, 256.

Ahenobarbus, Cn. Domitius, 217, 280.

Ahenobarbus, L. Domitius, 36.

Albucilla, 217 f., 280, 307 f.

Alexander the Great, 33, 70.

Alexandria, 83; famine in, 93.

Alpes Maritimae, province of, 29.

Amnesty, to friends of Sejanus, 208, 275, 281.

Amorgos, island of, 170.

Ampsivarii, German tribe, 73.

Amyntas, king of Galatia, 79.

Andecavi, people of Gaul, 138.

Annals of Tacitus, 2 f.; account of the relations of Nero, Otho, and Poppaea in, 236, 237, 253 f.; method of composition of, 252 f., 284 f.; single source theory, 233, 236; sources of, 3 ff., 248 ff., 254 ff., 259 ff.; *see also* Tacitus.

Antioch, rejoicings of people at recovery of Germanicus, 94.

Antonia, mother of Germanicus, absent from funeral of her son, 98, 259, 260; exposes Sejanus to Tiberius, 192 f., 226, 304, 308, 309.

Antonia Caenis, *see* Caenis.

Antoninus Pius, 109.

Antonius, *see* Primus.

Antony, attempt of, to conquer Parthia, 81; captures two Armenian princes, 83; daughter of, and Cleopatra, 150; granddaughter of, 79.

Apicata, wife of Sejanus, 198.

Appian Way, 292.

Appuleia, *see* Varilla.